A. Graeme Auld

Seeing David Double

Beihefte zur Zeitschrift für die alttestamentliche Wissenschaft

Edited by
John Barton, Reinhard G. Kratz, Nathan MacDonald,
Sara Milstein, and Markus Witte

Volume 550

A. Graeme Auld

Seeing David Double

Reading the Book of Two Houses
Collected Essays

DE GRUYTER

ISBN 978-3-11-105997-6
e-ISBN (PDF) 978-3-11-106027-9
e-ISBN (EPUB) 978-3-11-106078-1
ISSN 0934-2575

Library of Congress Control Number: 2022948968

Bibliographic information published by the Deutsche Nationalbibliothek
The Deutsche Nationalbibliothek lists this publication in the Deutsche Nationalbibliografie; detailed bibliographic data are available on the internet at http://dnb.dnb.de.

Typsetting: Meta Systems Publishing & Printservices GmbH, Wustermark
Printing and binding: CPI books GmbH, Leck

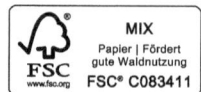

www.degruyter.com

Contents

Place of First Publication

Kings, Prophets, and Judges.
The Cambridge Companion to the Bible and Literature. Edited by Calum M. Carmichael. CUP, 2020, 80–97.

Tell נא How It Is. Placing הגד־נא within Biblical Hebrew.
From Words to Meaning. Studies on Old Testament Language and Theology for David J. Reimer. Edited by Samuel Hildebrandt, Kurtis Peters, and Eric N. Ortlund. HBM 100. Sheffield: Sheffield Phoenix Press, 2021, 63–76.

נפש אדם and the Associations of 1 Chronicles 5 in the Hebrew Bible.
Chronicles and the Priestly Literature of the Hebrew Bible. Edited by Jaeyoung Jeon and Louis C. Jonker. BZAW 528. Berlin: de Gruyter, 2021, 108–124.

Did the Assyrian Envoy know the *Venite*? What Did He Know? What Did He Say? And Should He Be Believed?
Torah and Tradition. Edited by Klaas Spronk. OTS 70. Leiden: Brill, 2017, 42–53.

Chronicles – Isaiah – Kings.
Imperial Visions. The Prophet and the Book of Isaiah in an Age of Empires. Edited by Reinhard Kratz and Joachim Schaper. FRLANT 277. Göttingen: Vandenhoeck & Ruprecht, 2020, 115–126.

“Divination” in Hebrew and Greek Bibles. A Text-historical Overview.
Prophecy and Hellenism. Edited by Hannes Bezzel and Stefan Pfeiffer. Tübingen: Mohr Siebeck, 2021, 55–67.

Deuteronomy and the Older Royal Narrative: Some Core Questions.
Deuteronomy in the Making. Studies in the Production of Debarim. Edited by Diana Edelman, Benedetta Rossi, Kare Berge, Philippe Guillaume. BZAW 533. Berlin: de Gruyter, 2021, 219–239.

Some Thoughts on the First Jeroboam.
Biblische Notizen 185, 2020, 45–53.

Ahaz and Jeroboam.
Characters and Characterization in the Book of Kings. Edited by Keith Bodner and Benjamin J. M. Johnson. LHBOTS 670; T&T Clark, 2020, 17–31.

https://doi.org/10.1515/9783111060279-201

David and His *Alter Ego* in the Desert.
David in the Desert. Edited by Hannes Bezzel and Reinhard G. Kratz. BZAW 514. Berlin: de Gruyter, 2021, 145–158.

Of Proust and Prophets: Samuel, Elijah, and Charles Swann.
Expository Times 133, 2021, 143–148.

Tracing the Origins of Kings with Nadav Na'aman and Klaus-Peter Adam.
Scandinavian Journal of the Old Testament 35, 2021, 259–275.

Reading Solomon with Three Eyes Open.
Scandinavian Journal of the Old Testament 36, 2022, 169–182.

Follow the Words: What's in a King's Name?
Scandinavian Journal of the Old Testament 36, 2022, 302–312.

Ruth. A Reading of Scripture?
The Oxford Handbook of the Writings of the Hebrew Bible. Edited by Donn E. Morgan. New York: OUP, 2019, 215–228.

I am grateful to the above-noted publishers for permission to re-use these fifteen essays in this volume. Apart from correcting an occasional error, I have kept the essays as first published except for creating a single bibliography and a unified footnote style.

Preview

This volume explores a beautifully crafted text that has lain hidden for millennia in plain sight within the biblical books of Samuel and Kings and of Chronicles. Finding it gives us access to a creative stage in Israel's thinking about its past; lets us inspect the writing of the books of Samuel, Kings, and Chronicles; and raises fresh historical questions. In the essays that follow, it is referred to variously as synoptic material, shared material, or the Book of Two Houses (BoTH). All the essays have appeared since the publication of *Life in Kings* (Auld 2017). That book made advances on three fronts; and was defective in a fourth.

(a) Forms of חיה and חיים are used much less frequently in synoptic portions (only 6 or 7 times) than in Sam-Kgs as a whole (some 80 times in non-synoptic portions). At the same time, the fact that the final two synoptic instances appear together in the Amaziah story suggests the significance of 'life' and 'live' to its author, an importance that developed as the narrative was expanded into Sam-Kgs (29–38). Other contrasts are the complete absence from synoptic material of 'today' and 'this day', as also of the little Hebrew word יש ('there is') – all these, like live/life, are common in non-synoptic Sam-Kgs (39–58).

(b) Judah's kings in Sam-Kgs were rewritten from their origins in BoTH (141–161) and particular attention was paid to the development of the Hezekiah story (163–189).

(c) The clustering of words and phrases used only in the reports of two kings, offering comparative and contrasting perspectives, is a feature of the synoptic narrative. A preliminary list (91–94) comprised some thirty unique pairs of words and phrases.

(d) The important studies of Trebolle (1980) and Schenker (1996) arguing that 3 Kgdms 12:24a–z preserves an older account of Jeroboam and Rehoboam than we find in 1 Kgs 11–14 (MT) were ignored.

Each of these issues is further explored in the essays that follow.

The first two were commissions written for the non-specialist reader. 'Samuel-Kings and Chronicles: Two Understandings of Israel's Past' was prepared for a collection of essays designed to be read in five minutes. Though amongst the latest to be written, its sketch of alternative developments of a shared older text provides a convenient overview of much that follows. 'Kings, Prophets, and Judges' includes a brief account (10–13) of the making of the books Judges, Samuel, and Kings. The next two essays augment the word studies early in *Life in Kings*. 'Tell נא How It Is. Placing הגד־נא within Biblical Hebrew' sets the text-critically complex attestation of this little particle in Sam-Kgs against the background of its

https://doi.org/10.1515/9783111060279-202

usage across the Hebrew Bible. 'נפש אדם and the Associations of 1 Chronicles 5 in the Hebrew Bible' notes that נפש is used only four times in texts shared by Sam-Kgs and Chr, but some 80× in non-synoptic Sam-Kgs. Typically, in synoptic usage, נפש occurs in two pairs. In non-synoptic Chr, forms of חיים are used twice and נפש once when describing the fate of those defeated in battle.

A third pair of studies augments the discussion of the Hezekiah narratives in Auld 2017. 'Did the Assyrian envoy know the *Venite*?' proposes that the Assyrian envoy was being mocked when the synoptic narrator had him claim that Hezekiah had instructed prostration before a unique altar in Jerusalem. 'Chronicles – Isaiah – Kings'[1] argues that Chr's shorter account of the envoy in Jerusalem is a better witness to the synoptic account than the much expanded versions in Isaiah and Kings. Then '"Divination" in Hebrew and Greek Bibles' offers an overview of Hebrew and Greek terms found in biblical discussions of divination (and sorcery), including the closely related 2 Kgs 21//2 Chr 33 and Deut 18, while 'Deuteronomy and the older royal narrative' sets this material in a wider framework as it compares the cores of Sam-Kgs and of Deut and their development.

The next pair addresses a principal defect in *Life in Kings*. The important studies of Trebolle (1980) and Schenker (1996) arguing that 3 Kgdms 12:24a–z preserves an older account of Jeroboam and Rehoboam than we find in 1 Kgs 11–14 (MT) had been ignored. 'Some Thoughts on the First Jeroboam' finds that this shorter and older account fits the synoptic narrative well. 'Ahaz and Jeroboam' develops the argument and sets alongside it the expansion in Kgs of the older synoptic presentation of wicked king Ahaz. Another pair also concerns developments from the older synoptic narrative to the familiar Sam-Kgs. 'David and his *alter ego* in the desert' traces some of the rewriting in Samuel and Kings of synoptic David and Jeroboam. 'Of Proust and Prophets: Samuel, Elijah, and Charles Swann' sketches key differences between Samuel, Elijah, and Elisha and the prophetic characters in the older narrative in whom they are rooted.

The next quartet is closely knit. 'Tracing the Origins of Kings with Nadav Na'aman and Klaus-Peter Adam' includes a complete listing of some 130 words and phrases, each found in synoptic narrative within reports of only two kings. This assemblage of unique pairings is more than four times longer than those tabulated in the 2017 monograph; and the much richer clustering permits greater precision over both the extent of the older narrative and how it may be interpreted. 'Reading Solomon with Three Eyes Open' notes that paired terms almost all occur in the same order within the accounts of Solomon in 1 Kgs (MT), 3 Kgdms (LXX), and 2 Chr despite considerable differences on other matters. 'Follow the

1 Delivered at the meeting in Göttingen of the Aberdeen Prophecy Network (18–21 October 2015).

Words: What's in a King's Name?' draws attention to the 'transparency' of many of the names in the synoptic narrative and concludes that these should be included in the list of significant word-pairs. 'Comparing Ahaziah and Jehoash' with David, Rehoboam (and Jeroboam), and Hezekiah further illustrates both the role of pairing and the transparency of names.

The sheer number of the unique links between elements found in Ruth and once elsewhere in the Hebrew Bible renders it most likely that its author was fully conscious of (most of) these connections. 'Ruth. A Reading of Scripture?' was not conceived as part of the larger project to which the other studies belong. Yet the allusiveness it documents holds a useful mirror to the doubling observed throughout the telling of the house of David. And Ruth is hardly a stranger in that house. 'Reading the Book of Two Houses' sets some 150 unique pairings in context.

I appreciate the enthusiasm with which the editors welcomed these essays into the Beihefte and thank the production team at de Gruyter for their friendly competence.

Graeme Auld, May Day 2023

Samuel-Kings and Chronicles: Two Understandings of Israel's Past

Samuel-Kings and Chronicles inherited the same account of Israel's early Kings, David and Solomon, followed by their successors' fraught relationship with Israel. The narrative had started at the death of Saul (1 Samuel 31//1 Chronicles 10) and finished with the death of Josiah (2 Kings 23//2 Chronicles 35). David and Solomon each occupied some 30% of the text and the fifteen successors from Rehoboam to Josiah only some 40% together. This older story explored the past not against standards drawn from Deuteronomy but through an intricate pattern of comparisons and contrasts. Each inheritor version added a prequel. 1 Samuel 1–30 dwells on the beginnings of kingship in Israel under Samuel and Saul and introduces David before he becomes king. More briefly, 1 Chronicles 1–9 sketches Israel's family tree from David and Saul right back to Adam. And both versions extended the shared narrative briefly down to the capture of Jerusalem by Babylon.

Samuel-Kings is some five times longer than the shared story; and the expansion has five components. (1) A parallel account of the kings of (northern) Israel is interleaved in 1 Kings 15 – 2 Kings 17. Its preface in 1 Kings 11–14 rebrands Jeroboam: no longer the neutral inheritor of most of Israel lost by Solomon's foolish heir Rehoboam (as in the older text preserved in Greek), he is now portrayed as instigator of a false cult rivalling Jerusalem in which each northern successor is entrammelled (2 Kings 17:21–23). (2) The pace of the synchronistic narrative slows in 1 Kings 17 – 2 Kings 10, mostly devoted to larger-than-life Elijah and his prophetic successor Elisha. (3) The Prequel too occupies the single lifespan of Samuel and Saul: one, the great prophet who prefigures Elijah/Elisha; the other, the king he anoints and tries to direct, but must later inform of divine rejection. Its second half (1 Samuel 16–30) features the struggle between rejected King Saul and secretly anointed David. (4) David's adultery with Bathsheba and the killing of her husband is preface to tumultuous scenes (2 Samuel 11–1 Kings 2): each of his three eldest sons is killed, leaving the succession to Solomon. (5) Of the smaller expansions, the most substantial relate to the kings reckoned most like David, Hezekiah and Josiah (2 Kings 18–20; 22–23).

The largest extensions in Chronicles to the source narrative precede and follow a lightly expanded David story (1 Chronicles 11–21): Israel's genealogy is sketched in chapters 1–9; and David's preparations for the temple-building by Solomon occupy 22–29 (like Samuel, Chronicles makes a substantial addition to the older David story). The account of Solomon (2 Chronicles 1–9) is shorter than in 1 Kings 1–11. It is closer in length to the shared source, but often adjusted to the wording of the longer (Hebrew) text of Kings. By contrast, most of the follow-

https://doi.org/10.1515/9783111060279-001

ing reports on Jerusalem's kings are longer than their (more original) counterparts in Kings: added details about warfare and fortifications; more attention to cultic matters; and insistence on the individual responsibility of each king. As in Kings, the accounts of Hezekiah (29–32) and Josiah (34–35) are much expanded. Less is said about Josiah's reforms and much more about his revived Passover. Then, while Kings deals at greater length with the deliverance of Jerusalem from Sennacherib, Chronicles concentrates on extensive cultic reform by Hezekiah following the depredations of his father Ahaz.

The narrative shared by Samuel-Kings and Chronicles is a highly artistic creation. Jerusalem twice prepares to attack the north, is twice invaded by the north, and twice partners the north militarily against Aram. Only Saul and David deal with Philistines, only Ahaz and Hezekiah with Assyrians; and Assyrians like Philistines scorn Israel and their god. Names, often transparent in Hebrew, contribute to the comparisons and contrasts: Ahaziah/Ahaz, Amaziah (Yahweh is firm)/ Hezekiah (Yahweh is strong) reinforce serial links. 'Joash' and 'Josiah' are more similar in Hebrew than in English; and in both episodes the priest produces a surprise hidden in the Temple – the one, a child; the other, a document. Ephraim, Lachish, and the wall of Jerusalem, all feature only twice and in combination with other such pairs. Jehoshaphat emulates Solomon in Red Sea trade in Tarshish-ships. Amaziah like David kills thousands of Edomites in the Valley of Salt. Two Pharaohs pass through the land, both with unwelcome consequences. Only David and Solomon sacrifice to Yahweh, but none of their successors; only they 'ask' or are asked of; only they 'practise justice and righteousness'. Yahweh's house functions more as national bank than national shrine. Israel is lost to David's house under Rehoboam, yet Huldah speaks to Josiah in the name of Yahweh god of Israel. Reform is a small part of the older Josiah story; it is more concerned with temple-repair, finding the document and having it validated by Huldah, celebrating Passover anew after many centuries, and a fatal encounter with the Pharaoh.

The much greater attention paid to David and Solomon anticipates the periodization developed in successor tellings of the past and discussed elsewhere in this volume. They were founders of a long-lasting dynasty, but most of Israel was lost to it after Solomon's death. The more leisurely telling of their story is also reflected in three of the expansions in Samuel-Kings: about Samuel, Saul, and the young David; about King David's dysfunctional family; and about Elijah and Elisha in the days of northern king Ahab and his house.

Levites play no role in the older history; and their very few appearances in Samuel-Kings seem late additions to these books. However, they have a large and always positive role in Chronicles, often alongside priests or supervising other functionaries (2 Chronicles 34:12–13). Prophets and men of God play an important role in the older royal story; and several more are added as the narrative is differently developed in Samuel-Kings and Chronicles. Those in Chronicles are more like Nathan, Gad, Ahijah, Micaiah, Isaiah, and Huldah – the royal advisers in the shared story. The stories of Elijah and the prophets of Baal (1 Kings 18) and Elisha in the campaign against Moab (2 Kings 3) are both indebted to the story of Micaiah and the two kings shared in 1 Kings 22//2 Chronicles 18. And Samuel, Hannah his mother, and Eli the priest (1 Samuel 1) may be developed from (future king) Joash, his aunt, and Jehoiada the priest in 2 Kings 11//2 Chronicles 23. But Samuel and Elijah and Elisha are larger-than-life movers and shakers; and Nathan in his new roles in 2 Samuel 12 and 1 Kings 1 like Isaiah in 2 Kings 19–20 resemble Samuel, Elijah, and Elisha more than their earlier selves depicted in 2 Samuel 7//1 Chronicles 17 and 2 Chronicles 32:20.

The older report on wicked King Manasseh, reigning for 55 years between Hezekiah and Josiah (both explicitly said to resemble David), is largely preserved in 2 Kings 21:1–9, 17–18. Going beyond even his grandfather Ahaz in wickedness (16:3–4), he raised altars in Yahweh's space in Jerusalem to gods other than Yahweh, (and) to Yahweh's heavenly court (21:3–7). Comparison and contrast with David are implicit, but unmistakable. In the older story only David and Manasseh were reported as 'sinning'. David constructed an altar for Yahweh as a *remedy for the sin* which he had admitted (2 Samuel 24:10, 17). Calling Manasseh's behaviour 'sin' (2 Kings 21:17) spells out the hint given in 'raised ... built ... built' (21:3–5), a combination of verbs that uniquely recalls David in 2 Samuel 24:18, 21, 25. Manasseh's altar-building *was sin.*

2 Kings 21:10–16 adds to the catalogue of wickedness and blames Manasseh uniquely and definitively for the catastrophe coming to Judah and Jerusalem. But 2 Chronicles 33:10–19 develops a wholly different account: captured by Assyria, the king repented when in Babylon and returned to Jerusalem where he restored the cult of Yahweh. Kings underscores the older story – after Manasseh there is no way back for Judah. But in Chronicles, even Manasseh shows the effectiveness of what Solomon had requested of Yahweh (1 Kings 8:46–49//2 Chronicles 6:36–39): the possibility of restoration following repentance in exile.

Most academic discussion understands the relatedness of Samuel-Kings and Chronicles differently. At the start of the 19th century, W. M. L. de Wette argued persuasively that the author of Chronicles worked not from separate sources but from a continuous narrative of monarchy in ancient Israel. But this he identified as Samuel-Kings, rather than simply the material shared with Chronicles. Most scholars have followed him and hold that when he made the characteristic additions noted above the Chronicler deleted from his source the unsuitable reports of David's dysfunctional family and of the women that led Solomon astray. He also removed the synchronistic history of the northern Israelite kings (and with it, more surprisingly, the stories of Elijah and Elisha) as no longer relevant to

Yehud of Persian or Hellenistic times. The David of the book of Samuel is the most closely drawn character in the Hebrew Bible. Was he too warm-blooded to survive the pious Chronicler? Or was he a brilliant development of the finely crafted older shared narrative and response to the many questions it left open?

Kings, Prophets, and Judges

Together, the three books Judges – Samuel – Kings tell the larger part of the story of Israel and Judah as more-or-less independent nations on their own land. Their principal focus is on 'rule', good rule and bad rule: mostly royal rule (by kings), but also 'rule' by judges and deliverers, and even by prophets. God too 'rules' in these books, but as judge rather than as king. Together with the book of Joshua, they constitute the sub-set of the Hebrew Bible called Former Prophets.

Judges starts where Joshua finishes, with the death and burial of Joshua under whose leadership Israel had gained her land – and the warning that, with the passing of the conquest generation, people were no longer aware of what Yahweh their God had done for Israel. The larger part of the book (chs 3–16) tells at greater length how a handful of 'deliverers' saved Israel from a series of external foes and reports quite briefly on a series of five men who in turn 'judged Israel'. The latter part of the book (chs 17–21) concentrates instead on problems that threaten Israel from within. Kingship makes a brief explicit appearance in the heart of the book (chs 8–9): victorious Gideon (also known as Jerub-baal) refuses Israel's offer of monarchy while behaving as if he had accepted it, and his concubine's son Abimelech is briefly king – not over Israel or even a large grouping within it, but locally in Shechem in the central mountains. Then its absence becomes the focus of the final chapters. Through these, we read a fourfold refrain: 'in those days there was no king in Israel'. The first and last of these go on to state, 'each person did what was right in their eyes' (Judg 17:6; 21:25). In the book of Kings, every king would be assessed as doing right or evil 'in Yahweh's eyes'. The actions recounted towards the end of the book of Judges leave readers in no doubt that 'right in their own eyes' – and the absence of kings – was very wrong.

Samuel reports the beginning of settled kingly rule in Israel. It opens with the birth and early development of Samuel (1 Sam 1–3) and reports the rise and fall of Israel's first king, Saul (1 Sam 9–31). But the figure that dominates 40 of its 55 chapters is David: from his secret anointing by Samuel, through his uneasy relationship with Saul, to his acceptance as king first by Judah and then by the rest of Israel, early external successes, his fateful adultery with the wife of one of his leading warriors whose death he then contrives, and growing tensions within his household and mirrored in his kingdom. Though known as 'Samuel', its contents suggest '[The Book of] David'. Moses may feature across four of the five books of the Torah or Pentateuch; but no biblical character is delineated in such detail as David.

Pace picks up again in Kings: its 47 chapters tell a tale that spans some 20 generations. Solomon, David's second son by Bathsheba, succeeds him, is prover-

https://doi.org/10.1515/9783111060279-002

bially wise, builds the temple in Jerusalem, enjoys international connections, but is corrupted by the religious implications of the many concomitant marriages (1 Kgs 2–11). The kingdom he inherited from David is divided between (the majority of) Israel to the north and Judah (ruled by his successors) to the south. Each of these kingdoms will have 19 kings before they collapse: Israel first, conquered by Assyria; and Judah, overthrown by Babylon some seven generations later. The central third of the book (1 Kgs 17–2 Kgs 10) is dominated not by kings, but by two prophets, Elijah and Elisha. The apostate character and subsequent demise of Israel is portrayed as a warning that Judah should have learned from (2 Kgs 17).

King David, his royal line over four centuries in Jerusalem, and the whole issue of kingship in Israel are together the main subject-matter of Judges, Samuel, and Kings. David himself dominates both books of Samuel. But many issues relating to his reign are seen more clearly from the part-earlier, part-overlapping story of Saul. When David becomes king of all Israel, he captures Jerusalem, defeats the Philistines, and brings into Jerusalem the sacred 'ark' – symbol of divine presence (2 Sam 5–6). He then proposes to the prophet Nathan building a house for the ark, only to receive the divine response that Yahweh needs no house but will create 'a house' for David (meaning 'a royal line') 'for ever'. 'For ever' is used more densely in 2 Sam 7 than any other biblical context: Nathan's words read like a promise that will not be recalled. No such promise was made to Saul at the time he was anointed king; but when Samuel told him of his rejection by Yahweh remarkably early in the story (1 Sam 13:13b–14a), he said: 'The Lord would have established your kingdom over Israel for ever, but now your kingdom will not continue.' And this issue of kingship 'for ever' is anticipated even earlier in the book. At the time of Samuel's birth and childhood, rule in Israel was exercised by Eli, hereditary priest at Shiloh. But in light of the gross failings of his sons, he was told by a man of God that the earlier grant of priesthood 'for ever' to his family was now anathema to Yahweh: 'those who honour me I will honour; and those who despise me shall be treated with contempt' (1 Sam 2:27–36). After the stories of promises to Eli and Saul being revoked, even the much-repeated 'for ever' in the account of David and Nathan should be read as conditional – like a modern contract for life, unless voided by bad behaviour.

Many of the great David-stories concern his relations with women. The first of these is preceded by a huge female chorus. After young David had killed Goliath, the giant Philistine champion, Israel's homecoming forces were greeted by women chanting: 'Saul has killed his thousands, and David his tens of thousands' (1 Sam 18:6–7). All Israel and Judah loved David, but Saul was furious. When he found that his daughter Michal was among the hero's admirers, he tried to bring David down by offering marriage and setting her bride-price at a hundred Philistine foreskins – but this challenge was met. Once his wife, Michal helped him escape her father's agents. Saul had already used his daughter against David; the next time we hear of her, he has given her to another man – in circumstances that are not explained. After Saul's death, David demands her return as part of his negotiations to succeed him in the north. We last see her watching the celebrations through a window as the divine ark is brought into Jerusalem; but this time she despises his behaviour – and significantly she is now identified as Saul's daughter and not as David's wife. She scolds him for exposing himself as he dances, but he assures her he will be honoured by the other women who see him. No longer is she seeing him like the majority of women; and her return to his 'house' anticipates the fate of the ten concubines he left in Jerusalem when he retreated during Absalom's revolt. Absalom had intercourse with them 'in the eyes of all Israel'; and when David returned he had them confined 'living as in widowhood'. So too Michal had no child till the day of her death.

Nabal (or Fool) is seen by many critics as a double of Saul (1 Sam 25). Between two episodes during Saul's hunt for David in the arid southern regions when the hunter came into the power of the hunted (1 Sam 24; 26), we find David providing 'protection' for the rich Fool and his flocks. Denied access to the party at the end of shearing, he moves to take revenge but is intercepted by Nabal's wife. Abigail is beautiful and has 'taste': she meets David with donkey-loads of provisions and wins him over in one of the longest and deftest speeches in the book. Nabal is a fool; but, when David becomes king, he should not have this death on his conscience. After the party, she tells Nabal what she has done, and he has a (divinely-induced) heart-attack. Abigail becomes David's wife: they are well matched.

Bathsheba is the most famous of his wives, and yet she remains elusive. Almost every aspect of the story in 2 Sam 11–12 is ambiguous: what sort of washing did David see her engaged in; did she come to him willingly when sent for; did her husband Uriah (one of David's officers, the Thirty) suspect why he was brought back from the battlefield and sent home to sleep with his wife; why did David mourn their baby before he died and not afterwards? In striking contrast to Abigail, accentuated by the length of the whole telling, Bathsheba says hardly a word. Her only reported utterance is her two-word message to the king, 'I'm pregnant': enough to set deception and murder to follow adultery. Through all the subsequent troubles in David's family, she is absent from the scene (2 Sam 13–20). When David is on his deathbed, his eldest surviving son Adonijah (son of another wife) claims the throne. Only then does she find her voice (1 Kgs 1) – or at least voices Nathan's strategy: Had not David promised that her Solomon would succeed him? Once Solomon is on the throne, she is happy to voice Adonijah's request of the new king (1 Kgs 2). Presumably she is confident this request will be his last: his unwise petition is for Abishag, the latest of his father's bedmates. Solomon reads a request for even one woman from his father's harem as a continuing claim on the throne and has him killed.

Is David careless or complicit over the rape of Tamar by her half-brother Amnon (2 Sam 13)? His love for her has made him sick, and he asks his father if Tamar may come and make 'heart-cakes' and feed him. In light of the Song of Songs (4:9–10), we may suppose these should have been suspect as less medicinal than aphrodisiac. But David gave his permission, and Amnon forced himself on her. Absalom was her brother; he had Amnon killed and fled to exile; brought back to Jerusalem through the skill of an unnamed wise woman from Tekoa (2 Sam 14), he launched a rebellion but perished in the civil war (2 Sam 15–18).

Other women play important, if briefly told, parts in the unfolding royal story. The Queen of Sheba (1 Kgs 10) has a much larger role in post-biblical storytelling (she is named Bilqis in Islamic legend). Huldah is the prophetess consulted by good king Josiah (2 Kgs 22). Athaliah in Jerusalem is a royal agent of the Baal-cult (2 Kgs 11). Only Jezebel, her counterpart in Samaria, is more fully narrated within Kings (1 Kgs 16–2 Kgs 9) – and has become proverbial. It is earlier in our story that we find a cluster of characters more like the women around David: Deborah and Jael and Sisera's mother (Jdg 4–5), Jephthah's daughter (Jdg 11), the mothers of Samson and Micah (Jdg 13; 17), Hannah mother of Samuel [kings' mothers are named but not described] (1 Sam 1), the Levite's abused concubine (Jdg 19), and the medium at En-Dor consulted by Saul (1 Sam 28).

But David's character is also explored in his dealings with Saul and his son Jonathan and with his own lieutenants, Joab and Abishai; in his murderous Negeb raids when a client of the Philistine king of Gath; and in civil war with his own son Absalom. We readers read twice (1 Sam 13:13–14; 15:17–26) about Samuel voicing the Lord's rejection of Saul as king; but each encounter had been private, for he does agree to save the king's face and accompany him as he leads his people in worship. Similarly, Samuel went secretly to Bethlehem to anoint David as the next king (1 Sam 16:1–13). We already know what the main characters only gradually intuit through the comings and goings reported in the second half of 1 Samuel.

The rule of his house over all Israel outlasted David only one generation. Solomon (1 Kgs 2–11), although builder of the temple in Jerusalem and proverbially wise, himself sowed the seeds of division; and his son, Rehoboam, was too feckless to prevent the split. 1 Kgs 12 – 2 Kgs 17 offers a synchronic account of the house of David in Jerusalem and Judah and the remainder of Israel in the north over two centuries till Israel's incorporation into the Assyrian empire. Then the final chapters of Kings report on David's last eight successors in Jerusalem till it too fell, this time to the Babylonians. This conclusion pays closest attention to good kings Hezekiah and Josiah (2 Kgs 18–20; 22–23), both explicitly compared with David.

The dynastic principle operates much more successfully in south than north. All the kings of Judah belong to the family of David. The line passes from father to son (or occasionally from brother to brother) over some four centuries. Even when queen mother Athaliah rules on for six years after the death of her son, this is a single isolated pause in the otherwise orderly succession; and she is overthrown in a putsch organised by Jehoiada the priest who had protected Joash, one of her grandsons, from her purge. The great majority of these 'sons of David' are assessed as having 'done what was right in the eyes of Yahweh' – four had 'done what was evil …' while one more had 'not done what was right …'. In a few cases, David is explicitly cited as setting the standard by which the ongoing generations are judged. The criteria are never spelled out; but he had secured Jerusalem as his capitol and brought there the ark, where the divine presence was encountered – and he is never associated with worship at 'high places' or service of 'other gods'.

In the north, however, there are several dynasties over only a couple of centuries. Jeroboam is succeeded by his son, but Nadab is quickly overthrown by Baasha. His son Elah soon shares Nadab's fate; but Zimri the assassin is quickly overthrown by Omri the army chief. Omri is succeeded by three of his family: by Ahab his son, then by Ahab's sons Ahaziah and Jehoram. J[eh]oram is overthrown by Jehu, whose rapid chariot ride to power has given our language 'driving like a Jehu'. He is followed by four generations of his family: Jehoahaz, J[eh]oash, Jeroboam, and Zechariah. Shallum struck Zechariah down and become king in his place, till he suffered the same fate at the hands of Menahem. Menahem was succeeded by Pekahiah his son; but he was overthrown by Pekah his army chief. An invasion by Tiglath-Pileser, king of Assyria, captured the northern and eastern districts of Israel; and Hoshea became king of the heartland centred on Samaria, till Shalmaneser suspected him of treachery, imprisoned him, and finally incorporated Samaria into his empire. Nineteen kings from seven families: only Omri and Jehu were followed in the throne by more than their own son. A complicated and violent story, but a single uniform judgment: each 'did what was evil in the eyes of Yahweh; he did not depart all his days from any of the sins of Jeroboam son of Nebat, which he caused Israel to sin'.

Assyrian inscriptions continued to refer to northern Israel as 'the house of Omri' even after his short-lived dynasty had been overthrown. But the book of Kings never uses this phrase and speaks instead of 'the house of Ahab', his son. At the same time, the narratives in 1 Kgs 16–22 make plain just how circumscribed was his authority. The towering figures in these chapters were Jezebel his wife and Elijah the prophet. The Ahab-problem is adumbrated in a couple of sentences (1 Kgs 16:30–31):

> Ahab son of Omri did evil in the sight of the Lord more than all who were before him. And as if it had been a light thing for him to walk in the sins of Jeroboam son of Nebat, he took

> as his wife Jezebel daughter of King Ethbaal of the Sidonians, and went and served Baal, and worshipped him.

A few verses later (1 Kgs 17:1), we learn of Elijah proclaiming to Ahab at their first reported meeting,

> As the Lord the God of Israel lives, before whom I stand, there shall be neither dew nor rain these years, except by my word.

Elijah declares to the king that it is he and not the king that is Yahweh's agent. It is he who stands before Yahweh, like the spirit among the host of heaven who volunteered to deceive the same Ahab (1 Kgs 22:21). Normally prophets state that they are proclaiming 'the word of the Lord'. Elijah instead asserts his proximity to Yahweh in the divine council and claims control over the rain by his own word.

At first sight, the synchronic history of the two kingdoms appears to be the result of interleaving once separate histories of each. On closer inspection, however, the account of the northern kings depends on the report of their southern counterparts, while the reverse is not true. The chronology of the successors of David in Jerusalem stands on its own: when he succeeds (mostly) his father, we are told the age of each new king and how many years he reigns. We still see this clearly in the book of Chronicles, which tells only the connected history of the southern kings and provides the same information. In Kings, however, we are not told the age of each northern king at his accession, but only in which year of the reign of their southern counterpart they come to the throne and how long they then reign. We need the southern data to understand the northern.

The development of the northern story is nicely illustrated when we compare two biblical accounts of Jeroboam. The older one is preserved only in the Greek Old Testament. In it, Jeroboam is an ambitious man, married to a relative of Pharaoh's wife and with a power-base in Ephraim near Shechem, who is ready to rule over most of Israel when Rehoboam follows reckless advice and loses much of what he inherited from his father Solomon. This account is limited to Jeroboam's role within the story of Rehoboam and offers no information on how he went on to rule in (northern) Israel. Its main components become re-ordered in the expansive retelling of the Jeroboam story we read in 1 Kgs 11–14 in Hebrew and English Bibles. The acted parable of a cloak torn into twelve tatters had reinforced a divine warning in the older version but is remodelled as a (conditional) promise offered to Jeroboam while still in Solomon's service. In this expansion, the divine promise once made to David is restated in Jeroboam's favour because of Solomon's misdeeds; and the Lord says to Jeroboam (1 Kgs 11:37) what Abner had once said to David: 'and you shall reign over all that your soul desires'

(2 Sam 3:21). However, once he becomes king in Shechem, he sets up a rival cult to Jerusalem. A bit-part in the story of one of Jerusalem's kings becomes the pattern for all of northern Israel's kings: every one of his successors followed him in 'the sins he caused Israel to commit'. He founded no dynasty but established a pattern.

The larger story of the fates of Israel and Judah is reflected in several of the lesser details. Jehoshaphat of Judah responds positively to an invitation from Ahab of Israel to campaign together against Aram for the return of Ramoth in Gilead (1 Kgs 22). This is the first occasion since the split in the kingdom that the house of David has made common cause with Israel. Ahab is wounded in the battle and dies; Jehoshaphat lives on. After the next joint battle against Aram at Ramoth, Joram son of Ahab is wounded – but survives only to be overthrown by Jehu. On this occasion, his ally Ahaziah does not long outlive him. There are also two instances of conflict between the kingdoms. Asa of Judah has to buy help from Aram to force Baasha of Israel to withdraw, and then outlives him. And later, even when Jehoash of Israel succeeds in destroying a section of the wall of Jerusalem, defeated Amaziah outlives him for 15 years. Israel is bigger; but when dealing with Judah, whether in cooperation or competition, its kings always go under first.

Each of these episodes is recounted within the report of the southern royal partner. This is most obvious in the cases of Asa (with Baasha), Ahaziah (with Joram), and Amaziah (with Jehoash). However, the story of Jehoshaphat, Ahab, and Micaiah son of Imlah is also thoroughly integrated within the whole history of the south. No corresponding account of cooperation or conflict between south and north is told within the report of a northern king. Despite first impressions, the synchronic account in the larger part of Kings resulted, not from splicing together two once-independent reports, but from supplementing the story of the south. After Solomon, we find the same number of kings in Israel as in Judah (nineteen). The connected story of separate Israel is less a northern record, and more a southern construct. The purpose of this supplement is spelled out in a lengthy epilogue after the fall of Israel's last king has been reported (2 Kgs 17): Israel was a mirror in which Judah should have seen itself and learned. The core of the argument is in vv. 18–20:

> Therefore the Lord was very angry with Israel and removed them out of his sight; none was left but the tribe of Judah alone. Judah also did not keep the commandments of the Lord their God but walked in the customs that Israel had introduced. The Lord rejected all the descendants of Israel; he punished them and gave them into the hand of plunderers, until he had banished them from his presence.

The story of Jehoshaphat invited by the king of Israel to make common cause in Gilead is one of the longest episodes in the book. Jehoshaphat first pledges solidarity with Israel, then requests enquiring of Yahweh's word before going further. Four hundred prophets give support to the campaign, but Jehoshaphat asks if any prophet was missing. Micaiah, who normally speaks against the king, first adds his voice to the supporters on the advice of the officer who summons him. When challenged to speak only the truth, he reports he has seen Israel scattered on the mountains and reinforces this first vision with a second – that Yahweh has sought a heavenly volunteer to be a lying spirit in the mouths of the prophets. As a result of his counsel, Micaiah is to be imprisoned till Israel's king returns in peace – if that happens, he retorts, Yahweh has not spoken by him.

This narrative plays a strategic integrative role. Firstly, it sounds many echoes of stories of the house of David from start (David) to finish (Josiah). Micaiah's vision of 'all Israel' as 'sheep' without a 'shepherd' (1 Kgs 22:17) recalls images uniquely associated with David: he was appointed to 'shepherd Israel' (2 Sam 7:7) and he called his endangered people 'these sheep' (2 Sam 24:17). And 'these have no master (literally lords)' (also 1 Kgs 22:17) again evokes David – for it is most often he that is addressed 'my lord king' (as in 2 Sam 24:3, 21). We have already noted that Ramoth-Gilead reappears only once, again as goal of a joint campaign against Aram. The prophets are asked if the king of Israel should 'desist' from his planned action (1 Kgs 22:6, 15), and Ahab's predecessor Baasha is the only other subject of this verb – and within the account of Asa of Judah (1 Kgs 15:21). 'Hide' and 'chamber' (1 Kgs 22:25) are repeated only when Joash is saved from his grandmother Athaliah (2 Kgs 11:2). And the two kings 'seek' Yahweh through Micaiah 'the prophet' (1 Kgs 22:7–8) as Josiah will do through Huldah 'the prophetess' (2 Kgs 22:13–14), while 'in peace' is uttered three times in the exchanges between Micaiah and the king of Israel and reappears only in the response of Huldah to Josiah.

Then, this Micaiah narrative has key links with the immediately surrounding chapters in which prophets play a larger role than kings. The rivalry between Micaiah and the 400 prophets is echoed in the story of Elijah at Mt Carmel in competition with 450 prophets of Baal and 400 prophets of Asherah; but here the account includes the mass slaughter of the rival prophets (1 Kgs 18). Then several features of the Micaiah story reappear in another campaign east of the Jordan undertaken by Jehoshaphat and Ahab's son (2 Kgs 3). This time the prophet is Elisha, Elijah's successor. Finally, and including a further massacre of prophetic servants of Baal, Jehu usurps the throne of Israel and brings to an end the house of Ahab (2 Kgs 9–10).

The prophets Micaiah (1 Kgs 22), Isaiah (2 Kgs 19–20), and Huldah (2 Kgs 22) do play a significant role in the reigns of Jehoshaphat, Hezekiah, and Josiah, kings of Judah, as do Nathan and Gad in the time of David (2 Sam 7; 12; 24). But prophets named and unnamed, singular and in groups, play a much larger role in the story of northern Israel. The two larger-than-life figures are Elijah (1 Kgs 17–19; 21; 2 Kgs 1–2) and Elisha, his one-time assistant (2 Kgs 2–9; 13). Theirs is the only biblical instance of prophetic succession; and their personalities are more clearly delineated than several of the kings of Israel with whom they dealt. We may speculate that prophetic charisma could not readily be passed on; but, whatever the reason, the only other instance of non-royal succession in the Bible is from Moses to Joshua. Not only so, but Elijah at Horeb (1 Kgs 19:11–13) recalls Moses on the mountain of God (Exod 33:12–23), Elijah and Elisha crossing the Jordan riverbed dryshod (2 Kgs 2:6–14) recalls Moses at the Sea of Reeds (Exod 14:15–29) and Joshua crossing near Jericho (Josh 3–4), and Elijah caught up into heaven (2 Kgs 2:9–12) echoes Moses buried where 'no one knows' (Dt 34:7) in this way – neither has a grave which could become a pilgrim-shrine.

While the biblical prophets from Isaiah to Malachi are known for their words, Elijah and Elisha are remembered instead for their actions. They are channels of divine power rather than bearers of the divine word. They bring healing to a widow's child or the commander of the armies of the king of Aram, provide the basics for survival in some poor families, and save a town from invasion. Elijah and the prophets of Baal at Mt Carmel, Elijah confronted by his god at Mt Horeb, the transfer of the divine spirit from Elijah to Elisha, and Elisha and the healing of Naaman the Syrian general, are just some of the great prophetic narratives set (mostly) in the north. Their role as national leaders is anticipated by Samuel.

Many important themes of Samuel and Kings are introduced in 1 Sam 1–8, though these chapters are far from typical of the whole. They open with a woman's story. Hannah, many years without child, takes the opportunity of the annual pilgrimage to make a vow: if she be granted a male child she will dedicate him for his whole life. At the first pilgrimage after Samuel is weaned, she brings him to the care of Eli the priest who had been witness to her vow at the temple. In a prayer, she sings about Yahweh her God, who turns things upside down – who makes poor and makes rich, brings low and also exalts (2:7). In the climax of her song (2:10b),

> Yahweh will judge the ends of the earth:
> he will give strength to his king,
> and exalt the power of his anointed.

Hannah, as she dedicates at the temple her small son who will become a prophet and the Lord's agent in instituting kings, sings about the divine role of a future anointed king. Hannah asks for and receives a son; and Israel asks for and receives a king (1 Sam 8–10). Because the name of the first king, Saul, means 'asked (for)', it is often supposed that the Hannah story originally led up to the birth of

Saul. Be that as it may, her song about kingship was probably appended to 1 Sam 1 long after that narrative identified her son as Samuel.

The young temple servant is contrasted with the rascally sons of Eli, who treat with contempt both the offerings made to God and the worshippers who bring them. Their father's rebukes go unheeded, and an unnamed man of God pronounces before him an extended oracle of rejection (2:27–36). This is followed by an even fuller account (3:1–18) of young Samuel's night-time 'audition' in the temple: Eli becomes persuaded that the voice calling Samuel is God's, and Samuel admits to the old priest that he has been informed that 'the iniquity of Eli's house shall not be expiated by sacrifice or offering for ever' (3:14).

Samuel was called as prophet in immediate proximity to the divine 'ark' (3:3); and this portable container of the divine presence becomes the principal actor in a major account (1 Sam 4–6) of war between Philistines and Israel. Brought into the battle by Eli's worthless sons, the ark is captured and both sons killed – the news causes old Eli's death. It is brought into the temple of Dagon in Philistine Ashdod; and, next morning, Dagon is found on his face before it and the people of Ashdod are suffering painful tumours. A way is found to return this dangerous ark with suitable gifts to Beth-shemesh in Israel. There is pleasure at its arrival and sacrifice is offered; but many people are killed by the Lord, and the ark is passed on to neighbouring Kiriath-jearim – it will be collected from there by David (2 Sam 6).

After some twenty years, Israel are concerned about their relationship with the Lord. Samuel convenes them at Mizpah and judges them there. The gathering provokes a hostile Philistine response, and Israel demands of Samuel that he not cease praying for them. The Philistines are duly vanquished, and many cities are returned to Israel. Samuel appoints his sons as judges in his place; but they prove as worthless as Eli's, and the people ask him to appoint instead 'a king like all the nations'. The divine answer to a displeased Samuel is that they have rejected God not Samuel: he should do as they ask, but first warn them how a king will behave. They reject the warning, and Samuel is instructed to listen to them (1 Sam 7–8).

Hannah sings of the potential of a king, and Eli learns that the divine promise to his fathers of priesthood 'for ever' is now revoked by God. Hannah sings of the potential of a king, and her son delivers a warning about how kings behave. Senior priests will play a key role when kings such as Joash and Josiah start their reigns as children (2 Kgs 11–12; 22–23). The ark, that will be hidden in the most holy inner sanctum of Solomon's temple (1 Kgs 8), is introduced as a potent and unmanageable force. The trouble it causes the Philistines leads on to an episode at Mizpah; and Mizpah will reappear at the end of Kings as the centre of administration, once the Babylonians have destroyed Jerusalem and plundered its temple (2 Kgs 25:22–26).

The book of Judges provides a rather wary prelude to the narratives about kings and prophets in Samuel and Kings. Though often described as a bridge linking these books with Deuteronomy and Joshua, most of its contents look forwards rather than backwards. The title given to it is derived from the second and third of three introductions (1:1–2:5; 2:6–3:6; and 3:7–11). In a time when what the Lord had done for Israel under Joshua was no longer remembered, Israel abandoned their god and served Baals and Astartes; God responded by giving them over to plunderers. In their distress, judges were raised up who delivered them; and this cycle was frequently repeated. The report of the first named deliverer (3:7–11) pulls out all the stops. Israel's evil deeds (serving gods other than Yahweh) led to him making them over to service of a foreign king. But when they cried out to him he raised up Othniel, known already from Joshua. Yahweh's spirit came on him, he judged Israel, went out to fight with Cushan 'the Doubly Bad', and had success resulting in a land at rest for forty years. The name of the opponent plus the use in a short account of many words and phrases we will meet throughout the book, though never again so many of them together, makes it likely that this is a contrived prelude to the stories of deliverers that follow. It introduces themes that follow and includes at the start a leader associated with the land of Judah, in the south.

The next deliverer (3:12–30) was Ehud, a left-handed 'Benjaminite' (the name suggests either southerner or right-hander). More double meanings follow in a tale reporting the nice trickery with which Ehud dispatches fat Eglon, escapes, and calls out his people who secure the Jordan crossings against escaping Moabites. A curious short note follows (3:31): Shamgar son of Anat (name of a Canaanite goddess) struck down 600 Philistines, and he too delivered Israel. No tribal affiliation is given, and he may not have been Israelite – perhaps just a case of my enemy's enemy being my friend.

Next time Israel are made over to Jabin, also familiar from the book of Joshua; and the divine answer was mediated through Deborah, described first as prophetess, third as judging Israel, while 'wife/woman of *lappidoth*' is a puzzle. Barak, her commander, will only move against rival Sisera if she goes too; and she agrees, warning him that his will not be the glory, for Yahweh will make over Sisera to a woman. Sisera's forces are routed and he flees towards home. Near Harosheth he is taken into her tent by Jael the wife of a Kenite (or smith); she kills him once asleep by a tent-peg in his head, then shows him off to the pursuing Barak. Already the longest single episode in the book so far (4:1–24), this narrative is now capped by a substantial victory song in praise of Yahweh (5:1–31), sung by Deborah (and Barak). His power demonstrated at (the mountains of) Seir and Sinai is first acknowledged (5:4–5). But this is not a song of the cult: it should be sung where people gather, as at watering places. The narrative had spoken only of forces from Zebulun and Naphtali (4:6, 10), and the song gives these tribes special praise (5:18). But it has first listed Ephraim, Benjamin, Machir, Zebulun, and 'Issachar faithful to Barak' among 'the people of Yahweh' (5:13–15a), before blaming Reuben, Gilead, Dan, and Asher for staying away (5:15b-17). Special credit is again given to Jael (5:23–27), before the song turns dramatically to Sisera's mother waiting for the return of her warrior son and encouraged by her ladies to suppose that the delay is due only to the division of the spoils from which her own neck will benefit (5:28–30). And it ends in all brevity (5:31) –

> So perish all your enemies, o Yahweh.
> But may your friends be like the sun as it rises in its might.

The next and still more detailed episode of deliverance (6–8) is introduced by a longer statement (6:1–6) of the blight caused by nomadic raiders. Yahweh's messenger greeted Gideon in fulsome terms as he was skulking in a wine-press (6:11–14). Commissioned to deliver Israel from Midian, he pleaded first that he was least among the weakest clan in Manasseh. After multiple episodes of reassurance, he moved against the invaders and terrified the Midianite camp into flight by a noisy stratagem. Naphtali, Asher, and all Manasseh were called out in pursuit. Finally, Ephraim too were called out. Protesting they should have been involved at an earlier stage, they were calmed by Gideon's charm (8:1–3).

Victory and pursuit east of the Jordan showed Gideon a changed man. Offered hereditary rule over Israel, he appeared to refuse it (8:22–23) but did institute a collection for a golden ephod which Israel worshipped in his town. He had seventy sons by many wives; but, when a secondary wife from Shechem bore him a son, he called him Abimelech ('my father is a king')! The note about Gideon's burial in the tomb of his father aligns him with only Joshua (2:9) and Samson (16:31) in the book of Judges. Anticipating David, and Jeroboam, and Jehu, each of whom started a new royal house, Abimelech had himself made king of Israel at Shechem (9:1–6). Just one of Jerubbaal's seventy sons escaped the slaughter, and this Jotham addressed the lords of Shechem from the top of (sacred) mount Gerizim in a memorable anti-royal parable of the different trees approached to be king, and then escaped his half-brother (9:7–21). The remainder of this lengthy chapter catalogues the several bloody stages through which Jotham's prediction to Abimelech and Shechem of their mutual destruction came to its culmination (9:22–57).

The next larger section of the book (10–12) opens more ambiguously in Hebrew than in NRSV: 'And there rose after Abimelech to deliver Israel Tola son of Puah …' No external oppressor is mentioned, and the suggestion may be that it was from the experience of Abimelech that Israel required deliverance. Tola is the first of five figures listed in almost formulaic terms as having each judged

Israel for so many years, two in 10:1–5 and three in 12:8–15. The notes about Tola and Jair are followed by a detailed account (10:6–16) of Israel's continuing apostasy from Yahweh in favour of the gods of all their neighbours. Israel then repented comprehensively, and Yahweh became impatient over the trouble they were having. When Ammon were called out against them, the leaders of Gilead wondered who would head their response (10:17–18).

The story backtracks to Gilead's (legitimate) sons expelling Jephthah, his son by a prostitute (an echo of the shorter Jeroboam story?). He had gone off and became leader of a group of 'empty fellows' (11:1–3). Under pressure from Ammon, Gilead's elders asked Jephthah to be their 'head'; energised by Yahweh's spirit, he moved against Ammon, but first vowed to offer in sacrifice whoever came through the doors of his house to greet him on his return. His victory is quickly noted (11:32–33); but the tragic tale of the sacrifice of his daughter, his only child, is sketched at greater length (11:34–40). Ephraim again complained at not being involved from the beginning. Jephthah was less diplomatic than Gideon; and it came to civil war by the Jordan, with the men of Gilead unmasking the fugitives from Ephraim who could not pronounce 'shibboleth' properly, but only say 'sibboleth' (12:1–6). The first mention of Jephthah 'judging Israel' comes in the last sentence we read about him (12:7).

Samson (13–16) anticipates Samuel (1 Sam 1–2; 7) in several ways, first of all in being born to a barren woman. Yet, while Samuel would be 'asked of' Yahweh by his mother, Samson's mother receives her divine instructions out of the blue from Yahweh's messenger (13), rather like Gideon (6:11–24). A man of great strength, provided he kept the Nazirite vow undertaken by his mother and did not cut his hair, each story about him starts with desire for a Philistine woman. Delilah is the only one of his women who is named. After she coaxes out of him the secret of his hair (16:4–22), he is blinded and shackled to a mill. His strength returns with his hair; and, summoned for his captors' entertainment to a great feast, he is able to pull down their temple on himself and them – killing more at his death than in his life (16:23–30). Burial in his family tomb follows (16:31); and there is not another burial in biblical story until Samuel (1 Sam 25:1).

If Samson anticipates Samuel, he also anticipates Saul and David. Samson is wholly and each king is importantly defined by their role in conflict with Philistines. And an unusual Hebrew idiom involving the divine spirit is found only in narratives about these three characters. NRSV offers different translations of the associated verb; and this unfortunately masks the deliberate comparison: 'rushed on him' (Judg 14:6, 19; 15:14); 'possessed him' (1 Sam 10:6, 10); 'came on Saul in power' (11:6); 'came mightily upon David' (16:13). Divine spirit is also credited with the success of Othniel, Gideon, and Jephthah.

If death and burial of Joshua and Gideon were followed by deplorable behaviour, it was no less so after Samson's end. In the final chapters of Judges, the key place-names evoke the narratives that follow in Samuel: Bethlehem, Gibeah, Jabesh, Shiloh. The story of Micah and his mother goes from bad to very much worse in just a few sentences (17:1–5); but, if Gideon's death was followed by a bad example of kingship, Micah and his mother exemplify a time when there was no king – and people set their own standards (17:6). Micah moved to improve the situation in his house-shrine by installing as priest a Levite from Bethlehem in place of his son: Yahweh would do good by him (17:7–13). The repeated notice (18:1) that in these days there were no kings this time introduces talk of the Danite tribe seeking land for itself; and that again implies setting its own standards rather than following Yahweh's. Micah then loses his Levite and his cult-objects to equally disreputable Danites according to a thoroughly discreditable tale about the origins of northern Dan, where King Jeroboam would set up one of his two shrines in opposition to Jerusalem (1 Kgs 12:27–33). We may wonder what Jephthah might have said to Micah's mother, had they ever met. Would he have reproved her for being careless with solemn words: she uttered a blessing on the thief she had cursed, when Micah confessed to the theft? Or would she have chided him for carrying out his vow at the cost of his daughter?

The next reminder that we are in a time of no kings (19:1a), introduces a new tale but with familiar elements. This time the Levite is resident in a distant part of the Ephraim hills, and his connection with Bethlehem of Judah comes through his concubine. She falls out with him and returns there to her family. After four months he goes to Bethlehem to persuade her to return with him and is generously welcomed by her father. When he finally tears himself away after days of hospitality, it is close to evening. As they reach Jebus (or Jerusalem), his servant presses him to stop for the night; but the Levite insists on continuing another few miles, and they end up in Gibeah (19:1–15), home town of King Saul.

An old man returning from the fields gives them hospitality in his house, but their evening is interrupted by the town's riff-raff who demand sex with the Levite. The householder offers his daughter and the visitor's concubine instead; and, when this is refused, the Levite simply pushes out his concubine. They abuse her through the night and leave her fallen at the door. Getting no answer from her in the morning, her master puts her on his donkey. On reaching his home, he anticipates Saul and the yoke of oxen (1 Sam 11:7), cuts the woman in twelve pieces, and sends her throughout 'all the territory of Israel'. All Israel gathers at Mizpah, hears the Levite's story, and determines to move against Gibeah immediately. Benjamin refuses to hand over the scoundrels from Gibeah and send their own forces to the town (20:1–17). Benjamin has the first success, and Israel take themselves weeping before Yahweh, presumably again at Bethel. Encouraged to try again (this whole situation is reminiscent of Josh. 7–8), they fail once more; but they succeed the third time (20:18–36a). Many further details of the end of the ambush and flight of Benjamin are added (20:36b-48).

The next cause of national weeping before Yahweh at Bethel is that one tribe is now lacking from the people, a situation made more acute by the oath Israel has taken at Mizpah to refuse intermarriage with Benjamin (21:1–4). Jabesh in Gilead had not participated in the campaign against Gibeah – its people are put to the sword except for four hundred young virgins that are provided to the defeated Benjaminites (21:5–14a), who are also invited to snatch girls as they dance at an annual festival at Shiloh (21:14b-24). No surprise that the book of Judges ends (21:25) by repeating in full its comment on the beginnings of the scandalous tale of Micah and his mother: 'In these days there was no king in Israel; all the people did what was right in their own eyes.'

A brief note about a change in circumstances for Jehoiachin, Judah's last king now blinded and in exile in Babylon, ends the book of Kings. Readers have long debated whether it brings a positive or negative conclusion to the story of David's house. The whole final chapter also serves as conclusion to Jeremiah (Jer 52), and several idioms used in the final note have significant echoes in one or both books. The fate of Jehoiachin, blinded and hence unfit for kingship, resonates with lame Mephibosheth (2 Sam 9) – the one son of Saul to outlive the catastrophe on Mt Gilboa. Was the promise of continued eating at court a benefit to be enjoyed, or a perpetual mockery because it was financed from their own land?

The kings in Jerusalem, whatever their qualities, ruled not because they embodied these qualities but simply in succession to their fathers. A few were ousted but always replaced by another member of the royal Davidic house. We catch an occasional glimpse of ability amongst the northern kings: Omri secured greater popular support than his rival pretender and not only became king but also founded Samaria as capitol city, a city whose name would long outlive the kingdom. However, for depictions of charismatic leadership, sometimes but not always attributed to divine spirit, we have to look to the narratives about Saul and David, and the deliverers in the book of Judges.

Tell נא How It Is. Placing הגד־נא within Biblical Hebrew

The main purpose of this essay is to review the usage of נא. It is one of the smallest Hebrew words but has a story larger than itself to tell. However, the occasion of the essay is to celebrate the work of a valued colleague and friend. One of David Reimer's key interests is semantic description of ancient Hebrew. When he became editor of T&T Clark's Old Testament Studies series, he invited me to prepare a collection of my (mostly text-historical) essays on Joshua (Auld 1998). It will come as no surprise that I seek to honour him by setting a little word in its text-historical context and probing what 'Biblical Hebrew' might mean.

The Mandelkern Concordance records five instances of [ו]הגד־נא (Jos 7:19; 1 Sam 23:11; 2 Sam 1:4; 2 Kgs 9:12; Jer 36:17); yet arguably none of these MT readings was original to its context. The whole clause הגד־נא לנו is absent from Jer 43:17 LXX (= 36:17 MT). In 1 Sam 23:11, 4Q52 reads not הגד־נא but הגידה and in 1 Kgdms 23:11 $LXX^{B\&L}$ also read the imperative without δή. δή is also lacking after the imperative in 2 Kgdms 1:4 (L and B) and 4 Kgdms 9:12 (L but not B) – we may suppose that the Greek translators worked from a text that read הגידה. If the use of נא in each case (and even a whole clause including נא in Jer 36:17) was part of a rewriting of the relevant book, such retelling may have been at least late-biblical if not post-biblical.

The entry on נא in Clines 2007, 576–577 includes extra-biblical evidence: a Lachish ostracon from the later monarchy and some Qumran texts. Within HB it is used in most books though not, among larger books, in Leviticus or Proverbs. It seems it was more prevalent in later texts than earlier.

1 Preliminary indicators: Psalms, Job, and the Book of the Twelve

In Psalms MT, we find נא only 3× within the first four books (Pss 1–106), though δή is also used in two further passages in LXX.[1] But in Book V (Pss 107–150), נא is read 13× in MT and δή 14× in LXX, of which 10 cases are identical.[2] In both MT

1 Ps 7:10; 50:22; 80:15 – LXX also attests נא in 66:2; 94:8.

2 Ps 115:2; 116:14, 18; 118:2, 3, 4, 25, 25; 119:76, 108; 122:8; 124:1; 129:1. LXX does not include δή in Ps 115:2 (נא is also lacking in $4QPs^b$); 116:14, 18; but does attest נא in Ps 122:6, 7 (before the shared instance in 122:8); and also in 133:1; 134:1 (both after הנה).

https://doi.org/10.1515/9783111060279-003

and LXX there are more instances of נא/δή in the latest collection than in the earlier ones. As we shall corroborate elsewhere, the evidence from the book of Psalms is not untypical. More than three-quarters of the modest core of thirteen instances common to MT and LXX are found in the last collection. Against that background, the pluses in both main textual traditions indicate that נא became still more prevalent as the corpus was recopied.

In Job, we read נא 22× in MT. In LXX the occurrences of δή are one or two less; but precision is not easy because of some variation in MSS between δή and δε. However, נא and δή coincide only seven times, three of these in Job 40.[3] In Job 38:18 LXX reflects הגד־נא of our title, while in MT we read simply הגד. At least twice (19:4, 9) δή is part of a good rendering of different Hebrew; and 'hear me' in Job 42:4 reflects not שמע־נא (MT) but שמעני. In both textual traditions, נא is attested some three times more often than the seven instances they share.

There is greater diversity among the so-called minor prophets. However, both in MT and LXX, נא is more densely attested in Haggai, Zechariah, and Malachi, universally recognised as containing much of the latest material in the Book of the Twelve. In MT, 10 of the 19 instances are in these books,[4] while the other 9 are found in Amos, Jonah, and Micah.[5] In the Greek Bible, δή is also attested in only 6 of the 12 books – but in Joel instead of Jonah; and again there are more instances in the final three books (9) than in the earlier ones (7).[6] Common to MT and LXX are 6 instances in Haggai-Malachi, 4 in Micah, and 1 in Amos. It is important to add that, in both MT and LXX, נא is wholly absent from five of the twelve: Hosea, Obadiah, Nahum, Habakkuk, and Zephaniah.

2 נא elsewhere in the Writings

The correspondence between נא and δή is unusually complete in three of the Megillot: twice in the Song of Songs (3:2; 7:9), twice in Lamentations (1:18; 5:16), and once in Qohelet (2:1). But the divergence in Ruth is substantial. They correspond only twice (2:2, 7) while δή is used six times in Ruth 1 (8, 11, 12, 13, 15, 20). δή corresponds to נא in Dan 1:12 in both LXX and Theodotion, but in 9:16 only in Theodotion. Each of the occurrences of נא in Ezra 10:14; Neh. 1:6, 8, 11, 11; 5.10, 11 is rendered by δή in II Esdras.[7]

---

3 Job 6:29; 12:7; 17:10; 22:21; 40:10, 15, 16.

4 Hag 2:2, 11, 15, 18; Zech 1:4; 3:8; 5:5; Mal 1:8, 9; 3:10.

5 Am 7:2, 5; Jon 1:8, 14; 4:3; Mic 3:1, 9; 6:1, 5.

6 Hag 1:1, 5; 2:2, 15, 18; Zech 3:8; Mal 1:1, 8; 3:10; and then Am 7:5; 8:4; Mic 3:1, 9; 6:1, 5; Joel 1:2.

7 The usage in 1–2 Chronicles will be noted in 9 below.

3 Isaiah, Ezekiel, and Jeremiah

There is much less commonality in Isaiah. MT and LXX share the נא/δή correspondence only twice (5:1 and 7:13) and one of these instances may not be ancient. 1QIsa[a] is generally close to MT in Isaiah but it does not include נא in 5:1 and opens the song of the vineyard simply אשירה לידידי in line with wider biblical usage (Williamson 2006, 331).[8] We read נא 15× more in MT[9] and δή 6× more in LXX.[10] As for Ezekiel, here too MT and LXX share נא/δή only twice (17:12; 18:25); but the total sample is much smaller: there are only three more instances of נא in MT: 8:5, 8; 33:30 and no more of δή in LXX.

There are eight unambiguous attestations in Jeremiah of the נא/δή correspondence: 5:21, 24; 18:11, 13; 37:3; 38:4; 40:15; 42:2. In Jer 4:31; 51:33 (= 45:3 MT), LXX *oimmoi* could equally represent אוי־לי as MT אוי־נא לי. Then נא is a simple plus 16×: 5:1; 7:12; 17:15; 18:11; 21:2; 25:5; 27:18; 28:17; 30:6; 32:8; 35:15; 37:20; 38:12, 20, 25;[11] 44:4; and twice it is part of a longer plus: 28:15; 36:17 (הגד־נא לנו noted above). Finally, in 43:15 LXX (= 36:15 MT), and just two verses earlier, πάλιν ('again') clearly represents ש[ו]ב, not שב־נא. In the opposite direction, δή is plus only twice: 8:6; 38:14 (= 45:14 LXX). The second of these occurs in the same chapter as נא is three times plus in MT. It is anachronistic to label MT and LXX as two 'editions' of the book of Jeremiah.[12] However, two pluses in LXX over against twenty-one in MT do constitute a fair sample of shorter LXX and longer – and broadly later – MT. Neither נא nor δή is used in Jeremiah's oracles 'against the nations'.

4 Samuel and Kings

In terms of the נא/δή correspondence, as in many other respects, the language of Jeremiah – and especially of the longer MT version – is more akin to Samuel-

8 None of the other ten instances of cohortative אשירה is followed by נא. Six of these (Ps 13:6; 27:6; 57:8; 89:2; 101:1; 104:33) are in Bks I–IV of Psalms where, see note 3 above, נא is very rare; two are in Ps 108:2; 144:9; and the remaining two are in Ex 15:1; Judg 5:3.

9 1:18; 5:3, 5; 7:3; 19:12; 29:11, 12; 36:4, 8, 11; 38:3; 47:12, 13; 51:21; 64:8. On two occasions (47:12 and 64:8), LXX νῦν may render MT נא.

10 3:1; 10:33; 22:17; 33:7; 39:8; 47:13.

11 After 'tell us' MT and LXX also differ over who spoke to whom: we read מה־דברת אל־המלך in MT while LXX retroverts to מה־דבר לך המלך.

12 When making this point in her contribution to the first meeting of the Edinburgh Prophecy Network, Rannfrid Thelle (2009) cited David Reimer's close attention to MT/LXX variants (Reimer 1993).

Kings than to the other Latter Prophets. However, the text-historical situation in the books of Samuel and Kings is different from that in Jeremiah and more complex too. Sam-Kgs is roughly twice as long as Jer (MT). Twenty-nine instances of נא in Jer (MT) would correspond to some sixty in Sam-Kgs. However, we find נא twice as often (119×) in MT. As for δή, it is even more frequent in LXX^B (125×) though less so in LXX^L (94×). These instances of נא and δή in Sam-Kgs correspond 79× in all three texts. Across all three textual witnesses, the broad pattern of usage is similar. The densest usage is found in 2 Sam 13 and 14 and in 2 Kgs 2. Then both נא and δή are very rare in 1 Sam 1–8; 2 Sam 1–12; 1 Kgs 3–16; and they are completely absent from 2 Kgs 10–17; 21–25.

Fifteen cases in LXX^L that are additional to the shared 79 are also found either in MT or LXX^B. On the other hand, MT has seventeen unique readings[13] and LXX^B has fourteen,[14] while they also share nineteen instances of נא/δή not in LXX^L.[15] This greater abundance of text-critical data from Sam-Kgs reinforces the impression already gained from other biblical books: late-biblical or post-biblical scribes tended to increase the frequency of נא in texts they were transmitting. In a scribal context congenial to נא, it was easy to transmit אל־נאבדה as אל־נא נאבדה (Jon 1:14) in the second of three נא pluses in that book – reading the first two letters of the verb as the particle before repeating them at the start of the verb. Similarly, though less strikingly, in קח־נא את־ (Jon 4:3) the second letter of added נא is the same as the first of the following את.

5 נא in Jos/Jud

In Joshua we find נא 4× in MT but δή not at all in LXX. Following the particle-plus at the start of 2:12 there is a whole clause-plus in MT at the end of the verse. Our titular instruction הגד־נא provides the second of two instances in 7:19. And the start of 22:26 has been rewritten in one direction or the other: MT reads ונאמר נעשה־נא לנו (And we said/thought, 'Pray let us act for ourselves ...') while LXX retroverts to the more straightforward ונאמר לעשות כן ('And we said/thought of acting thus ...').

Density of usage in Judges is much more like Sam-Kgs; but the proportion of instances shared between the main texts is smaller. In MT, we find the particle

13 1 Sam 2,36; 9,3; 14,29; 19,2; 20,36; 23,11; 30,7; 2 Sam 1,4; 13,28; 18,22; 1 Kgs 13,6; 14,2; 18,43; 19,20; 2 Kgs 4,26; 6,3; 19,19.

14 1 Kgdms 14,41; 17,32; 26,16; 28,9.9.21; 2 Kgdms 14,16; 18,31; 3 Kgdms 12,24k; 4 Kgdms 4,25; 5,11; 6,20; 9,26; 20,3.

15 1 Sam 15,30; 16,15; 28,22; 2 Sam 7,2; 13,25; 14,21; 24,10.14.17; 1 Kgs 20,31; 2 Kgs 4,13; 5,7.17.18; 6,17; 7,12; 8,4; 9,12; 18,26.

29 times; in LXX^A, 23 times; and in LXX^B, 27 times. Of these, 13 instances are shared.[16] In each of the three texts, despite the variation between them, some half of all instances are found in the Samson chapters (13–16) and the account of the Levite's concubine (19) which together occupy little more than one fifth of the book. There are substantial female roles in both these narratives, as also in 2 Sam 13–14 where the particle is densely used. The data can be reasonably explained as diverging scribal expansion from a common core.

6 נא in the Pentateuch

The usage of the particle in the 'first' books of HB is quite diverse. In Genesis, we find נא some 75 times, though never in the opening chapters (Gen 1–11). In Exodus, it is found 15 times (but only in 3 restricted contexts).[17] In Numbers, we read it 18 times (in 8 contexts within chaps 10–23, the final 6 in two Balaam chaps).[18] It is completely absent from Leviticus and found only twice in Deuteronomy.[19] In total contrast to נא, δή hardly appears in the Greek Pentateuch.[20] The four instances in Genesis (15:5; 18:4; 27:34, 38) are well attested in Greek MSS; but only the first two correspond to נא in MT.[21] The LXX version of Esau's repeated desperate plea in Gen 27 for his father's blessing may have read the first element of MT ברכני גם־אני as ברך־נא. But it would be unusual to express a stressed object by גם־אני alone without a preceding suffix.

In the context of the whole Bible, the situation in Gen 12–50 is doubly striking: the incidence of נא in MT is more than twice as dense as in the several texts of Sam-Kgs but is barely at all reflected in LXX. Then, though the particle is used much less frequently in Exodus or Numbers as a whole, the density in the portions where it is found is similar to Genesis.

---

16 4:19; 7:3; 8:5; 9:2; 10:15; 12:6; 13:8; 15:2; 16:28; 18:5; 19:9, 11, 23. A agrees with MT 5×: 11:19; 13:3, 15; 16:10; 19:24; B agrees with MT 7×: 6:39; 8:38; 11:17; 13:4; 16:6; 19:6, 8. 4× we read נא only in MT: 6:17, 18; 9:38; 14:12. And there are also LXX pluses – A+B together 3×: 14:15; 16:13; 18:25; A only 2×: 8:21; 19:30; and B only 4×: 1:15; 4:20; 11:37; 21:19. In 16:13 there is also support from Heb MSS.

17 6× in Ex 3:3, 18; 4:6, 13, 18; 5:3; 3× in Ex 10:11, 17; 11:2 and 6× in Ex 32:32; 33:13, 13, 18; 34:9, 9.

18 Num 10:31; 11:15; 12:6, 11, 12, 13, 13; 14:17, 19; 16:8, 26; 20:10, 17; 22:6, 16, 17, 19; 23:13, 27. In 16:8 and 20:10 LXX attests not נא but the sfx ני (cf above on Job 42:4). In 20:17 Sam followed by LXX reads נעבר as a statement; MT may have added נא to emphasise the change to cohortative נעברה

19 Deut 3:25; 4:32.

20 δή in Ex 12:32 is probably a corruption of δε. If δή does attest נא\נה in Deut 32:26, we may see a remnant in MT אשביתה where Sam/Qum read אשבית.

21 Yet נא appears 6× earlier in this narrative in Gen 27:2, 3, 9, 19, 21, 26 MT.

Timothy Wilt's sociolinguistic analysis of נא is based exclusively on narrative books and very largely on Genesis, Exodus, and Numbers.[22] His only remark (244, n. 15) about textual history identifies Num 16:8 as the only passage in which P uses נא, but that LXX attests the suffix ני. However, as remarked above (n. 18) and also noted in BHS, Num 20:10 provides an identical example; and we already observed the same shift in Job 42:4. If LXX attests the earlier reading in each of these passages, Wilt's case about נא being used in JE but not P is strengthened. However, a scribal context supportive of reading נא could explain (many?) other MT pluses – a possibility that his article does not address. The Syriac Peshitta complicates the issue in Numbers. Peter Hayman, who edited the book for the Peshitta project,[23] reports in a private communication: 'Everywhere except 12:6, 14:19, 16:8 and 20:10 it does not represent נא in its translation. In 12:6, 14:19, and 20:10 it translates נא with *hasha* (now) and in 16:8 with the emphatic particle *tubh* (also, yet, even, again). This evidence would suggest to me that the translator had נא in his exemplar in these four texts but not elsewhere in Numbers.' If ני as attested in LXX was the earlier reading in both 16:8 and 20:10, then the shift to נא was already attested in the Syriac translator's exemplar. But that exemplar may have included only four of the eighteen instances of נא in MT.

The incidence of נא appears to be related to literary-historical questions beyond JE/P, the issue identified by Wilt. Though more densely used in Genesis (and portions of Exodus and Numbers) than elsewhere in HB, the particle is used in only 24 of the 39 chapters in Gen 12–50. More strikingly in terms of JE/P, it is completely absent from Gen 1–11, the very narratives about creation and flood where the classic documentary theory was first tested. Instances in Exodus also suggest that the presence of נא indicates more than simply non-P: more positively, eight of the fifteen occurrences are in chaps 3 and 32–34 which share several distinctive features.

7 Literary history

There is great variation over the usage of נא both between books and groups of books in the Hebrew Bible and also within them. The particle appears to have become more prominent in the later stages of the production or transmission of the biblical material. Often the greater prominence had resulted from supplemen-

22 Timothy Wilt, 'A Sociolinguistic Analysis of na'', *VT* 46 (1996), 237–55. A. Shulman, 'The Particle נא in Biblical Hebrew Prose', *HS* 40 (1999), 57–82, appears to have a similar lack.

23 *The Old Testament in Syriac. Peshitta Version, Part I,2 and Part II,1b.* Leiden: Brill, for the Peshitta Institute, 1991.

tation of existing texts. But we have seen many cases where נא was not so much added as freshly recognised within a cluster that was also differently understood: when הגד־נא is read instead of הגידה or שמע־נא instead of שמעני, it is less a matter of *adding* than of *finding* the particle, or of reading with a different expectation.

The books of Samuel and Kings have a key evidential role. The usage of the particle is denser than in Psalms, Job, or the Latter Prophets, but not as heavy as in Gen 12–50 (at least in MT). Then the text-critical resources are much richer than for most of HB. Chronicles includes text closely related to about one fifth of Sam-Kgs. Much of Isa. 36–39 is even more closely related to 2 Kgs 18–20. The evidence from Qumran for Isaiah is remarkably complete, and for Samuel very much richer than for most biblical books. And there are important convergences between these alternative Hebrew texts and the LXX tradition(s) in the books of Kingdoms. At the very least, these several inter-related texts appear to document an almost random diffusion of the particle נא within the copying of otherwise relatively stable material. However, these books may also allow access to earlier stages in the development.

8 Synoptic texts

Variation in usage of נא between synoptic and non-synoptic portions of Sam-Kgs can be both compared and contrasted with other ways of expressing emphasis or nuance. Sam-Kgs is some five times longer than the synoptic material it shares with Chr, and Chr some two and a half times longer than the shared/synoptic material. (1) מאד (very) occurs 10× in synoptic texts[24] among 25 occasions in Chr – and hence the synoptic usage is typical of the usage of מאד in Chr as a whole. However, it is used not 50× but more than 70× in Sam-Kgs – some 40% more densely than in Chr and synoptically. (2) גם (even/also) is also used 9 or 10 times in synoptic texts;[25] and so similar density of usage would produce some 25 instances in Chr and 50 in Sam-Kgs – but the actual figures are some 45× in Chr and

24 1 Sam 31:4//1 Chr 10:4; 2 Sam 8:8; 10:5; 12:30; 24:10, 10, 14, 14//1 Chr 18:8; 19:5; 20:2; 21:8, 8, 13, 13; 1 Kgs 10:2, 10//2 Chr 9:1, 8. MT does not attest a second מאד in 2 Sam 24:14; but LXX agrees with 1 Chr 21:13.

25 1 Sam 31:5//1 Chr 10:5; 2 Sam 5:2, 2; 8:11; 21:20//1 Chr 11:2, 2; 18:11; 20:6; 1 Kgs 10:11; 15:13; 22:22//2 Chr 9:10; 15:16; 18:21; 2 Kgs 22:19//2 Chr 34:27; and also 2 Kgs 16:3, close to 2 Chr 28:2 (see reconstruction in Auld 2017, 259). And in synoptic contexts it is also found in 2 Sam 7:19 MT (גם אל while both LXX^B and LXX^L attest simply על with 1 Chr 17:17); 1 Chr 19:15 (in an expansive recasting of 2 Sam 10:15).

some 135× in Sam-Kgs. (3) הנה (look/behold) is also used 10× synoptically, more frequently (38×) in Chr, and very much more frequently (more than 220×) in Sam-Kgs.[26] (4) Pairing an infinitive absolute with a finite form of the same verb for emphasis is even rarer in synoptic contexts than the previous three examples. There are just five cases in Chronicles as a whole: 1 Chr 21:24 and 2 Chr 18:27 are identical to 2 Sam 24:24 and 1 Kgs 22:28; 2 Chr 32:13 is clearly related to 2 Kgs 18:33, as is 1 Chr 21:17 to the text of 2 Sam 24:17 attested in 4Q51 and LXX^{L}; and only 1 Chr 4:10 is non-synoptic. But this emphatic usage of the conjoined infinitive absolute is found in four further synoptic contexts (2 Sam 5:19; 1 Kgs 8:13; 9:6; and 2 Kgs 14:10) and more than seventy times in non-synoptic portions.

All of these four types of emphasis are more frequent in Sam-Kgs as a whole than in the 20% of text that these books share with Chr – and more frequent on a rising scale from מאד and גם to the infinitive absolute and הנה. In terms of greater relative frequency, נא is more like הנה and the conjoined infinitive. But the crucial difference between נא and all the others is textual (in)stability. With the others, there are occasional differences between MT and LXX and in synoptic portions between Sam-Kgs and Chr (the latter mostly over the infinitive absolute). However, the textual variety recorded in section 4 above over נא/δή is of a wholly different magnitude. A few cases had doubtless been accidental: MT has יתן את in 1 Kgs 2:21 while B and L attest יתן נא את – was this an example of accidental loss or gain? But it is hard to avoid the conclusion that scribes added this little particle to many contexts that had been drafted without it.

As noted above, the absence of δή from 1 Kgdms 23:11 (B&L) corresponds to the reading in 4Q52 (4QSam^{b}): הגידה without a following נא. In the phrase that gives this essay its title we are dealing with an *additional* case of the particle and yet it is hardly a *plus* like the example from Jonah. It was easy to present הגידה with its three syllables and five letters afresh as the similar-sounding הגד־נא. Similarly, 4Q53 (4QSam^{c}) in 2 Sam 14:32 shares both נא pluses attested in L. Then 1QIsa^{a} has a role in identifying נא as a later addition to the Hezekiah narrative in 2 Kgs 19:19 MT. Not only does LXX lack δή in 4 Kgdms 19:19 but the Isaiah texts of this synoptic narrative also lack נא and δή in the corresponding clause: MT, LXX, and 1QIsa^{a} all agree in Isa 37:20. LXX in Isa 39:8 uniquely includes δή in Hezekiah's closing wish. The Kings/Isaiah synoptic narrative helps identify the later spread of נא as texts were copied. However, comparing some synoptic narratives in Samuel-Kings and Chronicles may help us penetrate earlier stages in the development of biblical נא.

26 These relative frequencies in Sam-Kgs may be compared with Gen 12–50: מאד 23×; גם 50×; and הנה some 120×. The comparative and much lesser frequencies in Gen 1–11 are מאד 3×; גם 7×; and הנה 5×.

9 An older royal narrative

There are several small differences throughout the versions in Sam and Chr of the early scene between David and Nathan: there has certainly been rewriting in one direction or both (or several). In 2 Sam 7:2 (MT), the king's first words to Nathan the prophet are ראה נא אנכי יושב. LXX^B also attests the particle נא; but LXX^L does not and may instead reflect הנה אנכי יושב of synoptic 1 Chr 17:1. Elsewhere in Chr the independent 1st person pronoun is always אני, as normally in synoptic texts.[27] Its unique use here of אנכי may suggest that the wording in 1 Chr 17:1 faithfully followed its source. Addition of נא in 2 Sam 7:2 (MT and LXX^B) had been facilitated by the presence of the same two letters (though in reverse order) in the following אנכי. Adding נא, whether deliberate or accidental, could have been associated with altering הנה to ראה.

The only other synoptic chapter in Samuel where we find נא is 2 Sam 24. There we read it four times in MT and LXX^B (24:2, 10, 14, 17) though only the first of these in L. As noted above, the Lucianic text (LXX^L) of Sam-Kgs attests נא less frequently than MT or LXX^B. Our discussion of נא in 2 Sam 7:2 encourages viewing the start of this story too from the perspective of its synoptic parallel in 1 Chr 21. The opening verses of 2 Sam 24 and 1 Chr 21 in MT are set out in parallel below to assist comparison.

	2 Sam 24	1 Chr 21	
1	ויסף אף־יהוה לחרות בישראל	ויעמד שטן על־ישראל	1
	ויסת את־דוד בהם לאמר	ויסת את־דויד	
	לך מנה את־ישראל ואת־יהודה	למנות את־ישראל	
2	ויאמר המלך אל־יואב שר החיל אשר אתו	ויאמר דויד אל־יואב ואל־שרי העם	2
	שוט־נא בכל־שבטי ישראל מדן ועד־באר שבע	לכו ספרו את־ישראל מבאר שבע ועד־דן	
	ופקדו את־העם		
		והביאו אלי	
	וידעתי את מספר העם	ואדעה את־מספרם	
3	ויאמר יואב אל־המלך	ויאמר יואב	3
	ויוסף יהוה אלהיך אל־העם	יוסף יהוה על־עמו	
	כהם וכהם מאה פעמים	כהם מאה פעמים	
	ועיני אדני המלך ראות	הלא אדני המלך כלם לאדני לעבדים	
	ואדני המלך למה חפץ בדבר הזה	למה יבקש זאת אדני	
		למה יהיה לאשמה לישראל	

27 אני is the shared form in 5 synoptic verses: 2 Sam 7:8, 14//1 Chr 17:7, 13; 1 Kgs 22:16, 21//2 Chr 18:15, 20; and 2 Kgs 22:20//2 Chr 34:28. However, we find variation within 2 of these 3 contexts: אנכי in 2 Sam 7:18 and 2 Kgs 22:19 but אני in 1 Chr 17:16 and 2 Chr 34:27. Only 2 Sam 7:2 and 1 Chr 17:1 share אנכי.

4	ויחזק דבר־המלך אל־יואב ועל שרי החיל	ודבר־המלך חזק על־יואב	4
	ויצא יואב	ויצא יואב	
	ושרי החיל לפני המלך		
	לפקד את־העם את־ישראל		
5–7	[northwards through Transjordan]		
8	וישטו בכל־הארץ ויבאו	ויתהלך בכל־ישראל ויבא	
	מקצה תשעה חדשים ועשרים יום		
	ירושלם	ירושלם	

B in 2 Kgdms 24 represents a very literal rendering of MT. At two points where Sam differs from Chr, B offers different though equally appropriate renderings: החיל ('the force') is rendered in 24:4 by δυναμεως first and then ισχυος; and the command to 'roam' (שוט־נא) is translated by διελθε δη in 24:2 while the completion of the mission is reported as διωδευσαν in 24:8. L retroverts to a mixture of what we read in the first line of v. 2 in Sam MT and Chr MT and adds at the end 'in Jerusalem': אל־יואב ואל־שרי החיל אשר אתו בירושלם. In the 2nd line of 3 it retroverts to יוסף יהוה אלהיו על־העם. Unlike B, L does render שוט by the same verb in 8 as both do in 2.

Samuel provides a fuller version of the story, often using the same terms as Chronicles and then reusing them, sometimes making distinctions that are not part of Chronicles. Two implications of '[went about] in all Israel' (1 Chr 21:4) are explored in Sam: '[to review] the people Israel' (2 Sam 24:4) and '[roamed] in all the land' (24:8) – 'Israel' is both people and land. 'People' (עם) features in both versions but differently: they are the 'people' to be numbered in 2 Sam 24:2, 2, 4 and possibly increased by Yahweh (24:3), while in 1 Chr 21:2 Joab is their leader and those to be numbered are identified in 21:3 as his (Yahweh's) people. Sam has made both components of 'Israel' explicit (land and inhabitants). And it also makes a distinction among the occupants: while it uses עם for 'the people as a whole' Sam employs חיל for 'the people under arms' led by Joab (2 Sam 24:2, 4, 4, 9). This introduction is significant: חיל is used once each in three other synoptic passages[28] and it is much commoner in Chr than in Sam-Kgs – the Chronicler is hardly likely to have edited it out of his census source.

The more colourful imperative שוט ('roam') in 2 Sam 24:2 is addressed primarily to David's deputy in the singular, while the more prosaic and plural לכו ('go') in 1 Chr 21:2 includes the other chiefs alongside Joab. The use of a different verb at the start of the royal command continues the redrafting that had started in the opening verses. The enticement of David was attributed in 1 Chr 21:1 to an *agent provocateur*, a 'satan' (שטן). However, the prime mover in 2 Sam 24:1 has

28 1 Sam 31:12//1 Chr 10:12; 1 Kgs 10:2//2 Chr 9:1; 2 Kgs 11:15//2 Chr 23:14.

become Yahweh's wrath, a force that had already consumed Uzzah in the story of bringing the ark to Jerusalem (2 Sam 6:7). The troublemaker in the first clause of the story may have morphed into an iteration of Yahweh's wrath from the ark narrative, yet he has not disappeared. Each consonant of שטן has been preserved in the new start of David's instruction to Joab – שוט־נא. Whatever the relationship between the census story and the prologue to the book of Job, it is Joab here who must play the role of the satan there: 'roaming' through the land.

If after comparing the two versions of the royal command to count we note that נא is Sam+ here, just as in David's words to Nathan in 2 Sam 7, our recording is accurate; yet it is also rather banal. It is much more important to recognise the literary masterstroke through which the provocative dynamics of שטן have been re-presented. The spirit of the anonymous troublemaker, far from being removed from the story, has been re-embodied in roaming Joab. At the same time, Yahweh is explicitly recognised as the moving force, as in the tale at the start of the book of Job.

The absence of δή in the Lucianic text of 2 Kgdms 7:2 helped confirm the evidence in 1 Chr 17:1 that נא was not an original component of the story of David and Nathan. L's distinctive testimony in 2 Kgdms 24 is equally important but differently so. This chapter is within one of the *kaige* portions of Kgdms, where L is witness in general to an older form of the text than B or MT. The absence of δή from Lucianic 24:10, 14, 17 suggests that נא had played no role in the older narrative source. On the other hand, its exceptional presence in 24:2 supports the thesis proposed above. נא in this verse is not, as often in Sam-Kgs and elsewhere in the Bible, an almost accidental alteration in a changed scribal milieu. Instead, and as an integral element of שוט־נא, it is part of a deliberate allusion (admittedly easier to make within that new scribal milieu) to שטן in its source.

Of the three instances of נא in 24:10, 14, 17 (MT & LXX^{B})//1 Chr 21:8, 13, 17 only the last falls within the portion represented in fragments of 4Q51 (24:16–22). The final words of v. 17 are not preserved among these remnants. However, the reconstruction in DJD XVII, claiming to follow LXX^{L} and the Syriac,[29] does not include נא. Chr frequently shares readings with 4Q51 and LXX^{L}, not least in this narrative. However, as far as נא is concerned, it seems to have been 'corrected' (though only partially in LXX[30]) towards what emerged as the standard text in 2 Sam 24.

The particle is rare in non-synoptic Chronicles: beyond synoptic 1 Chr 21 and 2 Chr 18 we read נא only three times. In 1 Chr 22:5, given the negative testimony of B and L, it appears that MT אכינה נא is a case of accidental dittography.[31] (The

29 The second claim is a surprise, since Syr does not regularly render the particle.

30 Neither LXX^{B} nor LXX^{L} has δή in 21:17; and two of the five principal witnesses to LXX^{L} (19 108) lack it also in 21:8 (Fernández Marcos 1996, 53).

31 There are several instances in Qumran MSS of the particle written נה and even נו.

same scribal process may explain at least the first three of six δή pluses in Ruth 1: נא\נה had been added in the underlying Hebrew text to fem.pl. imperative forms לכנה in 1:8 and שבנה in 1:11, 12.[32]) Only LXX^L supports MT in 1 Chr 29:20. However, the case of 2 Chr 6:40 is doubly different: (a) the immediate context is synoptic; and (b) here LXX$^{B\&L}$ both agree with MT. Shorn of נא, this verse may have provided the original conclusion of Solomon's prayer, briefly restating 1 Kgs 8:29–30//2 Chr 6:20–21 at the end of the king's seven petitions (8:31–50//6:22–39). In (synoptic?) 1 Kgs 8:52 we read an expanded form of the text (but without נא), bracketed by Exodus tradition in 8:51, 53.

נא is only certainly found in one narrative shared by Kgs and Chr – of the two kings with Micaiah and the four hundred prophets (in 1 Kgs 22:5, 13//2 Chr 18:4, 12[33]). This story has some significant links with the account of David's census. (a) David calling his people 'sheep' (2 Sam 24:17//1 Chr 21:17) anticipates Micaiah seeing Israel in his vision as sheep without a shepherd (1 Kgs 22:17//2 Chr 18:16) – uniquely within synoptic material. (b) Both Joab (2 Sam 24:3//1 Chr 21:3) and Araunah/Ornan/Orna the Jebusite (24:21//21:23) addresses David as אדני המלך ('my lord king'). No one else in synoptic texts uses this wording; but its closest echo sounds when Yahweh notes in response to Micaiah's 'sheep without a shepherd' that they have no 'lord(s)'. (c) Only David and Jehoshaphat are involved with action at a threshing floor (גרן).[34] (d) The task set by David is to number 'Israel',[35] but totals are brought back to him for both Israel and Judah.[36] It will not be an accident that there are unique links in content with the story of Micaiah, where a king of Israel and a descendant of David in Judah pledge common military action – and fail. Given these several links, it is easy to understand how the particle travelled from 1 Kgs 22//2 Chr 18 to 2 Sam 24//1 Chr 21.

10 Conclusion

I have long argued that (something very like) the synoptic narrative provided the starting point for the development of the royal narrative in Samuel-Kings.[37] It

32 The other 3 instances are in Ruth 1:13, 15, 20.

33 2 Chr 18:12 includes נא only once, but 1 Kgs 22:13 twice. Some Lucianic witnesses (but again not 19 108) also attest the particle in a third verse: 1 Kgs 22:17 (Fernández Marcos and Busto Saiz 1992, 75).

34 2 Sam 6:6; 24:16, 18, 21, 24//1 Chr 13:9; 21:15, 18, 21, 22; 1 Kgs 22:10//2 Chr 18:9.

35 As easily noted in the texts set out in parallel above, 'Judah' is plus at the end of 2 Sam 24:1 and 'all the tribes [of Israel]' is plus in 24:2. The two pluses belong together.

36 BHS suggests Gk MS evidence for 1 Chr 21:5b being secondary.

37 Most recently in *Life in Kings*.

had functioned both as the root work out of which other episodes developed and as a framework to which other stories were attached. We can see within the growth of Sam-Kgs the same processes that we sketched in Psalms and the Book of the Twelve at the start of this essay: from sparse use of נא in the earlier material to greater use in the later material, then continuing and diverging diffusion of the particle within all textual witnesses. The synoptic royal narrative belongs at the earliest to the very end of the monarchy in Jerusalem. Very sparse use of the particle in a narrative of that period will correspond to its non-use in half the books of the Twelve. Greater use of נא in Samuel-Kings as it developed corresponds in part to the greater density in Book V of the Psalms and in Haggai-Zechariah-Malachi. But it results also – like denser usage of הנה \ מאד \ גם – from the increased proportion of speech, as also in Gen 12–50.

The radically different frequencies with which these three little words are used in synoptic narrative vis-à-vis Sam-Kgs as a whole are closely matched when we compare Gen 1–11 with Gen 12–50 (the totals were noted above in fn 26). The comparison is strengthened if we add יש and (the topic of this essay) נא. יש is absent from synoptic narrative and from Gen 1–11 but is used more widely in Sam-Kgs as also in Gen 12–50. נא is also absent from Gen 1–11. Recognising the varying densities in usage of this group of little words gives greater objectivity to analysis.

Back to where we began – but with new questions rather than answers. It is entirely proper to discuss what authorship may mean in terms of many books in the Hebrew Bible. However, if הגד־נא was never authorial (whichever meaning we give to that term) but always a feature of ongoing scribal tradition, in what sense is it an example of biblical Hebrew – or what does 'biblical Hebrew' mean? How often was adding נא a scribal device towards greater precision? Was it used more in Genesis because of the importance of this prologue to Torah? If increasing profusion of נא was a feature of ongoing scribal tradition, how far is the resultant textual evidence a proper object of *socio*linguistic research?

נפש אדם and the Associations of 1 Chronicles 5 in the Hebrew Bible

1 Introduction

The combination of *nephesh* and *'adam* (נפש אדם) occurs only once in the books of Chronicles: in 1 Chr 5:21, almost at the centre of 1 Chr 1–9 (at v. 197 out of 407). Although both components are unremarkable nouns, they are combined only rarely in the Hebrew Bible. As in Chr, נפש אדם is found in only one context in each of two further books. (a) Lev 24:17–18 distinguishes between killing 'any human being' (כל־נפש אדם) and killing an animal: איש כי יכה כל־נפש אדם מות יומת ומכה [נפש־]בהמה ישלמנה (LXX does not attest the repetition of נפש in v. 18). There is a difference in penalty: death for killing a human but payment for an animal. (b) Ezek 27:13 talks of humans being traded, humans as articles of exchange in Tyre's commerce: בנפש אדם וכלי נחשת נתנו מערבך. Lev 24 makes a distinction between humans and animals; however, by contrast, Ezekiel lumps humans along with lifeless bronze items as joint items of Tyre's trade. Then we find them on three occasions in Numbers: in Num 9:6 and 19:11, 13 in definitions of ritual uncleanness; and in Num 31:35, 40, 46 alongside animals, as in 1 Chr 5:21, among the prizes of war. Leviticus and Numbers are among the broadly 'priestly' books of the Pentateuch; and Ezekiel and Chronicles have many affinities with the priestly literature. Yet such priestly links may prove quite irrelevant to understanding how the few instances of נפש אדם are related.

Translations of 1 Chr 5:21 will be reviewed next (2). Then the wider paragraph (18–22) will be discussed under three main headings: Transjordanians and Levites in the books of Numbers, Joshua, and Chronicles (3); stories of victory, booty, and survival in Chronicles (4); and the sources of 1 Chr 5:18–22, 25–26 (5). Some conclusion will then be drawn (6).

2 Translation issues

נפש אדם may be near central in the Chronicler's prologue, but what does it mean? 1 Chr 5:21 is often paraphrased rather than translated literally. Roddy Braun's translation[1] is not untypical:

1 Braun, 70.

https://doi.org/10.1515/9783111060279-004

וישבו מקניהם	So they seized their cattle
גמליהם חמשים אלף	(fifty thousand camels,
וצאן מאתים וחמשים אלף	two hundred and fifty thousand from their flocks,
וחמורים אלפים	and two thousand asses),
ונפש אדם מאה אלף	together with one hundred thousand men whom they took alive.
כי־חללים רבים נפלו	Many others fell slain ...

1. מקנה overwhelmingly in HB refers to domestic animals, and the widespread choice to render מקנה by cattle/*Vieh*/livestock[2] gives priority to this usage over the primary sense of property or 'possessions', as rendered by Myers.[3]
2. Many agree in making a distinction between animals and humans – but that does not come straightforwardly from the simple Hebrew ־ו. Myers and Knoppers[4] seem to me to be correct when they include humans straightforwardly in the list of מקניהם.
3. כי at the start of 22 is taken as causal by some and emphatic by others.
4. How do the fallen רבים relate to what has gone before? Are they contrasted with the immediately preceding נפש אדם, or does their great number help to explain how the Transjordanians were able to take such huge amounts of plunder, including human slaves?
5. Whatever the answer to 4., the 'many fallen slain' at the start of 22 have influenced Braun, Willi, and Knoppers[5] to give separate value to נפש from אדם in translation.[6] However, Myers ('men') and Klein ('people') take נפש אדם as a single semantic unit.[7]

מקניהם can be read strongly as defining the possessed status of all the living creatures that follow:

They captured **their stock**:	their camels 50,000	וישבו **מקניהם** גמליהם חמשים אלף
	and sheep 250,000	וצאן מאתים וחמשים אלף
	and asses 2,000	וחמורים אלפים
	and humans 100,000	ונפש אדם מאה אלף

2 Rendering מקניהם at the start by '*live*stock' (as also NRSV) may not be sensitive to the issues of life and death in the context – simply 'stock' would be better.

3 Myers, 33.

4 Myers, 33 and Knoppers, 376.

5 Braun, 70, Willi, and Knoppers, 376.

6 Braun's expansive 'whom they took alive' corresponds more closely to [עשרת אלפים] חיים שבו in 2 Chr 25:12 (see section 4.3 below).

7 I am puzzled that Japhet, 139 finds in this verse 'the only occurrence in Chr of נפש alone meaning "person", which is the more common usage in the priestly stratum'; and I suspect that her Hebrew has suffered in English translation.

So read, נפש אדם may have been slaves of the Hagrites, a fourth element of Hagrite property. However, if the 100,000 were surviving Hagrites who escaped being among the many who fell (5:22), then נפש אדם is a second object of וישבו,[8] and co-ordinate instead with מקניהם:

They captured **their stock**: their camels 50,000	וישבו **מקניהם** גמליהם חמשים אלף
and sheep 250,000	וצאן מאתים וחמשים אלף
and asses 2,000	וחמורים אלפים
and humans 100,000	**ונפש אדם** מאה אלף

The absolute numbers are extraordinary, and even the proportions surprising. 100,000 human captives alongside a total of 302,000 animals is just credible. But Klein's extraordinary suggestion[9] that these 100,000 humans may all have been virginal females surely constitutes one argument against joining him in reading 1 Chr 5 in light of Num 31:35, 40, 46.[10]

3 Triangular relationship?

נפש אדם would be even closer to the centre of 1 Chr 1–9 if ch. 5 were organised more logically: vv. 23–24 belong logically with vv. 1–17, while vv. 25–26 naturally link with vv. 18–22.

5:1–10		Reuben	
5:11–17		Gad	
	5:18–22		all three together
5:23–24		half-Manasseh	
	5:25–26		all three together

However, to focus on the near-central location of נפש within the opening chapters of Chronicles would probably lead interpretation into a *cul de sac*. Yet there is more than one structural way to suggest significant links. Within the register of all Israel (1 Chr 4–8), we find Transjordan (5) and the Levites (5–6) at the centre: between the southern (4) and the northern (7–8) tribes west of the Jordan. A similar distinction between groups of tribes is achieved differently in Joshua by having Transjordan and Levites and refuge not separate south from north but set before (Josh 13–14) and after (20–22) south and north (15–19).

8 *Die Bibel (in heutigem Deutsch)*, 435 supplies a second verb for the second object: *Sie erbeuteten von ihnen … und nahmen 100,000 Mann gefangen.*
9 Klein 2006, 168.
10 See section 3.2 below.

1 Chr 4–8		Josh 13–22	
4	South	13–14	Transjordan and Levites
5A	Transjordan	15	South
5B–6	Levites and refuge	16–19	North
7–8	North	20–22	Refuge, Levites, and Transjordan

It is the same two groups that receive special attention at the end of Numbers: Transjordan (Num 32) and Levites and refuge (Num 35). Some key terms have similar prominence in these same books.

– אחזה (holding/possession) is concentrated at the end of Numbers (and related end of Deuteronomy), in Josh 21–22, at the end of Ezekiel, and in Chronicles.[11]
– In seven contexts in the narrative books, מקנה (possession/holding of livestock) denotes property belonging to David and subsequent kings in Jerusalem;[12] but ten times in the narratives listed below, all set between Exodus and monarchy, מקנה is exclusively associated with Israel in Transjordan or Reuben/Gad/half-Manasseh in particular.

Num	20:19	Israel and Edom
	31:9	Israel and Midian
	32:1, 4, 16, 26	Gad and Reuben
Deut	3:19	Reuben/Gad/half-Manasseh
Josh	22:8	Reuben/Gad/half-Manasseh
1 Chr	5:9, 21	Reuben, then Reuben/Gad/half-Manasseh

An eleventh case (Josh 14:2–4) explains how the Levites relate to the 12 tribes understood as 9½ west of the Jordan +2½ east.[13]

There is further evidence of a triangular relationship between the end of Numbers, the framework of Josh 13–22, and 1 Chr. מעל often appears in these books in contexts that have already used מקנה.

	מקנה	מעל
Numbers	31:9; 32:1, 4, 16, 26	31:16
Joshua	14:4; 22:8	22:20, 31
1 Chr	5:9, 21; 7:21	2:7; 5:25; 9:1; 10:13

11 Num 27:4, 7; 32:5, 22, 29; 35:2, 8, 28; Deut 32:49; Josh 21:12, 41; 22:4, 9, 19, 19; 1 Chr 7:28; 9:2; 2 Chr 11:14; 31:1; and 14× in Ezek 44–48.

12 1 Sam 23:5; 30:20; 2 Kgs 3:17; 1 Chr 28:1; 2 Chr 14:14; 26:10; 32:29. 1 Chr 7:21 provides the sole exception.

13 The Cisjordanians are described as 9½ tribes only in Num 34:13; Josh 13:7; 14:2.

Itzhak Amar draws attention, within his discussion of how the Chronicler portrays exile differently for Judah, Israel, and the Transjordanians,[14] to the several similarities noted by Zakovitch[15] between the portrayal of west and east in Num 32 and Josh 22. But he does not comment on the fact that Reuben and Gad are found in parts of these texts without half-Manasseh.

- They (mostly in the order Gad-Reuben) are the only players in Num 32:1–32, with half-Manasseh added only in 32:33–42.
- In Josh 22 MT, Reuben, Gad, and half-Manasseh feature throughout vv. 1–31 while only Reuben and Gad in the concluding vv. 32–34.[16]
- As already noted, 1 Chr 5 starts with Reuben alone, moves to Gad alone, then reports on all three together before a separate mention of half-Manasseh.

3.1 1 Chr 5 and Josh 22

The kinship between these chapters is marked not just by shared terminology – an argument over substance is also implied. 1 Chr 5:25 straightforwardly attributes the exile of Reuben, Gad, and half-Manasseh to a gross though unspecified breach (מעל) with the god of their fathers. In Josh 22, however, a specific accusation of מעל is laid by the western majority against the eastern minority and is vigorously rebutted by them. The western tribes first charge these easterners with מעל over a structure near the Jordan, but then become persuaded they had been wrong in making such a complaint. Possibly 1 Chr 5:25 is a brief reference to the extended narrative in Josh 22. It is equally possible that the debate reported in Joshua between tribes east and west of the Jordan was created in response to the charge recalled in 1 Chr 5. That long account is told differently in MT and LXX, with some of the differences reflected in the variant retellings in Josephus and Pseudo-Philo – and, in MT at least, Joshua himself is absent from the story.[17]

3.2 Num 31: a major locus for נפש אדם

Num 31 deals with living booty, human and animal, taken by Israel from Midian, and in much greater detail than 1 Chr 5 from the Hagrites. And this long chapter of 54 verses immediately precedes the report in Num 32 of Moses settling the

14 Amar, 367.
15 Zakovitch, 200.
16 LXX includes half-Manasseh throughout.
17 Auld 2012.

Transjordanians in a land entirely suitable for מקנה (32:1, 4, 16, 26 resonate with 1 Chr 5:9). The act of capture is stated in Num 31:9 using the same verb שבה as 1 Chr 5:21 (with the cognate noun שבי used in 31:12, 19, 26). The expressions for 'those going out to war', היצאים לצבא (31:27, 28) and היצאים בצבא (31:36), are similar to but not the same as the Chronicler's יצאי צבא (1 Chr 5:18; 7:11; 12:33, 36; 2 Chr 26:11). In fact, the Chronicler's usage is the same as we find when all Israel is counted earlier in Numbers (chs 1 and 26).

Later in the long chapter come instructions (unique to Num 31) about the division and taxation (מכס) of the booty (31:28, 37–41), both human (אדם) and animal (בהמה) – with the animals in three categories: herd (בקר), asses (חמרים), and flock (צאן). The taxation rate for all categories, animals and humans alike, is stated in v. 28 as one *nefeš* per five hundred (אחד נפש מחמש המאות).[18] The statement in v. 31 that 'Moses and Eleazar the priest did as Yahweh had commanded Moses' is at least an interim conclusion and may have marked the end of an earlier shorter draft. There are several shifts in terminology from the first to the second part of the chapter:

- The totals of the taxable remainder are listed in 31:32–35 in reverse order from v. 28: sheep, asses, cattle, and humans.
- The humans are now termed not אדם but נפש אדם (vv. 35, 40, 46) and narrowly defined in 31:35 as women who had not experienced lying with males (אשר לא־ידעו משכב זכר).
- The tax due on the three categories of animal is stated as a simple numeral, for example there were 36,000 cattle 'and the tax on them for Yahweh was seventy-two' (ומכסם ליהוה שנים ושבעים). However, the tax on the 16,000 נפש אדם is given in v. 40 not as 'thirty-two' but as 'thirty-two *nefeš*' (שנים ושלשים נפש).[19]

4 Camels, capture, and divine aid in Chr

In several respects, what the Transjordanians capture from the Hagrites anticipates several linked situations described in Chronicles.

4.1 Key terms

A pattern of recurrent terms readily illustrates this:

18 The first half of this chapter uses נפש just once more: כל הרג נפש (v. 19).
19 מלקוח (31:11, 12, 26, 27, 32) is used elsewhere in HB only in Isa 49:24, 25.

מקנה	1 Chr 5:9, **21**; 7:21; 28:1; 2 Chr **14:14**; 26:10; 32:29
רכוש	1 Chr 27:31; 28:1; 2 Chr 20:25; 21:14, 17; 31:3; 32:29; 35:7
גמלים	1 Chr **5:21**; 12:41; 27:30; 2 Chr 9:1; **14:14**
שבה	1 Chr **5:21**; 2 Chr 6:36, 37, 38; **14:14**; 21:17; 25:12; 28:5, 8, 11, 17[20]
עזר	1 Chr **5:20**; 12[5×]; 18:5; 22:7; 2 Chr **14:10, 10**; 18:31; 19:2; 20:13; 25:8; 26:7, 13; 28:16, 23; 32:3, 8

As the numbers in **bold** make clear, the report of the confrontation between King Asa and the Cushites (2 Chr 14:9–15) provides the closest parallel. And the relevance of this link is further marked by similar resources available to Asa and the Transjordanians: נשאי מגן (shield-bearers) is unique in HB to 1 Chr 5:18 and 2 Chr 14:7, while דרכי קשת (bow-drawers) is found additionally only in Jer 50:14, 29 and 1 Chr 8:40. The combination מגן וחרב (5:18) is known elsewhere only in Ps 76:4, while the passive participle למוד (5:18) and the combination שעמהם (5:20) are unique. But there is one key difference: in the case of Asa, as often in the other subsequent passages, the humans or animals captured are said to be 'very many' (רב מאד) or 'in quantities' (לרב). In all of Chronicles, it is only in 1 Chr 5:21 that we are provided with precise totals – as also in Num 31.

4.2 Arabic, camels, and corpses

The list of the defeated Hagrites starts with their camels, which can remind us of the joke that purports to explain how difficult it is to learn Arabic – because so many nouns in that language have at least four senses: a word means itself, and its opposite, and something obscene, and some part of a camel. And that observation, even if much exaggerated, leads back to the book of Numbers, even if not one camel can be found anywhere in its 36 chapters.

Num 9:4–5 opens: 'Moses spoke to all Israel of holding the Passover. And they held the Passover at first on the fourteenth day of the month …' The passage continues (9:6): ויהי אנשים אשר היו טמאים לנפש אדם ולא יכלו לעשת־הפסח ביום ההוא – 'And there were men who had become unclean in respect of a נפש אדם and they were unable to perform the Passover on that day.' How can one become unclean by way of or in respect of a living human being? The more specific Num 19:11, 13 apparently clarifies the situation: הנגע במת לכל־נפש אדם וטמא שבעת ימים – 'Whoever touches the dead of any human being will be unclean seven days.' It seems that נפש אדם, like any good Arabic word in the jest, can also mean its opposite; and certainly נפש in Qumran Hebrew (Clines

20 Half the non-synoptic instances in Chronicles of שבה are in 2 Chr 28 – Judah under Ahaz suffers incursions from Aram (v. 5), Israel (vv. 8, 11), and Edom (v. 17).

2001, 733b), like its cognates in Aramaic and Arabic, can refer to a memorial for the dead.

4.3 חיים in 2 Chr 25, מחיה in 2 Chr 14, and נפש in 1 Chr 5

According to the synoptic narrative, Amaziah and his people struck down 10,000 men of Seir (2 Chr 25:11//2 Kgs 14:7). But the Chronicler adds in the next verse that they captured (שבו) a further 10,000 alive (חיים): ויך את־בני שעיר עשרת אלפים ועשרת אלפים חיים שבו בני יהודה. These they then threw to their destruction from the top of a rock. Klein interprets this action in light of the observation by the unnamed man of God that Yahweh could give Amaziah much more if he discharged his northern mercenaries.[21] Troy Cudworth cautions in response that Chr 'never praises mere brutality for its own sake'.[22] However that may be, 'alive' (חיים) in this supplement to the older story is the result of a skilful re-reading of the immediate synoptic context. The story shared with the book of Kings about Amaziah's success over the Edomites and subsequent challenge to Joash of Israel uniquely contained two of the very rare[23] synoptic instances of this 'life/living' word.

The first response by J[eh]oash to the presumptuous Amaziah was verbal: couched in the form of a fable (2 Chr 25:18//2 Kgs 14:9). As often in a parabolic warning (distinct from an allegory), the relationship between the characters in the story and those in the real-life situation it addresses is flexible. On first hearing/reading the fable, we fairly suppose that the king of Israel is portraying himself as the cedar. But when he responds in action, he is experienced more like a 'wildlife' (חית השדה), an animal who would trample on a mere thistle. Defeat him he did; but the consequence was paradoxical: Amaziah out*lived* wild*life* Jehoash by fifteen years (25:25//14:17), till his reign ended in death in Lachish during an uprising against him. The Chronicler's addition to the Edom section of the story underlined a mismatch: between Amaziah's behaviour to 'the men of Seir' and his own lenient treatment at the hands of Jehoash. Ten thousand men of Seir were still *alive* after the battle; but, unlike Amaziah who would live fifteen more years after his defeat, they sur*vived* only to meet an immediate grisly fate.[24]

21 Klein 2010, 242.

22 Cudworth, 151.

23 There are seven at most: 2 Chr 6:31; 10:6; 18:13//1 Kgs 8:40; 12:6; 22:14; and 2 Chr 23:11; 25:18, 25//2 Kgs 11:12; 14:9, 17 (Auld 2017, 29–38). The seventh is 1 Chr 11:8, arguably part of a more original account of David taking Jerusalem than 2 Sam 5:6–9 (Auld 2011, 395–399).

24 The final synoptic instance of חיה was no less influential on the development of the book of Kings. I have argued that Amaziah's 15-year survival was the model for Hezekiah's survival from Sennacherib's invasion in his 14th year to his own death in the 29th year (Auld 2017, 184).

Asa's struggle with the Cushites is told in terms very reminiscent of 1 Chr 5. The defeat is no less decisive and is described in a single clause (2 Chr 14:12): 'and there fell of the Cushites till none of them had life' (ויפל מכושים לאין להם מחיה), though a great quantity of booty is also reported. Klein inserts 'wounded' in his paraphrase: 'some fell wounded beyond recovery'.[25] It should be stressed that מחיה in the Asa story and חיים in the Amaziah story are the only instances of words related to חיה in all of non-synoptic Chronicles.[26] The behaviour of kings Asa and Amaziah described in non-synoptic Chronicles matches that of their ancestor David in non-synoptic Samuel: in his southern raids (1 Sam 27:9, 11) 'he left alive neither man nor woman' (ולא יחיה איש ואשה). The cases of Asa and Amaziah are cited here partly to caution against Braun's rendering of נפש אדם in 1 Chr 5:21b – 'together with one hundred thousand *men whom they took alive*'.[27] Chr, supposing he was consistent in his usage, would have used some form of חיה to convey that meaning.

נפש and חיים are familiar in HB in poetic parallel, repeatedly so in Job 33.[28] Yet in Chronicles, these terms, each only sparsely used, are never found in proximity, whether in synoptic or non-synoptic contexts. While חיים largely corresponds to Latin *vita*, נפש in Chronicles might better be represented by *vitalitas*. In the case of the Transjordanians and Hagrites, booty is reported before casualties. The booty includes humans (נפש אדם) who, like the other livestock, will be found useful and not simply led off to a second stage of slaughter.

5 Development in 1 Chr 5:1–26

There are clear signs of development within this first section of 1 Chr 5. As in Num 32 and Josh 22, it appears that half-Manasseh has been added secondarily to Reuben (and Gad).[29]

---

25 Klein 2012, 208.

26 Given that Chr did add forms of חיה twice to the source-material he shared with Sam-Kgs, it seems unlikely that he also stripped out of his source more than one hundred instances of this word. It is more likely that he knew a shorter and earlier form of the book of Kings that did not yet contain them.

27 Section 2 above.

28 The densest cluster is in Job 33:20, 22, 28, 30; but there are several other instances in Job – 7:15; 9:21; 10:1; 12:10; 36:14.

29 See section 3 above.

5.1 From Reuben alone to Reuben/Gad/half-Manasseh

The account of joint action by Reuben/Gad/half-Manasseh in vv 18–22 – before half-Manasseh has even been mentioned as a separate unit – reuses each element of vv 9b–10 except for the specifics of place (‘in the land of Gilead’, 9b) and time (‘in the days of Saul’, (10a).

	1 Chr 5:9–10 >>	>>5:18–22	
9b	כי מקניהם רבו בארץ גלעד		
10a	בימי שאול עשו מלחמה עם־ההגראים	ויעשו מלחמה עם־ההגריאים	19a
	ויפלו בידם	וינתנו בידם ההגריאים	20a
		וישבו מקניהם	21a
		כי־חללים רבים נפלו	22a

‘They made war with the Hagrites’ (10a/19a) ends with the enemy ‘in their hands’ (10a/20a). But ‘their possessions’ at the start of 9b is resumed only in 21a, while the associated רבו ... כי (9b) is not resumed till 22a by רבים ... כי, where ‘they fell’ also resumes 10a. Time and place are not overlooked in this expansive retelling. However, they are apparently only rather loosely suggested in the concluding words (22b): ‘and they settled instead of them[30] till the exile’ – see further section 5.2 below.

Benzinger already noted the link with Hagrites in 5:10.[31] Klein observes that ‘[t]he vague expansion of Reuben into the lands of the Hagrites in v. 10 is modified in vv. 21–22 by the acquisition of an enormous amount of booty and the notice that the two and one-half Transjordanian tribes settled in their territory’.[32] However, his further comment is rather odd: that ‘[t]he word “livestock” מקניהם echoes the abundant “cattle” מקניהם of the Reubenites in v. 9’.[33] Such a shift in rendering is certainly anticipated in LXX (and differently in B and L); but it seems perverse to translate מקניהם differently *precisely where* a relevant link is being asserted.

LXX^B		LXX^L	
5:9	κτήνη	5:9	κτήνη
5:21	ἀποσκευήν	5:21	κτήσεις

30 וישבו תחתיהם is anticipated in 1 Chr 4:41. Cf וישבו תחתם in Deut 2:12, 21, 22, 23 – also in a Transjordanian context.

31 Benzinger, 20.

32 Klein 2006, 158.

33 Klein 2006, 168.

We are not dealing with a simple expansion or supplementation of the earlier note. It is more like a 'midrashic' development of the conclusion of the section on Reuben. And this is not unique within 1 Chr 5:1–26. The still earlier note (5:6) about the Assyrian king exiling a Reubenite prince is reapplied to the exile of the Reubenites, Gadites, and half-tribe of Manasseh as the development of the whole section ends (5:26). In Amar's account of the narrative as chiastic, 'the exile of the two and a half tribes' (25–26) corresponds to 'Reuben ... deprived of his birthright' (1–2).[34] These opening verses of the section on Reuben are of course also secondary: the opening words of v. 1 are recapitulated in v. 3. Amar also notes unique links between the core account of Reuben and the preceding report on Simeon as also between Reuben and Levi. As to the first, both 4:38 and 5:6 use נשיא 'prince' and both 4:38–40 and 5:9–10 'describe an increase in population and livestock'.[35] And, as to the second, 5:6 and 5:41 are the only mentions of a *single* person taken into exile.[36] The links he notes might preserve evidence of a Simeon – Reuben – Levi textual substratum, that was developed later into the Transjordanian/Levite pairing explored in section 3 above. These were after all the three senior sons of Jacob listed before Judah in Gen 29:32–35; 35:23.

Amar himself does not venture into literary-historical remarks about 1 Chr 5:1–26. However, I find in his own remark that '[t]he exile of the two and a half tribes is mentioned in 2 Kgs 15.29' an echo of how the author of 5:18–22, 25–26 read 5:3–10.[37] The verse in Kings does not in fact mention Reuben, Gad, or half-Manasseh: it lists Gilead as one of several areas of Israel taken from Pekah by Tiglath-Pileser and exiled. It is because of Amar's prior knowledge that he reads *all these tribes* into a mention of Gilead. Somewhat similarly, the author of 1 Chr 5:1–26 expansively re-presented 5:3–10 in light of his knowledge of all the Transjordanian tribes. Whatever prompted the author of the longer report to produce an account of joint action by 'the sons of Reuben and Gad and half of the tribe of Manasseh', much of the content was developed from a very local source. The source of much of the rest was also close to hand.

5.2 אדם, נפש, and שבה in Solomon's prayer

נפש אדם combines two common Hebrew words. It is of course possible that these were paired more frequently in classical Hebrew, even though this is rarely attest-

34 Amar, 365.
35 Amar, 359.
36 Amar, 363.
37 Amar, 359 (n. 6).

ed in HB. The author of 1 Chr 5:21 may even have been familiar with the passages already reviewed in Ezekiel or Leviticus or Numbers. But the more important question is not whether the Chronicler knew these texts, but whether in this detail he was influenced by them. We have already noted that 1 Chr 5:18–22 and 5:26 were spun in part from threads sourced very locally in 1 Chr 5:6, 9b–10a.

There are also several close links between this 'midrash' and the seventh and last request in Solomon's long prayer (2 Chr 6:36–39//1 Kgs 8:46–50a). Whether as part of the familiar book of Kings (the consensus view) or as one element of an older draft of Kings (my own view), Solomon's long prayer was part of the Chronicler's major source. נפש and אדם are both used in this final petition – separately. More significantly, the prayer includes alongside אדם (6:36) and נפש (6:38) the only synoptic instances of the verb שבה: twice in qal (36) and once in niphal (37). Not only so – a feature of this petition is the juxtaposition of the common and also assonant verb שוב ([re-]turn) with this repeated verb שבה (capture): והשיבו and ושבו are examples of שוב in v. 37, and נשבו and שבים of שבה; and in v. 38, ושבו is again related to שוב, but שבו and שבים to שבה.[38] Modelled on Solomon's intricate play, the 'midrash' concludes (5:22b) equally skilfully: וישבו תחתיהם עד־הגולה (and they dwelt in their place till the exile). גולה (exile) names the background implied in Solomon's plea; and וישבו (dwelt) is no less assonant with שבה than Solomon's שוב.

Num 31 also uses both שבה (v. 9) and נפש אדם (vv. 35, 40, 46), but not in the same immediate context. Then, though a long chapter, it uses neither of the assonant – and common – verbs שוב and ישב. Only Solomon's prayer in all of HB, like 1 Chr 5, uses both אדם and נפש (though not in actual combination), with שבה in close proximity.

6 Some conclusions

6.1 1 Chr 5 in light of Numbers and Joshua

Israel's Levites and the tribes east of the Jordan are odd associates from several points of view. Yet they share an important link that can be stated both negatively and positively. Neither has a share in the division of land west of the Jordan and both have requirements for grazing livestock. The holdings (מקנה) of the Transjordanians are described in terms of animals, while the Levites have a need for pasture (מגרש) near their appointed cities.

---

38 Non-synoptic 2 Chr 28:11 repeats the wordplay: והשיבו השביה אשר שביתם מאחיכם.

These two groups come to the fore in the final chapters of Numbers as joint exceptions within a 12-tribe Israel: counted once in Num 1 and again in Num 26 after forty years, this Israel is now facing the historical and topographical realities of settlement in a promised land west of the Jordan. In Josh 13–22, their exceptional situation is described before and after the division of that western land of promise; but in 1 Chr 5–6 they are listed at the heart of the people, between south (1 Chr 4) and north (7–8). For all that they are handled side by side in Numbers and Joshua as well as at the start of Chronicles, there is one major difference in the Chronicler's treatment of the two exceptional groups. Levites and priests will play a large role throughout Chronicles while the Transjordanians are restricted to 1 Chronicles:[39] they do not reappear in the text after the death of David has been reported. This textual disappearance – the 'actual' disappearance will not occur till much later – may support Amar's reading the Transjordanian exile as one without return.

The inter-relatedness of Num 32, Josh 22, and 1 Chr 5 as they present the Transjordanians does not simply belong to the final stage in the development of these texts. There is some evidence in each that the half-tribe of Manasseh has been added to a prior Reuben-Gad pairing. The materials in 1 Chr 5:18–22, 25–26 about the eastern tribes as a group are additional to the traditions about the three separate units. A key source of their wording is the section on Reuben (5:3–10). Then 1 Chr 5:26 states that the easterners were exiled because of מעל, while Josh 22 debates such a charge against them and finally rejects it. The Chronicler may have misremembered the narrative in Joshua or disagreed with it. Alternatively, as suggested above, the extended narrative in Josh 22 may have taken the brief note reported in Chronicles as the opportunity for an extended discussion of centre and periphery, of the legitimacy or otherwise of (cultic) life outside the western heartland. I am no longer committed to the view that the list of Levitic cities in 1 Chr 6 was the source of Josh 21; but I still find it equally unlikely that Josh 21 (MT or LXX) was the source of the list in 1 Chr 6. The ideal number 48, stated in Num 35 (4 cities from each of 12 tribes), has been imposed on a prior list which it cannot fit: Judah and Simeon have 9 cities and the Aaronites 13.[40]

In most of Num 31 (in vv. 11, 26, 28, 30, 47), the term for human (as distinct from animal) is simply אדם. But in the supplementary section about taxation (vv. 32–46) this is replaced (in vv. 35, 40, 46) by נפש אדם (human [person?]). The end of the supplement is marked by recapitulating much of vv. 30–31 in v. 47, including a return to using the simple אדם. If the author of the so-called midrash in 1 Chr 5:18–22 did draw on the expanded text of Num 31–32 with its variation

39 1 Chr 6:48, 63; 11:42; 12:9, 15, 38; 26:32; 27:16, 21.
40 Auld 1990.

between אדם and נפש אדם, then his נפש אדם too may signify little different from אדם; and, even if נפש does have its own significance within the pairing, it will simply mean 'person' or 'individual'.[41]

6.2 Victory and booty and life in Chronicles

In the victory story of Amaziah, continued living (חיים) on the part of the vanquished is mentioned only to be immediately extinguished. In the victory story of Asa, life/survival (מחיה) is mentioned only to be denied. These, we need to remember, are the only two instances of חיה/'life' in non-synoptic Chronicles; and, in the Chronicler's version of the story of Jerusalem's monarchs, both Asa and Amaziah came to a bad end. However, for the two-and-a-half tribes east of the Jordan, 100,000 נפש אדם are a vital human resource.

The victory-plus-booty report in 1 Chr 5:18–22 is the first in a whole series of such narratives in Chronicles; yet it is also distinct from those that follow. It states precise thousands of animals and humans captured while other reports simply claim 'large numbers'. Then, even within the sub-group of three that deal with the issue of continued existence for the defeated humans, the report about the Transjordanians takes its own path. Defeated Edomites equal in number to those who died in battle do leave the field 'alive' (חיים), though only to be killed elsewhere. As for the defeated Kushites, no 'life' (מחיה) survived. The Chronicler took over from his source only a small number of forms related to חיה. It is only in these two notes that Chr adds to this already sparing usage; and in one of them חית השדה and ויחי were already part of the inherited synoptic context (2 Kgs 14:9, 17//2 Chr 25:18, 25). However, the continuation of human life after the Hagrite defeat in 1 Chr 5:21 is differently expressed. Here the Chronicler uses נפש, a term similarly rare in both synoptic and non-synoptic Chronicles. 'Life' (חיים\מחיה) denotes the opposite of immediate death meted out by the troops of Amaziah or Asa. But human נפש has potential as a useful labour force. The Chronicler made at least a lexical distinction between the battlefield actions of the eastern tribes and of two kings in Jerusalem. Whether he intended thereby an ethical distinction is hard to determine. Unlike Achar/n before them (1 Chr 2:7) or Saul after them (10:13–14), their terrible fault (מעל) is left unspecified (5:25).

6.3 A 'midrash' indebted to Solomon

Two features of 1 Chr 5 do invite comparison with Num 31: specification of booty-totals unique within Chr; and the use of נפש [אדם]. However, three further

41 As … *ainsi que cent mille personnes* in *La Bible: traduction oecuménique*, 1813.

features of 1 Chr 5 – *in addition to* uniquely sharing the keywords אדם, נפש, and שבה – suggest an even closer relationship with the conclusion of Solomon's long prayer at the dedication of the temple: (1) The assonant play by Solomon on שבה and שוב is echoed in 1 Chr 5 by play on שבה with ישב. (2) The formula 'with all his/their heart and נפש' from the source-prayer (2 Chr 6:38) is repeated almost verbatim three times in non-synoptic Chr – Solomon's words were clearly important to this author.[42] (3) Several other elements of vv. 18–22 and vv. 25–26 are also midrash-like developments, in their case of material in vv. 1–10. In the source text, נפש and אדם both have a distinct role. That makes it more likely that they retain a separate function in 1 Chr 5:21 and that combined נפש אדם was not simply, as in the extension to Num 31, an expanded alternative to אדם.

Typical of many key synoptic terms in the older book of Jerusalem's kings, the four instances of נפש come in two pairs, with each member of the pair relating to a different king.[43]

1a	1 Chr 11:19 (//2 Sam 23:17)	כי בנפשותם הביאום
1b	2 Chr 1:11 (//1 Kgs 3:11)	ולא־שאלת את נפש שנאיך
2a	2 Chr 6:38 (//1 Kgs 8:48)	ושבו אליך בכל־לבם ובכל־נפשם
2b	2 Chr 34:31 (//2 Kgs 23:3)	בכל־לבבו ובכל־נפשו

1. David refuses to drink water brought by his heroes from Bethlehem at cost of their *lives* and Yahweh praises Solomon in his vision at Gibeon for not requesting the *life* of those who hate him.
2. In each of the second pair, נפש reinforces לב:[44] Solomon asks Yahweh to listen if his future exiled people commit *their whole hearts and lives* in turning back to him and Josiah covenants *with his whole heart and life* to follow Yahweh.

The non-synoptic usage of each in Chronicles nicely illustrates the thesis of organic development from the synoptic core.[45] Four of the five non-synoptic instances maintain the synoptic inheritance or modify it only minimally:

---

42 Japhet rightly finds the usages in 1 Chr 22:19 and 28:9 'characteristic of the Chronicler' (493, cf. 402), yet describes 2 Chr 15:12 as borrowing from a Deuteronomistic phrase (726).

43 Auld 2017, 92–93 included 29 significant pairings. These נפש-pairs are two of more than 130 listed in Auld 2021 f.

44 One half of all the synoptic occurrences of 'heart' are found in Solomon's prayer: 2 Chr 6:7, 8, 8, 14, 30, 37, 38//1 Kgs 8:17, 18, 18, 23, [38,] 39, 47, 48. Of these, it is the culminating instance that is paired with נפש.

45 The thrust of my work on Sam-Kgs and Chr has been less interested in Chr as such and more in what comparison between Chr and Sam-Kgs helps us to understand about Sam-Kgs: both Sam-

- 1 Chr 11:19 simply repeats the synoptic usage within the same verse.
- 1 Chr 22:19; 28:9; 2 Chr 15:12 repeat or lightly modify the use of נפש to reinforce לב that is already synoptic in 2 Chr 6:38; 34:31 and is most familiar now in the Shema and related texts.

If this short narrative builds on material from the source of Chronicles, and specifically the water brought to David from Bethlehem or the seventh request in Solomon's prayer, נפש אדם will carry the stronger sense of 'live humans' or even 'lively humans'.

An ancient writer could re-present details of a more ancient report about Reuben in his own account of the two-and-a-half tribes. A modern scholar familiar with Numbers and Joshua could read Gilead in Kings as a reference to these two-and-a-half tribes. And it is natural for other contemporary readers, familiar with the categories Primary History (Genesis-Kings) and Secondary History (Chronicles-Ezra-Nehemiah), to give priority to Numbers and Joshua when studying similar materials in Chronicles.[46] However, this essay has advised double caution in relation to the development of 1 Chr 5:1–26. (1) Even the latest elements in this narrative are derived from earlier material within Chronicles. (2) While there are clear links with late elements in both Num 31 and Josh 22, the direction of influence in each case was arguably from 1 Chr 5 to these 'partner texts'. Each such relationship between materials in the so-called 'Primary' and so-called 'Secondary' Histories must be assessed on its own merits.[47]

Kgs and Chr being organic developments from a much earlier book of Kings. The book of Chronicles may be one of the latest books in HB. However, in several cases I suspect that it also contains evidence about earlier stages in the so-called 'Primary History' (Genesis-Kings). See below.

46 The end of Auld 2002 probed these terms. 'Primary' in English is ambiguous: it can refer to greater authority (primacy) or simply greater age. Torah and Former Prophets (the Primary History) certainly have greater (canonical) authority; but does that necessarily derive from the greater age of all their materials?

47 Whichever way the influence runs between the 'generations' (תולדות) at the start of Genesis and the start of Chronicles, the fact that 1 Chr 1 and Gen 5 open with the same genealogy of Adam and that Gen 5 has a formal 'title' ('*This is the book* of the generations of Adam') may preserve evidence that 'the generations of heaven and earth' (Gen 1–4) are a later preface to the 'first' book of the Bible (Auld 2005).

Did the Assyrian Envoy Know the *Venite*? What Did He Know? What Did He Say? And Should He Be Believed?

Narrator and envoy in Chronicles

In its report on King Hezekiah, the book of Chronicles offers quite the longest reform report anywhere in the histories of the monarchies since David and Solomon. Much ground is covered in 2 Chr 29–31; but it is widely agreed that one key statement by the narrator (31:1) summarizes the action taken by 'all Israel who were present (at the festival of Passover and unleavened bread just celebrated)' – וישברו המצבות ויגדעו האשרים וינתצו את־הבמות ואת־המזבחת: 'and they shattered the pillars and they hacked the Asheras and they tore down the "high places" and the altars'. Later in the Hezekiah narrative (32:12), the Assyrian envoy is able to argue that the king deceives his own people when he claims that Yahweh will deliver them from the king of Assyria – הלא־הוא יחזקיהו הסיר את־במתיו ואת־מזבחתיו ויאמר ליהודה ולירושלם לאמר לפני מזבח אחד תשתחוו ועליו תקטירו: 'Is he not the one whose "high places" and whose altars Hezekiah removed and said to Judah and Jerusalem, "Before one altar you shall prostrate yourselves and on it offer incense?"' There is no conflict between the envoy and the Chronicler: the envoy certainly passes over what was done to the pillars and the Asherim. And by talking of simply 'removing' the *bāmôth* and altars he concentrates on the king's policy decision rather than the shattering and hacking and pulling down by the crowds with enthusiasm (the Hebrew verbs are emphatic *piels*). And Hezekiah's final instruction (ועליו תקטירו, 'and on it offer incense'), according at least to the Assyrian outside the walls, rights what the king had said was wrong at the very start of his reform (29:7): ויכבו את־הנרות וקטרת לא הקטירו ועלה לא־העלו בקדש לאלהי ישראל ('[our fathers] have put out the lamps, and even incense have they not offered and burnt offerings have they not made in the holy place to the god of Israel').

Prostration before a single altar does go beyond anything the narrator has told us about Hezekiah. But we tend to believe the envoy here – he has been well-informed and fair about everything else. And what he says fits the contrast that the narrator makes between Hezekiah and his father Ahaz. Previous kings in Jerusalem – even good ones – may have *failed* to remove the *bāmôth*; but Ahaz was *enthusiastic* in cultivating them (the verbs in 28:4 are *piels* as in 31:1). Ahaz also 'shut up the doors of Yahweh's house and made himself altars in every corner of Jerusalem' (28:24). 'One altar' (32:12, MT) is therefore a credible response from Hezekiah to his father's 'altars in every corner'. LXX reads 'this altar' like

https://doi.org/10.1515/9783111060279-005

the book of Kings, and may be more original. But, in a context of the son undoing the father's multiple mistakes, the difference between מזבח אחד and המזבח הזה may be immaterial: 'one' simply clarifies 'this'.

Narrator and envoy in Kings

When we turn from Chronicles to Kings, we find a rather different relationship between narrator and Assyrian envoy. This narrator's reform *note* (hardly a 'report') in 2 Kgs 18:4 states simply: הוא הסיר את־הבמות ושבר את־המצבת וכרת את־האשרה וכתת נחש הנחשת – 'he it was removed the "high places" and shattered the pillars and cut the Ashera and crushed the bronze snake'. The envoy in 2 Kgs 18:22 reports much like his counterpart in Chronicles: הלוא־הוא אשר הסיר חזקיהו את־במתיו ואת־מזבחתיו ויאמר לפני המזבח הזה תשתחוו בירושלם – 'Was it not [Yahweh[1]] whose "high places" and whose altars Hezekiah removed and said "Before this altar you shall prostrate yourselves in Jerusalem"?' Altars had *not* been included in the narrator's list of four destructions practised by Hezekiah. But by contrast, the envoy in Kings makes a *feature* of altars being *removed* and *this* altar chosen.

Again in Kings, it is sensible to compare Hezekiah with Ahaz. In 2 Kgs 16:4 (as in synoptic 2 Chr 28:4), his father had been enthusiastic about *bāmôth* (the *piel* verbs used are identical). But, when it comes to altars, the distinctive charge against Ahaz in 2 Kgs 16 concerns building a large new altar about which at least two things were wrong. It was constructed on the model of an altar Ahaz had seen in Damascus (16:10). And it replaced the Solomonic altar, which was moved aside and demoted (16:14). Against the background of Ahaz's actions, what does the envoy's '*this* altar' mean? And whose 'this' is it anyway? Is it the envoy's 'this' – this altar I am pointing to (from my vantage point overlooking your city)? Or is the envoy claiming to quote Hezekiah:

- this altar, not these *bāmôth*?
- this altar in Jerusalem, and not another elsewhere?
- this older Solomonic altar – not that new altar built by my father?

Envoy and narrators

In Chronicles, envoy and narrator appear to agree about Hezekiah's reforms. Hezekiah's people had torn down altars as well as 'high places' and Hezekiah

1 As in the similar-sounding authoritative claims אני יהוה ('I am Yahweh') and אני הוא ('I am he'), we may be dealing here with a play on הוא\יהוה.

had given instructions about reverence to be shown before a particular altar. But the envoy in Kings says more than the narrator – the narrator has not mentioned altars. Is the narrator using the envoy to spell out what he has already reported? Or is the narrator giving the envoy some independence? What does the envoy know? And, if he is at all independent, is the envoy a credible witness whether to what Hezekiah has done, or to how Jerusalem did worship at the time? It is the business of politicians and diplomats to be cleverly economical with the truth. The more the Assyrian envoy is seen to be a realistic character, the less perhaps we should believe him.

If the short reform note preserved in 2 Kgs 18:4 (without altars) was the tiny plant from which the huge tree of a complex reform narrative in 2 Chr 29–31 grew, then the addition of tearing down altars that we read in 2 Chr 31:1 may have been a graft from the envoy's speech. The expansive Chronicler had taken the envoy in his source at face value; but is this also true of the author of Kings?

Envoy in Kings and Isaiah

The Hezekiah narrative in Isa 36–39 is largely the same as in 2 Kgs 18–20. However, its starting point (Isa 36:1‖2 Kgs 18:13) is with Sennacherib's attack on the cities of Judah. Unlike the parallels in Kings or Chronicles, we are not offered any prior reform report – we have no information against which to assess the envoy's words, apart from our natural scepticism (do our enemies – or even opposition politicians – ever tell the whole truth about us, or even fully understand us?). And as we move to consider the evidence from Isaiah, the plot thickens. In Greek Isaiah, even the envoy does not offer a reform report: Isa 36:7–8 (LXX) is much shorter than MT (= 2 Kgs 18:22–23). The whole issue of prostration before whatever altar is absent from Isa 36:7 (LXX). The envoy's shorter argument here does make some sense, especially when read in Greek where *kurios* first reverently replaces 'Yahweh' before it refers to his own 'master'. He first disposes of Pharaoh as a credible ally; and then says, 'But if you say, "On the Lord our God we have put our trust", then [try?] my lord, the king of Assyria.' Whether or not this shorter text is more original, the Greek rendering of a key element may provide a clue about the envoy's character, his truthfulness. His recommendation runs as follows: התערב נא את־אדני המלך אשור (so MT in Isa 36:8 – 2 Kgs 18:23a offers the more grammatical התערב נא את־אדני את־מלך אשור). This is widely – but not wholly convincingly – rendered 'Make a bet with my lord, the king of Assyria'.

Up to six lenses have been proposed for inspecting verbal forms with the radicals ער"ב: ערב I: 'mix'; ערב II: 'stand surety'; ערב III: 'be pleasant'; ערב IV:

'be evening'; ערב V: 'offer'; and ערב VI: 'enter'.[2] This is not the place for a full review. 'Make a wager' is explained on the basis of ערב II.[3] A hitpael form התערב is found just 5× more in HB: Ps 106:35; Prov 14:10; 20:19; 24:21; Ezra 9:2. There is no doubt about the meaning of the first and fifth instances. Ps 106:35 talks of unwelcome 'mixing' of Israel with other nations: ויתערבו בגוים וילמדו מעשיהם ('and they mixed among the nations and learned their deeds'); and Ezra 9:2a adds explicit mention of intermarriage: כי־נשאו מבנתיהם להם ולבניהם והתערבו זרע הקדש בעמי הארצות ('and they took of their daughters for themselves and their sons; and they, the holy seed, became mixed among the nations of the lands'). LXX in Ps 106:35, as in both 2 Kgs 18:23 and Isa 36:8, renders התערב by *mignunai* pass (be mixed), but in 2 Esdras 9:2 by *paragein* pass (be diverted). *mignunai* corresponds to ערב I. This Greek verb can be used literally of sexual mixing, and also in metaphors that take off from that literal sense. In Prov 14:10, התערב is often rendered 'share', which could derived from ערב I or VI. 'Associate with' (Prov 20:19) could also relate to I or VI.[4] Whether he said 'Make a bet with my lord' or 'Get into bed with my lord, the king of Assyria' the envoy would be marked out as a figure of fun. He would be speaking more like a stock false prophet than a serious diplomat.

A fresh and very interesting proposal by Ronnie Goldstein[5] about התערב has the envoy inviting Judah to become auxiliary or mercenary troops of his master. He suggests that *urbi* (^{LÚ} urbī) used in three Akkadian texts, two of them inscriptions that record campaigns of Sennacherib, bears the sense of 'auxiliary forces' and is related to the root ער"ב with the basic meaning 'to enter', as Akkadian *erēbu*. (The term is apparently of West-Semitic origin, and it is probably used also in several passages within HB, Jer 50:37 for example). התערב נא would accordingly be rendered 'Become an auxiliary force [to my lord ...]'. And he notes that the cognate בני התערבות in 2 Kgs 14:14‖2 Chr 25:24 could also refer to such forces: the context makes clear that they are some sort of human 'booty' transferred from Jerusalem to Samaria by Jehoash of Israel, in addition to the gold and silver plundered from Yahweh's house and the royal treasury in Jerusalem. Given the many links between synoptic Amaziah and Hezekiah[6] – and even more between synoptic Amaziah and the developed Hezekiah of the Hezekiah/Isaiah legend in

---

2 Clines 2007, 546–549.

3 Clines 2007, 548.

4 In Prov 24:21, LXX implies a different consonantal text from MT.

5 At the meeting in Göttingen of the Aberdeen Prophecy Network (18–21 October 2015).

6 Both kings were 25 years old at their accession and both reigned for 29 years (2 Kgs 14:2‖2 Chr 25:1; 2 Kgs 18:2‖2 Chr 29:1); and, within text shared by Kings and Chronicles, Lachish is mentioned only in the reports of their two reigns (2 Kgs 14:19‖2 Chr 25:27; 2 Kgs 18:17‖2 Chr 32:9).

2 Kgs 18–20[7] – it can be argued that the author of non-synoptic התערב נא in the Hezekiah/Isaiah legend had been influenced by synoptic בני התערבות, which he found in 2 Kgs 14:14‖2 Chr 25:24.

The envoy on Hezekiah's reform

The Greek text of Isaiah's version of what the envoy says makes no mention of instructions from Hezekiah about an altar in Jerusalem. However, the Greek rendering (*mignunai*) of this rare Hebrew verbal form (התערב) encourages the suspicion that the envoy is not simply a mouthpiece for the narrator's views. Where 'altar' is part of the text, the big issue is not whether we should read 'this altar' or 'one altar – nor even which or where this one altar was. The elephant in this room is that no one else anywhere in HB ever prescribes or describes prostrating (השתחוה) before an altar[8] – not even sinking (כרע) or falling (נפל) or bowing (סגד) or kneeling (ברך) in front of an altar. Is this another obvious mistake put into the mouth of the envoy? In fact 'before' is very seldom linked with 'altar' in HB – and only once outside Kgs/Chr. The link is found 4 times synoptically in Kgs/Chr:

- 1 Kgs 8:22‖2 Chr 6:12 – 'Solomon ***stood*** before Yahweh's altar'
- 1 Kgs 8:31‖2 Chr 6:22 – 'if someone comes and swears before your altar'
- 2 Kgs 11:18‖2 Chr 23:17 – 'they killed Mattan, priest of Baal, before the altars'
- 2 Kgs 18:22‖2 Chr 32:12 – 'before this/one altar you shall prostrate yourselves'

and just 3 times elsewhere:

- 1 Kgs 8:54 (no ‖) – 'Solomon arose from before Yahweh's altar from sinking on his knees'
- 2 Chr 29:19 (no ‖) – 'see [the utensils rejected by Ahaz] are before Yahweh's altar'
- Zech 14:20 – 'the cooking pots in Yahweh's house will be like the bowls before the altar'

---

7 Non-synoptic Hezekiah is aligned in 2 Kgs 18:13; 20:6 with synoptic Amaziah who survived ('lived') for 15 years after defeat at the hands of northern Joash in a campaign that included severe threat to Jerusalem (2 Kgs 14:12, 17‖2 Chr 25:22, 25).

8 Throughout this paper, השתחוה has been rendered 'prostrate oneself' without further argument, although many public translations use the less specific 'worship'. More important is the fact that, however rendered, the elements השתחוה + לפני + מזבח are nowhere else combined in HB.

The words of Solomon's long prayer at the dedication of the temple are found almost identically in 1 Kgs 8:23–50a and 2 Chr 6:14–39; and they are also introduced in the same terms in 8:22‖6:12 – ויעמד שלמה לפני מזבח יהוה נגד כל־קהל ישראל ויפרש כפיו השמים ('And Solomon stood before the altar of Yahweh in the presence of all the assembly of Israel and spread out his hands to heaven.') 2 Chr 6:13 (without parallel in Kgs) inserts a correction between introduction and prayer – 'Solomon had made a platform ... and stood on it; and knelt on his knees (ויברך על־ברכיו) ... and spread out his hands ...'. Then (this time at the end of Solomon's long prayer) there is a corresponding plus in 1 Kgs 8:54 (without parallel in Chr) – 'Solomon arose from before Yahweh's altar from sinking on his knees' (מכרע על־ברכיו). Both versions that have come down to us of Solomon's prayer have modified the text they share, the text they inherited. In the older version of the narrative, Solomon simply stood in front of Yahweh's altar. Both successor versions have contrived to make him kneel.

The larger synoptic context seems relevant as well. Material shared by Sam-Kgs and Chr uses השתחוה ('prostrate oneself') in only four passages; and a foreign element is *always* involved: Arauna/Orna the *Jebusite* prostrates himself to David (2 Sam 24:20‖1 Chr 21:21); Solomon is warned against prostration to *other* gods (1 Kgs 9:6, 9‖2 Chr 7:19, 22) and Manasseh is blamed for such behaviour (2 Kgs 21:3‖2 Chr 33:3). Then, when the *Assyrian* envoy reports Hezekiah as commending prostration (2 Kgs 18:22‖2 Chr 32:12), how were the earliest readers intended to react to his words?

The next point is not a synoptic observation – at least not in the sense I am normally using the term in this paper. There is one other instance of השתחוה in the Hezekiah story as told in both 2 Kings and Isaiah: Sennacherib was killed by his sons as *he* prostrated himself in the house of his god Nisroch (2 Kgs 19:37‖Isa 37:38). Sennacherib's envoy outside Jerusalem may fairly have supposed that Hezekiah would have prescribed worship like his own master practised at home in Nineveh.

We have noted that the setting of Solomon's long prayer was re-framed in both Kings and Chronicles: the originally standing Solomon became kneeling Solomon. We find something analogous in both books in or near the Hezekiah narratives. In Chronicles, Hezekiah's cultic reforms began in the first year of his reign (2 Chr 29:3). When the temple and the altar and its utensils had been cleansed, the king ordered that a holocaust be offered on the altar (29:27). Each of the next verses reports prostration during or after the sacrifice: by the whole assembly (28), by the king and all with him (29), and by the levites (30). Fresh from reading this detailed report about prostration relating to sacrifice, we can hardly be surprised by the Assyrian envoy's statement that Hezekiah had required prostration before the altar (32:12).

In Kings, the similar point is made just before the start of the Hezekiah story, towards the end of the long peroration in 2 Kgs 17:7–41 on the fall of northern Israel. First of all, and unremarkably, four covenanted prohibitions[9] are listed *against* any sort of reverence or worship or sacrifice to *other* gods (v. 35):

לא תיראו אלהים אחרים	'you shall not fear other gods'
ולא־תשתחוו להם	'and you shall not prostrate yourselves to them'
ולא תעבדום	'and you shall not serve them'
ולא תזבחו להם	'and you shall not sacrifice to them'

The surprise comes in the following verse (36), where the first, second, and fourth prohibitions in respect of foreign gods reappear as *positive* demands in respect of Yahweh:

כי אם את־יהוה	'But Yahweh
אשר העלה אתכם מארץ מצרים	'who brought you up from the land of Egypt ...'
אתו תיראו	'him you shall fear'
ולו תשתחוו	'and to him you shall prostrate yourselves'
ולו תזבחו	'and to him you shall sacrifice'

The command of prostration to Yahweh has never before been stated, anywhere in the Former Prophets. Its unique promulgation here is reinforced by wordplay and by its position within 2 Kings.[10] The fact that ולו תשתחוו ('and to him you shall prostrate yourselves') is immediately followed by ולו תזבחו ('and to him you shall sacrifice') suggests that the envoy's unique formulation לפני המזבח הזה תשתחוו ('before this 'sacrifice-place' you shall prostrate yourselves') is in the mind of the author and is being adapted. The pairing of the verbs for prostration and sacrifice is quite unusual and is found only once more in HB (1 Sam 1:3). And the novelty of this significant transition from negative to balancing positive is neatly underscored in the shift from ולא־תשתחוו להם to ולו תשתחוו and from ולא תזבחו להם to ולו תזבחו. ולו ('and to him') in v. 36 corresponds in sense to להם ('to them') in v. 35, while at the same time ולו (*wlw*) retains the sound of the ולא (*wl'*) of the previous verse. The suggestion that Jerusalem's king had advocated prostration (2 Kgs 18:22) may have surprised earlier readers of the (synoptic) Hezekiah story. However, 2 Kgs 17:36, unlike 2 Kgs 18:4, has taken the Assyrian envoy at his word. And its carefully balanced contrast between *what not* to do to foreign gods and *what* to do to Yahweh is set only a few verses before

9 ויכרת יהוה אתם ברית ויצום לאמר – 'And Yahweh made with them a covenant and commanded them saying'.

10 The situation is similar in Deuteronomy: prostration to other gods is blamed 7× (4:19; 5:9; 8:19; 11:16; 17:3; 29:25; 30:17) but commanded only once – and towards the end (26:10).

the start of the Hezekiah story. Later readers of that narrative are being prepared, as in 2 Chr 29:28–30, NOT to share the surprise of its first readers.

Finally the Venite

Knees (ברכים) are well known in HB; they are often associated with birthing[11] and nursing[12] (and adoption[13]), as are weak knees with fear.[14] But only seldom are they explicitly linked with worship or entreaty: Elijah speaks of the 'knees that have not bowed to Baal' (1 Kgs 19:18); and an officer of the king of Israel pleads on his knees before Elisha for the life of his men (2 Kgs 1:13). The only explicit parallel to Solomon on his knees before Yahweh (1 Kgs 8:54 and 2 Chr 6:13, both non-synoptic) is provided by Ezra (9:5). On the other hand, apart from the Chronicler's Solomon, a Hebrew verb 'kneel' (ברך) is attested only once more, in Ps 95:6. There is also the instance in Aramaic of Daniel kneeling (6:11). These certainly late-biblical passages in Ezr 9:5 and Dan 6:11 help to set a context for the pluses relating to Solomon kneeling in Kings and Chronicles.

Psalm 95 (the *Venite*) includes more synonyms for bowing low before God than any other biblical psalm.[15] השתחוה is used just 9× across most of the Psalter (Books I–III and V):

5:8	אשתחוה אל־היכל־קדשך	'I will prostrate myself towards your holy temple'[16]
22:28	וישתחוו לפניך	'and there shall prostrate themselves before you'
22:30	וישתחוו כל־דשני־ארץ	'and all the earth-sleepers shall prostrate themselves'[17]
29:2	השתחוו ליהוה בהדרת־קדש	'prostrate yourselves to Yahweh in holy splendour'[18]
66:4	כל־הארץ ישתחוו לך	'all the earth, prostrate yourselves to him'
72:11	וישתחוו־לו כל־מלכים	'let all kings prostrate themselves to him'[19]
86:9	וישתחוו לפניך	'and there shall prostrate themselves before you'
132:7	נשתחוה להדם רגליו	'let us prostrate ourselves to his footstool'
138:2	אשתחוה אל־היכל־קדשך	'I will prostrate myself towards your holy temple'

11 Gen 30:3; Job 3:12.

12 2 Kgs 4:20; Isa 66:12.

13 Gen 48:12; 50:23.

14 Isa 35:3; Ezek 7:17; 21:12; Nah 2:11; Ps 109:24; Job 4:4.

15 In some Christian traditions, illustrated in the 17th century Book of Common Prayer of the Church of England, it is also privileged above all other psalms: only the *Venite* is recited every day of the month.

16 Ps 5:8 = 138:2.

17 Ps 22:28 = 86:9.

18 Ps 29:2 = 96:9

19 Compare השתחוו־לו כל־אלהים in Ps 97:7.

However, this verb is found as many as 6× in Book IV of the Psalms (Pss 90–106), the shortest book:

95:6	באו נשתחוו ונכרעה נברכה לפני־יהוה עשנו	'Come let us prostrate ourselves and bow down; let us kneel[20] before Yahweh our maker'
96:9	השתחוו ליהוה בהדרת־קדש	'prostrate yourselves to Yahweh in holy splendour'
97:7	השתחוו־לו כל־אלהים	'let all gods prostrate themselves to him'[21]
99:5	והשתחוו־להדם רגלו	'and prostrate ourselves to his footstool'
99:9	והשתחוו־להר קדשו	'and prostrate yourselves to his holy mountain'
106:19	יעשו־עגל בחרב וישתחוו למסכה	'they made a calf at Horeb and prostrated themselves to a casting'

Five of these instances are within the Psalms of Yahweh as king (Pss 93–100). And the first is quite distinctive:

1. The unusual assemblage in 95:6 of verbs of self-abasement has already been noted.
2. כרע normally connotes collapse or dread.
3. As a contribution to dating we may note a. that both 'prostrate oneself' and 'bow down' are *used* in Deutero-Isaiah, but not together;[22] b. that elsewhere in HB, כרע and השתחוה are only *paired* in two late contexts, 2 Chr 29:29 and Esth 3:2, 2, 5.
4. The indicator of direction (לפני, 'before') is also most unusual, whichever of the three verbs is deemed to be most prominent.
   a. Simple ל ('to') is the normal preposition used after the verb 'prostrate oneself' (השתחוה). Pss 5:8 and 138:2 commend prostration אל־היכל־קדשך ('towards your holy temple') and Ps 99:5, 9 'to his footstool' (להדם רגלו) and 'to his holy mountain' (להר קדשו). With more physical objects, אל and ל are used, but never elsewhere לפני. The fuller לפני ('before') is occasionally used if prostration is 'in face of' Yahweh or a suffix referring to him,[23] but it never precedes a physical object like an altar.
   b. כרע ('bow down') is never construed with לפני ('before').
   c. ברך ('kneel') is not construed with לפני ('before') in 2 Chr 6:13, the only other instance in Hebrew of this verb. Aramaic קדם אלהה (Dan 6:11)

---

20 ונבכה ('and let us weep') is attested in LXX.

21 Compare השתחוו־לו כל־מלכים in Ps 72:11.

22 כרע (Isa 45:23; 46:1, 2; 65:12); and השתחוה (44:15, 17; 45:14; 46:6; 49:7, 23; 60:14; 66:23). Another verb meaning 'bow' (סגד) is unique to Deutero-Isaiah. Probably original to 46:6 (ויעשהו אל יסגדו אף־ישתחוו, 'and [the craftsman] makes it a god – they bow down and even prostrate themselves'), it is re-used in the expansive 44:15, 17, 19.

23 Ps 22:28; 86:9; and elsewhere in Deut 26:10; 1 Sam 1:19.

would correspond to Hebrew לפני אלהיו ('before his god'), but it is separated from 'knelt on his knees' by two other verbs.
d. Num 11:20; Deut 1:45; Judg 20:23; 2 Kgs 22:19‖2 Chr 34:27 provide parallels to ונבכה לפני ('and let us weep before'), attested in LXX.

'No prostration before *other* gods' was a common biblical demand. But it is less easy to determine when kneeling before *Yahweh* was first positively articulated. Other gods are frequently dismissed as unworthy of attention on the ground that they are simply human fabrications. Here too Book IV of the Psalms repays closer inspection. מסכה ('a casting') and its close associate פסל ('a carving') appear only once each in the Psalter – and not just in the very same Bk IV as includes such dense usage of השתחוה but also in immediate association with two of these instances:

95:6	באו נשתחוה ונכרעה נברכה לפני־יהוה עשנו
96:9	השתחוו ליהוה בהדרת־קדש
97:7	יבשו כל־עבדי פסל המתהללים באלילים השתחוו־לו כל־אלהים
99:5	והשתחוו־להדם רגלו
99:9	והשתחוו־להר קדשו
106:19	יעשו־עגל בחרב וישתחוו למסכה

The two relevant passages state 'Let all servants of a carved object, who boast in idols, be ashamed; prostrate yourselves to him, all gods' (Ps 97:7) and 'They made a calf at Horeb and prostrated themselves to a cast object' (106:19).

Pss 97 and 106 may be an unintended pairing, with gods in Ps 97:7 called on to acknowledge Yahweh, while Israel's fathers 'had exchanged the glory of God for the image of an ox that eats grass' (106:20)! As noted by Anja Klein, the kingship of Yahweh collection (Pss 93–100) may once have concluded an earlier Psalter consisting of most of Pss 2–100.[24] The narrative pair 105–106 may also have been relatively late members of the expanded Psalm collection.[25] However that may be, the long historical review in the final Psalm of Bk IV, with its mention of prostration before a cast idol (106:19), is significantly anticipated by briefer reviews within the kingship of Yahweh collection in Pss 95 and 99.

The *Venite* makes the first reference to prostration in Bk IV (95:6), and by including two broad synonyms it underlines the importance of self-abasement before Yahweh. It then moves immediately to the first historical reminiscence in that book (95:7b-11), which opens היום אם־בקלו תשמעו אל־תקשו לבבכם כמריבה

24 Klein 2014, 299.
25 Klein, 304–306.

כיום מסה במדבר ('Today, if you will hear his voice, harden not your hearts as at Meribah, as on the day of Massah in the wilderness.'). The link between historical reminiscence and proper approach to Yahweh is also emphasized, though differently, in Ps 99. The opening call to praise the exalted god culminates in v. 5: רוממו יהוה אלהינו והשתחוו־להדם רגלו קדוש הוא – 'Extol Yahweh our god and prostrate yourselves to his footstool – holy is he.' The following reminiscence of the relationship with Yahweh enjoyed by Moses, Aaron, and Samuel (vv. 6–8) is then capped (v. 9) by a closing repetition of v. 5. Only in Pss 95:7b-11 and 99:6–8 within Pss 90–100 do we find an appeal to historical memory; and on both occasions the appropriateness of prostration to Yahweh is not simply noted but is stressed.

If the Assyrian envoy (or – better – the author of the Hezekiah narrative) knew the Psalms, and especially the *Venite*, he would have been aware of the importance of self-abasement in worship. However that may be, it was not from the Psalms – or indeed anywhere else in HB – that he learned about prostration *before Yahweh's altar*. Only five psalms mention an altar,[26] and none of these says anything about bowing or prostrating. There is good reason to believe that the Judahite historian responsible for the shorter narrative on which both Kings and Chronicles are based was mocking an Assyrian envoy misinformed about the details of Hezekiah's cultic reforms.[27]

---

26 Ps 26:6; 43:4; 51:21; 84:4; 118:27.

27 The next study engages more fully with the wide-ranging and clearly written study by Song-Mi Suzie Park of *Hezekiah and the Dialogue of Memory* (Park 2015). While there is very much to welcome, she continues to represent the wide consensus that the envoy's words about this/one altar reflect the narrator's own view of Hezekiah's reforming actions. The material in both studies is re-presented more briefly, but set in a wider context, in Auld 2017.

Chronicles – Isaiah – Kings

1 Fortschreibung und Trigonometrie

In this paper I am developing work presented in two contributions to the Utrecht meeting (in 2013) of the (then Edinburgh) Prophecy Network. My "Recovering the Oldest Prophetic Roles in Biblical Narrative" explored both the longer narratives and the short notes describing divine/human interaction that are reported in both Sam-Kgs and Chr – from David seeking divine rulings on whether he should attack Philistines to Josiah sending members of his court to Huldah the prophetess:

2 Sam 5:19, 23	David asks for divine guidance before attacking Philistines
2 Sam 7	Nathan on building a house, and David's prayer
2 Sam 24	Gad and David's choice between 3 punishments
1 Kings 3:4–15	Solomon's vision at Gibeon
1 Kings 8	Solomon prays at the dedication of the Jerusalem temple
1 Kings 9:1–9	Solomon's vision at Jerusalem
1 Kings 12:15	confimation of words spoken by Ahijah the Shilonite
1 Kings 12:22–24	oracle spoken by Shemaiah
1 Kings 22	Micaiah and the prophets with the two kings
2 Kings 18–20	Isaiah and Hezekiah
2 Kings 22:13–20	Huldah the prophetess and Josiah

The wording of these synoptic notes and stories is remarkably stable between the two books. The parade examples are Solomon's prayer, Micaiah and the two kings, and the consultation of Huldah. The greatest variety between Kgs and Chr comes in their accounts of Solomon's two visions. The paper as read in Utrecht simply noted the one large exception that proved the rule: the Hezekiah/Isaiah narratives. The expanded paper (Auld 2015) began a discussion of this major exception.

Then Reinhard Kratz's contribution to the Utrecht meeting was a discussion of "Isaiah and the Siege of Jerusalem" (Kratz 2015). I liked his application of the *Fortschreibung* model to exploring the history of this narrative but was not persuaded by all of his results. In principle, his use of the successive rewriting model and my interest in an even-handed synoptic approach to Samuel-Kings and Chronicles could be mutually supportive, and also mutually corrective; and I want to develop such an approach here. A synoptic approach to the Hezekiah narratives is all the richer because we have inherited not two but three principal biblical sources: 2 Kgs 18:13–20:19; Isa 36–39; and 2 Chr 32:9–32.

When mapping the earth, observations recorded from at least three known positions permit more accurate reconstruction. Each of the accounts in the books

https://doi.org/10.1515/9783111060279-006

of Kings, Isaiah, and Chronicles, about Hezekiah and the Assyrian embassy, Hezekiah's illness, and Hezekiah and the visit of messengers from Babylon, is unusual in its own immediate context. And each is sufficiently different from the others, although of course Kings and Isaiah are much closer to each other in length and detail than either is to Chronicles. In Kings, the very large role played by the prophet Isaiah is without parallel in the narratives about Jerusalem's kings. In Isaiah, no other piece of prose narrative is nearly so extensive. And in Chronicles, no other royal report is quite so different from – or so much shorter than – its synoptic parallel in Kings. However, comparisons between these three should permit reconstructions of their development that are more secure than if we possessed only two of these accounts. Triangulation helps.

Most scholars consider Chronicles irrelevant to the study of the development of 2 Kgs 18–20‖Isa 36–39, and this for two reasons. The first is the more general one: Chronicles as a whole is "known" to be a reworking of Samuel and Kings. The second is more particular. Most scholars accept Stade's division of 2 Kgs 18:13 + 18:17–19:37‖Isa 36–37 between two once-separate reports of the Assyrian embassy that were only secondarily combined (Stade 1886). Some elements of the shorter 2 Chr 32 correspond to material in one of these sources and some to material in the other. It follows that it must have been after their combination that the Chronicler had written his abbreviated account. However, just one of the benefits of a *Fortschreibung* or "successive rewriting" approach to the longer version in Kgs/Isa advocated by Kratz is this: that it enables the relationship with Chr to be reconsidered. What if Chr was based not on the completed report in Kings and Isaiah but on an earlier stage in its complex development? If the longer report had been drafted in several stages, not every element of the so-called "B1" need have been in its present position before "B2" began to be drafted: the several stages in the successive rewriting of B could in principle have included some changes to the order of the material. And, if B had its origins in a narrative much shorter than Stade's B1, then comparison with the relevant portion of 2 Chr 32 which is also shorter could be relevant and should be explored.

2 Isaiah in Chronicles and Isaiah/Kings

The relevant portions of all three books share the same three main topics: first and at greatest length in each, the Assyrian threat to Jerusalem; then more briefly the life-threatening illness of Hezekiah and the visit of a Babylonian embassy which was shown his wealth. But the relationships between the three topics are differently handled. In Kgs/Isa, the king prays first about the siege (19:15–19) and then about his illness (20:2–3); and two explicit *spoken* answers are recorded

(19:20; 20:5). In Chr too, the king prays twice (32:20, 24), but here the divine responses are simply acted, not spoken: a destroying מלאך is sent and a מופת is given. In Kgs and Isa, the two situations of national and royal distress are closely and explicitly linked (19:34; 20:6). And of course the precise dating of the invasion to Hezekiah's fourteenth year in 2 Kgs 18:13||Isa 36:1 already implies this linkage. In Chr, the king does pray twice; but the troubles of city and king are not explicitly connected – one simply follows the other, linked loosely by "in these days" (בימים ההם): no date is specified. Did Chr disentangle into its original elements what Kgs/Isa had secondarily put together? Or is Chr a witness to how these traditions were shaped before the Kgs/Isa linkage? By contrast, Chr like Kgs/Isa does link the Babylonian embassy with the king's illness (and recovery): in Kgs/Isa (20:12) Babylon had heard that Hezekiah had been sick (though not that he had surprisingly revived), while in Chr they came to enquire about the (unspecified) מופת done in the land (32:31) – in both versions Hezekiah had great riches.

If we focus on the king, the only major thematic difference between Isa/Kgs on the one side and Chr on the other concerns the explicit linkage in the two longer versions between the fate of Jerusalem and of Hezekiah. But, when we focus on the prophet, the differences are much greater. Isaiah is present in Chr only at the end of the first scene: as the king prays for his city, he is with him. However, he plays no role at all in the next two scenes. In Isa and Kgs, the prophet features in all three scenes and his words actually form part of the linkage between the first two scenes. It is he who articulates the explicit divine response to each of the king's prayers, and in the second response he speaks of delivering "you and this city" (38:6//20:6).

Did the Chronicler write Isaiah out of much of the Hezekiah narrative he inherited from the books of Kings or Isaiah? Or did he draw on a source very different from the alternative we know so well from both Former and Latter Prophets? I need to be more specific about what I mean by "the Chronicler". We should distinguish in principle between the main royal reports in Chronicles on the one hand, and on the other hand the references at the end of each section to an alternative account – at least until we find evidence to conflate them.

The sentence that immediately precedes the note of Hezekiah's death (2 Chr 32:33) reads as follows in MT: ויתר דברי יחזקיהו וחסידיו הנם כתובים בחזון ישעיהו בן־אמוץ הנביא על־ספר מלכי־יהודה וישראל ("As for the remainder of the deeds of Hezekiah and his acts of loyalty – they are clearly written in the vision of Isaiah son of Amoz the prophet, upon the book of the kings of Judah and of Israel".). LXX has two differences: " ... written in the *prophecy* of Isaiah son of Amoz the prophet *and in* the book of the kings ..." Two things are plain. The author of the cross-reference[s] was aware of the Hezekiah/Isaiah story as told in the books of Kings and/or Isaiah. And the author of the main text had a very different story to tell: not only radically shorter, but also very much less concerned with Isaiah. Indeed it is fair to ask whether the mention of Isaiah alongside the king at prayer was original to the main text, or whether it was added by the author of the cross-reference[s]. By associating Isaiah with the praying king (32:20), was he simply drawing on the alternative report in which Isaiah had played a much larger role in the story of Hezekiah – the alternative report identified in the cross-reference (or is it a double reference?) that immediately precedes the note of Hezekiah's death (2 Chr 32:33)? Perhaps not.

The only mention of Isaiah in the main body of 2 Chr 32 is at the end of the siege; and this corresponds to an important feature of how the prophet is portrayed in Kgs/Isa. We meet him first at the start of 2 Kgs 19||Isa 37 (towards the end of Stade's B1). He is approached by representatives of the king; and the scene mirrors Josiah's approach to Huldah. Like Huldah, and in fact all the synoptic intermediaries in Sam-Kgs and Chr, this Isaiah responds: he voices the divine answer to a royal question. However, the Isaiah we meet in the remainder of Kgs/Isa shows more initiative: he is more like Elijah or Elisha in non-synoptic Kings. Chr only mentions Isaiah at the same point in the story as Kgs/Isa first introduces him; and, at this first introduction, he behaves differently from the Isaiah who has left no trace in Chr. That other Isaiah is a later development.

3 Where Kings and Isaiah differ

It remains hotly debated whether the largely shared material in Isa 36–39 and 2 Kgs 18–20 had its origins more in one of these books or the other. Some of this argument is focused, not on what they do share, but rather on the two portions in which they are most different from each other.

(1) The short narrative in 2 Kgs 18:14–16 about Hezekiah paying off Sennacherib that immediately follows the shared opening verse (2 Kgs 18:13||Isa 36:1) is not represented at all in Isa 36.

(2) The end of the second topic, about the healing of Hezekiah, is written very differently in 2 Kgs 20:1–11 and Isa 38:1–22. The two versions of the healing start in almost identical terms (20:1–3||38:1–3);[1] then 20:4–6[2] is a little fuller than 38:4–6.[3] However, the reports in 20:7–11 and 38:7–8, 21–22 about signs and treatment by a compress of figs diverge still further:

1 LXX attests ויהי at the opening of Isa 38:1, but simply לאמר at the start of 38:3 where MT has ויאמר אנה יהוה.

2 In place of the puzzling לא יצא העיר (2 Kgs 20:4), "in the hall" (LXX) may attest בחצ[י]ר.

3 In Isa 38:5 "the sound of [your prayer]" is LXX+, while in 38:6 ואת העיר הזאת is MT+.

- Only Kgs talks of "healing" (רפא) in 20:5, 8 (but not Isa 38:5, 22, although this verb is commoner in Isaiah than Kings).
- Only Kings specifies "the third day" for the king's return to the temple in 20:5, 8 (but again not Isa 38:5, 22). "The third day" is specified elsewhere in Sam-Kgs;[4] however, it is never found in Isaiah, and appears in Chronicles only in the synoptic 2 Chr 10:12‖1 Kgs 12:12 (also but differently in 3 Kgdms 12:24p–q).
- Then the extra detail in 2 Kgs 20:10 (without parallel in Isa 38) about the direction in which the shadow should move includes נקל ("is easy"). This verb is found in several late portions of Sam-Kgs (a significant plus in 2 Sam 6:22 related to 1 Sam 18:23; 1 Kgs 16:31; and 2 Kgs 3:18[5]) but is never found in Isaiah.

On the other hand, Hezekiah's extended response to his recovery (the so-called "psalm" in Isa 38:9–20) has no parallel at all in Kings.

Yair Zakovitch, when exploring assimilation in biblical narratives, took his start from the version of the story in 2 Kings 20:1–11 and found that "verse 7 is not only contradictory to verse 8 but is also opposed to the general character of the story … the verse was added to enhance Isaiah's similarity to Elisha" (1985, 183). This narrative judgment found support in text-critical details of the version in Isa 38. For Zakovitch, the first stage of the story was "1 (*sic*) Kings 20:1–6, 8–11, reflected in abridged[6] form in 1QIs[a] 38:1–8, minus the later addition of verses 21–22".

Raymond Person's starting-point is text-critical, rather than literary; and he concludes that only a short text such as Isa 38:7–8 originally stood between 38:6 (= 2 Kgs 20:6) and 39:1 (= 2 Kgs 20:12). Five observations combine to suggest the secondary nature of all the other verses: that they were added in 1QIs[a] by a different, later hand at the end of a short line continuing into the margin; that we find them in different positions in Kings (both MT and LXX) over against Isa (MT, LXX, and 1QIs[a]); that Hezekiah's question in these verses does not receive an answer; that these verses are closely related to the addition in 2 Kgs 20:5; and that they are lacking in the parallel account in 2 Chr 32:24–26. He suggests that "a probable source for this addition is 19:29 which has references to a sign and three years" (Person, 72).

---

4 1 Sam 30:1; 2 Sam 1:2; 1 Kgs 3:18; 12:12; 2 Kgs 20:5, 8.

5 Here, significantly part of a divine promise through Elisha – late Isaiah was compared above with Elisha.

6 "Abridged" (185) does appear to be a deliberate choice of words, although it is less than clear in n. 21 just what is "original": "Note that the version of the story in Isaiah was originally shorter than that in Kings and lacked verse 8 – part of the original story – as well as verse 7. When 2 Kings 20:7 was interpolated in Isaiah, part of verse 8 was brought along as well."

In Kgs, and only there, we have a tension between Hezekiah paying a large tribute to Sennacherib of Assyria in 18:14–16 and (still) having a treasury to display to his Babylonian visitors in 20:12–19. Isa and Chr share only the display at the end; and 2 Chr 32:23 reports that Hezekiah's wealth was enhanced through gifts brought to the king after Sennacherib's withdrawal. Have Chr and Isa resolved the tension by omission, or has Kgs created it by the late addition of 18:14–16?[7] We shall return to this issue.

The fact that the relevant texts of Kgs and Isa are otherwise so similar to each other might already suggest that these two larger (sets of) differences arose at the latest stages in the development of each text. The different ordering of the shared verses towards the end (20:7–11 and 38:7–8, 21–22) reinforces the effect of the pluses in each text. The book of Isaiah stresses the piety of king Hezekiah, but the book of Kings emphasises the efficacy of the prophet Isaiah. Then the presence in Kgs at the beginning, and the absence there from Isa, of the short report about Hezekiah paying tribute to Sennacherib is also relevant to the estimate of king Hezekiah in each book. Ray Person has proposed that 2 Kgs 18:14–16 was added for the purpose of "downplaying Hezekiah as a model king" (79). Nadav Na'aman has dismissed Persons's case as "arbitrary": vv. 14–16 were omitted towards "the idealization of the figure of Hezekiah in exilic and postexilic periods" (Na'aman 2003, 203).

We may expand on the fifth "observation" of Ray Person noted above. There is no trace in Chr of material similar to any one of these significant shorter and longer pluses in Isa and Kgs. From our three-book point of view, this fact supports the suggestion that all of them were added quite late to Kings and Isaiah. At the very least, these shared absences give further encouragement to continue what we have already begun: comparing the shorter account in Chr with those portions of the longer versions that Kgs and Isa actually share.

4 Chronicles compared with shared Isaiah/Kings

The prophet has a major role in Isa/Kgs, but is only just mentioned in Chr, and may even be a secondary afterthought there. And there are two further very striking differences. "Life" and "hearing" are key terms of the longer version, but completely absent from 2 Chr 32. The Assyrians scorn Yahweh, though he alone is "a living god"; and Hezekiah, though illness brought him close to death, revives (literally "lives"). The life of Jerusalem's god and the life of its king are both

7 For Joseph Blenkinsopp, "The biblical account simply ignores the problem that Hezekiah had only recently handed over all his gold and silver to the Assyrians …" (2006, 42).

important to the longer narrative; but none of this is reflected in the shorter one. As for the common verb “hear” (שמע), it is used as many as 17× in portions shared by Isa and Kgs, but never in 2 Chr 32. Neither of these differences is unique within the wider synoptic narrative about the house of David – each has a single partner.

חרף (“scorn/taunt”) is used in only two contexts – the same two contexts – in Sam-Kgs and Chr. In 1 Sam 17 and 2 Sam 21:21‖1 Chr 20:7 (ויחרף את־ישראל) it describes the slighting behaviour of Philistines towards Israel and Israel’s god; and, in 2 Kgs 19:4, 16‖2 Chr 32:17, of Assyrians towards Israel’s god. 1 Sam 17:26, 36 and 2 Kgs 19:4, 16 – but not the parallels in Chr – are also the only passages in which Sam-Kgs speak of “living god”.

2 Sam 21:21//1 Chr 20:7	ויחרף את־ישראל (“and he scorned Israel”)
1 Sam 17:36	כי חרף מערכת אלהים חיים (“for he scorned the ranks of living god”)
2 Chr 32:17	לחרף ליהוה אלהי ישראל (“to scorn Yahweh god of Israel”)
2 Kgs 19:4, 16//Isa 37:4, 16	לחרף אלהים חי (“to scorn living god”)

Within the biblical accounts of monarchy, Yahweh is claimed as “living god” in only two narrative situations: in each case Sam-Kgs is dealing very much more expansively than Chr with the threat of an external and mocking foe.

By contrast with חרף and with אלהים חי, the common verb שמע is used throughout the royal narratives. When it comes to “hearing”, we find only minimal variation between Sam-Kgs and Chr across almost all synoptic contexts. But “hear” is also absent from the report in 2 Chr 1 of Solomon’s vision at Gibeon, though it is used twice in the synoptic version (1 Kgs 3:9, 11[8]) – and this, despite appearing 19× in the remainder of the Solomon story in 2 Chr 1–9. The total absence of this common verb from 2 Chr 32 is equally surprising. If we adopted the normal critical perspective, that Kgs has priority, we would expect at least some of the seventeen instances of the verb in the “original” version shared by Kgs and Isa[9] to have survived in Chr’s abridgement. Chr was manifestly not averse to this verb: he used it nearby in his own material both before ch. 32 in 29:5; 30:20, and after it in 33:13. From a synoptic viewpoint, we should suppose instead that “hear” was part of the more ample re-telling (*Fortschreibung*) within Kgs of both Solomon’s vision and the Hezekiah story. As often in the rewriting of Sam-Kgs, the narrative was amplified by drawing on synoptic material from

8 “A hearing heart” (לב שמע) is a combination unique to 1 Kgs 3:9; and “to hear a case” (לשמע משפט in 3:11) may represent the sole combination of these terms in this judicial sense – in Deut 5:1; 7:12, Israel is required to listen to divine “judgments”.

9 2 Kgs 18:26, 28, 31; 19:1, 4, 4, 6, 7, 8, 9, 11, 16, 16, 25; 20:5, 12, 16//Isa 36:11, 13, 16; 37:1, 4, 4, 6, 7, 8, 9, 11, 17, 17, 26; 38:5; 39:1, 5.

elsewhere. Hezekiah responds to the threat to Jerusalem by tearing his clothes (2 Kgs 19:1) and responds to his own illness by weeping (2 Kgs 20:3). Both of these reactions anticipate synoptic Josiah (2 Kgs 22:11, 19‖2 Chr 34:19, 27). In that synoptic passage, Huldah links Josiah "hearing" how Yahweh had spoken and Yahweh in turn "hearing" his response (22:19); and this exchange is also anticipated in Isaiah's interpretation of Yahweh and Hezekiah hearing each other. The final instance of שמע (2 Kgs 20:16) also has synoptic resonance. Micaiah prefaces his threat of disaster for the king (1 Kgs 22:19) in identical but uncommon terms: שמע דבר־יהוה. It seems unlikely that every single instance of "hear" would have been eliminated by a Chronicler abbreviating the longer Kgs/Isa narrative, especially since some of these constituted unique echoes of narratives which he retained in full.

5 2 Kings 18:14–16

Some of my results overlap with proposals made by Kratz or at least noted sympathetically by him (154–156). He also finds it possible that Isaiah was not original to the report of the embassy from Babylon but is less sympathetic to Würthwein's reconstruction of an original version of B1 without Isaiah at all (2.421). Not only has the second speech of the Rabshakeh been added,[10] but also the reference to Hezekiah's cultic reform in the first. However, there is one key point where our proposals are diametrically opposed.

My preliminary judgment that the brief report in 2 Kgs 18:14–16 about Hezekiah paying off Sennacherib is late, rests on the fact that it is unique to Kings and is not reflected at all in Isaiah or Chronicles. Kratz on the other hand accepts that "the tribute episode of version A is the oldest account of the siege of Jerusalem" (156) and supposes therefore that the B account is dependent on it. He also agrees with those who claim that the Isaiah narrative presupposes A even although it does not include it all: it does retain its opening verse (18:13) in 36:1. There are two separate issues at stake: (1) Was v. 13 drafted along with vv. 14–16? (2) Relative to the whole narrative, is the tribute-report early or late?

(1) 2 Kgs 18:14–16 need 18:13; but the reverse is not true. The date and the reported arrival of Sennacherib in Judah are an introduction to something; but the good sense evident at the start of Isa 36 demonstrates that that "something" need not be 2 Kgs 18:14–16. There is more: even although the *Fortschreibung* model

10 I note in support that the content of the single speech by the envoy in 2 Chr 32 is shared between the 1st and 3rd speeches in Kgs/Isa – the repetition in the 2nd is rhetorically significant but does not add fresh information or argument.

is in general very attractive to me, I have a problem with viewing even the kernel of Stade's B as *fortgeschrieben* from his A. The payment reported in A had presumably solved the Sennacherib problem, in the short term at least; and further military pressure of the sort reported in B would have gained nothing from empty coffers in Jerusalem. A and B, as these labels suggest, work better as different and even divergent sources than as successive stages in a linear development.

(2) There is nothing remarkable about Sennacherib's demands (v. 14), or the general statement about Hezekiah employing the resources he found in the treasuries of Yahweh's house and the king's house (v. 15). But the detail in the final verse 16 is more unusual, and therefore potentially diagnostic: בעת ההיא קצץ חזקיה את־דלתות היכל יהוה ואת־האמנות אשר צפה חזקיה מלך יהודה ויתנם למלך אשור – "At that time Hezekiah cut off [the gilt from] the doors of Yahweh's palace and the pillars which Hezekiah king of Judah had overlaid and gave them to the king of Assyria."

Kgs and Chr report the details of Ahaz's cultic innovations very differently; but they share in 2 Kgs 16:17||2 Chr 28:24 the unique instance in synoptic texts of the verb קצץ ("cut off"). The context there is Ahaz's destruction of (or removal of elements from) temple furnishings in favour of or under pressure from Aram and Assyria. The author of 2 Kgs 18:16 re-used a verb that his synoptic source had employed only once, in its report of Ahaz; and he thereby aligned Hezekiah's action with the behaviour of his wicked father. An author of Kings combines קצץ with היכל יהוה first in 2 Kgs 18:16 and only once again, in his report of the Babylonian sack of the temple (24:13)[11]: ויקצץ את־כל־כלי הזהב אשר עשה שלמה מלך־ישראל בהיכל יהוה. This fact encourages readers of this element of the Hezekiah story to see the king's action in 2 Kgs 18:14–16 as an anticipation of his foolish dealings with the envoys from Babylon in 2 Kgs 20:12–19.[12] However apparently credible the information, we are dealing in 2 Kgs 18:14–16 (as already in the date formula in 18:13) not with a historian's use of archive or of reliable memory, but with exegesis. Hezekiah's extra 15 years were not well used. The unusual date-formula in 18:13 (ובארבע עשרה שנה למלך חזקיה עלה סנחריב מלך־אשור על כל־ערי יהודה הבצרות ויתפשם) had set the divine action in favour of Jerusalem and Hezekiah in the context of Solomon building the היכל

11 Yahweh's temple in Jerusalem is routinely called his "house" (בית); and it is called היכל (literally "palace") in synoptic texts or contexts only in relation to its construction by Solomon (1 Kgs 6–7//2 Chr 3–4) and to actions by Hezekiah, differently reported in 2 Kgs 18:16 and 2 Chr 29:16.

12 Knoppers, while conceding the possibility "that Chron.'s *Vorlage* of Kings did not contain ... all the treasury incidents in Kings", does reckon that Chr not only removed this blot from Hezekiah's record but had him build and endow treasuries (1999, 201 n. 65).

יהוה, Josiah reforming cult and Passover, and the improved status of Jehoiachin in Babylon. The terms in which 18:16 is drafted hint at a similar arc stretching from Solomon to Babylon. Admittedly, that observation could be used to support the unity of Stade's A (13–16); but it serves quite as well to demonstrate sensitive exegetical development from an existing v.13 to a new v.16.

The opening date in Kgs/Isa and the developed role of Isaiah in these longer versions may both be secondary to an earlier, shorter telling of the story. The date is certainly not reflected in Chr, and Isaiah's bit-part in Chr may itself be a supplement to that version. It is likely that the presence of Isaiah and the date belong together. Both of these features relate intimately to the king's return to life after his illness. The initial specification of the fourteenth year implies the parallel between Hezekiah and Amaziah, who had surprisingly outlived disaster for fifteen years. And Isaiah, having first (2 Kgs 20:1) underscored "you are dying" (מת אתה) by "and you shall not live" (ולא תחיה), turns back to give explicit voice to the divine promise of life for a further fifteen years (20:7).[13]

6 אות and מופת

Trigonometry suggests that expansive rewriting can explain most of the divergences between our three accounts of Hezekiah. But at least one element of the drafting and redrafting of the several versions of Hezekiah was not linear: the shift from אות to מופת, or the other way round. The shorter version in 2 Chr 32:24, 31 is rather enigmatic: the king prays when close to death and Yahweh grants him a "portent" (מופת); and later the Babylonian envoys are sent to "examine the portent there has been in the land" (לדרוש המופת אשר היה בארץ). It is unclear what constitutes the מופת in the land; but we may presume it is one and the same as the divine response to the king's prayer. Chr never uses the term "sign" (אות); and "portent" (מופת) is found only once more – in the quotation of Ps 105:5 at 1 Chr 16:12.[14] Twice in Isaiah (8:18; 20:3) and quite frequently in several other books אות and מופת are found paired. Where this is not the case, אות is much more common than מופת (as, for example, in Isa 7:11, 14; 19:20; 44:25; 55:13; 66:19); and only אות is used in Sam-Kgs. I have the impression, in English at least, that "sign" is more open or positive than "portent". And William Johnstone has

---

13 Not only does Isaiah's presence alongside the praying Hezekiah in 2 Chr 32:20 seem secondary, but the chapter appears to lack any obvious borrowing from the book of Isaiah.

14 Ps 105:27 has אתות and מפתים in parallel, but the citation in 1 Chr 16 finishes at 105:15. The unique combination לדרוש המופת could allude to Ps 105:4–5 (= 1 Chr 16:11–12) as a whole, since the first of the Psalm verses opens with דרשו.

shown that in Exodus מופת on its own refers to bad things done to Egypt, while אות on its own refers to good things done to Israel (1993, 166–185). If there is an element of puzzling menace in מופת, then the Babylonian envoys may not have been alone in seeking to decode it.

In Kgs/Isa, two of the three instances of "sign" also concern the king's recovery, but are not reported in the same order. Isaiah is shorter in the relevant verses. Immediately after the double declaration that his god will lengthen the king's life and save both him and his city from the king of Assyria (38:6), the prophet first promises a "sign from Yahweh" that he will do what he has spoken (38:7). This sign is turning back the sun's shadow by ten steps on the steps of Ahaz (38:9). Then, at the end of the episode, the king asks for a sign that he will go up to Yahweh's house; but no response is offered (38:22). In Kings as in Isaiah, we read first the double promise (20:6||38:6). But here, Hezekiah goes on to request a sign that Yahweh will heal him and that he will go up to Yahweh's house on the third day (20:8, similar to but fuller than 38:22[15]), and the prophet announces a more complex version of the sign of the shadow on the steps immediately afterwards (20:9). In the relevant verses, Isaiah and Kings both use the word אות twice within very similar sentences. In Isa, the prophet promises one sign and the king later asks for another. In Kings despite using many more words, only one sign is narrated: the king asks for it and the prophet announces it.

Kgs/Isa has already reported a further sign in which Isaiah speaks of gradual relief and recovery of the land. This, his second response to Hezekiah's prayer (19:15–19||37:16–20), is set towards the end of the siege narrative (19:29–31||37:30–32). There is no immediate parallel in Chr's account of the siege, but the images in this sign of improvement to agriculture do resonate with "the portent there has been *in the land*".

7 Afterword

As we noted earlier, the only mention of Isaiah in the main body of 2 Chr 32 is at the end of the siege (v. 20); and this corresponds to an important (and earlier) stage in how the prophet is portrayed in Kgs/Isa. The first time we meet him in the longer version, he is reactive – like a synoptic Micaiah or Huldah. On later occasions, he is proactive, like non-synoptic Elijah and Elisha. It is also true, from the first mention of him in the Kgs/Isa Hezekiah story, that the prophet Isaiah is constructed from both the books Kings and Isaiah, and from Jeremiah too. Told

15 No one else in HB puts the question מה אות.

that Rab-shakeh has been sent "to scorn living god" (לחרף אלהים חי), he is reminded of (his "own" words according to) Isa 51:7 – אל־תיראו חרפת אנוש ומגדפתם אל־תחתו ("do not fear a human's scorn, and at their reviling be not broken"). These in turn inspire his response in 2 Kgs 19:6 – אל־תירא מפני הדברים אשר שמעת אשר גדפו נערי מלך אשור אתי ("do not fear before the words you have heard, with which the king of Assyria's lads have reviled me").[16] Then in 19:7, הנני נתן בו רוח ("see I am putting a spirit in him") is a unique repetition of Micaiah's words to the king of Israel (1 Kgs 22:23); ושמע שמועה appears to know Jer 49:14, 23; and והפלתיו בחרב ("and I'll make him fall by the sword") is said again in HB only in Jer 19:7.

Two final words: (1) This first and earliest Isaiah within the Kgs/Isa Hezekiah story develops a text drawn from II-Isaiah – it is subsequent Isaiahs within this story that engage with I-Isaiah. (2) In whatever literary contexts the Isaiah legends are developed – and Kgs and Isa and a once-independent literary unit have all been proposed – Isa 36–39 is a prime witness to a late stage in the development of 2 Kgs 18–20.

The material in this study is re-presented more briefly, but set in a wider context, in Auld 2017.

16 Strangely, Hans Wildberger notes the other occasions in HB where חרף and גדף appear together, but not this one instance in Isaiah (3.1410).

‘Divination’ in Hebrew and Greek Bibles: A Text-historical Overview

1 Greece and Israel

Introducing his study of divination in classical Greece, Michael Attyah Flower (5–6) writes:

> The focus of this book is on how divination functioned as a respected access to knowledge both for individuals and for communities in the Greek world, and, in particular, on the role of the seers in making divination a viable and useful social practice. The practitioners, the seers, were not marginal characters on the fringe of Greek society. They were not like the mediums and palm readers in modern Western cities who generally inhabit the fringe both spatially and intellectually, and who ply their trade in the seedy sectors of the urban landscape. Rather, a significant proportion of them were educated members of the elite, who were highly paid and well respected. There were, to be sure, practitioners of a lower order; but the seers who attended generals and statesmen were often the wealthy scions of famous families. They were at the center of Greek society.

Flower’s words may remind readers of the Hebrew Bible of the wide range of Jerusalem’s leaders listed in Isa 3:2–3. Eleven terms are assembled, with נביא (prophet?) and קסם (diviner) side by side, though no mention of king or priest. There are only a few mentions of נביא from (possibly) monarchic-period Jerusalem and nearby. They mostly appear in lists and summaries and hardly provide us evidence for a job-description. However, we might suppose from Mic 3:11 (ונביאיה בכשף יקסמו – ‘and her prophets – for money they divine’) that the verb קסם is a proper description of the activity of a נביא: that prophets divining *for money* is the problem for Micah, and not the act of divining in itself. In Isaiah and Micah, the association of נביא with קסם appears unremarkable. When these terms reappear together in Jer 27:9; 29:8 (both times followed by ‘dream[er]s’), people are warned against listening to them – they are no longer pillars of society.

2 Dating

It is very hard, if not impossible, to find neutral ground in the Hebrew Bible, and certainly not in matters relating to ‘religion’ or ‘the divine. My contributions to recent meetings of this group have marked stages in a research project. I argued, at the Utrecht meeting of the group in 2013, that the connected narrative from around the end of the Jerusalem monarchy shared in Sam-Kgs and Chron, which I now term the Book of Two Houses (BoTH), was the earliest recoverable prophet-

https://doi.org/10.1515/9783111060279-007

ically interpreted history (Auld 2015). There, Nathan the prophet (נביא) transmits a dynastic oracle received in a vision (חזון);[1] and Gad is described as David's 'seer' (חזה).[2] Jeroboam has dealings with Ahijah and Shemaiah, each of whom has or receives the divine word. Jehoshaphat and the king of Israel consult multiple נביאים; and one of these (Micaiah ben Imlah), identified as 'a prophet of Yahweh' (נביא ליהוה) transmits an oracle received in a vision (ראיתי in 1 Kgs 22:17, 19), like Nathan to David. Finally, Josiah sends representatives to consult Huldah the prophetess (2 Kgs 22). We see 'prophets' and 'seers' at work in this narrative from beginning to end, although we are never informed about how they received their oracles. However, in BoTH, several terms relating to 'divination' are confined to narratives about two wicked kings, Ahaz and Manasseh; and such 'divining' is never portrayed – it is only mentioned within the characterisation of one and possibly two bad kings near the end of the narrative. Manasseh's divinatory actions are characterised as foreign behaviour: they are listed (2 Kgs 21:6a) after reports of altars built for Baal and all the heavenly host and the construction of an Ashera (21:3–5) and are cast as abominations (תועבות) of the nations Yahweh had dispossessed in favour of Israel.

Further to a re-evaluation of the several Jeroboam narratives, I must restate my description of the prophetic contribution to BoTH rather more cautiously. I have argued more recently that the Jeroboam of BoTH is not to be found in the text shared by the very similar 1 Kgs 12:1–19//2 Chr 10:1–19, but rather in what that text shares with the relevant portion of the 'alternative' narrative preserved in LXX^{BL} (Auld 2020). The 'prophets' and other intermediary figures play an ambiguous role in BoTH. The extensive episode in 1 Kgs 22 offers a classic account, not only of prophetic conflict but also of a prophet of Yahweh – and yet 'Yahweh's prophet' had a mission to deceive. Also, and importantly, the shorter Jeroboam text does not include 1 Kgs 12:15b//2 Chr 10:15b, so important to von Rad's discussion of the Deuteronomist's 'theological proof ... by means of a whole structure of constantly promulgated prophetic predictions and their corresponding fulfilments' (1962, 340). In fact, 1 Kgs 8:20//2 Chr 6:10 (on which 12:15b//10:15b is modelled, but which does not name any intermediary) is the only synoptic (or BoTH) text among the many cited by von Rad. Incidentally, it is likely that the earliest datable instances in HB of verbal forms related to נביא are found within this narrative.[3]

The Utrecht paper and its successor, delivered at the following meeting of the Group in 2015 at Göttingen (Auld 2020b), were both preparatory studies for my

---

1 ככל־הדברים האלה וככל־החזיון הזה – 'according to all these words and according to all this vision' (2 Sam 7:17//1 Chr 17:15).

2 2 Sam 24:11//1 Chr 21:9.

3 niph in 22:12 and hitp in 22:8, 10, 28.

monograph *Life in Kings*. This present contribution in turn builds on that monograph. I already sketched there a proposal that the older royal narrative (BoTH) underlies the so-called centralisation requirement in Deut 12. Deuteronomy may have influenced (fully Deuteronomistic) Samuel-Kings. But I also argue that Deuteronomy is indebted to BoTH (2017, 195–202). Some 30 examples were tabulated in *Life in Kings* of words or phrases which occur only twice in BoTH, or at least only within the regnal reports of two kings (92–93). I have expanded this list to almost one hundred; and the last king paired in this way with any of his predecessors is Josiah. I deduce from this that BoTH had ended with the report of his reign, and therefore that a core-Deuteronomy indebted to BoTH must be post-Josianic.

In Isa 3 and Mic 3, נביא and קסם seem to be used without clear distinction. But in the developing royal narrative we find a two-fold change. Already in BoTH, קסם/קוסם is no longer used: now verbal forms of נבא are used to describe the action of the נביא instead of קסם as in Micah – prophets 'prophesy' rather than 'divine'. Then, in the expanded narrative we read in Sam-Kgs, we do find קסם/קוסם three or four times – but it is used in seemingly pejorative contexts. Worried Philistines consult their priests and diviners (1 Sam 6:2); Samuel warns Saul that divination is rebellion (1 Sam 15:23);[4] divination is one of the many sins listed in 2 Kgs 17:15–17. The only possibly neutral case relates to the medium at En-dor (1 Sam 28), who is a rather sympathetic character; but see further below (section 5).

3 Deuteronomy 18:9–14

The material under our consideration is concentrated in one half of the Hebrew Bible – in the narratives about the monarchy in Samuel-Kings and Chronicles and in the Latter Prophets and Daniel. However, the book of Deuteronomy provides a triply useful starting point for our quest: it is at least roughly datable; it includes more of the relevant terms than any other part of HB; and translation choices in the Greek Pentateuch are often said to be influential elsewhere in the Greek Bible. Deut 18:9–14 lists nine expressions relating broadly to 'divination',[5] before 18:15–22 introduces the prophet like Moses; and related material in Deut 12:29–

4 Here LXX οἰώνισμα may instead attest נחש. But Grillet and Lestienne (278) simply note that the term has the general sense of divination and does not envisage ornithomancy.

5 One notable absentee is חרטם, used in Gen 41:8, 24; Ex 7:11, 22; 8:3, 14, 15; 9:11, 11; Dan 1:20; 2:2.

13:6 adds the dreamer of dreams alongside the prophet. The context makes clear that each of the nine is the sort of person you should *not* have amongst you.

1	מעביר בנו־ובתו באש	περικαθαίρων τὸν υἱὸν αὐτοῦ ἢ τὴν θυγατέρα αὐτοῦ ἐν πυρί
2	קסם קסמים	μαντευόμενος μαντείαν
3	מעונן	κληδονιζόμενος
4	מנחש	οἰωνιζόμενος
5	מכשף	φαρμακός
6	חבר חבר	ἐπαείδων ἐπαοιδήν
7	שאל אוב	ἐγγαστρίμυθος
8	ידעני	τερατοσκόπος
9	דרש אל־המתים	ἐπερωτῶν τοὺς νεκρούς

The Greek renderings at 1 and 8 are unique, warning us immediately not to overestimate the influence of Pentateuch translators on subsequent books. The precise meaning of מעביר בנו־ובתו באש (1) is not clear; but מעביר is rendered straightforwardly by διάγειν (lead through) in 2 Kgs 16:3//2 Chr 28:3 and 2 Kgs 21:6//2 Chr 33:6, as also in the related 2 Kgs 17:17; 23:10. However, LXX at 1 means 'completely cleansing his son or his daughter in/by fire'; and in Jos 5:4, περιεκάθαρεν appears to be a euphemistic interpretation of the literal περιέτεμεν (circumcised) in 5:3, 5.[6] Then τερατοσκόπος or 'observer of portents' (8) is not only unique as a rendering of 'ידעני', but occurs only once more in LXX (Zech 3:8), corresponding there to אנשי מופת (although that Hebrew should be understood as 'men who are [themselves] a portent'). (1) and (8) may be free renderings, but the Greek in elements (2) and (6) does carefully replicate an idiom commoner in Hebrew than Greek: the objects are cognates of the verbs. Only in (7) is the Greek structured differently from the Hebrew. The Hebrew participial phrase, asking an *'ôb* or *'ôb*-asking, is replaced by the Greek noun corresponding to 'ventriloquist'. And here the difference is not just in shape but also in sense: the Hebrew participle means 'asking' while the Greek -μυθος implies telling – the Hebrew is seeking divine information while the Greek is providing it.

Taken as a whole, the nine Greek expressions are more transparent than their Hebrew counterparts. 'Thoroughly cleansing his son or his daughter in fire' (1) renders the Hebrew euphemistically but may also suggest that the translator did *not* reckon that this element of the parent text had any divinatory significance. For Richard Nelson (2002, 233), '[t]he context suggests that passing one's child through fire (v. 10) was a divinatory practice rather than a sacrifice to turn away a divinity's wrath or as part of the cult of the dead. Perhaps the survival

6 The by-form περικαθαρίζειν renders terms for circumcision (or pruning) in Lev 19:23; Deut 30:6.

or death of the child indicated a yes or no answer.' Divinatory practice certainly, and perhaps more appropriately, begins at (2) with Hebrew *qsm*. This may be the generic term for 'divine/ation' and is certainly more widely used in HB (some 30×) than any other element in the list.[7] It is almost always rendered in LXX by the family of terms based on μαντ- (giving English 'mantic'), itself the generic Greek term. The use of this verb with cognate object is found again in the closely related 2 Kgs 17:17 and twice in Ezekiel (13:23; 21:26). κληδον- (3) can mean simply 'rumour', as well as a more significant 'omen' or 'presage' detected in a chance remark.[8] οἰωνιζ- (4) is divining based on observation of birds – transparently so, since οἰωνός is a (large) bird. Φαρμακός (5) is a poisoner or sorcerer. ἀείδω (6) has the basic sense 'sing'; and the derived forms here mean 'incant an incantation' or 'enchant an enchantment' – or simply 'charm a charm'. ἐγγαστρίμυθος (7) is the normal LXX rendering for expressions including *'ôb*. ἐπερωτᾶν most frequently renders שאל, as here, though often דרש as well; but the combination ἐπερωτῶν τοὺς νεκρούς (9) is unique – in the similar Isa 8:19, ἐκζητεῖν corresponds to דרש.

4 העביר באש

Element (1) is part of extended pattern in which, though not shown on the table below, תועבה (abomination) is always part of the immediate context.[9]

2 Kgs 16:3		באש		העביר	וגם את־בנו
2 Chr 28:3		באש	את־בניו	ויבער	בגיא בן־הנם
2 Kgs 21:6		באש	את־בנו	והעביר	
2 Chr 33:6	בגיא בן־הנם	באש	את־בניו	והוא העביר	
Deut 12:31	לאלהיהם	באש		ישרפו	גם את־בניהם ואת־בנותיהם
Deut 18:10		באש	בנו ובתו	מעביר	

7 11 instances are found in just 3 portions of Ezekiel; but, even granted this concentration, the remaining instances are more numerous and are more widely spread than any of the other terms.

8 LSJ 959.

9 In the order of the table below, 2 Kgs 16:3//2 Chr 28:3; 2 Kgs 21:2//2 Chr 33:2; Deut 12:31; 2 Kgs 23:13; Jer 7:10 (further removed from 7:35 than elsewhere in this list); 32:35; Lev 18:22, 26, 27, 29, 30; 20:13.

2 Kgs 23:10	למלך	באש	את־בנו ואת־בתו	להעביר איש	לבלתי
Jer 7:31		באש	את־בניהם ואת־בנותיהם	לשרף	בגיא בן־הנם
Jer 32:35	למלך		את־בניהם ואת־בנותיהם	להעביר	בגיא בן־הנם
Lev 18:21	למלך			להעביר	ומזרעך לא תתן
Lev 20:2	למלך				אשר יתן מזרעך
Lev 20:3	למלך				כי מזרעו נתן
Lev 20:4	למלך				בתתו מזרעו

Seven of the statements tabulated include באש (in/by fire), five have למלך (see below), while 2 Kgs 23:10 includes both. Leviticus LXX always renders למלך as ἄρχοντι (dative, but without the article τῷ), while in 4 Kgdms 23:10 it is transliterated τῷ μολοχ. In Jer 39:35[MT 32:35] we find transliteration plus translation, τῷ μολοχ βασιλεῖ. In each context in Chronicles, as also in Jeremiah, the action is located בגיא בן־הנם (in the valley of the son of Hinnom) and the sons (and daughters) are plural.

If texts tend to grow, then the shorter versions in 2 Kgs 16:3; 21:6 and Deut 18:10 have most claim to priority among the formulations including באש – in each of them we read 'his son' (sg), while all of the others (plus LXX in 4 Kgdms 21:6) have plural forms.[10] Against Deut 18:10 is the inclusion of 'his daughter' alongside 'his son', while in 2 Kgs 21:6, בנו is unnecessarily prefaced by את (in 2 Kgs 16:3, by contrast, את is required to mark בנו as a pre-posed object). Whatever practice was earlier intended by העביר באש, it has been clearly disambiguated in Deut 12:31 and Jer 7:31 as 'burning their sons and their daughters'. In each of Lev 20:2, 3, 4, we read instead more neutrally of 'giving/gifting of [their] seed to "the King"'; but in Lev 18:21 this 'giving' specifically involves '*passing* [it] to the King'.

5 Remainder of Deut 18:10–11

Forms related to קסם (2) occur 31× in HB and are generally (28×)[11] rendered by forms of μαντ-. Each of the three exceptions is different. In Ezek 13:9 – and possibly in deliberate variation from the literally rendered 13:7 – ἀποφθεγγόμενοι

10 LXX has 'his sons' in Kgs but 'his children' (τέκνα) in Chr.

11 Num 22:7; 23:23; Deut 18:10, 10, 14; Jos 13:22; 1 Sam 6:2; 28:8; 2 Kgs 17:17, 17; Isa 44:25; Jer 14:14; 27:9; 29:8; Ezek 13:6, 9, 23, 23; 21:26, 26, 27, 28, 34; 22:28; Mic 3:6, 7, 11; Zech 10:2.

(plain speakers) is used. In Isa 3:2, where קסם is neighbour to נביא, the rendering by the unique στοχαστὴν (one who aims or guesses at something) may be pejorative alongside 'prophet'. Only in 1 Sam 15:23, where MT and LXX divide the line differently and there are other divergences, קסם corresponds to οἰώνισμα (4).

ענן (3) and נחש (4) are paired only in the sub-set of Deut 18 found also in Lev 18–20 and 2 Kgs 21//2 Chr 33. Whether as verb or noun, נחש is always (11×) rendered by a Greek form related to οἰωνιζόμενος.[12] In narrative, it is normally associated with foreign persons: Laban, Balaam, and (the envoys of) Ben-Hadad are all Aramaean; and Joseph became the vizier of Egypt.[13] And King Manasseh behaves like the nations Yahweh had removed in face of Israel. LXX in Lev 19:26 clearly understands both verbs as denoting divination by birds: οὐκ οἰωνιεῖσθε οὐδὲ ὀρνιθοσκοπήσεσθε.[14] In the four remaining instances in the sub-set,[15] LXX uses forms of κληδον- to render ענן (3);[16] and this rendering is also found in Isa 2:6. But in Jer 27[34]:9 we find οἰωνισμάτων. In Mic 5:11 as in Jer 27[34]:9, מעוננים are paired with כשפים (5), but this time rendered ἀποφθεγγόμενοι (plain speakers). In Judg 9:37, [the oak of the] מעוננים is rendered ἀποβλεπόντων (of those gazing upon).[17] And in Isa 57:3, the בני עננה – described as 'adulterous and whoring seed' – are rendered υἱοὶ ἄνομοι (lawless sons).

כשף (5) is always (13×) rendered by φαρμακ-.[18] However, φαρμακ- also corresponds to ל[ה]ט in Exod 7:11, 22; 8:3, 14; and to חרטם in Exod 9:11; Dan 2:27.[19] חבר (6) occurs in only two further contexts. In the first of these, in Isa 47:9, 12, it is again paired with כשף within an extended critique of Babylon/Chaldea and its vaunted powers. In both Isa 47:9, 12 and Deut 18:10–11 LXX renders it by ἐπαείδων ἐπαοιδήν. But in Ps 58[57]:6, where MT has מלחשים and חבר חברים in parallel,[20] we read in LXX *and in reverse order* ἐπαδόντων + φαρμάκου φαρμακευομένου.[21]

---

12 Gen 30:27; 44:5, 15; Lev 19:26; Num 23:23; 24:1; Deut 18:10; 1 Kgs 20:33; 2 Kgs 17:17; 21:6; 2 Chr 33:6.

13 Gen 30:27; Num 23:23; 24:1; 1 Kgs 20:33; and Gen 44:5, 15.

14 Pesh. also insists that this divination is 'by birds' (Milgrom 2000, 1686). But was it simply reflecting LXX usage, or does it offer independent testimony?

15 Deut 18:10, 14; 2 Kgs 21:6; 2 Chr 33:6.

16 Harl 1987, 231 gives proper sense as présager but here simply divine.

17 The Hebrew may be an alternative name of the oak known in Gen 12:6; Deut 11:30 as אלון מורה ('teacher's oak') – see Nelson 2017, 178.

18 Ex 7:11; 22:17; Deut 18:11; 2 Kgs 9:22; Isa 47:9, 12; Jer 27[34]:9; Mic 5:11; Nah 3:4, 4; Mal 3:5; Dan 2:2; 2 Chr 33:6.

19 חרטם in Exodus and Daniel is normally (6×) rendered by ἐπαοιδός – see further section 7 below.

20 It is widely held that נחש and לחש both represent a biradical חש meaning 'sound softly, whisper (a charm)' – see Milgrom 2000, 1686.

21 Dahood 1968, 60 renders חבר חברים by 'weaver of spells' on the basis of Phoenician *bny š'l l'štrt ḥbry tnt* ('mediums of Astarte and spell-casters of Tinnit').

Almost half the instances (7/16) of *'ôb* (7) in HB are in the plural and with article (הא[ו]בת).[22] Here the context is always negative: they are being blamed or destroyed; and in every one of these cases they are paired with and followed by הידענים (8), also plural and with article. All are rendered in Greek by plurals. Of the nine singular instances, four are again followed by ידעני, here also sg and also without article.[23] It must be stressed that ידעני and הידענים are completely unknown outside this pairing (11×). Outside the sub-set of five terms (1, 3–4, 7–8), found in Lev 18–20; Deut 18; and 2 Kgs 21//2 Chr 33, we find this pair only in Isaiah 8:19; 19:3 and in the episode of Saul and the medium. The remaining five cases of אוב, singular and independent, relate to the same two situations: Saul's consultation of the medium and the book of Isaiah.[24] In both 1 Sam 28:8 and 1 Chr 10:13, באוב is vocalised as articulated (*bā'ôb*) and is so translated in LXX. In the remaining three instances, the noun is unarticulated. In the En-dor narrative, the requested consultation is ב (of, or by means of) the known אוב of which the medium is owner or mistress (בעלה).

ἐγγαστρίμυθος (ventriloquist) corresponds at least 11× to אוב, or clauses in which it is used.[25] Whether it accurately catches their original sense is hard to decide; but two passages make this seem reasonable. In double parallelism, Isa 29:4 depicts in four expressions how 'the city where David encamped' (29:1) will sound after it has suffered the disasters of siege:

ושפלת מארץ תדברי	And low from the earth shall you speak
ומעפר תשח אמרתך	And from the dust shall your speech grow faint
והיה כאוב מארץ קולך	and your voice/sound shall be as an *'ôb* from the earth/underworld'
ומעפר אמרתך תצפצף	And from the dust your speech shall chirp

The sounds in the ruins will be hardly human, not readily sourced as from on the ground or from underworld. LXX paraphrases the third clause: καὶ ἔσται ὡς οἱ φωνοῦντες ἐκ τῆς γῆς ἡ φωνή σου ('and your voice/sound shall be as those voicing/sounding from the earth/underworld'). Then Saul makes two presumably related commands to the medium: (a) 'divine for me of/by the *'ôb*'; (b) 'raise up for me the one of whom I speak to you'. The *'ôb* will come from below to speak. In rendering the final two instances of אוב (in 2 Kgs 21:6; 23:24) as θελητὴν/ὰς, the translator assumed it to be cognate with אבה (wish/will).

---

22 Lev 19:31; 20:6; 1 Sam 28:3, 9 (sg in some MSS); 2 Kgs 23:24; Isa 8:19; 19:3.
23 Lev 20:27; Deut 18:11; 2 Kgs 21:6 (pl in some mss); 2 Chr 33:6 (pl in Gk).
24 1 Sam 28:7, 7, 8; 1 Chr 10:13; and Isa 29:4 (pl in Gk).
25 Lev 19:31; 20:6, 27; Deut 18:11; 1 Sam 28:3, 7, 7, 9, 9; 1 Chr 10:13; 33:6 – and probably also Isa 8:19; 19:3, as noted below.

The combination שאל אוב ('asking an *'ôb*') in Deut 18:11 is unique: in fact, there is no standard HB phrase.
- עשה אוב in 2 Kgs 21//2 Chr 33
- שאל אוב in Deut 18
- לשאול באוב לדרוש in 1 Chr 10:13
- קסם באוב in 1 Sam 28[26]

We also find פנה אל־האבת in Lev 19–20 and דרש אל־האבת in Isa 8:19; 19:3. In the related critique of king Manasseh, the phrase is עשה אוב (apparently 'making an *'ôb*') while Saul is reported in 1 Sam 28:8 as saying to the medium קסמי־נא לי באוב ('be sure to divine for me of/by the *'ôb*'). However, in noting the Saul episode, 1 Chr 10:13 specifies that king's malpractice as לשאול באוב לדרוש ('asking of/by the *'ôb*, seeking'), using both שאל and דרש. In this context, both Sam and Chr vary the usage of the older BoTH, which lacks קסם and never uses שאל and דרש together (שאל [ask] occurs only in narratives relating to David and Solomon while דרש [seek] is only used of later kings). Chr used the strong term מעל of Saul's behaviour with the medium, and so would hardly have recoiled from spoiling his reputation with קסם. Equally, if an author of Samuel has added this verb to the narrative in 1 Sam 28, it is hardly likely that this was done neutrally.

ידעני (8) is apparently related to one of the commonest verbs in Hebrew (ידע, know).[27] Since it is never found except following אוב, we may wonder whether it was intended to interpret that puzzling term. ידעני, which we know only as a masculine form, may have corresponded to the feminine בעלת־אוב (*'ôb*-mistress) from En-dor. Similarly, since in Isa 8:19 ידרש אל־המתים closely follows דרשו אל־האבות ואל־הידענים, we may suppose that 'the dead' clarify the sense of האבות. If so, we will be dealing in Deut 18:11b and Isa 8:19 with one category of diviner and not three.

Paradoxically, though we may find ידעני more transparent than אוב, the Greek translators exhibited greater variety in rendering it. In addition to the eccentric τερατοσκόπος in Deut 18, we find three further approaches in LXX to rendering ידעני of HB:

a) γνώστας (1 Sam 28:3, 9; 2 Kgs 21:6; 2 Chr 35:19a) and γνωριστὰς (2 Kgs 23:24) take it literally as 'knowing one(s)' – only in 4 Kgdms 21:6; 23:24 do we find the same literal renderings (θελητ- and γνω[ρι]στὰς) paired.

26 Grillet and Lestienne 1997, 395 note that ventriloquist is more restricted in sense than *'ôb*, and does not exactly meet the situation in 1 Sam 28 – Saul does not ask that she makes Samuel talk, but that she raise him; but are open to the view that by the time of the translation it had expanded to include necromancy (they cite parallel expansion of οἰωνισμός).

27 J. Tropper is cited as pointing out that noun formations like ידעני (with -ôn) 'mainly occur in younger strata of the language' (Cryer 1994, 261).

b) ἐπαοιδός (Lev 19:31; 20:6, 27; 2 Chr 33:6), meaning 'chanter/incantator/enchanter', corresponds in Deut 18 and Isa 47 to חבר (6). Though ἐπαοιδός properly relates to singing or chanting, its apparent component οιδ- ('know') resonates in both sound and sense with the ידע in ידעני.
c) τοὺς ἀπὸ τῆς γῆς φωνοῦντας καὶ τοὺς ἐγγαστριμύθους ('those sounding from the earth and the ventriloquists', Isa 8:19; 19:3). The first element appears to have its origins in the Greek rendering of Isa 29:4, noted above. Paired with 'ventriloquists', it certainly recognises האבות ... והידענים as a close semantic pair, seemingly offering a double rendering of האבות.

While Isa 8:19 LXX may agree with Deut 18:11 MT in reading elements 7–9 as a triplet, this does not seem to hold for Deut 18:11 LXX with its puzzling τερατοσκόπος for ידעני.

In short, after the apparently generic term קסם, only נחש and כשף have wider currency in HB; and it is these three more commonly used terms that have fixed renderings in Greek:
- נחש is always translated οἰωνι-
- כשף is always translated φαρμακ-
- קסם is almost always translated μαντ-

However, it may be sensible to conclude with Milgrom (2000, 1689) that 'their precise meanings remain nebulous'.

6 Subsets

Subsets of this list are found in other biblical texts. Five of the nine elements (1, 3–4, 7–8) appear in similar brevity in the synoptic critique of Manasseh (2 Kgs 21:6a//2 Chr 33:6a). And the same five members (granted the equivalence just observed over the first member) reappear within a more developed argument in Lev 18–20 that also includes the only instances in Leviticus of תועבה. It seems likely that the critique of Manasseh in BoTH is the prior text that has been expansively developed in different directions in Lev 18–20 and in Deut 18:9–14. Typical of the late-monarchic or early post-monarchic narrative of BoTH, the critique in 2 Kgs 21:6//2 Chr 33:6 is focused on King Manasseh. The more extended legislation in Lev 18–20 is for a people without a king. In each context, the five terms (or at least 2–5, the significance of the first being more obscure) concern 'divination', properly so called – probing the future. The development towards Deut 18 is of a different sort: the shorter older list is enhanced, but now includes some terms that describe 'sorcery' (changing the future) rather than 'divination' (Milgrom

2000, 1686). It has long been argued that the so-called 'Book of the Covenant' in Exod 21–22 (23) is a major source of core-Deuteronomy. The summary dismissal (Exod 22:17) of the sorceress as unworthy of life (מכשפה לא תחיה) may have influenced this expansion of the critique of Manasseh.

Two smaller subsets are shared with only one other biblical context each. The final element (9) is unique to Deut 18:11 and Isa 8:19, where it also follows elements 7 and 8. And the only other pairing of 5–6 is in Isa 47:9, 12, where critique is directed against Babylon. קסם (2) is quite the commonest term relating to divination in HB; but it is not used in BoTH. Apart from Deut 18:10, it is found in the Pentateuch only in the Balaam story (Num 22:7; 23:23[28]). It follows 'passing sons and daughters in fire' (1) only once again – in the clearly related (and non-synoptic) 2 Kgs 17:17; but there the next element is וינחשו (4 – cf Num 23:23).

The sub-set 1, 3–4, 7–8 is found in Lev 18–20, Deut 18, and 2 Kgs 21//2 Chr 33. Elements 5–6 are paired elsewhere only in Isa 47; elements 7–8 occur elsewhere only in 1 Sam 28 and Isaiah (the same two contexts where we find 7 on its own); and element 9 is appended to 7–8 only in Deut 18 and Isa 8. Outside Deut 18, it is only in the book of Isaiah that we find all of elements 2, 5–6, and 9.

7 Beyond Deut 18

Among relevant terms not found in the major list, the commonest is חרטם. The context is always the court of Egypt[29] or of Babylon.[30] In Genesis (the Joseph story) and mostly in Daniel, the context is the interpretation of dreams – Greek ἐξηγητὰς in Gen 41 offers a wholly appropriate rendering, for that term denoted the explanation of dreams and oracles before it was used for the interpretation of texts. In the Hebrew introduction to Daniel, the חרטמים are associated with the אשפים (1:20) and again with these plus the מכשפים and the כשדים (2:2). אשף occurs only in Daniel (in both Hebrew and Aramaic portions like חרטם) and is normally rendered by μάγος. Aramaic Daniel also delights in lists and these same terms recur:

- לכל־חרטם ואשף וכשדי (2:10)
- חכימין אשפין חרטמין גזרין (2:27)
- חרטמיא אשפיא כשדיא וגזריא (4:4)
- חרטמין אשפין כשדאין גזרין (5:11)

28 Alone in Num 22:7, while in 23:23 נחש (4) is used in parallel to קסם.

29 Gen 41:8, 24; Ex 7:11, 22; 8:3, 14, 15; 9:11, 11.

30 Dan 1:20; 2:2 (Heb); 2:10, 27; 4:4, 6; 5:11 (Aram).

In each case, the Greek has ἐπαοιδοί (σοφὸν in the main text at 2:10 may represent חכם rather than חרטם), and μάγοι for אשפין. In such lists – as perhaps also in Deut 18:10–11 and 2 Kgs 21:6//2 Chr 33:6 – the impression made by a collection of somewhat similar terms may be more significant than the exact sense of each. In Dan 4:6, Belteshazzar is summoned as רב חרטמיא and his business is clearly to interpret the king's dream. But in Exodus, the חרטמי מצרים are doers rather than interpreters. At first, Pharaoh's agents match Moses (snakes, river turned to blood, and frogs – 7:11, 22; 8:3), using their secret arts (בל[ה]טיהם). But they are then unable to keep pace with him and produce gnats; and they inform Pharaoh that Moses has acted by the finger of God (8:14–15). Finally, they are themselves overcome by the boils produced by Moses (9:11). In all but 9:11, these 'doers' are again called ἐπαοιδοί in Greek, while the arts at their disposal are φαρμακεῖαι; but in that final verse, they themselves are called φαρμακοὶ. By routinely employing ἐπαοιδοί, and occasionally φαρμακοὶ, the Greek translators reckoned that חרטמים belonged with the other 'divinatory' terms under discussion.

Ezekiel reports the king of Babylon standing at the parting of the ways in order to divine (21:26): he shakes the arrows, asks the teraphim, and looks at the liver. שאל בתרפים is unique to this passage (as is לשאול באוב in 1 Chr 10:13); but a divinatory role for teraphim is clear from Zech 10:2. Normally understood to be household gods, they are prized enough to be stolen by Rachel from Laban (Gen 31:19) and from Micah by Danites (Judg 18). Laban had earlier used the term נחש of himself (Gen 30:27), and the Danites were establishing a new cult.

8 קסם = divine?

Balaam is styled הקוסם in Josh 13:22, but not within the narrative in Num 22–24. However, when the elders of Moab and of Midian set off to recruit him (Num 22:7), they have in their hands קסמי[ה]ם (both Sam and Pesh attest the possessive suffix). LXX renders by μαντεῖα, for which LSJ 1079 offers 'rewards of divination' (citing only this passage). Early interpretations were divided between the money Balaam was to be offered and instruments for divination (Dorival 1994, 421). Balaam is asked repeatedly to curse Israel – to do harm to a people the king of Moab considered a menace. Whether the king's messengers were carrying tools or an inducement, Balaam was not being asked to 'explore' the future and report, but to change it. Like Egypt's חרטמים in contest with Moses, he should be a doer and not just a teller. חרטמים and קוסמים are never found in the same context, and in fact never in the same book: חרטמים belongs only to Genesis, Exodus, and Daniel; and קוסמים to Num 22–24, Deut 18, and several books in the Former and Latter Prophets (n. 19 above). 'Divining' in the stricter sense may be a fair label for the five-fold activities of Manasseh (repeated in Lev 18–20). But when this list was expanded within Deuteronomy, the addition of קסם קסמים in second place 'presaged' the incorporation of 'bad magic' such as מכשף and חבר חבר from Isa 47.

Deuteronomy and the Older Royal Narrative: Some Core Questions

1 Questions about a Deuteronomic core

Over the ages, readers have recognized the many obvious links between the books of Deuteronomy and Kings. The broad sweep of scholarship holds that the history of Israel from its settlement in Canaan to the fall of Jerusalem to Babylon was told in the books from Joshua to Kings in standards and language drawn from Deuteronomy. More precisely, in the prevailing understanding, the authors of the principal structuring narratives were familiar with the "code" of Deuteronomy (chs. 12–26).

I have challenged this hypothesis in *Life in Kings* (2017), where I advance a three-fold case for recognizing the narrative shared by Samuel-Kings and Chronicles as the core of the royal narrative. My three arguments are as follows. (a) The so-called synoptic material shared between Samuel-Kings and Chronicles is a quite distinctive sub-set of Samuel-Kings. (b) Detached from its present setting(s), this sub-set emerges as an integrated, coherent, and even artistically created text. Finally, (c) the synoptic material was not simply *one* major source alongside others that contributed to Samuel-Kings. It was, instead, its core or alternatively, the seedbed out of which much of Samuel-Kings developed through further exploration of the implications and resources of the older stories. Since the houses of Yahweh and of the king are prominent throughout, I call it the *Book of Two Houses* (henceforth BoTH).

Many nouns, verbs, names, and even whole phrases occur just twice each in the synoptic text – or, where found more than twice, then still are repeated within the accounts of only two kings. Some examples: a shot from a bow only kills Saul and Ahab. The verbs "save" (הושע) and "deliver" (הציל) are used only in narratives about David and Hezekiah; after Saul and David, there is no further mention of Philistines. Many of these pairs occur in clusters. For example: not only "save" and "deliver," but also "scorn" (חרף) and "Yahweh's messenger" (מלאך יהוה) are unique within the synoptic narrative to the accounts of David and Hezekiah. Then, though the verb "prostrate oneself" (השתחוה) occurs four times in BoTH, these clearly form two pairs: one concerns prostration before gods other than Yahweh; the other provides a further link between David and Hezekiah.

Auld 2017, 92–93 noted some 30 such pairings. However, more than 130 are identified below (pp. 153–161). On the one hand, this much larger total strengthens the claim that BoTH was an integrated and artistically purposeful text. On the other, it provides (negative) evidence about the original extent of BoTH. Josiah's

https://doi.org/10.1515/9783111060279-008

successors, the last four kings of Jerusalem, do all feature at the end of Kings and Chronicles; but the shared text relating to them is much sketchier than in the rest of BoTH. Hence it seems probable that BoTH started with the death of Saul and finished with that of Josiah. In support of this conclusion, not one of the eleven dozen paired links relates to any of these four last kings, while of the kings before Josiah, only Amon is without an explicit link. It is possible that Amon is blamed for serving the same detestable deities that Asa had much earlier removed and that later censors removed their names from 2 Kings 21:21 and 1 Kings 15:13.

Scholarship over many generations has termed chs. 12–26 of Deuteronomy its "code," with the most comprehensive statement about the place chosen by Yahweh at its start and pilgrimage to that place with first fruits at its close. This "code" is also widely reckoned to be its "core." However, several features of Deuteronomy 26:1–15 make me question whether it should be reckoned part of the core of the book.

(1) Its theme of the offerings to be taken to the sanctuary from the produce of the land has already been outlined at 14:22–23; thus, ch. 26 can fairly be described as an expanded statement of the requirement.

(2) That earlier statement of the theme (14:22–23) immediately follows the well-known injunction about the kid and its mother's milk (14:21b). These same themes are paired (though in reverse order) among the *mišpāṭîm* of the so-called Covenant Code (Ex 23:19b, 19a). The link with that code, together with the terseness of the formulation in Deuteronomy 14, are both indications of the priority of Deuteronomy 14 over Deuteronomy 26. The kid, which will not concern us further here, has been usefully discussed by Stefan Schorch (2010) and Philippe Guillaume (2011).

(3) Deuteronomy 26:1–15 includes the injunction to prostrate oneself (השתחוה) *before Yahweh* (v. 10). The negative counterpart, *not* to prostrate before *other* gods, is common (see Table a in the Appendix). However, this positive command is not found in any other part of Deuteronomy. In Samuel-Kings, prostration before Yahweh is found only in non-synoptic portions, most of them in 1 Samuel (1 Sam 1:3, 1:19, 1:28, 15:25, 15:30, 15:31, 28:14; 2 Sam 12:20; 2 Kgs 17:36).

(4) A fourth criterion, the wording לשכן שמו שם in Deuteronomy 26:2, is discussed below in section 2.

All in all, ch. 26, with its restatement of the first-fruits command that includes the requirement of prostration before Yahweh, should either be reassigned to the outer chapters of Deuteronomy or taken as our first sample of secondary material within Deuteronomy 12–26. Aside from this, I simply accept as a starting point in this paper the opinion about the central chapters of Deuteronomy that is widely shared (though not by Guillaume 2021, especially p. 214).

In my Samuel commentary, I had already argued that most of 1 Samuel (and chs. 1–30 include seven of the nine instances just noted of prostration before Yahweh) was extrapolated from – developed from and projected backwards from – the shared account of Jerusalem's kings.[1] It was a fresh prequel to the older royal story told in BoTH. The development from the major speech of synoptic Solomon (1 Kgs 8//2 Chr 6) to the major speech of non-synoptic Samuel (1 Sam 12) is just one example.[2] In the monograph I claimed that the process of re-appropriating the synoptic royal story continued beyond the prophet Samuel in the same direction – backwards in time – to Moses.[3] Here I will develop my earlier insight further by arguing that the teaching attributed to Moses in Deuteronomy 12 about the place chosen by Yahweh is also indebted to the synoptic account of David and Solomon in BoTH. I note fresh indications of how the whole synoptic narrative of BoTH (and especially the reports about kings Ahaz and Manasseh) may have informed Moses's teaching in Deuteronomy 13 and 18 about prophecy and divination.

The relationship of non-code to code material in Deuteronomy has several similarities to that of non-core to core material in Samuel–Kings. Deuteronomy 1–11 and 1 Samuel 1–30 provide substantial, fresh prequels to the older materials; and there are new tail-pieces in Deuteronomy 27–34 and 2 Kings 24–25. There will also have been many interpolations within the framework of the older materials, some of them quite large. These can be more readily identified in Samuel-Kings, granted that synoptic/non-synoptic corresponds to core/non-core. The core of Samuel-Kings (BoTH) lacked not only the prequel (Samuel and Saul) and the tail-piece (Jerusalem's four last kings) but also most of the story of David and his family in 2 Samuel 9–20, most of the prophetic narratives in 1 Kings 17–2 Kings 10 in which Elijah and Elisha are prominent, and all the connected account of the kings of northern Israel. However, within the Deuteronomic Code (chs. 12–26), we have no similarly objective criterion of verbatim or almost verbatim materials found in two separate books for distinguishing between earlier and later or core and non-core; instead, we must operate with clusters of details, as in the above discussion of Deuteronomy 26:1–15.

2 The place of divine choice

Within Deuteronomy, Moses's wording about Yahweh's "choice" (בחר) of a "place" (מקום) appears not only first but also repeatedly in Deuteronomy 12 (vv. 5, 11, 14,

1 Auld, *I & II Samuel*.
2 Auld, 103–5, 108–9.
3 Auld, 195–202.

18, 21, and 26). Only in Deuteronomy 16:2, 6, 7, 11, 15, and 16 is the density of usage greater. The other occurrences in Deuteronomy are at 14:23, 24, 25; 15:20; 17:8, 10; 18:6; 26:2; 31:11 (see also Guillaume 2021). This phrasing re-mints coinage from the divine promise through Nathan to David which, as cited by Solomon, had been extended to include the divine choosing of Jerusalem.

In each of the five synoptic mentions of Yahweh's choice of "the city" (העיר) or Jerusalem, the stated purpose is that his name should "be" there or that he should "set" it there. On four occasions, Kings and Chronicles present the same wording and they differ only on the second.

1 Kgs 8:16	להיות שמי שם	להיות שמי שם	2 Chr 6:6
1 Kgs 8:29	אמרת יהיה שמי שם	אמרת לשום שמך שם	2 Chr 6:20
1 Kgs 9:3	לשום את־שמו שם	לשום את־שמו שם	2 Chr 7:16
1 Kgs 14:21	לשום את־שמו שם	לשום את־שמו שם	2 Chr 12:13
2 Kgs 21:7	אשים את־שמי לעולם	אשים את־שמי לעולם	2 Chr 33:7

The setting of Yahweh's name in the city of Jerusalem (or indeed anywhere else) is never mentioned in Samuel–Kings outside these five synoptic instances.

The phrase "to set his name there" is also used three times in Deuteronomy in connection with the divine choice of a "place," two of them in ch. 12 (vv. 5 and 21) and the third in 14:24. However, six times (12:11, 14:23, 16:2, 16:6, 16:11, 26:2) we find an alternative formulation never replicated in Samuel-Kings but also found in Jeremiah 7:12 and Nehemiah 1:9: לשכן שמו שם ("to let his name *dwell* there"). Lauren A. S. Monroe has proposed the perfectly cogent argument that שכן in these contexts is a calque of Akkadian *šakanu*, which bears the same sense as Hebrew שים or שום ("set/place").[4]

However, an alternative and inner-biblical explanation of this variant in Deuteronomy is both perfectly safe and also convergent with a feature of non-synoptic Samuel-Kings often observed in *Life in Kings*. It can be argued that לשכן שמו שם simply draws on and combines two separate elements of BoTH: (a) לשום את־שמו שם (see 1 Kgs 9:3, 14:21; cf. 2 Kgs 21:7) and (b) שכן from 1 Kings 8:12–13//2 Chronicles 6:1–2, a poetic fragment telling that Yahweh had spoken of "dwelling" (שכן *qal*) in darkness, and a house was built for him to live in forever. Combining these two synoptic themes had been eased by עולמים at the end of 1 Kings 8:13 and לעולם at the end of 2 Kings 21:7, both meaning "forever" and functioning as catchwords. Similar talk of Yahweh "dwelling" in the holy "place" had probably been the original intention of Jeremiah 7:3 and 7:7. In unvocalized Hebrew, ואשכנה\ושכנתי אתכם במקום הזה is ambiguous: with the verbs read as *qal*, it

4 Monroe, 2011.

means “and I shall dwell with you in this place.” However, with the verbs read as *piel* in the standard text, it means “and I shall let you dwell in this place.” Assuming a shift from earlier *qal* to current *piel*, a theologically bold promise about Yahweh’s presence in the heart of the temple has been tamed to express a promise about Israel continuing in its land. In Deuteronomy, similarly, having the “name” of Yahweh “dwell” in the “place” avoided the bluntness of describing Yahweh (himself) dwelling in the temple, even in darkness.

If לשכן שמו שם is judged secondary to the synoptic formula לשום שמו שם shared with BoTH, two options remain available to us. The primary Deuteronomic legislator could have created this coinage and used it alongside the synoptic formula; or the primary legislator could have adopted the synoptic formula, while the new coinage indicates the work of a subsequent author. The alternative formulations appear in neighbouring verses only in Deuteronomy 14:23 and 24. Within Deuteronomy 12 they belong to different paragraphs: לשום is used in vv. 1–7 and vv. 20–28, and לשכן in vv. 8–12. There is consensus over the paragraphing implicit in Deuteronomy 12 (vv. 1–7 / 8–12 / 13–19 / 20–28 / 29–31), and wide agreement that the oldest form of the statement about the place of divine choice is within 12:13–18[19], although Simeon Chavel has argued that this paragraph is the latest in the chapter.[5] The final instance of the non-synoptic formula (“to let his name dwell”) is found in 26:2, within the restatement of the first fruits topic discussed above. If Deuteronomy 26:1–15 should still be reckoned part of the core of Deuteronomy, it should be seen as part of a secondary (or later) stratum within it and compared with 12:8–12. If לשכן שמו שם was also a secondary addition to 14:23, we should perhaps deduce that Deuteronomy 16:1–16, with its three instances of the non-synoptic formula, is also not primary.

Several features of Deuteronomy 12 are clearly related to synoptic 2 Samuel 7 and 1 Kings 8 (and linked passages). However, לשכן שמו שם, though twice as common in Deuteronomy as לשום את־שמו שם, is never found in Kings. Similarly, the chosen *place* (מקום), so common in Deuteronomy and found once in 2 Chronicles 7:12b, is never found in Kings. Instead of reading Kings from the perspective of Deuteronomy, we should read Deuteronomy from the perspective of BoTH. “Place” (מקום) is used in different senses in BoTH, but always “of a location where something of the deity has been invested, whether that be destructive force or more benign choice and commitment.”[6] However, in the context of the Jerusalem temple, “place” in BoTH was specifically the “holy of holies” where the ark was deposited. Deuteronomy instead conflated “place” with “house” or “city/Jerusalem.”

---

5 Chavel 2011, 316–19.

6 Auld, *Life in Kings*, 77–78.

(a) The divine choice of a "place" from all your sceptres/tribes (מכל־שבטיכם) to set his name there (12:5) recalls BoTH's wording of "a city" (1 Kgs 8:16) or "Jerusalem, the city" (1 Kgs 14:21) or "Jerusalem" (2 Kgs 21:7), chosen by Yahweh "from all the sceptres/tribes of Israel" (מכל־שבטי ישראל).

(b) במקום אשר יבחר יהוה באחד שבטיך שם תעלה עלתיך ושם תעשה כל אשר אנכי מצוך in Deuteronomy 12:14 again uses "choose" from BoTH but combines it instead with the unique "one of your tribes/sceptres," which draws on the equally unique באחד שבטי ישראל ("one of the sceptres/tribes of Israel") in synoptic 2 Samuel 7:7.

(c) Deuteronomy 12:21 repeats from 12:5 "the place" and "chosen by Yahweh" and "to set his name there," but without "from all your tribes." The same wording (with "set" and without "from all your tribes") occurs just once more. Only in 12:21 and 14:24 do we find the provision, "if the place is too far from you" (כי־ירחק ממך המקום). If "far" is also an echo of BoTH, it may be recalling the "far land" in Solomon's prayer (1 Kgs 8:41, 46//2 Chr 6:32, 36). In any case, David is the only other user in BoTH of "far," again in connection with "house": "and you have spoken even to the house of your servant from afar" (2 Sam 7:19//1 Chr 17:17).

Simeon Chavel has argued that Deuteronomy 12:20–28 results from splicing together two originally separate although overlapping formulations: v. 20 originally introduced vv. 22–25, and v. 21 headed vv. 26–28.[7] We have noted that "far" (v. 21) may echo BoTH, and this is also true of "place." However, the corresponding conditional clause that opens v. 20, "if Yahweh your god *widens* your *border*" (כי ירחיב יהוה אלהיך את גבולך), uses terms not found in BoTH. When "widens your border" is used again in Deuteronomy 19:8, it is much expanded: "… as he swore to your fathers and gives you all the land which he spoke of giving to your fathers." It is now explicit that the phrase refers to the completion of the promised land-taking and that Deuteronomy 12:20 and 12:22–25 mirror 12:8–12.

(d) It is important to note that "you" is plural in the opening paragraphs, Deuteronomy 12:1–7 / 8–12, but singular in 12:13–19 / 20–28 / 29–31. The singular "you" also helps to clarify the relationship between the declarations to Israel in Deuteronomy 12:20–28 and the divine promise to David, particularly as represented in 2 Samuel 7:12–16. The correlation is particularly striking at the culmination of vv. 20–28: Israel is addressed in the singular, in terms used of her first king, and charged to do "what is right in the eyes of Yahweh" like every good king that followed him. The synoptic royal story had told of fathers dying and being buried, followed by their sons, and each summarily assessed by whether he had or had

7 Chavel, "Literary Development," 312–16.

not done "what was right in the eyes of Yahweh." In Deuteronomy, Moses speaks in closely related terms: in 12:25, 28 (as also in 4:40), "to you and your sons" is followed by "after you" (אחריך) as in 2 Samuel 7:12 (BoTH), and there with "seed" (זרע) rather than "sons." And in BoTH, the divine promise to David and his *seed* is "forever" (2 Sam 7:13, 16//1 Chr 17:12, 14). "Forever" is used much more densely in synoptic material than in non-synoptic Samuel–Kings (see Table b in the Appendix). The account in 2 Samuel 7//1 Chronicles 17 of the divine commitment to David mediated by Nathan and David's response uses "forever" most densely of all (six times). It is precisely with these several synoptic "forever" passages that Deuteronomy 12 shares so much; and yet it mentions "forever" only in 12:28 (and not even in the related 12:25). This important chapter culminates in 12:28. (As will be noted in 4. below, 12:29–31 has a close link with 13:1–6.) In 12:25 and 28, Moses addresses Israel as a singular "you." לך ולבניך is not a common pairing (Ex 12:24; Lev 10:15; Num 18:8, 9, 11, 19; Deut 4:40, 12:25, 12:28; Josh 14:9); but it is almost always linked with עולם, though not in Numbers 18:9 nor Deuteronomy 12:25, and in Deuteronomy 4:40 it is linked with כל־הימים instead. However, there is one crucial difference between the words of Moses and the synoptic narrative – "forever" in Deuteronomy 12:28 is now conditional–– "Watch and listen to all these words that I am commanding you in order that it may be well for you and your sons after you forever, *supposing you do what is good and right in the eyes of Yahweh your god* (כי תעשה הטוב והישר בעיני יהוה אלהיך)." The optimism of the older royal ideology represented in BoTH has become blunted.

Just two linked chapters in BoTH have provided several of the key terms in Deuteronomy 12. One narrates the divine promise to David (2 Sam 7) and the other Solomon's actualization of that promise as he dedicates the Jerusalem temple (1 Kgs 8). Viewing this supposed introduction to the core of Deuteronomy from the perspective of BoTH contributes to the analysis of Deuteronomy 12. Positively, Israel (sg) is addressed like one of its (former) kings; and this in turn supports the long-standing critical judgment that the earliest component in Deuteronomy 12 is vv. 13–18. Negatively, vv. 8–12 are stated in language unknown in BoTH: not only the לשכן (let dwell) formula in v. 11, itself part of a secondary combination of elements from BoTH, but also the nouns מנוחה ("rest") and נחלה ("allotment") in v. 9 and the cognate verbs מנחיל ("allot") and הניח ("give rest") in v. 10.

Deriving the wording in Deuteronomy about divine "choice" of a "place" from portions of BoTH also sets a major text-critical issue in a fresh light. Throughout Deuteronomy, and starting from Deuteronomy 12, MT refers to the place "which Yahweh *will/may choose*" (יבחר יהוה), but the Samaritan text always offers "which Yahweh *chose*" (בחר יהוה) – understood as performative *qatal*, בחר could also be rendered "chooses." Innocent Himbaza has attractively argued for a future perfect interpretation, "which Yahweh will have chosen," of the more original בחר (2016). The linked passages in BoTH also use perfect/*qatal*: דברתי in 2 Samuel 7:7, בחרתי in 1 Kings 8:16, and בחרת in 1 Kings 8:44 and 48. If Deuteronomy borrowed from BoTH, it is natural to suppose that the law-giver simply adopted the perfect/*qatal* from the parent text and produced what we read in the Samaritan text. Only later was the verb adjusted in MT. Adrian Schenker marshals the evidence from Greek, Coptic, and Latin mss that the earliest Greek translation of Deuteronomy used the preterite "chose" in agreement with the Samaritan text (2010, 113–116). Only after the shift in MT had LXX been adjusted to agree.

In summary, the following three-stage development is plausible:

1. Yahweh chooses Jerusalem/the city to set his name there (BoTH)
2. Yahweh chooses "the place" to set his name there (Deut^1)
3. Yahweh chooses "the place" to let his name dwell there (Deut^2).

If the older portions of Deuteronomy 12:13–28 were indebted to the completed *Book of Two Houses*, which came to its end with the death of king Josiah, then the purpose of Deuteronomy 12 was not to enjoin *centralization* of "worship" under Josiah or any other king (see also Halpern 2021). According to BoTH, David and Solomon had already offered holocaust sacrifices in Jerusalem, and BoTH has nothing to report about holocausts offered up elsewhere. A Deuteronomic legislator working from BoTH after the fall of Jerusalem had no reason to commend centralization but had every reason to restate principles already normative in BoTH for a new and still emerging situation. The kings had always represented the nation; now without kings, the nation is addressed directly. There had been and must still be a centre for key cultic practices. Given the uncertain status of Jerusalem, this centre is not (yet) named. The divine promise "forever" is too deeply rooted in the old traditions to surrender; but its restatement now comes with clear conditions.

3 Prophets and dreamers

It can be argued that both sections of Deuteronomy that deal with prophecy or divination (chs. 13 and 18) were also developed from and respond to (portions of) BoTH (see the previous essay). I have described BoTH as "the oldest 'biblical' prophetic narrative" (Auld 2015). Prophets, along with a seer and men of God, certainly play an important role – from David asking Nathan about building a house for Yahweh to Josiah sending representatives to Huldah after hearing the words from the scroll found in the temple. And Solomon received two divine visions or dreams. However, I prefer now to define the section that dealt with Rehoboam and Jeroboam in BoTH more tightly (see the next essay). If this was more like the "alternative story" preserved in LXX^{BL} than what we read in 1 Kings 12:1–19 (MT and LXX^{A})//2 Chronicles 10:1–19, then neither Ahijah nor Shemaiah was originally styled a "prophet." Furthermore, the religious interpretation now found in 1 Kings 12:15b// 2 Chronicles 10:15b had not yet been added, stating that Rehoboam's disregard for the people was "a turn originating from Yahweh in order to establish his word which he spoke through Ahijah the Shilonite." Recognizing as secondary that explicit formulation of word + fulfilment permits a more nuanced view of the earlier role of prophets according to BoTH: they play important parts in the story, but their words do not provide an authoritative interpretation.

The extended story at its heart about Micaiah and the two kings is instructive for two reasons: (a) it pits one "prophet of Yahweh" over against hundreds of prophets who are never said to be in the cause of any other god; and (b) it depicts Yahweh's prophet as involved in Yahweh-inspired deception of the kings. Several significant pairings link the stories in BoTH of Micaiah (1 Kgs 22:5, 22:7, 22:8, 22:17, 22:20, 22:27, 22:28, 22:31) and of Huldah (2 Kgs 22:13, 22:14, 22:18, 22:20, 23:2). Jehoshaphat and Ahab seek (דרש) Yahweh through Micaiah the prophet (הנביא), as only synoptic Josiah will do again through Huldah the prophetess (הנביאה). Small (קט[ו]ן) and great (גדול) are paired only in the Jehoshaphat and Josiah reports. In peace (בשלום) is uttered three times in the exchanges between Micaiah and the king of Israel and reappears only in the response of Huldah to Josiah. Many generations of readers have been surprised at Josiah dying on the battlefield (2 Kgs 23:29–30) after being told by Huldah that he would be gathered to his grave in peace (22:20), but they may have misread the prophetess.

If its author was familiar with BoTH, it is appropriate that Deuteronomy 13:2–6 expresses caution about the advice that might be given by prophets and dreamers of dreams. They might promise things that do not happen; and, even if they do happen, they might go on to encourage following other gods. This would constitute a test from Yahweh. Deuteronomy 18:15–22 returns to the theme of prophets and the danger of following other gods. Moses promises that Yahweh will raise up a prophet like him: he will speak what Yahweh will put in his mouth, and Yahweh will take action against those who do not listen. If the prophet speaks and what is indicated does not happen, then that word was not from Yahweh. It is easier to see these paragraphs in Deuteronomy as responses to the narratives in BoTH about kings and prophets than as statements of the principles that later became operative in these narratives (see also Turton 2021).

4 King Manasseh's shadow

Each of these two paragraphs relating to prophets immediately follows a paragraph that deals with "divination" (in the broadest sense) and is also closely related to BoTH – in this case, not to the broad sweep of the narrative, but only its sections on the wicked kings Ahaz and Manasseh.

In BoTH (2 Kgs 21:2//2 Chr 33:2), Manasseh, like Ahaz his grandfather (2 Kgs 16:3//2 Chr 28:3), followed the "abominable actions" (תועבות) of the nations dispossessed before Israel by Yahweh. BoTH uses this abhorrent term only twice. In the case of Ahaz, only one notorious example is cited of his abominations: making his son pass in fire. In the second case, we are also told that Manasseh built altars for Baal, made an Asherah, and built altars for the whole host of heaven (2 Kgs 21:3–5//2 Chr 33:3–5) before, like Ahaz, he "passed his son through fire" (העביר את־בנו באש). This much longer, hostile report goes on to state that Manasseh also practised divination, described in 2 Kings 21:6//2 Chronicles 33:6 in two pairs of expressions: ועונן ונחש and ועשה אוב וידעונים. Whether there was any relationship between divination and what was done with his son and fire remains an open question.

These materials are rebuilt in Deuteronomy 18:9–14. The two pairs of terms from BoTH have become eight (18:10–11). However, unlike the case of Manasseh (2 Kgs 21:3–5//2 Chr 33:3–5), there is no mention in Deuteronomy 18 of altar-building for Baal, the making of an Asherah, or the service of the whole host of heaven. Hence, its instruction not to learn to act according to the abominations of these nations (18:9) is now immediately followed by an enhanced list of "divinatory" practices (vv. 10–11) that has not only supplemented the shorter list in BoTH but may also have changed its character.

Deut 18:10–11	**Parallels**
מעביר בנו־ובתו באש making his son/daughter pass in fire	BoTH on Ahaz and Manasseh
קסם קסמים one divining divinations	(see below)
מעונן ומנחש a soothsayer and an augur	BoTH on Manasseh
ומכשף וחבר חבר and a sorcerer and a charmer of charms	Isa 47:9–12
ושאל אוב וידעני and an *'ôb*-asker and a "familiar"	BoTH on Manasseh
ודרש אל־המתים and one enquiring of the dead	Isa 8:19

The two pairs of terms shared with BoTH on Manasseh concern divination in the strict sense: discovering and stating what the future will be. "Enquiring of the dead" (דרש אל־המתים), the new final term, restates the second pair – and is also linked with them only in Isaiah 8:19. But the interpolated pair of terms, shared only with Isaiah 47:9–12, describe sorcery: attempting to change the future. As for קסם, it is quite the commonest of all these terms in the Hebrew Bible (some 30 times, including appearances in Isa 3:2; 44:25). Though normally rendered "divine(r)," it is applied to Balaam, whom the Moabite king recruits to curse Israel and so change Moab's future for the better. If we knew the original import of "making one's son (or daughter) pass in fire," we would know whether sorcery was an original component of the charge-sheet against Ahaz and Manasseh in BoTH. The warning is underscored in vv. 12–14, and only after this comprehensive description of false approach to the deity does Moses present the "prophet like me" that Yahweh will raise up for Israel (18:15–22).

The preceding passage on prophets and dreamers (Deut 13:2–6) also follows a short paragraph related to both Ahaz and Manasseh (Deut 12:29–31). When Yahweh cuts off the nations whose land Israel will settle, Israel should not be ensnared into consulting their gods: the nations had done for their gods every abomination that Yahweh hates – even burning their sons and daughters by fire for their gods. This solitary example given of abominable action is reminiscent of BoTH on Ahaz. However, the threefold mention of "their (unnamed) gods" recalls Manasseh's actions in favour of Baal, Asherah, and the host of heaven. The element of the BoTH critique of Manasseh that we did not find replicated in Deuteronomy 18:9–11 is provided in Deuteronomy 12:30–31 and 13:3. And in case this allusion to Manasseh's actions has not been spotted, his name מנשה (*mnšh*) is immediately played on in 13:4: wherever prophets commend serving other gods, Yahweh is "testing" (*mnsh*/מנסה) Israel. All other instances of נסה in Deuteronomy occur outside chs. 12–26, in 4:34, 6:16, 8:2, 8:16, 28:56, and 33:8.

Each "divinatory-leading-to-prophetic" section of Deuteronomy resumes תועבת הגוים and הוריש from Ahaz and Manasseh in BoTH. This is explicitly so in Deuteronomy 18:9 and 14 and occurs with small modifications in Deuteronomy 12:29–31 (ירש *qal* is used twice in 12:29 and תועבה sg occurs in 12:31). Making another small change, both 12:31 and 18:10 add daughters alongside sons in whatever is done to children "by fire." Deuteronomy 12:31 makes its understanding clear that Canaanites were burning their sons and daughters "to their gods." These are named in 2 Kings 21:3–5 but remain typically anonymous in Deuteronomy. Deuteronomy 13:4 also plays on the name of Manasseh without actually using it. Then Deuteronomy 18:10–11 adopts all the details listed in 2 Kings 21:6 and adds more. The critique of two wicked kings in the older royal narrative has driven the presentation in Deuteronomy of divination and prophecy, both false and true – and not the other way around. Four of the eight terms in the expanded Deuteronomy 18:10–11 (קסם, כשף, חבר, דרש אל־המתים) are neither synoptic nor found elsewhere in Deuteronomy – and this despite the fact that קסם is quite the commonest "divinatory" term in the Hebrew Bible.

There is evidence that the Ahaz and Manasseh narratives from BoTH were influential beyond Deuteronomy. There are striking parallels in a still larger section of Leviticus 18–20. Within Leviticus, "abominations" appear only in these chapters (18:22, 18:26, 18:27, 18:29, 18:30, and 20:13). Not only so – the four divinatory terms used in pairs in 2 Kings 21:6 appear in the same two pairings, לא תנחשו ולא תעוננו (Lev 19:26) and אל־תפנו אל־האבת ואל־הידענים (Lev 19:31), precisely between the mentions in Leviticus 18 and 20 of the abominable "gift" of children. Just as Deuteronomy 12:31 takes the burning (שרף) of children as the prime example of abominable behavior, so, too, the only uses of תועבה in Leviticus follow "giving" children to Molech (18:21, 20:2, 20:3, 20:4, and 20:5). Molech is found elsewhere in the Hebrew Bible only three times: Solomon built a "high place" (במה) for this Ammonite god (1 Kgs 11:7); Josiah's defilement of the Topheth in the Hinnom valley (2 Kgs 23:10) was "lest any man cause his son or daughter to pass in fire to the Molech" (לבלתי להעביר איש את־בנו ואת־בתו באש למלך); and Jeremiah complained against those who had built "high places" for Baal in Hinnom for this purpose (32:35).

From the perspective of BoTH, each positive panel in Deuteronomy 12–13 evokes David and Solomon and is preceded by a warning about continuing in the way of the two most recent evil kings. Deuteronomy 12:5–28 legislate for a central altar, like David and Solomon, "forever"; before this, 12:2–4 warn Israel against behaving like Ahaz and Manasseh and their cultivation of the במות. Deuteronomy 13:2–6 evokes good kings, such as David and Solomon, who were attentive to prophets and dreams, following the warning in 12:29–31 against replicating Ahaz and Manasseh and their abominations.

5 Deuteronomic core and non-core

In each case just discussed, the material is found within the central chapters of Deuteronomy and barely appears beyond their confines. The chosen place is introduced in Deuteronomy 12 (6 times), mentioned 13 times in Deuteronomy 14–18 (14:23, 14:24, 14:25, 15:20, 16:2, 16:6, 16:7, 16:11, 16:15, 16:16, 17:8, 17:10, and 18:6); then, after a substantial gap, there are two final instances in Deuteronomy 26:2 (probably not part of the core: see above) and 31:11 (certainly outside the core). In the royal story, mention of the choice of Jerusalem or "the city" is found in only two non-synoptic contexts: 1 Kings 11:13, 11:32, 11:36, and 2 Kings 23:27. Both of these conclude by re-using synoptic formulae (לשום שמי שם and יהיה שמי שם) – neither adopts the Deuteronomic לשכן שמו שם. That could indicate (but it would be only an argument from silence) that the non-synoptic authors were not yet familiar with the later Deuteronomic usage.

Correlation over prophecy and divination is more complex. Deuteronomy does not mention divination at all outside the central chapters (or indeed prophecy, except for the concluding note about the special prophetic status of Moses in Deut 34:10–12). BoTH features divination only in the case of Manasseh and possibly Ahaz. However, non-synoptic Samuel–Kings includes four mentions and, at least in MT, each uses a form of non-synoptic קסם, apparently now the generic term (נביא experienced a similar development). In 1 Samuel, Philistines consult their priests and “diviners” (6:2); Samuel warns Saul against “divination” (15:23); yet, despite this, Saul asks the medium to “divine” by means of a *’wb* and she raises up Samuel (28:8). However, in 1 Kingdoms 15:23, LXX may attest not to קסם but נחש. Finally, in 2 Kings 17:16b–17a, and within a wider critique, fallen (northern) Israel is blamed for behaving in many ways like Manasseh: “they made an Asherah, prostrated themselves to the whole host of heaven, and they served Baal; and they made their sons and daughters pass in fire, divined divinations, and practised augury.” Within the first three complaints, serving Baal comes third instead of first with Manasseh. Within the second three, the first and third items are as in the critique of Manasseh, but the second (מעונן) has been replaced by ויקסמו קסמים, presumably under the influence of the enhanced list in Deuteronomy 18:10–11. “Divining divinations” is also in second place there.

6 Conclusion

In each of these topics, chosen place and divination/prophecy, the development appears to have started the same way: moving from BoTH to core-Deuteronomy (no more than Deut 12–25 – but see Table c in the Appendix). Yet, there are differences between them all. The developing critique of “divination” proceeds from synoptic Manasseh, via Deuteronomy 18, to non-synoptic exiled Israel (2 Kings 17). However, the “choosing” of Jerusalem in non-synoptic portions of Kings is not similarly influenced by Deuteronomy: the chosen “place” plays no part in 1 Kings 11:13, 32, 36 or 2 Kings 23:27. Again, several prophets play a higher, more normative role in non-synoptic Samuel–Kings than any of their counterparts in BoTH. Yet here, the trajectory of development appears to be from BoTH, via non-synoptic Samuel–Kings, to Deuteronomy 18 with its talk of “a prophet like [Moses].”

Non-synoptic materials in Samuel–Kings may find their counterparts either within Deuteronomy 12–25 or within the outer chapters of that book. An example of the first is Samuel’s warning about the nature of kingship in 1 Samuel 8 and the law of the king as delivered by Moses in Deuteronomy 17:14–20. One striking instance of a topic found *only* in *non-core* Deuteronomy and *non-synoptic* Kings is the renegade construction of the golden calf and worship before it in Deuteronomy 9:8–21 and 1 Kings 12:25–33.

Mainstream scholarship links the origins of Deuteronomy closely to a reform by Josiah near the end of the monarchy in Jerusalem and reckons that its teachings were drafted in response to the long experience of monarchy. The claims made above are convergent but more specific. Much of the *wording* at the core of the book called דברים had been influenced by the history of Jerusalem’s monarchy as told – as *worded* – in the *Book of Two Houses.*

Appendix: Word counts

Relationships between Samuel-Kings and BoTH and between the central chapters of Deuteronomy (12–25) and the remainder of that book, and indeed between both, can be sketched in a series of word-counts. Many of the totals tabulated below suggest parallel developments, on the one side from BoTH to Samuel-Kings and on the other from Deuteronomy 12–25 to the whole of Deuteronomy. However, in assessing them, we need to recall that not all materials now in the *central* chapters of Deuteronomy (12–25) had been original components of its *core*.

Life in Kings was so titled because "live," "life," and "alive" or "living" are so sparingly used in BoTH that they provide an excellent indicator of its difference from Samuel–Kings as a whole.[8] As in the synoptic narrative (BoTH), these terms are also used very sparingly in the heart of Deuteronomy. The outer chapters of Deuteronomy comprise roughly twice as much text as the central chapters. Hence, 14 occurrences in chs. 1–11 and 26–34 would reflect a similar density of usage to 7 occurrences in chs. 12–25. Non-synoptic Samuel–Kings is three to four times longer than the synoptic kernel; hence 21 occurrences in non-synoptic Samuel-Kings would reflect a similar density of usage to 6 occurrences in BoTH. The numbers in parentheses in the final two columns of this table and of those that follow indicate the totals across these longer texts, supposing the same level of usage as in their cores. Taking that into account, the "life"-family appears more than twice as densely (32 times) in the outer chapters of Deuteronomy as would be projected from the core (14 times). And in non-synoptic Samuel-Kings, the life-family is used some five times as frequently as a projection from the synoptic core. Development is not simply a matter of increased frequency but also of fresh coinages. For example, "living god" (אלהים חיים or אל חי) is found only in non-core Deuteronomy and in non-synoptic Samuel-Kings.[9]

Tab. a: BoTH < Non-BoTH Sam–Kgs *and* Deut 12–25 < Deut 1–11; 26–34.

	BoTH	**Deut 12–25**	**Deut 1–11; 26–34**	**Non-BoTH Sam–Kgs**
חיה etc	6[10]	7[11]	32[12] (14)	c110 (21)

8 Auld, *Life in Kings*, 29–38.

9 Deut 5:26; 1 Sam 17:26, 17:36; 2 Kgs 19:4, 19:16.

10 1 Kgs 8:40, 12:6, 22:14; 2 Kgs 11:12,14:9, 14:17. Here, as in all other BoTH references, mention is made only of the relevant passages in Sam–Kgs and not the synoptic portions in Chr.

11 Deut 12:1,16:3, 16:20, 17:19, 19:4, 19:5, 20:16.

12 Deut 4:1, 4:4, 4:9, 4:10, 4:33, 4:42, 5:3, 5:24, 5:26 (twice), 5:33, 6:2, 6:24. 7:22, 8:1, 8:3 (twice), 28:66 (twice); 30:6, 30:15, 30:16, 30:19 (thrice), 30:20, 31:13, 31:27, 32:39, 32:40, 32:47, 33:6.

Tab. a (continued)

	BoTH	Deut 12–25	Deut 1–11; 26–34	Non-BoTH Sam–Kgs
משפט	5[13]	12[14]	25[15] (24)	35[16] (17)
חק[ה]	2[17]	3[18]	26[19] (6)	18[20] (7)
מצוה\ות	2[21]	4[22]	35[23] (8)	19[24] (7)
צוה (subj. YHWH)	6[25]	4[26]	30[27] (8)	21[28] (21)
צוה (subj. Moses)	0[29]	15[30]	39[31] (30)	1[32]

13 2 Sam 8:15; 1 Kgs 8:45, 8:49, 9:4, 10:9.
14 Deut 12:1, 16:18, 16:19 17:8, 17:9, 17:11, 18:3, 19:6, 21:17, 21:22, 24:17, 25:1.
15 Deut 1:17 (twice); 4:1, 4:5, 4:8, 4:14, 4:45, 5:1, 5:31, 6:1, 6:20, 7:11, 7:12, 8:11, 10:18, 11:1, 11:32, 26:16, 26:17, 27:19, 30:16, 32:4, 32:41, 33:10, 33:21.
16 1 Sam 2:13, 8:3, 8:9, 8:11, 10:25, 27:11, 30:25; 2 Sam 15:2, 15:4, 15:6, 22:23; 1 Kgs 2:3, 3:[11], 3:28 (twice), 5:8, 6:12, 6:38, 7:7, 8:58, 8:59, 11:33, 18:28, 20:40; 2 Kgs 1:7, 11:14, 17:26 (twice), 17:27, 17:33, 17:34 (twice), 17:37, 17:40, 25:6.
17 1 Kgs 9:4, 9:6.
18 Deut 12:1, 16:12, 17:19.
19 Deut 4:1, 45, 45:6, 45:8, 45:14, 45:40, 45:45, 5:1, 5:31, 6:1, 6:2, 6:17, 6:20, 6:24, 7:11, 8:11, 10:13, 11:1, 11:32, 26:16, 26:17, 27:10, 28:15, 28:45, 30:10, 30:16.
20 1 Sam 30:25; 2 Sam 22:23; 1 Kgs 2:3, 3:3, 13:4, 6:12, 8:58, 8:61, 11:11, 11:33, 11:34, 11:38; 2 Kgs 17:8, 17:13, 17:15, 17:19, 17:34, 17:37.
21 1 Kgs 9:6; 2 Kgs 23:3.
22 Deut 13:5, 13:19, 15:5, 19:9.
23 Deut 4:2, 4:40, 5:10, 5:29, 5:31, 6:1, 6:2, 6:17, 6:25, 7:9, 7:11, 8:1, 8:2, 8:6, 8:11, 10:13, 11:1, 11:8, 11:13, 11:22, 11:27, 11:28, 26:18, 27:1, 27:10, 28:1, 28:9, 28:13, 28:15, 28:45, 30:8, 30:10, 30:11, 30:16, 31:5.
24 1 Sam 13:13; 1 Kgs 2:3, 2:43, 3:14, 6:12, 8:58, 8:61, 11:34, 11:38, 13:21, 14:8, 18:18; 2 Kgs 17:13, 17:16, 17:19, 17:34, 17:37, 18:6, 18:36.
25 2 Sam 5:25, 7:7, 7:11; 1 Kgs 9:4; 2 Kgs 14:6, 21:8.
26 Deut 13:6, 18:18, 18:20, 20:17.
27 Deut 1:3, 1:19, 1:41, 2:37, 4:5, 4:13, 4:14, 4:23, 5:12, 5:15, 5:16, 5:32, 5:33, 6:1, 6:17, 6:20, 6:24, 6:25, 9:12, 9:16, 10:5, 26:13, 26:14, 26:16, 28:8, 28:45, 28:69, 31:14, 31:23, 34:9.
28 1 Sam 2:29; 13:13, 13:14 (twice), 25:30; 2 Sam 17:14; 1 Kgs 8:58, 11:10 (twice), 11:11, 11:38, 13:9, 13:21, 15:5, 17:4, 17:9; 2 Kgs 17:13, 17:15, 17:34, 17:35, 18:6.
29 In one synoptic *context* (2 Kgs 21:8), Moses is the subject of "commanded" – compare non-synoptic 1 Kgs 8:56 and 2 Kgs 18:12. However, the synoptic parallel in 2 Chr 33:8 is stated differently.
30 Deut 12:11, 12:14, 12:21, 12:28, 13:1, 13:19, 15:5, 15:11, 15:15, 17:3, 19:7, 19:9, 24:8, 24:18, 24:22.
31 Deut 1:16, 1:18, 2:4, 3:18, 3:21, 3:28, 4:2 (twice), 3:40, 6:2, 6:6, 7:11, 8:1, 8:11,10:13, 11:8, 11:13, 11:22, 11:27, 11:28, 27:1 (twice), 27:4, 27:10, 27:11, 28:1, 28:13, 28:14, 28:15, 30:2, 30:5, 30:8, 30:11, 30:16, 31:5, 31:10, 31:25, 31:29, 33:4.
32 2 Kgs 18:12.

Tab. a (continued)

	BoTH	Deut 12–25	Deut 1–11; 26–34	Non-BoTH Sam–Kgs
השתחוה (other gods)	2[33]	1[34]	6[35] (2)	10[36] (7)
עבד (other gods)	4[37]	5[38]	13[39] (10)	18[40] (14)
עבד (Yahweh)		1[41]	5[42] (2)	8[43]
ירא את־יהוה	3	10	22 (20)	13 (11)
אהב\אהבה	1	7	16 (14)	25 (4)

Moses is never the subject of "to command" in BoTH and is only once in Samuel-Kings. Prostration before Yahweh is not explicit in BoTH – synoptic 2 Kgs 18:22// 2 Chr 32:12 report the Assyrian envoy telling his Jerusalem hearers that Hezekiah had ordered prostration "before this/one altar" but do not endorse this foreigner's words. Of the 10 non-synoptic instances, 6 belong to just two chapters of 1 Samuel (chs. 1 and 15). Serving (עבד) Yahweh is never mentioned in BoTH; yet its sole mention in the central chapters of Deuteronomy (13:5) comes within a passage partly based on BoTH (section 3 above).

Tab. b: BoTH > Non-BoTH Sam–Kgs *BUT* Deut 12–25 < Deut 1–11; 26–34.

	BoTH	Deut 12–25	Deut 1–11; 26–34	Non-BoTH Sam–Kgs
תורה	4[44]	3[45]	19[46] (6)	7[47] (14)

33 1 Kgs 9:6; 2 Kgs 21:3.

34 Deut 17:3.

35 Deut 4:19, 5:9, 8:19, 11:16, 29:25, 30:17.

36 1 Kgs 11:33, 16:31, 22:54; 2 Kgs 5:18 (thrice), 17:16, 17:35,19:37,21:21.

37 1 Kgs 9:6, 9:9; 2 Kgs 21:3, 21:21.

38 Deut 12:2, 12:30, 13:7, 13:14, 17:3.

39 Deut 4:19, 4:28, 7:4, 7:16, 8:19, 11:16, 28:14, 28:36, 28:64; 29:17, 25; 30:17; 31:20.

40 1 Sam 8:8, 12:10; 1 Kgs 16:31, 22:54; 2 Kgs 10:18 (twice), 17:12, 17:16, 17:33, 17:35, 17:41, 21:21 (twice).

41 Deut 13:5.

42 Deut 6:13, 10:12, 10:20, 11:13, 28:47.

43 1 Sam 7:3, 7:4, 12:10, 12:14, 12:20, 12:24, 26:19; 2 Sam 15:8.

44 2 Kgs 14:6, 21:8, 22:8, 22:11.

45 Deut 17:11, 17:18, 17:19.

46 Deut 1:5, 4:8, 4:44, 27:3, 27:8, 27:26, 28:58, 28:61, 29:20, 29:28, 30:10, 31:9, 31:11, 31:12, 31:24, 31:26, 32:46, 33:4, 33:10.

47 2 Sam 7:19; 1 Kgs 2:3; 2 Kgs 10:31, 17:13, 17:34, 23:24, 23:25.

Tab. b (continued)

	BoTH	Deut 12–25	Deut 1–11; 26–34	Non-BoTH Sam–Kgs
עדה\עדות	2[48]		3[49]	2[50] (7)
עמים	3[51]	2[52]	19[53] (4)	4[54] (10)
גוים	6[55]	4[56]	20[57] (8)	14[58] (21)
לעולם	4[59]	1[60]	2[61]	3[62] (14)
כל־הימים	5[63]	4[64]	8[65]	15[66] (17)

תורה plays a much larger part in non-central Deuteronomy than in non-synoptic Samuel–Kings; and עדה\עדות (admittedly rare in Samuel-Kings) is absent from Deuteronomy 12–25.

Except in the outer chapters of Deuteronomy, גוים is at least twice as common as עמים. Both terms are used more densely in non-core Deuteronomy than in the central chapters of that book but less densely in non-synoptic Samuel-Kings than in BoTH. Within BoTH, עמים is found in more central sections and גוים nearer start and end; that may have influenced word-choice in the development of neigh-

48 2 Kgs 11:12, 23:3.
49 Deut 4:45, 6:17, 6:20.
50 1 Kgs 2:3; 2 Kgs 17:15.
51 1 Kgs 8:43, 9:7, 22:28.
52 Deut 13:8 (around you near or far); 20:16 (apparently same as גוים in 15).
53 Deut 2:25, 4:6, 4:19, 4:27, 6:15, 7:6, 7:7, 7:14, 7:16, 7:19, 10:15, 28:10, 28:37, 28:64, 30:3, 32:8, 33:3, 33:17, 33:19.
54 2 Sam 22:48 (= Ps 18:48); 1 Kgs 5:14, 8:53, 8:60.
55 2 Sam 7:23, 8:11; 2 Kgs 16:3, 18:33/19:12, 21:2, 21:9.
56 Deut 15:6, 17:14 (around), 18:9 (of the land), 20:15 (same).
57 Deut 4:27, 4:38, 7:1, 7:17, 17:22, 9:1, 9:4, 9:5, 11:23, 26:19, 28:1, 28:12, 28:65, 29:15, 29:17, 29:23, 30:1, 31:3, 32:8, 32:43.
58 1 Sam 8:5, 8:20; 2 Sam 22:44, 22:50 (= Ps 18:44, 18:50); 1 Kgs 5:11, 11:2, 14:24; 2 Kgs 17:8, 17:11, 17:15, 17:26, 17:33, 17:41, 19:17.
59 2 Sam 7:29, 7:29; 1 Kgs 10:9; 2 Kgs 21:7.
60 Deut 23:7.
61 Deut 5:29, 32:40.
62 1 Kgs 1:31, 2:33; 2 Kgs 5:27.
63 1 Kgs 8:40, 9:3, 12:7, 14:30; 2 Kgs 8:19.
64 Deut 12:1, 14:23, 18:5, 19:9.
65 Deut 4:10, 4:30, 4:40, 5:26, 6:24, 11:1, 28:29, 28:33, 31:13, 31:29.
66 1 Sam 1:28, 2:32, 2:35, 18:29, 20:31, 23:14, 27:11, 28:2; 2 Sam 13:37, 29:14; 1 Kgs 5:15, 11:36, 11:39; 2 Kgs 13:3, 17:37.

bouring non-synoptic portions. For example, synoptic 8:43 and 9:7 with עמים bracket non-synoptic 1 Kings 8:53 and 8:60, and 5:14 is also part of the expanded Solomon narrative. Similarly, 2 Kings 17:8, 17:11, and 17:15 mention the "nations" Yahweh dispossessed in favor of Israel and use the same term גוים as we find in the same context just before and after, in synoptic 2 Kings 16:3 and 21:2 and 21:9.

The usage of כל־הימים ("all the days"/"for all time") is remarkably stable across both "core" and "non-core" portions of Deuteronomy and Samuel–Kings. But the usage of "forever" decreases from "core" to "non-core." Later tradition became less optimistic about the older, monarchic claims of "forever."

Tab. c: BoTH < Non-BoTH Sam–Kgs *BUT* Deut 12–25 > Deut 1–11; 26–34.

	BoTH	Deut 12–25	Deut 1–11; 26–34	Non-BoTH Sam–Kgs
נפש	4[67]	20[68]	13[69] (40)	74[70] (14)
כהן (sg)	8[71]	3[72]	2[73]	51 (27)
כהנים (pl)	5[74]	1[75]	0	40 (18)
הכהנים הלוים		4[76]	1[77]	1[78]

67 In two pairs of pairs: 1 Kgs 8:48//2 Chr 6:38 with 2 Kgs 23:3//2 Chr 34:31 and 2 Sam 23:17//1 Chr 11:19 with 1 Kgs 3:11//2 Chr 1:11.

68 Deut 12:15, 12:20 (twice), 12:21, 12:23 (twice), 13:4, 13:7, 14:26 (twice), 18:6, 19:6, 19:11, 19:21, 21:14, 22:26, 23:25, 24:6, 24:7, 24:15.

69 Deut 4:9, 4:15, 4:29, 6:5, 10:12, 10:22, 11:13, 11:18, 27:25, 28:65, 30:2, 30:6, 30:10.

70 1 Sam 1:10, 1:15, 1:26, 2:16, 2:33, 2:35, 17:55, 18:1 (twice), 18:3, 19:5, 19:11, 20:1, 20:3, 20:4, 20:17, 22:2, 22:22, 22:23, 23:15, 23:20, 25:26, 25:29, 26:24, 26:24, 28:9, 28:21, 30:6; 2 Sam 1:9, 3:21, 4:8, 4:9, 5:8, 11:11, 14:7, 14:14, 14:19, 16:11, 18:8, 18:13, 19:6; 1 Kgs 1:12, 1:29, 2:4, 2:23, 11:37, 17:21, 17:22, 19:2 (twice), 19:3, 9:4 (twice), 19:10, 19:14, 20:31, 20:32, 20:39 (twice), 20:42 (twice); 2 Kgs 1:13, 1:14, 2:2, 2:4, 2:6, 4:27, 4:30, 7:7, 9:15, 10:24 (twice), 12:5, 23:25. [1 Sam 28 ties; 2 Sam 13 times; 1 Kgs 20 times; 2 Kgs 13 times].

71 2 Kgs 11:9, 11:10, 11:15 (twice), 11:18, 12:3, 22:4, 22:10.

72 Deut 17:12, 18:3, 20:2.

73 Deut 26:3, 26:4.

74 2 Sam 8:18; 1 Kgs 8:6, 8:10, 8:11; 2 Kgs 23:2.

75 Deut 18:3.

76 Deut 17:9, 17:18, 18:1, 24:8.

77 Deut 27:9.

78 In 1 Kgs 8:3, the priests carry the ark into the new temple; but in synoptic 2 Chr 5:3 it is the Levites. When mentioned again in 1 Kgs 8:4, they have become הכהנים הלוים; but in synoptic 2 Chr 5:5, הכהנים והלוים. However, this second mention is not part of the shorter and more original text in 3 Kgdms 8 and so is not here reckoned part of BoTH.

Tab. c (continued)

	BoTH	Deut 12–25	Deut 1–11; 26–34	Non-BoTH Sam-Kgs
הכהנים בני לוי		1[79]	1[80]	1[81]
הלוי (landless)		7[82]	3[83]	
שבט [ה]לוי		1[84]	1[85]	
הלוים		1[86]	2[87]	2[88]

Like the "life"-family (6.1), נפש is very rare in BoTH and very common in Samuel-Kings; but, unlike חיה\ים, it is relatively commoner in central Deuteronomy than in the outer chapters of the book. However, it is also true that נפש is used in more senses in Deuteronomy than in BoTH, where the four occurrences are in two pairs. Twice in BoTH (2 Sam 23:17; 1 Kgs 3:11) נפש bears the sense of "life" (as opposed to death), and this is one of the senses found much more often in the central chapters of Deuteronomy (12:23 [twice]; 19:6, 19:11, 19:21, 22:26, 24:6, 24:7, and 24:15) and only once outside (27:25). It is twice paired with "heart" (1 Kgs 8:48 and 2 Kgs 23:3) – and this linking of Solomon and Josiah is replicated in non-synoptic 1 Kings 2:4 and 2 Kings 23:25. We find this usage once in the "code" of Deuteronomy (13:4), but 8 times in the outer chapters (4:29, 6:5, 10:12, 11:13, 11:18, 30:2, 30:6, and 30:10). The "self" with desires appears in Deuteronomy 12:15, 12:20 (twice), 12:21, 14:26 (twice), 18:6, and 23:25 but outside only in 4:9 and 4:15.

Similarly, the usage of "priest" and "priests" is denser in non-synoptic Samuel-Kings than in BoTH, but this pattern is not at all replicated between the central and outer chapters of Deuteronomy. The table above also illustrates at a glance that BoTH makes no mention of Levites and wider Samuel-Kings only minimal mention of them. By contrast, both Levites and Levitical priests are concentrated in the central chapters of Deuteronomy. Landless Levites are mostly mentioned in the same contexts where the secondary לשכן formula is used. There is no

79 Deut 21:5.
80 Deut 31:9.
81 1 Kgs 12:31 – here the negative: priests that were not "sons of Levi."
82 Deut 12:12, 12:18, 12:19, 14:27, 14:29, 16:11, 16:14.
83 Deut 26:11, 26:12, 26:13.
84 Deut 18:1.
85 Deut 10:18.
86 Deut 18:7.
87 Deut 27:14, 31:25.
88 1 Sam 6:15; 2 Sam 15:24.

mention at all in the outer chapters of the (landless) “Levite” or of “priest[s]” who are not explicitly “Levitical.” From the perspective of the royal narrative, whether synoptic (BoTH) or non-synoptic, priests and Levites may have been central to Deuteronomy, but they were hardly part of its core.

Some Thoughts on the First Jeroboam

1 Introduction

Adrian Schenker has argued powerfully (1996) that 1 Kgs 11–14 represent a thorough recasting of the much shorter alternative narrative (henceforth AN) preserved in some Greek Bible manuscripts after 3 Kgdms (1 Kgs) 12:24. Marvin Sweeney mentioned Schenker's work at the start of his own case for setting in the later 2nd century BCE (what he perceived as) a shorter 'midrash' (2007b). However, he did not properly engage with Schenker's arguments, and drew a quick and appropriate riposte from him (Schenker 2008). I also overlooked them in my more recent discussion of how the royal traditions in the Hebrew Bible were shaped and reshaped (Auld 2017). The purpose of this article is not to re-enter the long debate about priority, except tangentially, but to advance in a somewhat different direction from Schenker's final remarks. His results mesh rather well with the larger case I argued in *Life in Kings*; however, accepting them would require adjustment to the detail presented there about Rehoboam and Jeroboam (Auld 2017, 223–229).

More recent contributors to that debate have agreed on one point at least: that Zipora Talshir's account of *The Alternative Story* has settled definitively that AN is a faithful Greek rendering of a text written originally in Hebrew.[1] Her analysis was based exclusively on the Vaticanus text (LXX^B^) of AN; but she did note towards the end of her study a small number of variants in the Lucianic or Antiochean text (LXX^L^). She did not find these significant; and her judgment here too appears to have been influential. Despite the fresh publication in the same period of the five principal Lucianic witnesses (Fernández Marcos 1992), discussion has remained concentrated on LXX^A^ and LXX^B^. The textual puzzle is that LXX^B^ and LXX^L^ include AN but not a (second) report of Jeroboam's sick son, while LXX^A^ and MT include 1 Kgs (3 Kgdms) 14:1–20 but not AN. The Spanish edition has succeeded in adapting LXX^L^ to the familiar biblical chapters and verses. Instead of presenting AN as 12:24a.b … z (where these divisions are normally longer than typical verses), AN occupies 47 verses denoted 12:25 to 13:32; then the end of 1 Reyes 13 (33–41) corresponds to the familiar 1 Kgs 12:25–33, 1 Reyes 14:1–34 corresponds to 1 Kgs 13:1–34, and 1 Reyes 14:35–45 corresponds to 1 Kgs 14:21–31. However, given that discussion of AN always identifies its sections using a to z, that will be followed here.

1 Talshir 1993 has been widely commended. An English translation of AN is also available in Sweeney 2007a, 165–167, but without comment. However, Sweeney 2007b offers a defence of the priority of the MT.

https://doi.org/10.1515/9783111060279-009

2 The shorter narrative

Partly because AN is shorter, partly because its range is more restricted, but importantly also because of the nature of the main 'pluses' in the longer version, Schenker should be followed in arguing that the AN gives us access to an older account of Jeroboam than we find in the Hebrew Bible. This shorter, less familiar, account can be presented in three stages.

We learn first (b–f) that Jeroboam had responsibility for Solomon's building works both in Ephraim and in Jerusalem and that he aspired to kingship. Solomon sought to kill this potential rival, and he took refuge in Egypt till Solomon's death. When he asked permission to return, the pharaoh offered him a relative of his own wife in marriage. They married and had a child in Egypt. On his return to Ephraim (and so quite some time after the death of Solomon), his whole tribe gathered to him and he built a fort in his home town.

The second act (g–n1) starts with the serious illness of his son by the princess. Jeroboam requested his wife to ask God about the child: she should take a gift of several foodstuffs to the man of God in Shiloh. As she approached, Ahijah asked his lad to meet her and tell her that Yahweh had a bad message for her. When she came before the man of God, Ahijah said to her: 'Why have you brought me the foodstuffs, for I have bad news for you? When you come to your town, your maids will meet you and tell you your child has died.' In fact, the response she receives from him is much worse than they could have expected. Not only will the sick child die as soon as she returns home (l), but any male offspring of Jeroboam will be 'cut off' and their corpses scavenged by dogs in the towns and birds in the country (m). The first part of the divine threat is validated by the lamentation that greets her return home.

Jeroboam next assembled all Israel's tribes to Shechem, in Ephraim's hill-country (n2–u). 'Rehoboam son of Solomon' too 'went up' (n). This common verb often implies attack, but there is nothing to suggest hostility here: when David 'went up' to Hebron (2 Sam 2:2), he was simply making a journey with his two wives. Before any more is reported, Jeroboam receives a second divine oracle (o) that comes in the form of an acted parable and involves a torn garment. The type of the cloak seems integral to the message; for the same four Hebrew letters (*slmh*) can be read either as *śalmâh* (cloak) or as *šᵉlōmōh* (Solomon). Shemaiah's tearing of the pristine cloak is deliberate and twin conclusions are implied: Jeroboam will receive only (the larger) part of the whole kingdom; and even that part will be severely damaged – in ten tatters. Jeroboam had convoked the tribes and may have been involved in their discussion with Rehoboam as they probed him about his style of government (p–t). On his harsh response, they rejected the family of David, and he returned to Jerusalem to rule over Judah and Benjamin only. Jeroboam is not actually mentioned again till the very end, where he is the target of Rehoboam's planned invasion of the north (x).

The shorter account of Jeroboam is set entirely within the Rehoboam story. Before it starts, we read simply the formal report of Solomon's death and burial and the succession of Rehoboam his son, who 'did what was evil in the eyes of Yahweh and did not walk in the way of David his father' (a). And it ends in the year following the debacle in Shechem (x–z), when Rehoboam assembles Judah and Benjamin and goes up to Shechem to make war on Jeroboam but is prevented by Yahweh's word to Shemaiah (almost exactly as in 1 Kgs 12:21–24//2 Chr 11:1–4). Not only is this version of the Jeroboam story framed by the Rehoboam story, but significantly it also interrupts the Rehoboam story as soon as that has begun. The purpose of this story of the first Jeroboam is to help explain how Rehoboam's kingdom lost the north, the larger part of its territory – the rest being down to Rehoboam's own folly.

Shishak's spoiling of the Jerusalem temple in Rehoboam's fifth year (1 Kgs 14:25–26//2 Chr 12:2, 9) is one of the very few precise dates provided in the Book of Two Houses,[2] apart from the ages of kings at accession and the length of their reigns. I have suggested that at least some dates in non-synoptic portions of Kings or Chronicles are secondary.[3] However, as a detail in BTH immediately after AN, it is quite suggestive. The debacle at Shechem had taken place after the death of Solomon had been reported in Egypt, then after Jeroboam's subsequent marriage, then after the birth of his child, then after his return home and the fortification of his town, then after his convocation of Israel's whole leadership. Whether before or after the Egyptian incursion in Rehoboam's fifth year, it was presumably quite close to it. And it was Jeroboam, not Rehoboam, who now had the marriage-link with Pharaoh once enjoyed by Solomon. (In the expanded and familiar story in 1 Kgs 11:14–22, it was another exile in Egypt, an Edomite, who became husband to the Pharaoh's sister-in-law.)

3 The longer narrative

The Jeroboam of 1 Kgs 11–14 has been developed out of this older Jeroboam, in part by thinking him together with the David of the older (synoptic) accounts. The two largest single additions to AN within the longer narrative (1 Kgs 11:32–39; 14:7–9), both within prophetic oracles, explicitly align Jeroboam with the tradi-

---

2 My name for the narrative about the houses of Yahweh and David shared by Samuel-Kings and Chronicles.

3 Particular attention to Hezekiah's 14th year is paid in Auld 2017, 86, 178, 185.

tions about David. In the shorter version, David is mentioned – but only twice, and both in connection with his grandson: Rehoboam does not follow David's example (a); and, when the people reject Rehoboam, what they say is 'we have no portion in David' (t). In specific content, the references to David in the two prophecies are wholly additional to AN. Yet in BTH, David and Jeroboam already played analogous roles: each as successor to his one-time master. Israel had offered kingship to David on the death of Saul on two grounds (2 Sam 5:1–2//1 Chr 11:1–2): because they were his 'bone and flesh' and because, under Saul, he had already been commander in chief: 'he had led them out and in'. Northern Israel coalesced round Jeroboam after Solomon's death because he was an Ephraimite and so one of them, and because he had been a principal agent of Solomon on his building projects. Kinship and proven leadership are crucial to both these accounts of non-dynastic succession. Thinking these two figures together may even have been a two-way process in the writing of Samuel and Kings. As an author of 1 Samuel was developing the account about the earlier David before he became king, Jeroboam's exile in Egypt and preferment by Pharaoh may have suggested the theme of David's parallel exile among the Philistines and the patronage of Achish king of Gath.

Influence on Samuel-Kings from the first Jeroboam may have been wider still. Jeroboam 'exalting himself as far as the kingship' (b), may have suggested the wording of (non-synoptic) 1 Kgs 1:5, where we read of the failed attempt by Adonijah (David's eldest surviving son) to become king when his father's strength was failing; and Jeroboam's many chariots (also b) recall Absalom too at the start of his revolt (2 Sam 15:1). Both AN(t) and 1 Kgs 12:16 pit the whole people against Rehoboam with their rallying cry ('What share do we have in David ...?'). But, while AN(u) has the king followed to Jerusalem by Judah and Benjamin (both will soon jointly muster against the north), the more expansive 1 Kgs 12:17–20 insists that only Judah supported him. Similarly, in non-synoptic 2 Sam 20:1–2, when the same rallying cry is attributed to Sheba ben Bichri of Benjamin, he is followed by every man of Israel and only the men of Judah stick with David. Beyond David in 1 Samuel, Shemaiah and his cloak may have contributed to the cloak-scene between Samuel and Saul: there the cloak is not torn in many tatters, and the whole kingdom passes from Saul to David. AN may also have contributed themes to an author of Judges. Jephthah like the first Jeroboam was a bastard son who was forced into exile and lost his child; and the conclusion of his story also uses 'Ephrathite' as adjective corresponding to Ephraim (Judg 12:5). Then Abimelech, son of (similarly named) Jerub-baal, also ruled in Shechem (Judg 9).

4 From shorter to longer narrative

The two divine oracles received by Jeroboam and his wife are reported almost side by side at the heart of AN (k-m; o); and Schenker argues that the second reinforces the first (1996, 227). However, the greatly expanded versions of the acted parable of the torn cloak and the response about his sick child are set towards the outer frame of 1 Kgs 11–14 (11:29–39; 14:5–16); and the first of these is reported within the limits of an extended Solomon narrative. Two of the details in this longer account can be read as admitting the radical changes made by their author. (1) The seemingly banal remark about Rehoboam's elders (12:6 but not q), that they 'had attended his father Solomon while he was still alive' (Rehoboam's 'elders' could hardly have been attending his father after he was dead!), may recognise the larger Solomonic role in the expanded account. (2) In AN the man of God who acted the parable of the torn garment was called 'Shemaiah' (o), but he is named as 'Ahijah the prophet' in 1 Kgs 11:29. Significantly, when Jeroboam asked his wife to make enquiries about their son of Ahijah the prophet, he added (14:2 but not h): 'it was he who spoke about me as king over this people' – his remark to his wife deftly 'corrected' the older record.

The first of these details requires reconsideration of a prominent element in my argument. I note that 'life' and '[a]live' (*ḥy*/*ḥyh*/*ḥyym*) only occur six times in texts shared by Samuel-Kings and Chronicles, but more than one hundred times in Samuel and Kings (Auld 2017, 29–38). And I argue that these were favourite terms of the expansive rewriters of the royal narratives. One of the six shared instances is 'while [Solomon] was still alive' (1 Kgs 12:6//2 Chr 10:6). However, this phrase seems bland and unnecessary and it is not part of the corresponding sentence (q) in AN. We should reckon that at least one of the six instances, though shared, was not part of the oldest text. In the other direction, when their child falls ill, Jeroboam asks his wife to visit the prophet. In the normally longer text (1 Kgs 14:3), he says briefly to her: 'he will tell you what will happen to the child'. In AN, however, he says to her at greater length (g): 'Go, inquire of God concerning the child whether he will "live" (i.e. recover) from his sickness'. The wording of the final (and supplementary) clause is similar to the enquiry King Ahaziah sent after a serious fall (2 Kgs 1:2). In each version of the Jeroboam story, we find '[a]live' in a plus relative to the other version.[4]

4 Although the broad lines are clear, reconstructing the first Jeroboam is not wholly straightforward. The familiar 'canonical' version has reordered the story and made additions large and small, but also some important changes of detail – the son of a prostitute, father unknown, has become son of a widow, whose father was Nebat.

This is consistent with, and indeed supports, my wider case that forms of the word 'live' tended to be added as portions of Kings were expansively rewritten from shorter drafts in BTH. But, at the same time, it calls into question my general rule of attributing to BTH all material common to Kings and Chronicles. I did recognise as a single exception the shorter LXX text of 1 Kgs 8:1–5 as prior to 1 Kgs 8:1–5 (MT)//2 Chr 5:2–6 (Auld 2017, 208–209); however, I need to pay closer attention to Julio Trebolle Barrera's remarks (2007) about a triple textual tradition. Is the more complex material relating to Solomon the exception that proves the rule?

In other respects, AN fits perfectly within what I call the Book of Two Houses (BTH), the larger narrative of the house of David in Jerusalem. The role of Jeroboam as simply part of the Rehoboam story is entirely typical of the several kings of northern Israel who feature in the shorter and older narrative shared by Kings and Chronicles: each is there solely for his contribution to the Jerusalem story. The north is mentioned in synoptic texts (those shared by Kings and Chronicles) only where it bears on the story of the south; and in these texts no northern leader features in reports of more than one southern king.

5 Concluding remarks

The first two of Schenker's final remarks (1996, 236) should be restated in light of the above. His first is that 'HA' (what he calls AN) is the original Jeroboam story, and that it was reworked by a redaction preserved in MT; and the second that, while HA has Deuteronomistic marks, its concise and dramatic stories resemble those in Judges and Samuel, and so it could be Deuteronomistic in the same sense as they are. The implication is that the original as well as the redacted account was part of the (Deuteronomistic) book of Kings – that the redaction was part of the textual history of the book of Kings. However, the contention of this paper is that the expansive rewriting of the earlier Jeroboam story was part of the creation of the Book of Kings out of the Book of Two Houses. If accepted, it also requires a restatement of my discussion of 'Redrawing Jeroboam' (2017, 131–133).

Schenker cites just two Deuteronomistic marks in AN and neither is persuasive. Within the context of BTH, the formula of succession from Solomon to Rehoboam (a) is unremarkable; and it can be argued that the formulaic evaluation of the several kings already in BTH as 'doing evil (or right) in Yahweh's eyes' has influenced Deuteronomic language rather than the other way round. And the memorably stated threat (m) to every male of Jeroboam's household ('who pisses against the wall') will simply have been adopted from AN by the author[s] of 1 Sam 25:22, 34; 1 Kgs 16:11; 21:21; 2 Kgs 9:8 as they in turn expansively rewrote BTH.

Schenker's final observation is more puzzling. His starting point is uncontroversial, that AN does not report the religious schism described in detail in 1 Kgs 12:26–33. But he then adds that this difference could well explain why the Deuteronomistic History does not seem to have a negative attitude regarding the cult of the northern kingdom – because this narrative about the religious schism did not figure in its original state. One could ask in response: If it was not the act of setting up the northern cult, what was the "sin" of Jeroboam from which none of his successors could escape?

In two important senses, the first Jeroboam (of AN and BTH) was not Jeroboam I (of the Book of Kings). The first Jeroboam was recast to become Jeroboam I, the first of the kings of northern Israel. In himself, however, he had been only an occasional bit-player, even if an important one, in the story of Rehoboam as told in the Book of Two Houses. In that prior history, he neither inaugurated a dynasty nor started an apostate trend. By contrast, Jeroboam I within the Book of Kings was the first of nineteen kings of northern Israel, among whom there was also a Jeroboam II (unmentioned in BTH). Though followed only by his son on the northern throne, we find his name repeated in the reports of all his successors: every one of them 'walked in the way of Jeroboam' or 'did not depart from the sins Jeroboam caused Israel to sin'. Through the book of Kings, his name echoes more often and even more resoundingly than David's.

Ahaz and Jeroboam

Two bad kings

Ahaz and Jeroboam 'enjoy' two of the worst reputations in the book of Kings. About one half of David's successors in Jerusalem are introduced as having done 'what was right in the eyes of Yahweh'. Among them, Hezekiah (2 Kgs 18–20) and Josiah (22–23) are explicitly ranked alongside David. The other half are said to have done 'what was evil in the eyes of Yahweh'. Ahaz (2 Kgs 16) must be ranked alongside this latter group but is doubly unique. First of all, the preliminary assessment of him is in two parts: 'He did not do what is right in the eyes of Yahweh his God, as his father David had done, but he walked in the way of the kings of Israel.' Then the first of these is not said of any other king. Unlike these kings of Judah with their different ratings, each successor of David and Solomon in (northern) Israel after the first is introduced the same way: 'He did what was evil in the eyes of Yahweh; he did not turn from the sins of Jeroboam son of Nebat, which he caused Israel to sin.' What complicates this plot is the fact that Jeroboam himself is presented as something of a second David (1 Kgs 11–14).

We have wicked Ahaz who is not like David and sinful Jeroboam who is like David. At least part of this conundrum is down to different stages in the writing of Samuel and Kings. Ahaz is unlike one presentation of David and Jeroboam is part of another David story. David was always a nuanced character as far back as we can probe the tradition. However, as part of the general discrediting of kingship in the Former Prophets, more and more doubts and negatives accumulated in his record. Ahaz was contrasted with 'good old David', while the Jeroboam of the familiar book of Kings has his place in a fresh development of the story of Israel's kings. The following essay will take account of the biblical rewriting of each.

Ahaz

Sometimes explicitly and sometimes implicitly, Ahaz is compared and contrasted with several other kings (Auld 2017, 69–76 and 150–151). The introduction starts in standard fashion: Ahaz was 20 years old when he succeeded as king on the death of his father Jotham; and he reigned for 16 years (2 Kgs 16:2a). But it goes its own way when it comes to assessing Ahaz. Ahaz is doubly unique: he is accorded a negative assessment in two parts, and the first part is not repeated elsewhere: (a) he did *not* do what was right in Yahweh's eyes like David his father; (b) he walked in the way of the kings of Israel. It may be that the narrator is less

https://doi.org/10.1515/9783111060279-010

interested in a contrast between Ahaz the David of the distant past, but more in a contrast with Hezekiah his own son and Josiah in the immediate future, both of whom *did* what was right just like David his father. The second part, walking in the ways of the kings of Israel, aligned Ahaz instead with Jehoram and his son Ahaziah (namesake of Ahaz), who had been reported as walking in the ways of the house of Ahab (2 Kgs 8:18, 27). Ahaz is *not* like David, or Hezekiah, or Josiah; but he *is* like Jehoram and Ahaziah of Israel. As he moves to specifics, the narrator continues to suggest comparisons and contrasts. Ahaz (16:3) anticipated wicked Manasseh (21:6): 'he even made his son pass in/through fire'. And such behaviour was 'according to the abominations of the nations who Yahweh drove out in face of the sons of Israel', another formula found only in the introduction to Manasseh (21:2). There can be no doubt about the two comparisons with Manasseh: they are stated in exactly the same terms.

The contrast with Solomon that follows is, however, less than fully explicit (though rather more suggestive in Hebrew than in English). 'He sacrificed ... on the "high places" on the hills' (16:4) alludes to two elements of the Solomon story: Solomon had offered sacrifice at the great 'high place' at Gibeon before receiving a first vision from Yahweh (1 Kgs 3:4) – and, in its very name, Gibeon (*gb'wn*), the peak that towers over Jerusalem from the NW, was a 'hill' (*gb'h*) *par excellence*. Then, though Solomon had sacrificed (*zbḥ*) at Gibeon, a more intensive form of the same verb is used to describe his 'enthusiastic sacrificing' as the divine ark was brought into the new temple in Jerusalem (1 Kgs 8:5) – and exactly this (piel) form of the verb 'sacrifice' is now used to describe Ahaz's cultic behaviour 'on the "high places" on the hills'. Solomon had *pro*gressed from Gibeon to the new national sanctuary in Jerusalem; but Ahaz's cultic practices were *re*gressive and were carried out at several sites. The synoptic tradition certainly observes that 'high places' were not removed in the time of kings Asa and Jehoshaphat; but none of the kings between Solomon and Ahaz is said to have sacrificed at one of these – the book of Kings states (and the book of Chronicles may well imply) that it was just the people that frequented such local sanctuaries. Ahaz was unlike David and Hezekiah and Josiah, but like the kings of Israel; like Manasseh (whose long reign would follow between Hezekiah and Josiah), but unlike Solomon. With these broad stroke introductory comparisons 2 Kgs 16 and 2 Chr 28 are in full agreement: this is the common or assured biblical tradition. This so-called 'synoptic' tradition offers a further unique royal pairing: it mentions Assyria and its king(s) only in connection with Ahaz and his son Hezekiah, so inviting readers to compare or contrast these kings as they relate to the great imperial power.

Between this introduction and the largely formulaic conclusion (2 Kgs 16:17–18//2 Chr 28:26–27), Kings and Chronicles tell a story with several shared elements, but very differently.

2 Kgs 16		2 Chr 28	
5	War with Aram and Israel	5–15	War with Aram and Israel
7	Appeal to Assyria	16	Appeal to Assyria
6	Trouble with Edom	17	Trouble with Edom
		18	Philistine raids
		19	Judah brought low by Ahaz
8	Treasures sent from Jerusalem	21	Treasures sent from Jerusalem
9	Assyria does respond	20	Assyria does NOT respond
10–16	Copy made of Damascus altar		
		22	Ahaz still more faithless
		23	Ahaz sacrificed to gods of Aram
17	Cut up temple furniture (detail)	24	Cut up temple furniture (summary)
18	Other Jerusalem changes		
		25	'High places' in every city of Judah

It is a useful principle that the shorter version of a shared tradition is the older. On that basis, we would see the summary statement of the war with Aram and Israel (2 Kgs 16:5) as prior, with 2 Chr 28:5–15 as secondary expansion. On the other hand, Chr states the appeal to Assyria more briefly (28:16), while Kgs includes the terms of Ahaz's message to the Assyrian king (16:7). His words are quite extraordinary: 'I am your servant and your son. Come up and rescue me …'. Out of all the kings in Jerusalem, only David and Solomon have ever called themselves 'your servant' – and only when speaking to Yahweh – or been called 'my servant' by Yahweh. Then, except for its regular, literal genealogical sense, 'son' only appears in that synoptic tradition where Yahweh makes a promise to David: he will be 'father' to one of David's offspring who in turn will be 'son' to Yahweh (2 Sam 7:14). In this longer version of the appeal for help (2 Kgs 16:7), Ahaz is making a commitment to the king of Assyria in terms that he would have used only before Yahweh, had he been like David or Solomon. Furthermore, in synoptic narratives, 'rescue' and 'save' are only found in narratives about David and Hezekiah. Now the Chronicler has not a single good word to say about Ahaz. We have already noted that Ahaz and Manasseh share key elements of negative assessment. Yet, according to 2 Chr 33:12–19, even wicked Manasseh will come to see the error of his ways. This king does not. On his death, 2 Kgs 16:20 reports the burial of Ahaz in ‘the city of David’ – the royal necropolis; but 2 Chr 28:27 insists he was *not* brought into ‘the tombs of the kings’. There was therefore no reason for the Chronicler to delete this compromising passage from 2 Kgs 16:7, if it was part of his source. It is more sensible to conclude that the author of 2 Kgs 16:7b has added ‘I am your servant and your son; come up and rescue me’, to blacken Ahaz still further. For the same reason, he added the pejorative word ‘bribe’ (or ‘present’) to the report in 16:8 of sending state treasures to Assyria in return for help.

Quite the largest ‘plus’ in 2 Kgs 16 vis-à-vis 2 Chr 28 serves the same function. According to this extended report (vv. 10–16), Ahaz visits Tiglath-Pileser of Assyria in Damascus, sees an impressive altar there, and sends a model of it to Uriah his priest in Jerusalem with instructions to make a precise copy. On his return to Jerusalem, he inspects it and offers various sacrifices on it. Having inaugurated the new altar, he moves the old bronze altar to its side, and gives extended instructions to Uriah: the new ‘great altar’ should be used for the morning and evening sacrifices of king and people – and the bronze altar will be for the king’s own use (for exactly what purpose is not clear). When the synoptic introduction to the Ahaz story invoked memories of Solomon, it was only in order to suggest a clear distinction between these kings over resort to ‘high places’. Ahaz himself, and not just his people, had been involved in cultic practices at a plurality of ‘high places’ – presumably outside Jerusalem. This added narrative in Kings now does concern Jerusalem and makes further allusions to the king who had built its temple: (1) No other king since Solomon has been reported as presiding at sacrifice there. (2) The altar Ahaz describes as ‘great’ is a striking reminder of the ‘great high place’ visited by Solomon at Gibeon. (3) In synoptic tradition, only David and Solomon offered the sacrifices called *shelamim* (‘offerings of wellbeing’ in 2 Kgs 16:13, NRSV). And in Samuel-Kings as a whole, apart from David and Solomon, no other king but Saul has offered these sacrifices. Ahaz is presented as a large-scale innovator. Indeed, the detailed ritual instructions from this king to his priestly deputy remind us not so much of Solomon as of Moses passing divine instructions to Aaron.

The detailed report on the new altar is followed by a couple of verses (17–18) that are clearly related to 2 Chr 28:24a but say something very different. Most obviously, both state that Ahaz ‘cut up’ or ‘cut off’ something that had to do with ‘the house of Yahweh’. Kgs talks of removing a king’s outer entrance to the temple, Chr simply of closing the doors (of Yahweh’s house). Most puzzling, the verb ‘close’ (*sgr*) in 2 Chr 28:24 is cognate with the plural noun *msgrwt* in 2 Kgs 16:17. These were some attribute or accompaniment of the ‘stands’ or ‘supports’ by which the great ‘sea’ was held clear of the ground and are often translated ‘frames’. Whatever earlier form of words had linked these shared elements, Kgs reports radical alterations within the Jerusalem temple while Chr states clearly that Ahaz closed it: in its place 'he made himself altars in every corner of Jerusalem' – the multiple 'high places' he supported outside the city were now matched by multiple altars within it.

The opening overview (shared by Kgs and Chr) sketches an Ahaz who is not like Hezekiah and Josiah but is aligned instead with Jehoram and Ahaziah and Manasseh. It also introduces a contrast between Ahaz and Solomon; and this is more fully developed within Kings in the narrative about the new 'great' altar in Jerusalem. On the two occasions when the added material introduces Ahaz's own words, we must deduce that they are being cited against him: his readiness to replace loyalty to Yahweh with loyalty to the king of Assyria (16:7) and to impose new cultic arrangements on his priest (16:15).[1]

Jeroboam

There are two (obviously related) versions of Ahaz, one in Kings and the other in Chronicles. For Jeroboam, the textual evidence is more complicated. We shall concentrate here on the two different versions within Kings – at least in the ancient Greek translation of that book. The standard Hebrew text preserves just one; and that means that in 1 Kgs 11–14 our English Bibles also make only that one available to us. Greek Kings includes a translation of most of this longer Jeroboam account, but not the final part about the sickness and death of his first son in 1 Kgs 14:1–18. However, at the heart of the remainder (between 12:24 and 12:25), Kings in Greek also contains an alternative, shorter, and quite differently arranged, Jeroboam story. This story, though available to us only in Greek, clearly did have a Hebrew original; and this was presumably part of the edition of the Hebrew book of Kings available to the Greek translator.[2] Partly because it is shorter, partly because its range is more restricted, but partly also because of the nature of the main 'pluses' in the longer version, I suspect that the alternative text preserved in Greek gives us access to an older account of Jeroboam than we find in our Hebrew or English Bibles.[3] Be that as it may, reading the two versions of Jeroboam together helps our appreciation of each.

1 For a more sympathetic account of a historical Ahaz, see Sweeney 2007a, 378–386.

2 Talshir 1993 has been widely commended. The divisions of this story, mostly longer than traditional biblical verses, are normally numbered a to z. An English translation is also available in Sweeney 2007a, 165–167 – but without comment. The priority of the MT is defended in Sweeney 2007b.

3 Adrian Schenker has argued strongly for the priority of the shorter variant account, notably in Schenker 1996. And he could be said to have demolished Sweeney 2007b in Schenker 2008.

The shorter, less familiar, account is presented in three stages. (1) We learn first (b–f) that Jeroboam had responsibility for Solomon's building works both in Ephraim and in Jerusalem and that he aspired to kingship. Solomon sought to kill this potential rival, and he took refuge in Egypt till Solomon's death. When he asked permission to return, the pharaoh offered him a relative of his own wife in marriage. They married and had a child in Egypt. On his return to Ephraim, his whole tribe gathered to him and he built a castle in his home town. (2) The second act (g–n1) tells of the serious illness of his son by the princess. Jeroboam asked his wife to ask God about the child: she should take a gift of several foodstuffs to Ahijah, the man of God in Shiloh. As she approached, he asked his lad to meet her and tell her that Yahweh had a bad message for her. When she came before the man of God, Ahijah said to her: 'Why have you brought me the foodstuffs, for I have bad news for you? When you come to your town, your maidens will meet you and tell you your child has died.' A divine threat against Jeroboam's wider progeny followed. As she reached her town, she was met by lamentation. (3) Jeroboam's next move was to assemble all Israel's tribes to Shechem, in Ephraim's hill-country (n2–u). They were joined there by 'Rehoboam son of Solomon'. The word of Yahweh came to Shemaiah, 'Take to yourself a new garment that has not entered water and tear it into twelve tatters before you put it on. Give Jeroboam ten tatters and say to him, "This is what Yahweh says: 'Take to yourself ten tatters to put on.'"' And Jeroboam took them, and Shemaiah said to him, 'This is what Yahweh says, "Over the ten tribes of Israel shall you be king."' The people then probed Rehoboam about his style of government in terms familiar from 1 Kgs 12:4–14. On his harsh response, they rejected the family of David, and he returned to Jerusalem to rule over Judah and Benjamin only.

This account of Jeroboam has the Rehoboam story as its outer frame. At its start, we have the formal report of Solomon's death and burial and the succession of his son, who 'did what was evil in the eyes of Yahweh and did not walk in the way of David his father' (a). And it ends in the year following the debacle in Shechem (x–z), when Rehoboam assembles Judah and Benjamin and goes up to Shechem to make war on Jeroboam but is prevented by Yahweh's word to Shemaiah (almost exactly as in 1 Kgs 12:21–24//2 Chr 11:1–4). This version of the Jeroboam story is framed by the Rehoboam story. Its contribution within the larger house of David/Jerusalem narrative is to offer a part-explanation of how Rehoboam's kingdom lost the north, the majority of its territory – the rest was down to Rehoboam's own folly.

The clues to Jeroboam's characterization are ambiguous from the start of the shorter account. To start with his mother: she is introduced as a prostitute, and there is no mention of his father. We are inevitably reminded of Jephthah (Judg 11:1–11), another bastard son who was also forced into exile. On the other hand, we are told his mother's name (b), and the actual form of words used ('and the name of his mother was X') is only used within the Bible's royal story (from Rehoboam onwards, in both Kings and Chronicles) where a new king is being introduced. In fact, we find this formula only once more in all the Hebrew Bible: in Lev 24:10–12, a piece of legislation that appears to include some coded references to the story of Jeroboam. It may be significant that when Rehoboam 'comes up' (n) to join the assembly at Shechem he is called 'son of Solomon', so stressing his legitimate birth. Then, when Jeroboam is described as 'exalting himself as far as the kingship' (b), the wording is very similar to 1 Kgs 1:5, where we read of the failed attempt by Adonijah (David's eldest surviving son) to become king when his father's strength is failing; and his many chariots (also b) recall Absalom at the start of his revolt (2 Sam 15:1). Marrying a close relative of Pharaoh (e) compares Jeroboam with Solomon himself, just as favour shown to him in Egypt evokes memories of Joseph. [Re-]Building his own town, on his return to Ephraim from Egypt, is typical business of a king (f). And Shishak's spoiling of the Jerusalem temple in Rehoboam's fifth year (1 Kgs 14:25–26) can be read as the Pharaoh's reaction to the events at Shechem not long before.

The response Jeroboam's wife receives from the man of God in Shiloh is much worse than they could have expected. Not only will the sick child die as soon as she returns home (l), but all Jeroboam's male offspring will be 'cut off' and their corpses scavenged by dogs in the towns and birds in the country (m). The first part of the divine threat is validated by the lamentation that greets her return home. However, nothing daunted, Jeroboam assembles all the tribes (or sceptres) of Israel in Shechem; and Rehoboam too 'went up' (n). This common verb often implies attack, but there is nothing to suggest hostility here: when David 'went up' to Hebron (2 Sam 2:2), he was simply making a journey with his two wives.

Before any more is reported, Jeroboam receives a second divine oracle (o). This comes in the form of an acted parable; and, as in other biblical stories, it involves a torn garment (see below on 1 Sam 15). The type of cloak is part of the message; for the same four Hebrew letters (*slmh*) can be read one way as *salmah* (cloak) and another way as *Shelomoh* (Solomon). Shemaiah's tearing of the pristine cloak is deliberate and twin conclusions are implied: Jeroboam will receive only (the larger) part of the whole kingdom; and even that part will be severely damaged – in ten tatters. Jeroboam had convoked the tribes and may have been involved in their discussion with Rehoboam (p-t). But he is not actually mentioned again till the very end, where he is the target of Rehoboam's planned invasion of the north (x). In the shorter story, David is mentioned only twice: Rehoboam does not follow David's example (a); and, when the people reject Rehoboam, what they say is 'we have no portion in David' (t).

In the longer and more familiar account within 1 Kgs 11–14 (MT), Jeroboam is also introduced as responsible for Solomon's labour-gangs (11:28). But in this version the start of the Jeroboam story is told within the parameters of the whole Solomon narrative.[4] On one occasion, as he was on the way from Jerusalem, Ahijah the prophet found him, grasped the garment he was wearing and tore it in twelve tatters, and said: 'Take to yourself ten tatters; for this is what Yahweh has said, "I am tearing the kingdom from the hand of Solomon and shall give you the ten tribes ..."' (11:29–39). Solomon sought to kill him, and he escaped to Egypt (11:40). However, in this version, Jeroboam is only the third of three such troublemakers for Solomon; and it is the first of them, an Edomite prince and also a refugee in Egypt, that marries the Egyptian princess (11:14–22).

Then comes the formulaic report of Solomon's death and burial and the succession of Rehoboam (11:41–43); and that is followed by Rehoboam going to Shechem, where 'all Israel' had come to 'king' him (12:1). As in the shorter version, but without mention of an Egyptian royal marriage, Jeroboam comes home on learning of Solomon's death (12:2). Jeroboam is mentioned among the representatives of Israel who put critical questions to Rehoboam (12:3). The new king's rejection of their concerns is attributed to Yahweh turning events to establish his own word spoken through Ahijah to Jeroboam (12:15). Before the shared account of Rehoboam's return to Jerusalem and subsequent attempt to recoup his losses by force, we read of his sending Adoram, who was over the forced labour, whom 'all Israel' stoned to death (12:18).

The story of Jeroboam's sick son is not told in 1 Kings till 14:1–18, after the account of his cultic activities at Bethel and Dan (12:25–33), and after the narrative about the visit to Bethel of the man of God from Judah and its lengthy aftermath (13). It is followed by a summary of Jeroboam's reign and the succession of Nadab his son (14:19–20). Neither longer nor shorter element of 14:1–20 (in Hebrew, or English) is represented in the Greek rendering of the (mostly) longer Jeroboam narrative. LXX mentions Nadab for the first time in 15:25, at the start of its short report on his reign. That means that the only report preserved in Greek on the son who died despite appeal to the man of God is the second 'act' of the shorter alternative history.

In each of the episodes that are (broadly) shared between the shorter and longer narratives, there are small differences and also several ambiguities; and these bear on our assessment of characterization. The larger contrasts are of two sorts and both are 'theological' – though quite differently – in that they concern the prophetic interpretations of the action. Shemaiah explains his acted parable

4 Bodner 2012 offers a very fine reading of this longer version but does not enter the discussion of alternative texts (n. 7 on p. 7).

of the torn garment only in terms of Jeroboam becoming king over part(s) of Israel (o); and the people then turn to bargain with Rehoboam. All of this takes place within the assembly at Shechem; and readers of the shorter version may fairly assume that both people and Rehoboam witnessed or were made quickly aware of what Shemaiah had done and said. In the longer version of the acted parable (this time ascribed to Ahijah), Solomon is still alive and Jeroboam (somewhere not far from Jerusalem) is still his servant. Ahijah starts his explanation with an extended indictment of Solomon (11:31–33) and moves on to offer Jeroboam (11:37) terms like Abner had offered David over northern Israel (2 Sam 3:21). The immediate result is that Jeroboam must flee to Egypt till his king dies.

The shorter (alternative) history has nothing to say about the implications of the (Rehoboam and) Jeroboam narratives for the larger story-line in Kings about the divine promises to David and the divine demands on his house. However, in the longer (familiar) history, these implications are spelled out in great detail, most densely in 1 Kgs 11:31b-39 but also within the prophecy about the sick child (14:7–9). Such theological/dynastic explanations are not only completely absent from the shorter alternative version but are also integrally related to the order in which the whole longer narrative is presented. It is not just that the longer (Ahijah) form of the parable (the earlier of the divine words in the familiar version) blames Solomon, offers Jeroboam a role as a part-replacement David, and hence leads to his immediate exile. The shorter (Shemaiah) form of the ten tatters comes on the heels of Ahijah's oracle delivered to Jeroboam's wife, warning that the death of their first son will be only the start of the divine threat to his house. Heard against that threatening background, the offer of ten tatters to wear from a larger garment is less a promise than a threat. It is not that the longer narrative has a religious component while the shorter does not, but rather that the shared prophetic actions are quite differently arranged and developed in each. Only in the longer version do the extended prophetic oracles explain how the story of Jeroboam relates to the divine promises to David and the iniquitous behaviour of Solomon.

The Jeroboam who will receive a promise analogous to David is differently introduced in the longer version: his father is named (Nebat) and his mother is not a prostitute but a widow (11:26). 'All Israel' had come to Shechem to 'king' Rehoboam; Jeroboam had returned from Egypt; Israel summoned him, and they jointly put questions to Rehoboam (12:2–3, 12). After the threat of invasion from the south was averted on prophetic advice, we learn of building operations by Jeroboam: not at his own town of Zeredah, as in the alternative version (f), but at Shechem which he made his residence and at Penuel (12:25). Penuel (Gen 32), Shechem (Gen 33), and of course Bethel (Gen 28), all have positive resonance in the story of Jacob/Israel. Like the comparison with David, these echoes tie this

Jeroboam son of Nebat positively into the larger biblical narrative. However, fearing that continuing worship in Jerusalem will lure his people back to Rehoboam, he furnishes cult-centres at Bethel and Dan with golden calves (12:26–30). And this time the echo from the books of Moses is quite negative: the golden calf fashioned by Aaron in the absence of Moses, that nearly led to the destruction of the people (Ex 32; Dt 9). Jeroboam's people did worship before his calves; and this 'became a sin'. And this 'sin' was the only element of the Jeroboam story to be recalled throughout the account of northern Israel in the books of Kings: each of his successors, without exception, is blamed for continuing 'in the sin which Jeroboam caused Israel to sin'. David had also sinned (2 Sam 24:10); but he had sought to clear his own sin by building an altar in Jerusalem and sacrificing at it (24:25). Adding iniquity to iniquity, Jeroboam appointed priests who were not Levites and instituted a fresh sacral timetable (12:30–33).

When Jeroboam himself was presiding at the altar over offerings by fire, a man of God from Judah arrived and proclaimed a divine oracle against the Bethel altar itself. The king stretched out his hand, commanding that the intruder be seized, and his hand withered – echoing the fate of the worthless shepherd in Zechariah's vision, who deserted the flock (11:17). Jeroboam making such offerings is in dubious company in the book of Kings: with Solomon at the 'high places' (1 Kgs 3:3), with Solomon's wives to their several gods (11:8), with 'the priests of the high places' (13:2), and with Ahaz at his new altar (2 Kgs 16:13, 15). At the same time as he lost power in his hand, the altar was 'torn' (1 Kgs 13:3, 5). This verb is most often used of tearing clothing, as in the acted parable, where it symbolised tearing the kingdom. Jeroboam was the beneficiary then but is the loser now.

Jeroboam now asks the man of God to 'soften Yahweh's face' (13:6), to entreat him to change his mind. It is a phrase with significant echoes. Yahweh tells Moses when still on the mountain that his people are worshipping a golden calf, that he will destroy them, and start a new people from Moses. But Moses successfully softens his face (Ex 32:11). Saul tells Samuel that, in expectation of a Philistine advance, he knew he had not softened Yahweh's face; and he forced himself to offer up a holocaust. Another golden calf, and another rejected king. In this instance, the man of God did successfully intercede – as had Moses. The king now offers the man of God a meal and a gift, but these are roundly rejected: even for half the king's house he would neither eat nor drink in this place. It is another uncanny echo: again, in the temple in Bethel but now in the time of the much later king Jeroboam, Amos (also from Judah) is warned by the priest to return south and eat his bread there – not practise his prophetic craft in the national shrine of the northern kingdom (Amos 7:10–17).

We meet Jeroboam for the last time, anxious about his sick son. As in the alternative shorter version, he does not go himself but sends his wife to the man of God in Shiloh. Again, she should take gifts of food; but, in this version, she should also not be recognised: she should 'alter herself' (14:2). The words are different, but we are inevitably reminded of Saul who 'disguised himself and put on other clothes' before going to En-Dor to consult the medium (1 Sam 28:6). Jeroboam also remarks to his wife that it was Ahijah who had said of him that he would be 'king over this people'. This note may well have a double function. On the surface, consulting the prophet who had promised him kingship again compares the relationship between Jeroboam and Ahijah with that between Saul and Samuel. However, the narrator may also be using Jeroboam to tell readers aware of the other version, which told that Shemaiah made the prediction to him, that it had really been one and the same Ahijah. There is a similar tell-tale note in 1 Kgs 12:6. The shorter version simply reports that Rehoboam consulted the elders (q); but the longer continues 'who had attended his father Solomon while he was still alive'. The longer version makes more of Solomon in the story; and, as a general rule, the words 'live', 'life', and 'alive' play a much larger role in later than earlier elements of Samuel and Kings (Auld 2017, 29–38).

Yahweh briefs Ahijah in advance, telling him that his visitor is 'playing a stranger' – the verb is used just once more in the Bible: at the first meeting of Joseph with his brothers in Egypt, he recognizes them but to them he seems a stranger (Gen 42:7). Ahijah's response to Jeroboam's wife is much more extensive than in the other version. As with Samuel and Saul at Endor, the divine response goes far beyond the immediate enquiry, be it Philistine pressure there or a child's illness here. Whether Saul or Jeroboam, in both cases the royal house is lost. The sick child dies and is buried and mourned by the people. But we are told nothing about any involvement of his father; and, in fact, we do not meet Jeroboam himself again.

In the shorter version, Jeroboam is a social nobody who is given status by Solomon and then Pharaoh. Despite a prophetic threat to his house and a 'torn' warning about his prospects, he gains what is forfeited through Rehoboam's stubborn folly. In the familiar and much longer version, his father Nebat is acknowledged and again he becomes Solomon's servant, responsible for construction labour. He has to flee to Egypt, not because of his own royal pretensions, but because of a detailed divine oracle predicting that he will reign over most of Solomon's kingdom: ten tribes will be lost to the house of David because of *Solomon's* behaviour. Rehoboam's folly at Shechem simply eases the process of realising of the divine promise to Jeroboam and its counterpart, the threat to the house of David. In what follows, Jeroboam is presented as cultic innovator, along with Solomon's wives and King Ahaz; and he also uncannily echoes Saul who lost divine favour – and his kingdom to David.

A balance struck?

Neither Kings nor Chronicles has a good word to say about Ahaz. The tradition they share contrasts him with both David and Solomon. Kings attributes to him two statements. In one he makes a pledge to the king of Assyria in terms David and Solomon only used in relation to their God. In the other, he institutes new ritual instructions. Bad has become worse.

Jeroboam is more complex. In the shorter and less familiar account, told wholly within the Rehoboam story, he is not a cultic innovator, but he does have royal pretensions. Rehoboam may have himself to blame for losing much of his kingdom; but Jeroboam, despite prophetic warnings, is very ready to gain what Solomon's son is losing. This narrative helps to explain how, in human terms, much of Israel was lost to Jerusalem and the line of David. But the longer and familiar story locates Jeroboam within a much larger narrative, stretching back to David and even Jacob. Solomon's faults are now in play, and not just those of his son. Jeroboam's own father is now named. The ten tatters are clearly presented as promise and not threat – Jeroboam will be something of a new Davidic king of Israel while at the same time the genealogically Davidic line will not lose everything. However, because of his cultic innovations, Jeroboam becomes a failure. In the one account, he is a self-server; in the other, he is a servant of God gone bad.

We noted as we began that the name of David is differently used in the presentations of Ahaz and Jeroboam. As we proceeded, we found that the reputation of Solomon is also important in both. He is never mentioned in so many words in connection with Ahaz; but the attentive reader of the synoptic introduction understands that the king who sacrifices with enthusiasm at 'high places' on hills is as unlike synoptic Solomon as he is unlike David. He has lapsed and returned to behaviour from which Solomon had moved on. But Solomon too was re-evaluated – for the worse – as the whole progression of kings became increasingly blamed for the collapse of Jerusalem. Whereas Ahaz in all versions was distanced from synoptic Solomon, now Solomon actually takes on traits of wicked Ahaz. The older Solomon story had told of his visit to the great 'high place' at Gibeon (1 Kgs 3:4//2 Chr 1:3); but now we are told that this was just one of many such visits, for 'he sacrificed and offered incense at the high places' (3:3, not shared by 2 Chr 1). This new preliminary verse is an interesting mix: it starts by saying that Solomon *loved* Yahweh and walked by David's statutes (3:3a) – just the opposite of Ahaz who was not like David but walked in the ways of the kings of Israel; but it goes (3:3b) on to compare Solomon with Ahaz who *sacrificed at 'high places'*. And it foreshadows 1 Kgs 11:1–8 (also not in Chr), which starts by saying that Solomon *loved* many foreign women and finishes by noting that these women burned incense and *sacrificed to their gods at the 'high places'* he built for them around Jerusalem. Solomon's behaviour in 1 Kgs (3:3) 11:1–8 is precisely what Ahijah complains about in his oracle to Jeroboam (11:33). The Solomon who now resembles wicked Ahaz is part of the background to the divine promise to Jeroboam in the longer of the two accounts.

Jeroboam is promised an 'enduring' or 'sure' house (11:38) just like David (2 Sam 7:16), provided he is loyal to Yahweh as David had been. The parable of the twelve tatters had been something of a poisoned chalice when uttered by Shemaiah at Shechem in the shorter account. But in the longer version ascribed to Ahijah near Solomon's Jerusalem (11:29–31) there is no hint of curse; instead, the parable introduces an explicit promise. And the acted promise has complex resonances. Like what had once passed between Saul and Samuel (1 Sam 15:30–31), it concerns a torn garment. There, as Samuel turned to leave Saul, the king grabbed his cloak and it tore; and Samuel responded that Yahweh similarly was to tear his kingdom from Saul and give it to another – in this case, all his kingdom. At this early stage in the story, Jeroboam corresponds to the David who inherited another's kingdom. Rather like David and Jonathan with Saul, Jeroboam is Solomon's agent while Rehoboam is his son. But, by the time his wife hears Ahijah's words about their son(s), Jeroboam is more like Saul than David – a promise wasted and a dynasty without future. The prophetic voice is already significant, when expressed first by Shemaiah and then by Ahijah at the heart of the shorter version. But its importance is even greater when both expanded oracles are voiced by Ahijah, promise at the start and threat at the end of the whole story.

The alternative and shorter story of Jeroboam preserved in the Greek Bible is simply a component, though an important one, of the story of Rehoboam; it is only a footnote within the larger story of the Jerusalem royal house from David to the fall of Jerusalem. This Jeroboam, like several subsequent kings of northern Israel, has a 'walk-on' part in the southern story. But the expansively rewritten Jeroboam story constitutes a principal scene within an extensive re-presentation of the Bible's royal story in which a connected account of northern Israel's kings has been created and interleaved with the Jerusalem story. The new rebuilt Jeroboam heads that fresh account. Unable to establish a dynasty, he did inaugurate a lasting fateful trend.

David and His *Alter Ego* in the Desert

1 Text-criticism and the BoTH project

Developing proposals made in my Samuel commentary (Auld 2011), *Life in Kings* (Auld 2017) defends three claims:

- BoTH (earlier BTH), the synoptic narrative common to Sam-Kgs and Chr, is a very distinctive sub-set of Sam-Kgs.
- BoTH is cohesive and artistically constructed: it could have existed independently.
- Many portions of non-synoptic Sam-Kgs can be explained as developments from BoTH, normally where two or more of its separate components have been thought together.

As much as 40% of the text of 1–2 Samuel (1 Sam 16–31; 2 Sam 1–4; 9; 21:1–14[1]) concerns the relationship first between David and king Saul and then between David and Saul's house after that king's own death. And the story of Saul before David is told in 1 Sam 9–15. Saul and his house feature in more than half of the book. But in the source-material in BoTH there are only three mentions of Saul:

- the short chapter that tells of the death of the former king on Mt Gilboa (1 Sam 31//1 Chr 10)
- the note that when Saul was king David commanded the army (2 Sam 5:2// 1 Chr 11:2)
- and the reference to Michal, identified as 'Saul's daughter', scorning David as he brought the ark into Jerusalem (2 Sam 6:16//1 Chr 15:29)

It is of course possible that the authors of Samuel had access beyond BoTH to other older sources about Saul. Yet such an assumption may not be necessary. The broad terms of the whole David/Saul conflict – and indeed of the earlier Saul story – could have been derived imaginatively from thinking together some details in synoptic 1 Sam 31 with others from 2 Sam 5–7 and 24.

My interest in Kings and Chronicles as divergent expansions from a shared source was sparked in part by working with Jeremiah (both MT in a big way and LXX in a small way are expansions from a shorter source-text), in part by noting similar prophetic language in Jeremiah and Kings, but not Chronicles (Auld 1984). Yet, despite this text-historical background, I made almost no reference to text-

---

1 The route from BoTH to Samuel is sketched in Auld 2011 (especially 9–14) and Auld 2017 (esp. 103–115).

https://doi.org/10.1515/9783111060279-011

criticism in *Life in Kings*. I did not want to complicate things. I hoped to carry with me more conservative readers: readers who might more easily accept arguments if they saw that they were based on the traditional Hebrew texts of Kings and Chronicles, and not on what they could characterise as 'private scholarly reconstructions'. Then I knew from Samuel that there was a wide convergence between LXX readings and synoptic parallels in Chronicles. Where Samuel and Chronicles agreed in MT, there was little need to complicate matters with the LXX!

I should have known that matters were less simple with Solomon. I did feature the much shorter report in LXX of the ark being brought into the new temple, over against the longer version including Levites largely agreed between 1 Kgs 8:1–5 (MT) and 2 Chr 5:2–6 (Auld 2017, 208–209). And I mentioned – but know now I did not take seriously enough – the advice offered in my own FS (Trebolle 2007) about a triple as well as double textual tradition in Solomon. I hope my overall case is not too vulnerable.

Adrian Schenker (1996) has offered a careful demonstration that the shorter Jeroboam story preserved in Greek after 1[3] Kg[dm]s 12:24 is prior to the familiar version in 1 Kgs 11–14 (MT). He accepts Zipora Talshir's demonstration (1993) that a Hebrew text underlies the Greek version, but not her literary-historical analysis. She is among the majority in regarding this shorter (originally Hebrew) text as secondary to the familiar version. I agree with his comparative evaluation of the texts and differ from him only over the wider literary-historical assessment at the end of his essay (see previous essay). I find that an older and shorter Jeroboam story fits perfectly into BoTH. Equally, this shorter Jeroboam (without Beth-el and Dan) cannot have formed part of a book of Kings, properly so called: Frank Moore Cross was surely correct when he insisted (Cross 1973) that the sins of Jeroboam (completely absent from the older story) provided one of the two principal themes of that book. The Jeroboam of the book of Kings, while not a dynastic founder, sets the religious trend for all his successors. This earlier Jeroboam was simply joint agent when David's family, in the person of unwise Rehoboam, lost most of Israel. BoTH had no interest in what Jeroboam went on to do in an Israel detached from Jerusalem – what the book of Kings calls 'the sins he made Israel to sin'. After my decision to follow the shorter LXX on bringing the ark into the new temple, I should have included this text in my reconstruction instead of 1 Kgs 12:1–19 and the very similar 2 Chr 10:1–19.

Near its start, BoTH had sketched two similar triangular relationships. One threesome was Saul/his sons/David, and the other Solomon/his son Rehoboam/Jeroboam. In each case – and uniquely so in all of BoTH – kingship passed not to the dead king's son but to someone who had previously been a leading servant of the king. In the first case, the former head of the army succeeded to all Israel – Saul's sons, after all, had died with him in battle. In the second case, the former corvée chief succeeded to most of Israel, while Solomon's son retained power in Jerusalem. Importantly, it is not just in *content* that the two triangles are similar: BoTH also *presents* the stories of Saul/David and Solomon/Jeroboam in similar fashion – neither David nor Jeroboam is mentioned until the old king's death has been reported. In each case a prior relationship had existed: David with Saul and Jeroboam with Solomon; but we learn this only in retrospect.

In BoTH, in the precursor narrative, the David flashback was stated much more briefly even if its implications were open-ended: Israel's leaders come to Hebron and say to him 'When Saul was king, it was you who led Israel out and in' (2 Sam 5:2//1 Chr 11:2). The Jeroboam flashback is also introduced immediately after the report in 3 Kgdms 12:24a of the old king's death but is much more extensive (12:24b–f). We are told about his origins, his service in Solomon's building projects, and his royal pretensions; that Solomon tried to kill him, but he escaped to Egypt where he fared well under the Pharaoh's protection; that sometime after Solomon's death, he returned to Ephraim. In this version it was only at the Shechem assembly – not before he ever went to Egypt – that Jeroboam received the acted oracle from the man of God about the cloak torn in twelve tatters.

Religious or theological structuring is much less overt throughout BoTH than in Samuel and (even more so) in Kings. The author of this older history leaves much of its significance to be deduced by the reader from an intricate web of paired situations and descriptions. Many pairings clearly suggest comparison or contrast, though some resist easy analysis. Such quiet, unexplained, parallels as we have just noted in the introductions to David and Jeroboam are entirely typical of BoTH.

LXX^{B+L} are our best witnesses to BoTH on Jeroboam. While they tell a story much shorter than the familiar one, they do include some small +'s vis-à-vis that mostly longer version. One of these relates to the very issue that provided my title for *Life in Kings* and the content of its second chapter (pp. 29–38). In 1 Kgs 14:3, when Jeroboam dispatches his wife to Shiloh, he says that the prophet will tell her what will happen to their son. But in 3 Kgdms 12:24g, he tells her: 'Go, ask the deity about the lad, whether he will *live* (ie survive) from his illness.' By contrast, while Rehoboam in 3 Kgdms 12:24q, when confronted by the people's demands at Shechem, first consults 'the elders' (so described, without any elaboration), their introduction in 1 Kgs 12:6 continues '... who stood before Solomon his father when he was *alive*'. Each version is expansive: both include a quite different and unnecessary supplement containing the word 'live'. Each version exhibits – at a different place – one of the commonest characteristic differences between Sam-Kgs and its core. Any future attempt to reconstruct the text of BoTH must identify what is common not just to Sam-Kgs in Chr in MT but to a wider of range of witnesses.

Questions such as the following arise naturally out of synoptic David and the death of Saul:

1. Why was Saul followed as king by David, who was not of his family? For two reasons: (1) because all Saul's sons, or at least all his able-bodied sons, had died with him on the battlefield (1 Sam 31:6–7); and (2) because David had previously been Saul's commander-in-chief (2 Sam 5:2).
2. If David had previously been Saul's commander-in-chief, what was his relationship with Saul's sons? Jonathan had died with his father on Gilboa. Had David been friend or rival to Saul's son and heir?
3. We read in BoTH (2 Sam 6:16) that, as David brings the ark into Jerusalem, he is despised by Michal, termed significantly 'Saul's daughter'. How to explain this? Was there a previous relationship? Had the brave commander previously married the king's daughter, as in many good stories – and often in history too?
4. In BoTH, 'asking' (*š'l*) is associated only with David and Solomon: they alone 'ask Yahweh'; and only of them do others 'ask' (make requests). Their immediate predecessor bears the cognate name 'Asked' (*šā'ûl*). Did Shaul also ask Yahweh, even if this is not reported?
5. Why did Saul fail against the Philistines, but David succeed? Is this related to the previous question: David asked Yahweh (שאל ביהוה) before he engaged in battle (2 Sam 5:19, 23), but Saul did not or could not?
6. Why, if David had been commander-in-chief, was he not at Gilboa?

These issues arise naturally out of synoptic David and the death of Saul. Such questions are just waiting for able story-tellers to provide the answers; and many of the answers are organic developments out of BoTH. The synoptic text supplies not only the questions, but also much of the material for the answers. Of course, the author[s] of Samuel may have had alternative sources available to help answer some of these questions. However, since we have at best internal evidence for such sources, it may be better to give credit to creative storytellers, when we can at least identify some of the problems they had wanted to solve.

2 David and Jeroboam in Samuel and Kings

I propose that the narrator[s] responsible for the latter chapters of 1 Samuel and for 1 Kgs 11–14 (and especially ch. 11) thought together the two triangular relationships identified above. For both David and Jeroboam, what BoTH had sketched in flashback is now told in real time – and more expansively. Jeroboam's origins, his early career, and his flight from Solomon to Egypt, are now narrated not after but *within* the Solomon story (1 Kgs 11:26–40). And the acted parable of the torn cloak is moved to an earlier position within the narrative, to help motivate Jeroboam's flight: he has received a word from the deity before he escapes from Solomon. The new narrator not only moves some of the pieces on the Solomon/Jeroboam chess board but also adds two new pieces. One gives explicit recognition to what had been implicit in BoTH: the similar situations of David and Jeroboam. Using language from Nathan in BoTH (2 Sam 7:16) the torn-cloak prophet now promises Jeroboam a בית נאמן (1 Kgs 11:38): provided he is obedient he will be a new David. The second piece helps explain why what was originally reported in flashback is now being retold in real time: it is not Rehoboam's kingdom that is being divided but Solomon's (11:31) and divided because of Solomon's religious mistakes (11:33) – only, not in Solomon's lifetime (11:34–35).

David makes these important contributions to the retelling of the early Jeroboam; but Jeroboam contributes much more to the retelling of the early David. Flight from the old king helps explain why the one-time commander-in-chief was not with his king for the decisive battle with Philistines. David enjoyed success in Philistine territory (1 Sam 27), like Jeroboam in Egypt. And David too had been addressed by a prophet about kingship while the old king was still alive (1 Sam 16). The authors of 1 Samuel used the Jeroboam framework as they explored the David and Saul questions identified above. Of course, David accumulating features from other characters in BoTH is no scholarly novelty: it has long been observed (Auld 2011, 13) that El-Hanan killed Goliath (in 2 Sam 21:18–22//1 Chr 20:4–8) before David did (in 1 Sam 17)!

Moving more specifically to the theme of David in the desert, there has been much discussion of the narrative architecture of 1 Sam 24–26 (for a brief account see Auld 2011, 311–313). One debate that goes backward and forwards concerns the relative priority of the two very similar stories of David when he has Saul in his power: what should he do with his rival? In my commentary, I opted for 1 Sam 24 as prior. I do not want to argue that again here, but simply note in possible support that David cutting part of Saul's cloak in the cave (1 Sam 24:4–6) may carry an echo of Shemaiah's acted parable in front of Jeroboam with the robe torn in tatters (1 Kgs 12:24o). Schenker argues (226–227), I think successfully, that in the older shorter story of Jeroboam this acted parable meant threat rather than promise: 'Take these pieces if you like. They represent most of a robe, but it's in tatters and may not do you any good.'

When we read 1 Samuel from start to finish, 1 Sam 24 reminds us of Saul tearing Samuel's robe back in 1 Sam 15. Of course, 1 Sam 15 like 1 Sam 26 may be from a later stage in the growth of 1 Samuel than 1 Sam 24. Whatever the truth of that, if instead we see the scene in the cave from the perspective of Shemaiah and Jeroboam in BoTH, David may have realised (before it was too late) that cutting Saul's robe could presage dividing the kingdom he hoped to inherit. If 1 Sam 24 was older than 1 Sam 25–26, then it is more likely that it resonated with the older form of the Jeroboam story.

Several details of the David-Nabal-Abigail story use elements already part of the old Jeroboam tale in BoTH.

- Nabal rejects David (1 Sam 25:10) in a double question, with 'David' and 'son of Jesse' in unusual parallel ('Who is David, and who the son of Jesse?'), modelled on Israel rejecting Rehoboam (1 Kgs 12:24t).[2]
- David's retort is drawn from the same text: he tells his men he will leave Nabal with none to piss on a wall (1 Sam 25:22) and repeats the phrase as he assures Abigail of what he would have done had she not intervened (25:34). This expression occurs just once in BoTH, in Shemaiah's oracle to Jeroboam's wife (1 Kgs 12:24m).

However, both of these details are also part of the developed Jeroboam narrative; and we cannot be sure which stage of that story influenced David in the desert. Other details clearly align the David-Nabal-Abigail story with the expanded account of Jeroboam.

- Abigail speaks to David rather like Shemaiah and Ahijah, the two men of God with oracles for Jeroboam (25:28, 30). Like Ahijah addressing Jeroboam (1 Kgs 11:38; 14:7), she takes both נגיד and בית נאמן from Nathan's words to David in BoTH (2 Sam 7:9, 16).[3]

Further links between 1 Sam 25 and 1 Kgs 11 are mediated by the Abner episode in 2 Sam 3.

- When Abner comes to David with a group of men (2 Sam 3:20), David makes a feast for him – the only משתה in the books of Samuel apart from Nabal's, from which David and his men were excluded (1 Sam 25:36).
- At that party, Abner (2 Sam 3:21) makes the same promise to David as Ahijah will make to Jeroboam (1 Kgs 11:37): ומלכת בכל־אשר תאוה נפשך – 'you will be king in all that your *nephesh* desires'.
- David laments that Abner (2 Sam 3:33) has died like a fool/Nabal; and he regrets that Abner has fallen before בני עולה (3:34), scoundrels known elsewhere in the narrative books only in 2 Sam 7:10 (BoTH).[4]

2 Sheba ben Bichri will do the same in 2 Sam 20:1.

3 This theme is also anticipated in the threat to Eli in 1 Sam 2:35.

4 The fact that יסף hiphil is also used in both 2 Sam 3:34 and 7:10 makes it more likely that 3:34 has drawn on synoptic 7:10.

– Delicious wordplay in 1 Sam 25:34, 36 between *mšth* (feast) and *mštyn* (pissing) reinforces the 1 Sam 25 – 2 Sam 3 – 1 Kgs 11 link. David recalls to Abigail the threat against Nabal he had made to his men, 'there won't be left for Nabal till morning light anyone pissing on the wall' (עד אור הבקר משתין בקיר). She then goes back to her house and finds her husband: 'and he had a feast in his house like the king's feast' (והנה־לו משתה בביתו כמשתה המלך); but says not a word to him 'till morning light' (עד אור הבקר). When she does speak to him at morning-light, he is effectively finished too.

Similarities between the earlier accounts in BoTH of David succeeding Saul and Jeroboam succeeding Solomon encouraged authors of the prequel in 1 Samuel to BoTH to use the outline of Jeroboam in exile as they mapped David in flight from Saul. Much of their detail was also drawn from the older royal narrative.

3 From BoTH to 1 Samuel

1 Samuel represents an extension – a projection – into earlier time of the David story told in BoTH. But it is also much more than a prequel to the familiar story: in important respects 1 Samuel takes us into a new story-world. Several minor elements of the synoptic David story play a much more prominent role in non-synoptic Samuel; and five of these will be briefly examined. All of them extend the narrative, but some clearly alter it as well. I would take 'asking of God/Yahweh' (שאל באלהים\ביהוה) as an example of simple extension, whereas prostration (השתחוה) before a human, concern with the king's 'life', and the category 'Yahweh's anointed' seem better examples of the second; and addressing the king as 'my lord [king]' (אדני [המלך]) is harder to pronounce on. Each of these expressions is not only rare in BoTH but also rare elsewhere in HB.

3.1 Though at first sight 'to ask [of] Yahweh/God' is not a remarkable expression, its usage within HB is restricted to Judges and Samuel[5] – שאל ב is found 3× elsewhere,[6] but never שאל ביהוה or שאל באלהים. We find the end of the Judges/Samuel series in 2 Sam 5:19, 23 (//1 Chr 14:10, 14), where David twice seeks divine clearance before attacking Philistines, and twice receives a positive response. These are the only synoptic instances; and, I suspect, far from marking the last of the series, they are the start of it all. What is reported twice about synoptic David is anticipated three times about non-synoptic David:

5 Apart from synoptic 1 Chr 14:10, 14.
6 במשפט (Num 27:21) or בתרפים (Ezek 21:26) or בעצו (Hos 4:12).

- In 1 Sam 23:2, 4, before defending Keilah against Philistine attack, David also puts the question to the deity twice, just as in 2 Sam 5 – and Philistines are again the enemy.
- In 1 Sam 30:8, David asks before attacking Amalekites.
- In 2 Sam 2:1, the context is no longer explicitly military, but David's question is again in two parts: 'Shall I go up into any of the cities of Judah?' 'Yes.' 'To which shall I go up?' 'To Hebron.'

Where David always succeeds in his asking, Saul is never successful. The contrast between the two kings is all the more obvious, because Philistines are the enemy putting pressure both on Saul in 1 Sam 14:37 and 28:6, and on David in 1 Sam 23:2, 4 and 2 Sam 5:19, 23.

The phrase is used in just two further contexts. Saul accuses the priest Ahimelech of treason claiming that he had consulted the deity on behalf of Saul's rival David (1 Sam 22:10, 13, 15). And my last example is in fact the first that we meet in the book (1 Sam 10:21–22). שאול בן־קיש is identified by lot as the divinely chosen king; but he cannot be found because he is hiding, and his location is discovered by 'asking of Yahweh'. This is not the first time that the verb שאל is used in the story of Saul;[7] but it is the first time that this verb is used so close to the name שאול. Here Saul is not the subject of the enquiry, but its object. This asking by the people succeeds, just like each asking by David; but on each occasion when Saul initiates the asking, he fails. The whole series of 'askings' is part of a new narrative prologue that sets out to explain the opening stages of an older text (BoTH): Saul has faced the Philistines and been killed, and there has been no mention of Yahweh; David becomes king, consults Yahweh, and defeats the Philistines.[8]

3.2 The only instance of prostration within the synoptic David story comes at its end (2 Sam 24:20//1 Chr 21:21). When the Jebusite saw David and his men approaching, he went out and prostrated himself before the king. The verb השתחוה will occur in only three other contexts in BoTH: Solomon is warned against prostration before other gods (1 Kgs 9:6, 9//2 Chr 7:19, 22); Manasseh is blamed for prostration before the host of heaven (2 Kgs 21:3//2 Chr 33:3); and the Assyrian envoy tells Hezekiah's people that their king had instructed prostration before

7 It is not the first time we have met the verb שאל at all within the story of Saul. That comes in 1 Sam 10:4, where Samuel promises Saul a sign: three men will meet him and greet him – will wish him well (ושאלו לך לשלום).

8 Outer portions of the book of Judges (1:1; 18:5; 20:18, 23, 27) take up the theme of asking Yahweh; but that belongs to another topic.

one particular altar in Jerusalem (2 Kgs 18:22//2 Chr 32:12). In all four cases in the BoTH narrative, a foreign element is present: there should be no prostration before 'other' gods; one non-Israelite prostrates before David; and another non-Israelite quotes – or misquotes – Hezekiah. You can't trust foreigners.

In non-synoptic Samuel, eight other characters prostrate before David: Abigail (1 Sam 25:23, 41), the Amalekite who reports Saul's death (2 Sam 1:2), Mephibosheth (9:6, 8), the wise woman from Tekoa (14:4), Joab (14:22), Absalom (14:33), Ziba (16:4), and Ahimaaz (18:28). Suitors also prostrate before Absalom (15:5), as does the Cushite messenger before Joab (18:21). And David himself prostrates before Jonathan (1 Sam 20:41) and Saul (24:9). David is involved in almost every scene, and even the two exceptions are very close to his person: Absalom his son and Joab his senior commander. The picture is similar in non-synoptic Kings. Bathsheba prostrates before David (1 Kgs 1:16, 31), as does Nathan (1:23). Then both David (1:47) and Adonijah (1:53) prostrate before Solomon, as does Solomon himself before his mother Bathsheba (2:19). Only two instances in Samuel-Kings are unrelated to David or to the Solomon of 1 Kgs 1–2: 'the sons of the prophets' prostrate before Elisha, recognizing him as *successor* to Elijah (2 Kgs 2:15), as does the Shunammite woman (4:37). And the very fact of a *succession* from Elijah to Elisha is suggestive of their quasi-regal – or alternatively regal – portrayal. Elsewhere in HB, we find prostration before a human mostly in parts of Genesis.[9]

3.3 There is a significant overlap between prostration before humans in Samuel-Kings and the use of the deferential 'my lord [king]' (אדני [המלך]).[10] The overlap is already noticeable in the synoptic tradition. Jebusite Araunah is the only character who prostrates before a human anywhere in BoTH. So too, the only synoptic instances of 'my lord king' are uttered by Joab and then the Jebusite in the same census narrative (2 Sam 24:3, 22//1 Chr 21:3, 23). Just as David is the only person to prostrate before Jonathan and Saul, so too only he addresses Saul as 'my lord king'; and he then addresses the Philistine Achish the same way.[11] David, prior to becoming king, expresses before current royal houses the deference that should become his due.[12] 'Lord' is paired with 'king' once each in relation to Solomon and Rehoboam, and three times in stories about Elisha.[13] Elsewhere in HB is it found only in 2 Kgs 18:23//Isa 36:8; Jer 37:20; 38:9; and Dan 1:10.

---

9 Gen 23:7; 27:29, 29; 33:3, 6, 7, 7; 37:10; 42:6; 43:26, 28; 47:31; 48:12; 49:8; Exod 11:8; 18:7; Ruth 2:10; Esth 3:2, 2, 5.

10 [my] lord [king] from 2 Sam 24+1 Kgs 22 to 1 Sam 24:7, 9, 11; 25:10, 14, 17, 24, 25, 25, 26, 26, 27, 27, 28, 28, 29, 30, 31, 31, 31, 41; 26:15, 16, 17, 18, 19. This is discussed in Kucová, 248–249.

11 1 Sam 24:9; 26:15, 17, 19; 29:8.

12 2 Sam 3:21; 4:8; 9:11; 26× in 2 Sam 13–19; and 12× in 1 Kgs 1.

13 1 Kgs 2:38; 12:27; 2 Kgs 6:12, 26; 8:5.

3.4 BoTH reports only two anointings: of David and Joash, the only kings who did not immediately succeed to their fathers. The verb ‘anointed’ is plural in both 2 Sam 5:3//1 Chr 11:3 and 2 Kgs 11:12//2 Chr 23:11. In the case of David, ‘the elders of Israel’ are the subject. In the case of Joash, the subject of the verb ‘anoint’ is unstated (hence similarly general) in 2 Kgs 11:12, while the Chronicler supplies ‘Jehoiada and his sons’. In neither case is there mention of divine initiative, such as we find in the narratives of Samuel anointing Saul and David (1 Sam 9:15–10:8; 16:1–13). The divine role in the anointing of Saul and David offers a narrative explanation of the title משיח יהוה (‘Yahweh’s anointed’). Beyond the ‘prequel’ narratives of Saul in David’s power then mourned by him,[14] משיח יהוה is found in 8 psalms[15] and is rare elsewhere.[16]

3.5 I gave *Life in Kings* its title because חי\חיה\חיים (life/live/alive) are so much more prominent in Sam-Kgs than in BoTH. The proportions are no less striking for נפש: 4× in BoTH and 78×[?] in non-synoptic Sam-Kgs.[17] Not only so: נפש and the חי-family never coincide in BoTH, though both are found (8 verses apart) in Solomon’s long prayer.[18] However, their conjunction is another distinctive feature of our chapters. חי נפשך (‘as your “self” lives’) occurs alongside the much commoner oath-formula חי יהוה (‘as Yahweh lives’) in 1 Sam 20:3 and 25:26 (and 8× more in Sam-Kgs[19]). חי יהוה is used more frequently:

- once in BoTH (1 Kgs 22:14, and so not in its David story)
- 30× in Sam-Kgs (more than half of these in the David story)
- And some 10× elsewhere in HB[20]

14 1 Sam 24:7, 7, 11 and 26:9, 11, 16, 23; 2 Sam 1:14, 16, 21.

15 Ps 2:2; 18:51; 20:7; 28:8; 84:10; 89:39, 52; 105:15; 132:10, 17. Ps 18 also appears as 2 Sam 22; and Ps 105:1–15 is included in 1 Chr 16:8–22 and Ps 132:8–10 in 2 Chr 6:41–42.

16 1 Sam 2:10, 35; 12:3, 5; 16:6; 2 Sam 19:22; 23:1; Isa 45:1; Hab 3:13; Lam 4:20; Dan 9:25, 26.

17 In non-synoptic Sam-Kgs it is used 74× (32× in 1 Sam, of which 4× in the substantial MT+ 1 Sam 17:55–18:5 – the others are 1 Sam 1:10, 15, 26; 2:16, 33, 35; 19:5, 11; 20:1, 3, 4, 17; 22:2, 22, 23; 23:15, 20; 24:12; 25:26, 29, 29, 29; 26:21, 24, 24; 28:9, 21; 30:6).

18 נפש in 2 Sam 23:17//1 Chr 11:19; 1 Kgs 3:11//2 Chr 1:11; 1 Kgs 8:48//2 Chr 6:38; 2 Kgs 23:3//2 Chr 34:31; and חי etc indisputably in 1 Kgs 8:40//2 Chr 6:31; 1 Kgs 22:14//2 Chr 18:13; 2 Kgs 11:12//2 Chr 23:11; 2 Kgs 14:9, 17//2 Chr 25:18, 25 – in light of the earlier discussion of Jeroboam, 1 Kgs 12:6// 2 Chr 10:6 has been removed from the list. It was argued in Auld 2017, 29–30 that the plus in 1 Chr 11:8 about Joab ‘letting live’ or ‘restoring to life’ the remnant of Jerusalem should be taken seriously as witness to BTH; oddly, the plus in the parallel narrative (2 Sam 5:8) includes נפש דוד, although there is much textual variety over how that phrase relates to the verb ‘hate’ (Auld 2011, 394–395).

19 1 Sam 1:26; 17:55[M+]; 2 Sam 11:11; 14:19; 2 Kgs 2:2, 4, 6; 4:30.

20 Auld 2017, 33–34.

נפש חיה ('living self') occurs 13×, mostly early in Genesis.[21] And נפש is obj of חיה (in the sense of 'preserve life') some 10×.[22] Other usages are few (4×).[23]

About one-third of all instances of נפש and the חי-family combined are in Sam-Kgs, including every instance of חי נפשך – this oath-formula is unknown elsewhere in HB, and is in fact unique to stories involving David or Elisha. A few sentences after uttering it, Abigail demonstrates that her use of this unusual oath is far from simply formulaic by adding in explanation והיתה נפש אדני צרורה בצרור החיים ('and my lord's self will be bound in the bundle of the living', 25:29).[24]

Persistent use of נפש starts with 1 Sam 19:5, 11; of אדני in 20:38; and of השתחוה before a human with 20:41 – and the first instance of חי נפשך is in 20:3. Though both Saul and David were anointed at divine instigation in the first half of 1 Samuel, only in 1 Sam 24 and 26 are the implications explored of what it meant to be משיח יהוה. Each of these expressions may have its roots in BoTH; and their (minimal) role in synoptic David does warrant discussion elsewhere. As in BoTH, they play only a tiny part in the portrait of kingship in Israel and Judah that we find elsewhere in HB. By contrast, the role they play together in the books of Samuel (and to a lesser extent Kings) is quite novel and remarkable. Massed in the later chapters of 1 Samuel, they are elements of a narrated world that is *rooted* in BoTH yet *radically* different from it.

The later chapters of 1 Samuel develop relationships already implied in BoTH: David is compared with Jeroboam and is both contrasted and compared with Saul. But other pairings suggested in BoTH are also in play. I noted earlier that only stories relating to David and Solomon use שאל. In the account of Solomon's first vision, Yahweh promises him as a bonus what he had not asked for: ולא שאלת נפש איביך; and Abigail anticipates this promise to David.[25] Then, in BoTH, only David and Joash are anointed; a covenant is associated with both anointings; and Joash also reigns for 40 years. When Joash is anointed, the people also shout יחי המלך ('[long] live the king') – no empty formula: he was only seven, and all his siblings had been murdered. Abigail's והיתה נפש אדני צרורה בצרור החיים is an evocative elaboration of their shout. We could even propose יחי המלך as motto for the whole David-in-the-Desert story. Among her many qualities, Abigail was an intelligent reader of BoTH.

---

21 Gen 1:20, 21, 24, 30; 2:7, 19; 9:10, 12, 15, 16; Lev 11:10, 46; Ezek 47:9.

22 Gen 19:19; 1 Kgs 20:31; Isa 55:3; Jer 38:17, 20; Ezek 13:18–19; 18:27; Ps 22:30; 119:175.

23 Ps 49:19; 66:9; Job 10:1; 12:10.

24 If I were determined to find a root in BoTH for as much as possible in Sam-Kgs, I would look to the poignant tale of David's heroes bringing him water from Bethlehem for the origin of בכל־אשר תאוה נפשך and related expressions. It is only there that BoTH uses any form of אוה; and one of only four instances of נפש is part of the same short episode.

25 1 Kgs 3:11//2 Chr 1:11 (though there the clause ends with שנאיך, 'your haters'); and 1 Sam 25:29.

Of Proust and Prophets: Samuel, Elijah, and Charles Swann

Interest over the discovery of Marcel Proust's '75 leaves' (*Soixante-quinze feuillets*) and their first publication (Proust 2021) goes beyond French literary circles. They had been written sometime around 1908 as he was beginning work on his complex and much discussed masterpiece, *À la recherche du temps perdu*. The novel was published in seven parts between 1913 and 1927, some of them after his death in 1922. In Proust's view these large 'leaves' adumbrated many of the main themes of his great work. Their publisher, Gallimard, claims they are nothing short of the oldest version of the novel. If this is fair description, the most notable absence from the 75 pages is any mention of the completed novel's principal character, Charles Swann.

As soon as I read of this literary find, I was struck by the analogy, even if only partial, that it offers to the account I have advocated of the origins of the biblical books of Samuel and Kings (Auld 2017). I find the source or seedbed of Sam-Kgs to consist of a much shorter draft of their narrative stretching from the death of Saul (1 Sam 31) to the death of Josiah (2 Kgs 23). The draft was only some 20% of the extent of Samuel and Kings and essentially comprised simply those parts of the text that we find both in Sam-Kgs and in Chronicles. A key similarity with the stages in Proust's work is that the dominant prophetic figures, Samuel, Elijah, and Elisha, are completely absent from the 'synoptic' narrative shared by Sam-Kgs and Chr.

These three towering characters and others associated with them – Eli with Samuel and Jezebel with Elijah and Elisha – feature in many of the most memorable stories in Sam-Kgs. While none of them had appeared in the source, many of their components were already there. Samuel and Eli of course could not be in the source – they belong to the major prequel in 1 Samuel to the royal narrative of David and his house (2 Samuel-2 Kings). The first half of the completed biblical narrative actually now bears Samuel's name; and the roles played along with him by Elijah and Elisha help explain why these books (along with Joshua and Judges) are known in Jewish tradition as the Former Prophets.

As he bursts on the scene (1 Kgs 17:1), Elijah's first words are 'As Yahweh lives, before whom I stand'. He will repeat them once (18:15) and Elisha, twice (2 Kgs 3:14; 5:16); but these are the only four instances in the Hebrew Bible. Each element, oath and servant-formula is familiar elsewhere – but separately. Even separately, we find them in the same context only once in the Hebrew Bible (1 Kgs 22). In the whole synoptic source, Micaiah is the only character to utter the oath (22:14). It heads his response to the officer sent to bring him to the two kings,

https://doi.org/10.1515/9783111060279-012

who encouraged him to fall into line with the other prophets. Micaiah replies under oath that he will follow divine instructions. Then, challenged now by a fellow prophet, he answers by reporting a vision of the heavenly court (22:19–22): by coming forward and 'standing before' the divine king, a spirit accepts a divine invitation to deceive the kings. Micaiah utters the oath under challenge from the officer and reports the vision when challenged by a fellow prophet. His opening declaration portrays Elijah as an amalgam of Micaiah the prophet loyal to Yahweh and the spirit-volunteer familiar with the divine court. Elijah's first words may be drawn from the major source of the book of Kings; but they also present him as a figure different from any in that early draft. His opening words show that he will brook no challenge.

Elijah's contest on Mount Carmel (1 Kgs 18) pits him against greater odds than Micaiah faced: not just 'about four hundred prophets' (22:6), but as many as 'four hundred and fifty prophets of Baal and the four hundred prophets of Asherah who eat at Jezebel's table' (18:19). Micaiah's rivals are not reported as serving another god; indeed, the only prophetic opponent specifically identified (22:11, 24), Zedek-*iah*, has a Yahweh name just like Mica-*iah*. Even the wicked queen in the synoptic source is named Athal-*iah*, who had usurped the throne in Jerusalem on the death of her son Ahaz-*iah* (2 Kgs 11:1–2). Overthrown in a plot devised by Jehoiada the priest, she was killed near the Horses Gate (11:16). Then, after Jehoiada had mediated a covenant between Yahweh, the newly anointed king, and the people, the people tore down the temple of Baal and killed Mattan his priest (11:17–18). This second synoptic narrative (in 2 Kgs 11–12) has supplied several details for the story of Jehu in 2 Kgs 9–10.[1] Anointed at Elisha's command, he had Jezebel killed on his arrival in Jezreel – thrown from a window, she was trampled by horses (9:33) so echoing Athaliah's fate. After having the remnants of Ahab's family massacred in Jezreel, Jehu moved on to Samaria. There he summoned all the servants/prophets of Baal to a great sacrifice in the temple of Baal – at its conclusion, they were all killed and the temple and its sacred pillar destroyed (10:12–27). Their fate mirrored the killing of Elijah's opponents in the open air on Carmel.

Episodes in the older synoptic narrative provided or suggested many of the details of the younger stories in Kings. The account in 2 Kgs 3 of the campaign against Moab by Jehoram of Israel and Jehoshaphat of Judah repeats several details of the campaign against Aram over Ramoth by Jehoram's father and Jehoshaphat reported in synoptic 1 Kgs 22. The kings pledge unity in the same terms (3:7); and the Micaiah role of prophet *loyal to Yahweh* (22:7) is now played by Elisha, successor to Elijah (3:11–12). But there's a difference. Elisha's instruc-

1 Others are listed in Auld 2017, 124–125.

tions for a determined and ruthless campaign against Moab (3:19) are followed by the kings (3:25); and only when the king of Moab sacrifices his firstborn on the city wall does Israel withdraw with 'great wrath' upon them (3:27). Like the spirit volunteer in the synoptic source, Elisha has given effect to Yahweh's dissatisfaction with his people.

Elijah and Jezebel and Elisha and Jehu have clear links with synoptic Micaiah and Athaliah and Jehoiada. But the newer stories that feature them involve large increases in numbers and intensity. Four hundred prophets have become more than double that number. Their loyalty is now specifically to Baal and Ashera, to gods other than Yahweh. A temple of Baal and its priest have become a temple of Baal packed with its worshippers. Death by the Horses Gate has become a death followed by trampling by horses. The narrative rhetoric has been cranked up. And the Elijah who has in him something of both Micaiah the loyal prophet and Jehoiada the loyal priest speaks with all the assurance of a divine spirit who has seen Yahweh and received his commission in the heavenly court.

The four hundred prophets did not suffer for their enthusiastic support for Ahab's campaign against Ramoth in Gilead – it was instead Micaiah who was committed to prison on short rations to be released only when Ahab returned victorious (1 Kgs 22:27). Elijah in flight from Ahab was also hungry (1 Kgs 17) but was fed first by ravens (or were they Bedouin? – the Hebrew letters *'rbym* can be read both ways) and then by a starving widow near Sidon. In the source narrative, the king of Israel is the only reported casualty in a deliberately focussed campaign (1 Kgs 22:31–35); however, if the deaths in Moab matched the extent of the collateral damage, they were of a different order. Elijah, like Jehu, instructed the massacre of his prophetic rivals (18:40). The new stories are memorable, but they also include some appalling details.

Synoptic Joash and Jehoiada may also have helped inspire the start of the prequel. Young Samuel delivered by his mother to the care of Eli the priest at the sanctuary in Shiloh (1 Sam 1) reminds us of baby Joash delivered by his aunt to the care of Jehoiada the priest at the sanctuary in Jerusalem. Eli of Shiloh unable to see (1 Sam 4:15) anticipates Ahijah, the blind prophet at the same sanctuary (1 Kgs 14:4). The narrative of the ark in Philistine hands draws on both ark episodes in BoTH. The first tells of David bringing the ark to his new capital from Baala/Kiriath-jearim west of Jerusalem and close to Philistine territory (2 Sam 6). The prequel now explains that it had once been captured by the old enemy: it had been returned there when Yahweh triumphed over them. And the multiple play on *kbd* ('where is the glory?' and 'give glory to Yahweh') in 1 Sam 4 anticipates the climax of Solomon bringing the ark into the temple, when Yahweh's 'glory' filled his house (1 Kgs 8:11). The great tale of the uneasy relationship between Saul and David fills the second half of the prequel (1 Sam 16–30) and is the response of a brilliant narrator to the sparsest of clues at the start of the older narrative: Israel approach David as their former commander in the time of Saul (2 Sam 5:2), yet he and his men were absent from the battle with the Philistines where the old king and his sons were killed (1 Sam 31). David prospering in Philistine exile from Saul anticipates Jeroboam's success in Egyptian exile from Solomon.

A case can certainly be made for understanding many non-synoptic portions of Sam-Kgs as drawing on and inspired by the shorter synoptic narrative. To this extent the analogy with Proust's 75 pages holds. The introduction of new characters who come to dominate the expanding story make the analogy more secure. But there is also a major difference. Not much more than a decade separates the completion of Proust's seven volumes from their seedbed in the 75 pages. However, there is at least a generational and probably an epochal gap between the synoptic narrative and the books of Samuel and Kings.

Elijah and Elisha have not just been added to the story – they have taken it over. Micaiah is the most substantial prophetic character in BoTH; and his depiction there has influenced how Elijah and Elisha are portrayed. Yet these belong to a different world. Micaiah, like Nathan and Gad and Huldah in the older royal story, is a prophet consulted by kings. In that monarchic context, unwelcome advice can lead to abuse and imprisonment. But Elijah is not consulted: he initiates. From commanding a drought, through defying king and queen, to being caught up into heaven, he is quite unlike any synoptic prophet. Elisha is no less unique within the Hebrew Bible: a prophetic servant become successor (2 Kgs 2), who continues to work miracles from his grave (2 Kgs 13:20–21). The nearest biblical analogy to such a quasi-royal succession is from Moses to Joshua. The shift from earlier prophetic category to later is nicely caught where we first meet Samuel as an adult (1 Sam 9–10). Saul and his attendant, failing in their search for lost donkeys, seek advice from Samuel, a seer. What they expect belongs to the older narrative world. However, their encounter ends with the seer seizing the initiative and anointing Saul king. Later, when Saul proved a disappointment as king, Samuel announced his end (1 Sam 13:13–14; 15:26–29) and anointed his successor (1 Sam 16).

In the world of the synoptic source, kings rule and occasionally consult prophets. When the king happens to be a child, as with Joash and Josiah who become king aged seven and eight, the leading roles are played by priest and scribe/secretary (2 Kgs 11; 22). But the Elijah/Elisha stories in 1 Kgs 17 – 2 Kgs 10 feature not a single scribe; the only priests mentioned are priests of Baal (2 Kgs 10:11, 19); and kings have been reduced almost to pawns. The older role played by Jehoiada the priest in having Baal's house and priest destroyed is transformed into the spectacular contest between Elijah, prophet of Yahweh, and the prophets of Baal and of Ashera. Whether or not the old narrative was written before or after the fall of Jerusalem, the royal house and the temple and priesthood that it portrays represent that world before the collapse. But Samuel and Elijah and Elisha belong in a different narrative world.

Oracles against Eli's house in 1 Sam 2 and 3 suggest at the outset that the function of the prequel is not simply to describe how kingship in Israel began. They also point beyond inherited office, whether priestly or royal. There is a future beyond kings. The first, delivered by an unnamed 'man of God', declares that Eli's house will be replaced by a house that is 'established' or 'trustworthy'. The second, delivered through the young Samuel, makes no mention of a replacement priestly house; the chapter ends instead with the recognition that Samuel himself was 'established' as 'Yahweh's prophet'. Prophets in the older royal narrative may have been part of the elite, along with scribes and priests. Samuel, like Elijah and Elisha, combines characteristics of three traditional roles: prophet and priest and king. It is hardly surprising that Jewish tradition calls these books 'Prophets' and names the first half of the story 'Samuel'.

Tracing the Writing of Kings with Nadav Na'aman and Klaus-Peter Adam

1 Klaus-Peter Adam on Jepsen

Within an interesting collection of *Soundings in Kings*, Adam (2010) contributed a substantial re-presentation of Alfred Jepsen's account of the sources of Kings (Jepsen 1956). Jepsen's synchronistic chronicle had started with Solomon (1 Kgs 2:10–12) and finished with Hezekiah (2 Kgs 18:1–2, 8). Adam notes that more synchronistic chronicles from Mesopotamia have been recovered since Jepsen's work, focussing on dynastic succession, securing frontiers, and rebellions; and setting Jepsen's proposals in a richer ANE context. Adam does not specify in detail his own view of the original extent of the Judah/Israel chronicle but devotes close attention to a pair of similarly structured narratives inserted near start and finish: about Asa (1 Kgs 15:16–22) and Ahaz (2 Kgs 16:5, 7–9) seeking help from Aram or Assyria when under threat from Israel. Both narratives 'assume some form of a covenantal agreement between Israel and Judah before the outbreak of the war' (2010, 65), each 'emphasizing Judah's tactics and the switching of covenantal relationships as a very successful political move' (66).

2 Nadav Na'aman

Na'aman (2017) offered a critique in *SJOT* 31 of Adam's attempt to revive Jepsen's account of an early Judahite-Israelite synchronistic chronicle. While not disputing Adam's attention to links between Asa and Ahaz, he set these within more intricate patterns (2017, 85–88). Not only did Amaziah and Hezekiah each accede to the throne aged 25 and reign for 29 years,[1] but their successors (Azariah/Uzziah and Manasseh) were the only kings in Jerusalem reported as reigning for more than 50 years. Similarly, Joash and Josiah were the youngest of Jerusalem's kings at accession; and, Na'aman notes, their immediate predecessors (Ahaziah and Amon) also had the shortest reigns. From these several correspondences between groups of earlier and later kings in Jerusalem, he deduces that this material was not authored before the time of Josiah. 'The same author wrote the histories of the [five] kings of Judah from Ahaz to Josiah and those of five earlier Judahite kings (Asa, Jehoshaphat, Jehoash, Amaziah, and Uzziah) according to the same

1 Noted also within a sketch of wider significant pairings in Auld 2017, 92–94 – expanded below (153–161).

https://doi.org/10.1515/9783111060279-013

literary and historiographical pattern.' The link between Asa and Ahaz was real; but they did not bracket a pre-Josianic narrative. Instead, each was the first element in a matching group of five kings. In previous studies, Na'aman had argued a Josianic date for a major source of Kings; but at the end of this article he notes that an exilic date is equally possible.

The strength of Na'aman's case rests on the richness of the patterning, for some strands are clearly stronger than others. Joash and Josiah are clearly linked as major reformers; but it is hardly surprising that they were also the youngest kings at accession when their fathers also had the shortest reigns. It may be more surprising that Uzziah and Manasseh had such long reigns following fathers who each lived to 54. His arguments explicitly challenge the dating element of Adam's case. Since the patterning includes – indeed is based on – material relating to Josiah and his four predecessors, it is likely to have been devised after that king's death. However, there is also an implicit challenge to any attempt to portray this source as already synchronistic. If kings were presented in patterns in this earlier story and if dates were sometimes integral to these patterns (as in the case of Amaziah and Hezekiah), we must deduce that these dates had not simply been transcribed from archived diaries: they were not [all] intended to be read literally. The author of Kings, however, did not share his source's attitude to dates: there we breathe a different numerical atmosphere. Composing this book of Kings, thinking together the royal story of northern Israel with the account of Jerusalem's kings, elaborating a whole series of synchronisms (see further in 7 below), implied a new view of dates – implied taking numbers literally (or strictly 'numerically'?).

3 Asa and Ahaz

Most of Na'aman's correspondences work in Chronicles as well as Kings – the relevant portions of text are synoptic; and this is also true of Adam's main worked example with which Na'aman starts (Asa and Ahaz), though not as both scholars present it. According to Kgs,[2] each king 'sent' (שלח) a 'present' (שחד) in the hope of military intervention against Israel, Asa to Aram and Ahaz to Assyria. In both cases, שלח is synoptic[3] but שחד is not. שחד is found in Kgs only in these two passages: I propose that Kgs has built on its synoptic source and enhanced the correspondence. Na'aman's evidence (2017, 82–83) that שחד is a pejorative term for gift, a bribe, tells against Adam's favourable reading of the Asa report (Adam

2 1 Kgs 15:19; 2 Kgs 16:8.

3 1 Kgs 15:19//2 Chr 16:3; 2 Kgs 16:8//2 Chr 28:16.

2010, 55, 176–177). However, just as the Chronicler did not remove 'life'-words from his source on Hezekiah, we should not suppose with Japhet (1993, 733) that he has deleted a pejorative term from the narratives about Asa and Ahaz. שחד was part of an addition to the older, synoptic version. The much commoner term throughout Sam-Kgs for 'present/offering/tribute' is מנחה. In synoptic portions, the recipient may be human (David or Solomon)[4] or divine (Yahweh);[5] and this is equally true of the more numerous non-synoptic contexts.[6] However, cultic and non-cultic senses are never found in textual proximity. It may be this that explains the choice of שחד in 2 Kgs 16:8 – and hence also in the paired 1 Kgs 15:19. In the following larger plus about Ahaz's new great altar (16:10–15), the author mentions cultic 'offerings' three times and naturally calls them מנחה. When adapting v. 8, he employs שחד instead of the (synoptic) near-equivalent מנחה.

Confidence is impossible over the exact shape of the text that underlies the rather different 2 Kgs 16:8 and 2 Chr 28:16, 21; but they agree that Ahaz took from the contents of *the house of Yahweh* and of *the king's house* and *sent* them to the king of Assyria. The same three terms are linked in the narrative about Asa.[7] These two 'houses' were plundered in the days of Rehoboam and Amaziah by conquering forces, Pharaoh Shishak and Jehoash of Israel.[8] However, of all the kings of Jerusalem up to Josiah, only Asa and Ahaz within synoptic narratives actually initiated the purchase of help from a more powerful state using the resources of the two houses built by Solomon. When the author of Kgs specifies what these two kings 'sent' as שחד, he is simply underlining a unique paired cluster already attested synoptically.[9] When probing sources of the Jerusalem royal narrative, the safest starting point is where Kgs and Chr agree.

Whether Adam was correct in presenting the actions of Asa and Ahaz as examples of astute policy is another matter. Ahaz is most certainly not evaluated positively in the formal introduction (2 Kgs 16:2–4 or 2 Chr 28:1–4). To assess Asa within the larger synoptic narrative, two further sets of paired accounts are rele-

---

4 In David's case (2 Sam 8:2, 6//1 Chr 18:2, 6) the 'offerings' were a response to his military might; in Solomon's (1 Kgs 10:25//2 Chr 9:24), the 'whole earth' brought them when they came to hear his wisdom.

5 1 Kgs 8:64//2 Chr 7:7.

6 It signifies a present to a human in 1 Sam 10:27; 1 Kgs 5:1; 2 Kgs 8:8, 9; 17:3, 4; 20:12; and the sense is cultic in 1 Sam 2:17, 29, 29; 3:14; 26:19; 1 Kgs 18:29, 36; 2 Kgs 3:20; 16:13, 15, 15.

7 1 Kgs 15:18//2 Chr 16:2.

8 1 Kgs 14:26//2 Chr 12:9; 2 Kgs 14:14//2 Chr 25:24.

9 Hezekiah's capitulation to Sennacherib over tribute is different again. The report is not synoptic: it is carried only in 2 Kgs 18:14–16, but not Isa 36 or 2 Chr 32, and immediately follows the added specification that the invasion was in his 14th year (Auld 2017, 183–185).

vant. Typically, each possible relationship between the Davidic house and Israel is sketched twice:

- Rehoboam and Amaziah initiate moves against Israel;
- Asa and Ahaz buy outside help when threatened by Israel;
- Jehoshaphat and Ahaziah cooperate with Israel against Aram.

Under Rehoboam the treasuries of both 'houses' had been plundered and Asa had paid out from both treasuries before Jehoshaphat became yoked in an unequal alliance with Ahab. Judah was always under Israel's shadow; despite buying help from Aram under Asa, Judah under Jehoshaphat found itself losing against Aram.

4 Clustered pairings

Some of Na'aman's findings nicely overlap with Auld 2017, published in the same year. My convergent interest in patterning in the book of Kings also came from trying to identify its source material, though by a quite different route. I had proposed (Auld 1994) that Samuel-Kings and Chronicles had developed in different directions from the (synoptic) material they shared. Returning to the issue (Auld 2017), I started by defending two apparently contrary propositions. (1) In both content and language, the synoptic material is a very distinctive sub-set of Sam-Kgs. (2) At the same time, it is also the seedbed from which much of Sam-Kgs is developed.

In a third methodical step, with the familiar emphases of the authors of Sam-Kgs and Chr removed, or at least lessened, it was important to pay fresh attention to their common 'synoptic' source. The structure of this 'text' was obviously provided in part by a storyline continuous from the death of Saul and the accession of David. I proposed that in part it was also provided by a complex series of 'pairs' and clusters of 'pairs': words, phrases, or names that occur only twice in the synoptic text, each in the report of a different king – or, where more than twice, still only within the accounts of two kings. Auld 2017, 91–94 provided a preliminary sketch of some 30 pairs, including the feature, noted also by Na'aman, of Amaziah and Hezekiah each starting their reigns aged 25 and reigning for 29 years! To this I added in confirmation that Lachish appears synoptically only in their stories. The listing tabulated below has multiplied more than fourfold and allowed the detection of many more interwoven patterns like those discussed by Na'aman. These start with the death of Saul, who is contrasted with David and compared with Ahab, and finish with the death of Josiah (the pattern of pairings includes no king after Josiah). David and Solomon are praised for practising משפט וצדקה; only narratives about David or Hezekiah use the standard verbs for save/deliver (הושע\הציל); Solomon and Jehoshaphat are associated with trade from Ezion-geber in Tarshish-ships; and over a hundred more unique links in wording are preserved jointly by Sam-Kgs and Chr. The conclusion imposes itself: implicit comparisons and contrasts are the very DNA of the synoptic material.

25 + 29 yrs[10]	Amaziah	Hezekiah
אבתיך[11]	David	Josiah
אבן יקרה[12]	David	Solomon
הכה אדום[13]	David	Amaziah
אדני[14]	David	Jehoshaphat
איבים[15]	David	Solomon
אילת[16]	Solomon	Azariah
אלהינו[17]	David	Hezekiah
נאמן[18]	David (but diff in Sam/Chr)	Solomon
האמין[19]	Solomon (Sheba)	Hezekiah (in 2 Chr 32:15)
אמר (to Yahweh)[20]	David	Solomon
אני[21]	Solomon	Jehoshaphat
הארון[22]	David	Solomon
אשור[23]	Ahaz	Hezekiah

10 2 Kgs 14:2//2 Chr 25:1; 2 Kgs 18:2//2 Chr 29:2.
11 2 Sam 7:12//1 Chr 17:11; 2 Kgs 22:20//2 Chr 34:28 – both in promises spoken by a prophet.
12 2 Sam 12:20//1 Chr 20:2; 1 Kgs 10:2, 10, 11//2 Chr 9:1, 9, 10.
13 2 Sam 8:13//1 Chr 18:12; 2 Kgs 14:7//2 Chr 25:11.
14 2 Sam 24:3//1 Chr 21:3; 1 Kgs 22:17//2 Chr 18:16.
15 2 Sam 5:20; 7:9//1 Chr 14:11; 17:8; 1 Kgs 8:33, 37, 44, 46//2 Chr 6:24, 28, 34, 36.
16 1 Kgs 9:26//2 Chr 8:17; 2 Kgs 14:22//2 Chr 26:2.
17 2 Sam 10:12//1 Chr 19:13; 2 Kgs 18:22 and 19:19//2 Chr 32:11.
18 2 Sam 7:16 and 1 Chr 17:23, 24 (at different points in the chapter); 1 Kgs 8:26//2 Chr 6:17.
19 1 Kgs 10:7//2 Chr 9:6; 2 Chr 32:15 (but בטח in 2 Kgs 18:30).
20 2 Sam 7:18//1 Chr 17:16; 1 Kgs 8:22//2 Chr 6:14.
21 1 Kgs 9:27; 10:22//2 Chr 8:18; 9:21; 1 Kgs 22:49–50//2 Chr 20:36–37.
22 2 Sam 6//1 Chr 13; 15–16; 1 Kgs 8:1–11//2 Chr 5:2–14.
23 2 Kgs 16:7, 8, 9//2 Chr 28:16, 20, 21; 2 Kgs 18–20(22×)//2 Chr 32(8×).

(continued)

אשרה[24]	Asa	Manasseh
הבמות לא סרו[25]	Asa	Jehoshaphat
בנה\בית[26]	David	Solomon
בעד[27]	David	Josiah
בעל[28]	Joash	Manasseh
בקר[29]	David	Solomon
בקש[30]	David	Solomon
ברזל[31]	David	Jehoshaphat
ברך[32]	David	Solomon
בשם\כסף\זהב[33]	Solomon (Sheba)	Hezekiah
בגיא־מלח[34]	David	Amaziah
גבעון\גבעה[35]	Solomon	Ahaz
גדל[36]	David	Solomon
גדל\קטון[37]	Jehoshaphat	Josiah
הגוים[38]	David	Hezekiah
גרן[39]	David	Jehoshaphat

24 1 Kgs 15:13//2 Chr 15:16; 2 Kgs 21:3, 7//2 Chr 33:3, 7.
25 1 Kgs 15:14//2 Chr 15:17; 1 Kgs 22:44//2 Chr 20:33.
26 2 Sam 7:5, 7, 13, 27//1 Chr 17:4, 6, 12, 25; 1 Kgs 5:19//2 Chr 1:18; 1 Kgs 8:13, 16, 17, 18, 19, 19, 20, 27, 43, 44, 48//2 Chr 6:2, 5, 7, 8, 9, 9, 10, 18, 33, 34, 38; 1 Kgs 9:11, 24; 10:4//2 Chr 8:1, 11; 9:3.
27 2 Sam 10:12//1 Chr 19:13; 2 Kgs 22:13//2 Chr 34:21.
28 2 Kgs 11:18–20//2 Chr 23:17–21; 2 Kgs 21:3//2 Chr 33:3.
29 2 Sam 6:6; 24:22//1 Chr 13:9; 21:23; 1 Kgs 7:25; 8:63//2 Chr 4:4; 7:5.
30 2 Sam 5:17//1 Chr 14:8; 1 Kgs 10:24//2 Chr 9:23.
31 2 Sam 12:31//1 Chr 20:3; 1 Kgs 22:11//2 Chr 18:10.
32 2 Sam 6:12, 18, 20; 7:29; 8:10//1 Chr 13:14; 16:2, 43; 17:27; 18:10; 1 Kgs 8:14//2 Chr 6:3.
33 1 Kgs 10:2, 10, 10, 25//2 Chr 9:1, 9, 9, 24; 2 Kgs 20:13//2 Chr 32:27.
34 2 Sam 8:13//1 Chr 18:12; 2 Kgs 14:7//2 Chr 25:11.
35 1 Kgs 3:4//2 Chr 1:3; 2 Kgs 16:4//2 Chr 28:4 (Solomon at a great במה and Ahaz בבמות).
36 2 Sam 5:10//1 Chr 11:9; 1 Kgs 10:23//2 Chr 9:22.
37 1 Kgs 22:31//2 Chr 18:30; 2 Kgs 23:2//2 Chr 34:30.
38 2 Sam 7:23; 8:11//1 Chr 17:21; 18:11; 2 Kgs 18:33; 19:12//2 Chr 32:14.
39 2 Sam 6:6; 24:16, 18, 21, 24//1 Chr 13:9; 21:15, 18, 21, 22; 1 Kgs 22:10//2 Chr 18:9.

(continued)

דבר[40]	David	Solomon
דרש\הנביא[ה][41]	Jehoshaphat	Josiah
הלך בדרך בית אחאב[42]	Jehoram	Ahaziah
הרג[43]	David	Joash
זבח[44]	David	Solomon
זבח[45] piel	Solomon	Ahaz
זקני ישראל[46]	David	Solomon
זקנים[47]	Rehoboam	Josiah
חבא\ה[48]	Jehoshaphat	Joash
חדל[49]	Asa	Jehoshaphat
חדר[50]	Jehoshaphat	Joash
חומה\חומת ירושלם[51]	Amaziah	Hezekiah
חזק[52] piel	Joash	Josiah
חלל[ים][53]	Saul	David
חנית[54] cf הרג	David	Joash
חסד[55]	David	Solomon
חק\חקה[56]	Solomon	Josiah

40 2 Sam 24:13//1 Chr 21:12; 1 Kgs 8:37//2 Chr 6:28.
41 1 Kgs 22:5, 7, 8//2 Chr 18:4, 6, 7; 2 Kgs 22:13, 18//2 Chr 34:21, 26.
42 2 Kgs 8:18//2 Chr 21:6; 2 Kgs 8:27//2 Chr 22:3.
43 2 Sam 10:18; 23:21//1 Chr 19:18; 11:23; 2 Kgs 11:18//2 Chr 23:17.
44 2 Sam 6:13//1 Chr 15:26; 1 Kgs 8:62, 63//2 Chr 7:4, 5.
45 1 Kgs 8:5//2 Chr 5:6; 2 Kgs 16:4//2 Chr 28:4.
46 2 Sam 5:3//1 Chr 11:3; 1 Kgs 8:1//2 Chr 5:2.
47 1 Kgs 12:6, 8, 13//2 Chr 10:6, 8, 13; 2 Kgs 23:1//2 Chr 34:29.
48 1 Kgs 22:25//2 Chr 18:24; 2 Kgs 11:3//2 Chr 22:12.
49 1 Kgs 15:21//2 Chr 16:5; 1 Kgs 22:6, 15//2 Chr 18:5, 14. Subject both times is a king of Israel.
50 1 Kgs 22:25//2 Chr 18:24; 2 Kgs 11:2//2 Chr 22:11.
51 2 Kgs 14:13//2 Chr 25:23; 2 Kgs 18:26//2 Chr 32:18.
52 2 Kgs 12//2 Chr 24; 2 Kgs 22:5, 6//2 Chr 34:8, 10.
53 1 Sam 31:1//1 Chr 10:1; 2 Sam 23:8, 18//1 Chr 11:11, 20.
54 2 Sam 21:19; 23:21//1 Chr 20:5; 11:23; 2 Kgs 11:10//2 Chr 23:9.
55 2 Sam 7:15; 10:2//1 Chr 17:13; 19:2; 1 Kgs 3:6; 8:23//2 Chr 1:8; 6:14.
56 1 Kgs 9:4//2 Chr 7:17; 2 Kgs 23:3//2 Chr 34:31.

(continued)

חצר[57]	Solomon	Manasseh
חקר[58]	David	Solomon
חרף[59]	David	Hezekiah
יבסי[60]	David	Solomon
צאת ובא[61]	David	Solomon
בירושלם אשים את־שמי[62]	Rehoboam	Manasseh
בירושלם אשר בחר יהוה\ בחרתי מכל שבטי ישראל לשום את־שמו\י[63]	Rehoboam	Manasseh
הוריש יהוה מפני[64]	Ahaz	Manasseh
הושע[65]	David	Hezekiah
הכהן[66] PN	Joash	Josiah
כנרות ונבלים[67]	David	Solomon
הכעיס[68]	Manasseh	Josiah
כרוב[ים][69]	David	Solomon
כרת ברית[70]	David	Joash + Josiah
מכתף הבית הפנמית[71]	Solomon	Joash

57 1 Kgs 8:64//2 Chr 7:7; 2 Kgs 21:5//2 Chr 33:5.
58 2 Sam 10:3//1 Chr 19:3; 1 Kgs 7:47//2 Chr 4:18.
59 2 Sam 21:21//1 Chr 20:7; 2 Kgs 19:4, 16, 22, 23//2 Chr 32:17.
60 2 Sam 5:6, 8; 24:16, 18//1 Chr 11:4, 6; 21:15, 18; 1 Kgs 9:20//2 Chr 8:7.
61 2 Sam 5:2//1 Chr 11:2; 1 Kgs 3:7//2 Chr 1:10.
62 1 Kgs 14:21//2 Chr 12:13; 2 Kgs 21:4//2 Chr 33:4.
63 1 Kgs 14:21//2 Chr 12:13; 2 Kgs 21:7//2 Chr 33:7.
64 2 Kgs 16:3//2 Chr 28:3; 2 Kgs 21:2//2 Chr 33:2.
65 2 Sam 8:6, 14; 10:11, 19//1 Chr 18:6, 13; 19:12, 19; and 23:10//11:14 (תשועה); 2 Kgs 19:19, 34//2 Chr 32:22.
66 2 Kgs 11:9, 10, 15; 12:3, 6, 11//2 Chr 23:8, 9, 14; 24:2, 5, 11; 2 Kgs 22:4//2 Chr 34:9 – כהן is + in 2 Kgs 12:7, 8, 9, 10(2×), 17; 22:8, 12, 14.
67 2 Sam 6:5//1 Chr 13:8; 1 Kgs 10:12//2 Chr 9:11.
68 2 Kgs 21:6//2 Chr 33:6; 2 Kgs 22:17//2 Chr 34:25.
69 2 Sam 6:2//1 Chr 13:6; 1 Kgs 6–8//2 Chr 3–5.
70 2 Sam 5:3//1 Chr 11:3; 2 Kgs 11:4, 17//2 Chr 23:3, 16.
71 1 Kgs 7:39//2 Chr 4:10; 2 Kgs 11:11//2 Chr 23:10.

(continued)

בלילה[72]	David	Solomon
לכיש[73]	Amaziah	Hezekiah
מגנים[74]	Solomon	Rehoboam
מלאך יהוה[75]	David	Hezekiah
עשי המלאכה[76]	Joash	Josiah
מנה[77]	David	Solomon
מנחה[78]	David	Solomon
מעשה ידי אדם[79]	Hezekiah	Josiah
משח[80]	David	Joash
נא[81]	David	Jehoshaphat
נביא[82]	David	Hezekiah
נביא[ה][83]	Jehoshaphat	Josiah
נגע[84]	Solomon [n]	Azariah [piel]
נוס + נגף[85]	David	Amaziah
נפש[86]	David	Solomon

72 2 Sam 7:4//1 Chr 17:3; 1 Kgs 3:5; 8,28//2 Chr 1:7; 6:20.
73 2 Kgs 14:19//2 Chr 25:27; 2 Kgs 18:17//2 Chr 32:9.
74 1 Kgs 10:17//2 Chr 9:16; 1 Kgs 14:26–27//2 Chr 12:9–10 – there are no other dedicated shields in Sam-Kgs.
75 2 Sam 24:16//1 Chr 21:15–16; 2 Kgs 19:35//2 Chr 32:21.
76 2 Kgs 12:12, 15, 16//2 Chr 24:12, 13; 2 Kgs 22:5, 9//2 Chr 34:10, 12, 13, 17 – compare 1 Kgs 7:40// 2 Chr 4:11; however, the similar but non-synoptic expressions relating to Solomon's projects in 1 Kgs 9:23 and 2 Chr 8:9 appear secondary.
77 2 Sam 24:1//1 Chr 21:1; 1 Kgs 8:5//2 Chr 5:6.
78 2 Sam 8:2, 6//1 Chr 18:2, 6; 1 Kgs 10:25//2 Chr 9:24.
79 2 Kgs 19:18//2 Chr 32:19; 2 Kgs 22:17//2 Chr 34:25.
80 2 Sam 5:3, 17//1 Chr 11:3; 14:8; 2 Kgs 11:12//2 Chr 23:11.
81 2 Sam 24:10, 14, 17//1 Chr 21:8, 13, 17; 1 Kgs 22:5, 13//2 Chr 18:4, 12. Both versions of Solomon's prayer attest it, but at different points (1 Kgs 8:26 and 2 Chr 6:40.)
82 2 Sam 7:2//1 Chr 17:1; 2 Kgs 19:2//2 Chr 32:20.
83 1 Kgs 22:7//2 Chr 18:6; 2 Kgs 22:14//2 Chr 34:22.
84 1 Kgs 8:37//2 Chr 6:28; 2 Kgs 15:5//2 Chr 26:20.
85 2 Sam 10:15–18//1 Chr 19:16–19; 2 Kgs 14:12//2 Chr 25:22.
86 2 Sam 23:17//1 Chr 11:19; 1 Kgs 3:11//2 Chr 1:11.

(continued)

נפש\לב[87]	Solomon	Josiah
נשא כלי[88]	Saul	David
הציל[89]	David	Hezekiah
ספר[90]	David	Solomon
סופר[91]	Joash	Josiah
עבד [יהוה][92]	David	Solomon
עון\העוה[93]	David	Solomon
עזב [יהוה] [94]	Solomon	Josiah
עלות[95]	David	Solomon
עמי\עמך\עמו[96]	David	Solomon
Israel as Yhwh's עם[97]	David	Joash
על־העמוד[98]	Joash	Josiah
עציון־גבר[99]	Solomon	Jehoshaphat
נעצר[100]	David	Solomon
עשה משפט וצדקה[101]	David	Solomon
פלשתים[102]	Saul	David

87 1 Kgs 8:48//2 Chr 6:38; 2 Kgs 23:3//2 Chr 34:31.

88 1 Sam 31:4, 4, 5//1 Chr 10:4, 4, 5; 2 Sam 23:37//1 Chr 11:39.

89 2 Sam 23:12//1 Chr 11:14; 2 Kgs 18–20 (9×)//2 Chr 32 (8×).

90 2 Sam 24:2//1 Chr 21:2; 1 Kgs 8:5//2 Chr 5:6.

91 2 Kgs 12:11//2 Chr 24:11; 2 Kgs 22:9, 10, 12//2 Chr 34:16, 18, 20.

92 2 Sam 7:5, 8, 19, 20, 21, 25, 26, 27, 28, 29//1 Chr 17:4, 7, 17, 18, 19, 23, 24, 25, 26, 27; 24:10//1 Chr 21:8; 1 Kgs 8:24, 25, 26, 28, 29, 30//2 Chr 6:15, 16, 17, 19, 20, 21 – and 2 Kgs 8:19 (but not 2 Chr 21:7).

93 2 Sam 24:10//1 Chr 21:8; 1 Kgs 8:47//2 Chr 6:37.

94 1 Kgs 9:9, 6//2 Chr 7:22, 19; 2 Kgs 22:17; 23:3//2 Chr 34:25, 31.

95 2 Sam 6:17–18; 24:22, 24, 25//1 Chr 16:1–2; 21:23, 24, 26; 1 Kgs 3:4; 8:64; 9:25//2 Chr 1:6; 7:7; 8:12.

96 2 Sam 5:2, 12; 7:7, 8, 10, 11, 23, 24; 8:15//1 Chr 11:2; 14:2; 17:6, 7, 9, 10, 21, 22; 18:14; 1 Kgs 3:9; 8:16, 33, 34, 38, 44//2 Chr 1:10; 6:6, 24, 25, 29, 34.

97 2 Sam 7:24//1 Chr 17:22; 2 Kgs 11:17//2 Chr 23:16.

98 2 Kgs 11:14//2 Chr 23:13; 2 Kgs 23:3//2 Chr 34:31 (LXX).

99 1 Kgs 9:27; 10:22//2 Chr 8:18; 9:21; 1 Kgs 22:49–50//2 Chr 20:36–37.

100 2 Sam 24:21//1 Chr 21:22; 1 Kgs 8:35//2 Chr 6:26.

101 2 Sam 8:15//1 Chr 18:14; 1 Kgs 10:9//2 Chr 9:8; and משפט on its own occurs only in 1 Kgs 8:45, 49; 9:4//2 Chr 6:35, 39; 7:17.

102 1 Sam 31//1 Chr 10; 2 Sam 5; 8; 23//1 Chr 11; 18; 20.

(continued)

פקד[103] qal	David	Joash
פרץ[104]	David	Amaziah
פרשים[105]	David	Solomon
צאן[106]	David	Jehoshaphat
צבא השמים[107]	Jehoshaphat	Manasseh
ציון[108]	David	Solomon
מצות[109]	Solomon	Josiah
[מלך] צר[110]	David	Solomon
צרר[111]	David	Solomon
הקדיש[112]	David	Solomon
ויבא את־קדשי אביו כסף וזהב וכלים[113]	Solomon	Asa
הקהיל[114]	Solomon	Rehoboam
קטר[115]	Ahaz	Josiah
קנה[116]	David	Josiah
קרע\בגדים[117]	Joash	Josiah
קשת[118]	Saul	Jehoshaphat
ראמת גלעד[119]	Jehoshaphat	Ahaziah

103 2 Sam 24:2, 4//1 Chr 21:6; 2 Chr 11:15//2 Chr 23:14.
104 2 Sam 5:20; 6:8//1 Chr 14:11; 13:11; 2 Kgs 14:13//2 Chr 25:23.
105 2 Sam 8:4//1 Chr 18:4; 1 Kgs 10:26//2 Chr 1:14.
106 2 Sam 24:17//1 Chr 21:17; 1 Kgs 22:17//2 Chr 18:16.
107 1 Kgs 22:19//2 Chr 18:18; 2 Kgs 21:3//2 Chr 33:3.
108 2 Sam 5:7//1 Chr 11:5; 1 Kgs 8:1//2 Chr 5:2.
109 1 Kgs 9:9, 6//2 Chr 7:22, 19; 2 Kgs 22:17; 23:3//2 Chr 34:25, 31.
110 2 Sam 5:11//1 Chr 14:1; 1 Kgs 5:15//2 Chr 2:10.
111 2 Sam 24:14//1 Chr 21:13; 1 Kgs 8:37//2 Chr 6:28.
112 2 Sam 8:11//1 Chr 18:11; 1 Kgs 9:3, 7//2 Chr 7:16, 20.
113 1 Kgs 7:51//2 Chr 5:1; 1 Kgs 15:15//2 Chr 15:18.
114 1 Kgs 8:1//2 Chr 5:2; 1 Kgs 12:21//2 Chr 11:1.
115 2 Kgs 16:4//2 Chr 28:4; 2 Kgs 22:17//2 Chr 34:25.
116 2 Sam 24:24//1 Chr 21:24; 2 Kgs 22:6//2 Chr 34:11.
117 2 Kgs 11,14//2 Chr 23,13; 2 Kgs 22,11.19//2 Chr 34,19.27.
118 1 Sam 31:3//1 Chr 10:3; 1 Kgs 22:34//2 Chr 18:33.
119 1 Kgs 22:3, 4, 15, 20//2 Chr 18:2, 3, 14, 19; 2 Kgs 8:28//2 Chr 22:5.

(continued)

רחוק[120]	David	Solomon
רכב[121] (cum פרשים)	David	Solomon
שרי הרכב[122]	Jehoshaphat	Jehoram
הרכיב[123]	David	Josiah
רעה[124]	David	Jehoshaphat
רצים[125]	Rehoboam	Joash
שלמה[126]	Solomon	Rehoboam (not C)
שמחים[127]	Solomon	Joash
שרף[128]	Asa	Josiah
שאל obj Yahweh[129]	David	Solomon
שאל obj king[130]	David	Solomon
השתחוה[131]	David	Hezekiah
other gods השתחוה[132]	Solomon	Manasseh
השחית[133]	David	Jehoram
שכן[134] (cf משכן)	David	Solomon
בשלום[135]	Jehoshaphat	Josiah
שלטים[136]	David	Joash

120 2 Sam 7:19//1 Chr 17:17; 1 Kgs 8:41, 46//2 Chr 6:32, 36
121 2 Sam 8:4//1 Chr 18:4; 1 Kgs 9:19; 10:26//2 Chr 8:6; 1:14.
122 1 Kgs 22:31, 32, 33//2 Chr 18:30, 31, 32; 2 Kgs 8:21//2 Chr 21:9.
123 2 Sam 6:3//1 Chr 13:7; 2 Kgs 23:30//2 Chr 35:24.
124 2 Sam 5:2; 7:7//1 Chr 11:2; 17:6; 1 Kgs 22:17//2 Chr 18:16.
125 1 Kgs 14:27–28//2 Chr 12:10–11; 2 Kgs 11:13//2 Chr 23:12.
126 1 Kgs 10:25//2 Chr 9:24; 1 Kgs 11:29–30 and 3 Kgdms 12:24o.
127 1 Kgs 8:64//2 Chr 7:10; 2 Kgs 11:14//2 Chr 23:13. Cognate שמחה is used in the synoptic ark narrative (2 Sam 6:12//1 Chr 15:25).
128 1 Kgs 15:13//2 Chr 15:16; 2 Kgs 23:20 and 2 Chr 34:5.
129 2 Sam 5:19, 23//1 Chr 14:10, 14; 1 Kgs 3:4–15//2 Chr 1:7–13.
130 2 Sam 8:10//1 Chr 18:10; 1 Kgs 10:13//2 Chr 9:12.
131 2 Sam 24:20//1 Chr 21:21; 2 Kgs 18:22//2 Chr 32:12.
132 1 Kgs 9:6, 9//2 Chr 7:19, 22; 2 Kgs 21:3//2 Chr 33:3.
133 2 Sam 11:1; 24:16//1 Chr 20:1; 21:15; 2 Kgs 8:19//2 Chr 21:7.
134 2 Sam 7:10//1 Chr 17:9; 1 Kgs 8:12//2 Chr 6:1.
135 1 Kgs 22:17, 27, 28//2 Chr 18:16, 26, 27; 2 Kgs 22:20//2 Chr 34:28.
136 2 Sam 8:7//1 Chr 18:7; 2 Kgs 11:10//2 Chr 23:9.

(continued)

שלמים[137]	David	Solomon
שלשים[138]	David	Solomon
בשם יהוה[139]	David	Jehoshaphat
שפט[140]	Solomon	Jotham
משקל[141]	David	Solomon
תועבת הגוים[142]	Ahaz	Manasseh
תרשיש[143]	Solomon	Jehoshaphat

5 An exception and a rule

There are many discrepancies between Sam-Kgs and Chr within broadly synoptic contexts and of course many differences in each of these books between MT and the main ancient versions. Both sorts of difference are particularly prevalent in the Solomon narratives. Remarkably, however, the many dozens of patterned pairings listed above appear text-critically reliable. Half of them (some 60) involve the Solomon narratives: around 40 of these compare and contrast him with David and some 20 with several of their successors. To prove the textual stability rule, I cite the sole exception. Concerning the labour force that Solomon recruited from the non-Israelite left-over peoples, we read:

1 Kgs 9:21 בניהם אשר נתרו אחריהם בארץ אשר לא־יכלו בני ישראל להחרימם
2 Chr 8:8 מן־בניהם אשר נותרו אחריהם בארץ אשר לא־כלום בני ישראל

These texts share כ־ל־ו exactly where they begin to differ. As the shorter version of the two, the Chronicler's may well be primary; but the issue here is more interesting than priority. החרים is used in just one other synoptic context: the Assyrian envoy will talk of the lands or nations that his people had *put to the*

137 2 Sam 6:17–18//1 Chr 16:1–2; 1 Kgs 8:64//2 Chr 7:7.
138 2 Sam 23:8//1 Chr 11:11; 1 Kgs 9:22//2 Chr 8:9.
139 2 Sam 6:18//1 Chr 16:2; 1 Kgs 22:16//2 Chr 18:15.
140 1 Kgs 3:9; 8:32//2 Chr 1:10; 6:23; 2 Kgs 15:5//2 Chr 26:21.
141 2 Sam 12:30; 21:16//1 Chr 20:2; 1 Kgs 7:47; 10:14//2 Chr 4:18; 9:13.
142 2 Kgs 16:3//2 Chr 28:3; 2 Kgs 21:2//2 Chr 33:2.
143 1 Kgs 9:27; 10:22//2 Chr 8:18; 9:21; 1 Kgs 22:49–50//2 Chr 20:36–37.

ban (2 Kgs 19:11//2 Chr 32:14). And כלה piel is also used in just one other synoptic context: Zedekiah wearing his iron horns will say (1 Kgs 22:11//2 Chr 18:10), 'With these you will gore Aram till *finishing them off*.' Each textual option in the Solomon narrative is part of its own unique pairing. This exception that proves one rule is at the same time an exception *within* the rules.

There are at least two further 'wheels within this wheel': (1) In the 'main text' of Greek Kings, most of this portion of text is found, not following 9:9, but after 10:22. (2) Of all the notes in the compendious 'miscellanies' in the Greek text of 1 Kgs [3 Kgdms] 2, the only materials that feature also in Chronicles are parts of 2 Chr 8:1–16 (the broadly synoptic parallel to 1 Kgs 9:10–25 MT). The correspondences are as follows:

3 Kgdms	1 Kgs	2 Chr	Topic
2:35f2	9:24a	8:11a	Pharaoh's daughter to her own house
2:35g	9:25	8:12	Offerings 3× per year
2:35h	9:23	8:10	Solomon's chief officers
2:35i	9:15–19	8:5b–6	Towns built by Solomon
2:46d	9:18	8:6	Baalath etc

Granted the very different arrangement of the Solomon story in 1 Kgs 1–11 and 3 Kgdms 1–11 and 2 Chr 1–9, it is remarkable that almost all sixty or so words and phrases with a unique 'paired partner' in the records of other kings appear in the same relative order in otherwise diverse Solomon narratives. They seem part of an established core. In such a context, this paragraph about the non-Israelite labour force may have been a late comer to an already settled synoptic text: a late comer looking for the right place, for the right wording, for the right paired partner. Whatever the answer, לא כלום\לא יכלו להחרימם (1 Kgs 9:21//3 Kgdms 10:22b//2 Chr 8:8) is a 1 in 130 exception.

6 Amaziah and Hezekiah

The distinctiveness of the synoptic material over against the wording of Sam-Kgs is objectively measurable. The proposal that it is also the seedbed from which much of Sam-Kgs developed may be suggestive but cannot be demonstrated with the same level of objectivity. However, the existence of well over one hundred unique verbal pairings, text-critically assured, and many of them in clusters, is – like the distinctiveness of the synoptic material – a simple matter of fact. In many cases the clustering of *identical* pairs encourages our detection of additional relevant comparators. The case of Amaziah and Hezekiah is instructive. Only they reigned for 29 years after coming to the throne aged 25; and Lachish appears only in connection with them. These are simple textual facts: they are incontrovertible. Next, their names אמציהו and חזקיהו have very similar meanings: חזק ואמץ is a familiar formula of encouragement. The evidence provided by identical or very similar wording may stop there, but the links continue. Both kings had seen Jerusalem in danger, both had received and ignored 'advice' from their enemies (Jehoash in his parable of the trees and Sennacherib's envoy by the walls of Jerusalem), and each of the enemy kings who had threatened their capitol had died soon afterwards. The comparison of these two kings operates at several different levels.

Beyond these many shared elements, the synoptic report on Amaziah makes very effective use of one of the distinctive features of the whole 'text' shared by Sam-Kgs and Chr: a very sparing use of 'life' and 'live'.[144] Only in this narrative is it used twice. Jehoash warns Amaziah that the thorn bush that represents him in his tale of the trees will be trampled by a wild animal – literally, a 'field *life*' (חית השדה). In the short term, the king of Israel's prediction comes true: he defeats Amaziah and seizes treasures from Jerusalem. However, Jehoash of Israel then dies, while Amaziah '*lived* on' (ויחי) for 15 years after his death. This paradoxical story of the (initially successful) *life*-force that is itself out-*lived* obviously appealed to the imagination of the authors of Kings and Chronicles and was quite differently developed by each.

The Chronicler is even more economical with the 'life' word than his sparing source: he adds only two more cases. One of these supplies a third instance to the Amaziah story.[145] That king, after defeating Edom, had 10,000 prisoners thrown *living* (חיים) from a rock: Amaziah hardly deserved his own more generous fate after defeat by Israel. The author of Kings, by contrast, developed the several intricate connections between Amaziah and Hezekiah that he inherited by making two linked additions in his Hezekiah story, each based on Amaziah living on for 15 years. (1) He dated Sennacherib's attack on Judah to the 14th year of Hezekiah – on the understanding that he like Amaziah would have 15 more years before dying in the 29th year of his reign. (2) He made 'live' and 'life' into one of the key themes of his expansively rewritten account of that king[146] – that 'life' word that is so rare in synoptic texts, though used twice in the Amaziah

144 1 Kgs 8:40//2 Chr 6:31; 1 Kgs 12:6//2 Chr 10:6; 1 Kgs 22:14//2 Chr 18:13; 2 Kgs 11:12//2 Chr 23:11; 2 Kgs 14:9, 17//2 Chr 25:18, 25.

145 2 Chr 25:12; the other is in 2 Chr 14:13.

146 In four verses shared by Kgs and Isa (2 Kgs 19:4, 16; 20:1, 7//Isa 37:4, 17; 38:1, 21) and also in separate pluses (2 Kgs 18:32; Isa 38:9, 16, 20). See more fully Auld 2017, 163–189.

story, and completely absent from Chr's version of Hezekiah. As we have just observed, far from tending to remove 'life' from his source, Chr was able to add it very effectively. The synoptic tale of Amaziah had been told very effectively, so encouraging similarly effective re-tellings.

7 Dates

Studying Kings and Chronicles from the perspective of the temporal material they share is doubly informative. On the one side, imprecise expressions like 'then' (אז) and 'afterwards' (אחרי־כן) are used more often in synoptic than non-synoptic texts (Auld 2014). On the other, both Kgs and Chr introduce more precision as they rewrite narratives from the older synoptic history. Asa becomes ill in his old age in 1 Kgs 15:23, but in the 39th of the 41 years of his reign in 2 Chr 16:12. Chr dates activities to Hezekiah's 1st year (2 Chr 29:3) and Josiah's 8th year (2 Chr 34:3) that are not found in Kgs. In the opposite direction, priestly failure to repair the temple leads to royal action dated to the 23rd year of Joash in 2 Kgs 12:7, but not in synoptic 2 Chr 24:5. However, the date-formula used, ויהי בשנת עשרים ושלש שנה למלך יהואש (with a second שנה), is never found in Chronicles but is a frequent element of synchronistic instructions throughout Kgs.[147] It was a feature of the creation of the book of Kings, when an account of the north-Israelite monarchy was interwoven with the (synoptic) story of Jerusalem. Since the very same date marks the accession in Samaria of Jehoahaz (2 Kgs 13:1), some relationship may have been intended (Auld 2017, 250). As with שחד just discussed, this date was added to the source narrative by the author of Kings, not subtracted by the author of Chronicles.

Most synoptic chronological details concern the age of each king at accession and the length of his reign. However, a few precise dates are also provided *within* royal reports. The first of these concerns the start of building the temple and is wholly exceptional in its detail – not just in the 4th *year* of Solomon's reign, but in the 2nd *month* of that year (1 Kgs 6:1//2 Chr 3:2). A second instance of precision within a royal report is the note that Amaziah lived for fifteen years after the death of Jehoash of Israel who had defeated him (2 Kgs 14:17//2 Chr 25:25). Kings and Chronicles share only two more dates, each stated as 'year x of King N': the 5th year of Rehoboam saw Shishak king of Egypt going up (עלה) against Jerusalem (1 Kgs 14:25//2 Chr 12:2); and Josiah in his 18th year began repairs to the temple and also held a Passover as specified in the book found during this maintenance.

147 1 Kgs 16:8, 15, 23; 2 Kgs 8:25; 13:1, 10; 14:23; 15:1, 8, 13, 17, 23, 27; 16:1.

Given the many paired patterns in the synoptic text, we should not be surprised that the Josiah story ends with the only other synoptic king of Egypt 'going up' (עלה, 2 Kgs 23:29//2 Chr 35:20) – and with even more disastrous consequences for Josiah.

8 Compare and contrast

Na'aman identifies clusters of similarities between Ahaz, Hezekiah, Manasseh, Amon, and Josiah and five of their predecessors. Such clusters – contrasting as well as comparing – are operative from the very start of the synoptic narrative. The table above demonstrates how these are signalled lexically. *Philistines* are responsible for Saul's death and reappear (in a very different role) only in narratives about David. This contrasting pairing is underscored further through word choices: many men of Israel fall (fatally) *pierced through* (חללים) by Philistines and are stripped by them, while Philistines are pierced through by David's heroes. חללים is found in synoptic material only in 1 Sam 31//1 Chr 10 and 2 Sam 23//1 Chr 11; and that is also true of נשא כלים (*armour-bearer/bodyguard*).[148] The proximity of these paired terms in the Chronicler's account of Saul and David (1 Chr 10 and 11) may reflect the synoptic source better than their separation in Samuel (1 Sam 31 and 2 Sam 23). As with Amaziah and Hezekiah (6 above), explicit lexical pairings invite exploring implicit comparisons or contrasts nearby. In synoptic texts, גברים appear only in narratives about David.[149] Listing dozens of David's *heroes* in 2 Sam 23//1 Chr 11 underscores the relative solitariness of Saul and his sons as they perish on Gilboa, where no heroes of Israel are listed in their company.

Some comparisons are of more distant kings. Defeating many thousands of Edomites in 'Salt Valley' is attributed to King Amaziah in 2 Kgs 14:7//2 Chr 25:11 but also to (three figures in) the Davidic period: to David himself in 2 Sam 8:13, to Abishai in synoptic 1 Chr 18:12, and to Joab in Ps 60:2. Only these four closely linked notes in HB describe the Dead Sea region as Salt Valley (גיא מלח). More important: within synoptic material, only reports relating to David and Amaziah use פרץ (burst through)[150] or describe defeat in terms of נגף (be smitten) followed by נוס (flee).[151] Either a memory of Davidic times was reassigned to Amaziah or, perhaps more likely, part of the Amaziah record found three different

148 חלל[ים] in 1 Sam 31:1, 8//1 Chr 10:1, 8 and 2 Sam 23:8, 18//1 Chr 11:11, 20; and נשא כלי in 1 Sam 31:4–5//1 Chr 10:4–5 and 2 Sam 23:37//1 Chr 11:39.

149 2 Sam 10:7; 23:8, 9, 22//1 Chr 19:8; 11:11, 12, 24.

150 2 Sam 5:20; 6:8//1 Chr 13:11; 14:11 and 2 Chr 14:13//2 Chr 25:23.

151 2 Sam 10:13–19//1 Chr 19:13–19 and 2 Kgs 14:12//2 Chr 25:22.

echoes in memories of more ancient times. Jehoshaphat features in two similar unique links, one forwards and one backwards in time. Jehoshaphat and Solomon shared a concern for *shipping* (אני[ות]). The relevant reports include unique mention of *Ezion-geber* (עציון־גבר),[152] showing that the trade was on the Red Sea; and in each case the ships are of *Tarshish* (תרשיש) – presumably specifying their type. Then *Ramoth in Gilead* features synoptically only as goal of two joint expeditions against Aram: one mounted by Jehoshaphat and Ahab and the other by Ahaziah (grandson of Jehoshaphat) and Joram (son of Ahab).[153]

9 Historical caution

This discussion has indicated three cases where we can see the author of Kings at work on his major source. One (7 above) specified a date not provided there (2 Kgs 12:7). Another (3 above) necessitated changing the inherited (synoptic) nomenclature of diplomatic 'gifts' or 'inducements' from מנחה to שחד (2 Kgs 16:8). The third is much more important for today's historians. If King Hezekiah's 14th year (6 above) – reported in 2 Kgs 18:13 (and Isaiah) but not Chronicles – is an exegetical development based on intricate literary patterns already in the source, then it must not be treated as a date from an archive and hence misused. It should *not* be combined with any external date for an Assyrian invasion of Judah in order to compute fixed dates for Hezekiah's accession and death – and especially not, if the period of 29 years attributed to that king's reign was itself part of earlier patterning.

10 Concluding remarks

With Adam we have agreed that presenting Asa and Ahaz in parallel was no innovation by the author of Kings; but against him we have concluded that calling their tribute שחד was part of a later heightening of the parallel. With Adam we agree that the repeated interactions of David's successors with northern Israel were a crucial element of the royal narrative; but against him we see no evidence of formal synchronisms till a later stage in the retelling of Kings.

---

152 1 Kgs 9:27; 10:22//2 Chr 8:18; 9:21; 1 Kgs 22:49–50//2 Chr 20:36–37.

153 1 Kgs 22:3, 4, 15, 20//2 Chr 18:2, 3, 14, 19; 2 Kgs 8:28//2 Chr 22:5. Thought the second narrative is very briefly told, it shares הלך למלחמה – חלה – ויכ־ as well as mention of Ramoth-Gilead, Aram, and Ahab.

With Na'aman we identify interlocking clusters of Jerusalem's kings up to and including Josiah; however, our even closer attention to word-choice has two benefits: it adds further substance to comparisons based on narrative content and more stereotyped terminology; and it shows that the clustering starts not with Asa but already with the death of Saul. Na'aman's work shows that the accounts of the five kings from Ahaz to Josiah had helped [re]shape those of their predecessors. This in turn may make it more likely that Amaziah's exploits in Edom and Jehoshaphat's on the Red Sea were prior to their parallels in the time of David and Solomon. Na'aman (2017, 86) repeats his earlier argument that 'the story of Athaliah and Jehoash is a late composition, written to provide an equivalent Judahite story to Jehu's rebellion'. In turn, I prefer to adhere to the opposite view (Auld 2017, 122–124).

Adam writes of his synchronistic chronicle and Na'aman of the integrated clusters of narratives as *sources* of the book of Kings. I have used similar language in the past but prefer now to describe the synoptic narrative as an earlier *version* of that book. It is not source-material from which an author drew but rather a substantial draft that later authors reworked. It is not so much a mine of information as a text woven with rich texture. It may be possible to identify still earlier stages and even sources. But the material shared by Kings and Chronicles is more like a snapshot of one stage in the process of writing Kings. Clustered pairings were already a major element in what made that draft succeed as a literate text; and they continued to multiply as it was rewritten. Specifying the sending of silver and gold to foreign powers on two occasions as שחד and bringing Hezekiah into even closer paired convergence with Amaziah were just two samples of expanding the synoptic narrative towards Kings. Both additions advanced the 'pairing dynamic' of the older text.

Reading Solomon with Three Eyes Open

1 Introduction

In the previous essay, I argued that '[w]hen probing sources of the Jerusalem royal narrative, the safest starting point is where Kgs and Chr agree' but recognised that '[c]onfidence is impossible over the exact shape of the text that underlies them' (p. 151). I provided a list of 134 words and phrases, each used in the synoptic reports of only two of Jerusalem's kings. חדל (desist), for example, is used only in the reports of Asa and Jehoshaphat[1] – in each case about a king of Israel: Baasha desisted from his attack on Judah, when Asa bought help from Aram; and Ahab, after inviting help from Jehoshaphat, asked for prophetic advice whether he should attack Aram or desist. The shared word helps us focus on the artistry of the telling. Then it is only in the synoptic reports of the same Asa and Jehoshaphat that we are told about the continued existence of 'high places' (הבמות לא סרו)[2] – Kgs and Chr developed differently this common inheritance (Auld 2017, 70–76). My conclusion in the previous essay (p. 159) was that such 'implicit comparisons and contrasts are the very DNA of the synoptic material'.

Almost half (65) of the listed pairs compare or contrast Solomon with either David (43) or one or other of eleven of his successors (22). Remarkably, despite the many differences between 1 Kgs 1–11 (MT), 3 Kgdms 1–11 (LXX) and 2 Chr 1–9 over the extent and shaping of the Solomon story, these 65 paired terms are almost all attested in the same relative order in all three witnesses to synoptic Solomon, thereby supporting the view that this shared material should be recognised as 'one stage in the process of writing Kings'.

2 Pharaoh's Daughter, the King of Tyre, and the Queen of Sheba

Solomon's relationship with Hiram of Tyre is introduced in substantial paragraphs in each of 1 Kgs 5:15–25 and 2 Chr 2:2–15. These share a modest substratum of wording that has been expanded in each version. This fresh relationship between Tyre and Jerusalem builds on the fruitful links between Hiram and David; and the report of it introduces one of the most frequently recurring themes of the Solomon story: building a house. Hiram commits a master craftsman to work

1 1 Kgs 15:21//2 Chr 16:5; 1 Kgs 22:6, 15//2 Chr 18:5, 14.
2 1 Kgs 15:14//2 Chr 15:17; 1 Kgs 22:44//2 Chr 20:33.

https://doi.org/10.1515/9783111060279-014

on Solomon's temple project (1 Kgs 7:13–14//2 Chr 2:13–14) whose role in the process is twice explicitly specified (1 Kgs 7:40, 45//2 Chr 4:11, 16). Cities are passed between Hiram and Solomon (9:10–14//8:1–2); and three brief notes report their shared maritime trade (9:26–28; 10:11–12, 21–22//8:17–18; 9:10–11, 20–21). The first two of these notes about their merchant fleets bracket a fuller report about the visit of the queen of Sheba (10:1–10//9:1–9). While there are many differences between Kgs, Kgdms, and Chr over the order in which they present their narratives on Solomon, Hiram and the Queen of Sheba are synoptic fixed points.

In striking contrast, the daughter of Pharaoh moves round the text as well as moving quarters within Jerusalem; and there are also important differences over what is said about her. In both MT (3:1) and the first 'miscellany' in LXX (2:35c), his Egyptian wife is introduced before the report of Solomon's visit to Gibeon and his vision there, but later – and just before the first mention of the king of Tyre – in the 'standard' Greek text (5:14).

3:1 MT	2:35c LXX	5:14 LXX
ויתחתן שלמה את־פרעה מלך מצרים		
ויקח את־בת פרעה	ויקח את־בת פרעה	ויקח את־בת פרעה לו לאשה
ויביאה אל־עיר דוד	ויביאה אל־עיר דוד	ויביאה אל־עיר דוד
עד כלתו לבנות	עד כלתו	עד כלתו
את־ביתו ואת־בית יהוה	את־ביתו ואת־בית יהוה בראשנה	את־בית יהוה ואת־ביתו
ואת־חומת ירושלם סביב	ואת־חומת ירושלם סביב	ואת־חומת ירושלם

There is ambiguity in 2:35c over Solomon's 'taking' her and bringing her to the city of David; but 5:14 adds that she is taken as his wife and this is also made clear by the prejudicial introduction in 3:1 that Solomon became an in-law of the king of Egypt. She is brought to the city of David till the completion of Solomon's building operations in Jerusalem. Here 5:14 is briefest: 'Yahweh's house and his house and the wall of Jerusalem'. Both 3:1 and 2:35c reverse the order of the houses and add round about after the city wall. 2:35c also adds at first after 'Yahweh's house', leading to further ambiguity: (a) The two houses are completed first and the city wall afterwards. (b) Despite 'his house' being mentioned ahead of 'Yahweh's house' (as also in 3:1), the building of 'Yahweh's house' was of course completed 'at first'.

Though Chr will mention the Egyptian princess later in the Solomon narrative (2 Chr 8:11), he nowhere reports either the fact of the marriage or her arrival in Jerusalem. 'The wall of Jerusalem' (חומת ירושלם) plays no part in Chr's Solomon story and is synoptic only in the reports of Amaziah's defeat by Jehoash of Israel (2 Kgs 14:13//2 Chr 25:23) and of the Hezekiah story (2 Kgs 18:26//2 Chr 32:18). In Kgs (MT), we find the wall in 3:1 and again in 9:15; and it occurs even more frequently (4×) in Kgdms – 2:3/35c, 10/35k; 5:1/14a; 10:23/22a, always and only in connection with Pharaoh's daughter. However, Chr's reason for her relocation is not the progress of Solomon's building work, but ritual appropriateness.

The arrival of the queen of Sheba is reported between the first two notes about Solomon and Hiram co-operating in trade using the port of Ezion-Geber; and a link between their Red Sea operations and Solomon's visitor from the south may well be intended. The Tyre and Sheba narratives are also linked verbally and they share with each other and with Solomon's great prayer a significant connection: the only three instances anywhere in synoptic narrative of 'Yahweh my/your god'. Solomon says 'Yahweh my god' to both Hiram (5:19//2:3) and Yahweh (8:28//6:19); and the queen blesses 'Yahweh your god' to Solomon (10:9//9:8).

Solomon had a further link with Egypt: his trade over horses is another fixed point in the synoptic tradition (10:28//9:28). But no connection is ever suggested between such trade and marriage to a daughter of the Egyptian king. It seems possible, therefore, that this moving element was a later arrival in the Solomon story. The statement in 1 Kgs 3:1a (MT only) that her marriage to Solomon was a case of (unwelcome) 'intermarriage' will have been the latest addition to the tradition. The only element shared with Chr, about her move within Jerusalem to a different house, may have been the first. That short report could well have stood alone; for it contained sufficient information to generate the note about her marriage and arrival in Jerusalem. And like the divergent report about Solomon and the indigenous aliens it is found at a different location in Kgdms from Kgs and Chr.[3]

3 Levites, ark, and Jeroboam

Levites receive only two mentions in the standard book of Kings (MT) – at 1 Kgs 8:4 and 12:31. The first instance is more straightforward. In 3 Kgdms 8:1–5, which is very much briefer than 1 Kgs 8:1–5//2 Chr 5:2–6, Levites play no role in bringing the ark into the new house of Yahweh. In this shorter version, there are only four 'players': king Solomon, the elders of Israel, the priests, and all Israel. In the longer and almost identical texts of Kgs (MT) and Chr, an augmented cast adds heads of tribes (ראשי המטות),[4] patriarchal leaders (נשיאי האבות),[5] Levites, and congregation of Israel (עדת ישראל).[6] It is likely that none of these was repre-

3 1 Kgs 9:20–21 and 24; 3 Kgdms 10:22a and 9:9a; and 2 Chr 8:7–8 and 11.

4 The only other instance in Sam-Kgs of מטה in the sense of 'tribe' is 1 Kgs 7:14; and that is presented differently in 2 Chr 2:13.

5 This combination is unique; but ראשי [ה]אבות, while never in Sam-Kgs, is found in 1 Chr 8:10, 13, 28; 9:9, 33, 34; 15:12; 23:9, 24, 32; 26:21; 27:1; 2 Chr 1:2; 26:12.

6 עדה is not found elsewhere in Chr but is used in 1 Kgs 12:20 as well as widely in Num and Josh.

sented in the Hebrew text of Kings from which the oldest Greek translation was made (Auld 2017, 208–209).

The second instance is more complex. At several points in Kgdms (LXX), we find duplicate traditions: one more like and the other less like the standard text of Kings (MT). It is likely that an older text has been preserved alongside an updated or corrected text. The shorter story of Rehoboam and Jeroboam told in Greek after 1 Kgs/3 Kgdms 12:24 in the standard text has nothing to say at all about cultic innovations at Bethel and Dan, and hence nothing to report about Jeroboam making priests who were not of Levitical stock (as in 1 Kgs 12:31 and similarly in 2 Chr 11:13–15). Scholars have long differed over the relationship between the longer and shorter versions. The shorter is set entirely within the report of Rehoboam's reign. Jeroboam plays an important role in the break-up of Rehoboam's kingdom; but nothing is said about him as subsequent ruler or innovator in the north. In recent discussions, I have supported Adrian Schenker's argument that the shorter account is prior; and I have proposed that it had been drafted for an earlier version of the book of Kings, focused on Jerusalem, that did not yet include the familiar synchronistic account of all the kings of northern Israel.[7]

Levites play a large role in the book of Chronicles – witness the expansive rewriting of (something like) 2 Sam 6 into 1 Chr 13–16 and small additions like 2 Chr 7:6 to the account of Solomon's dedication of the temple. It seems likely that extending the account of bringing the ark into the new temple was of a piece with these although here the textual evidence is different. In 1 Kgs/3 Kgdms 8:1–5, the older text is preserved only in Greek: Kgs MT and Chr exhibit the same expansion.

The text-historical situation relating to Jeroboam is much more complex. 1 Kgs 12:1–19 and 2 Chr 10:1–19 are very similar and jointly present a slightly longer account of the assembly at Shechem than 3 Kgdms 12:25. However, while the shorter story is silent about Jeroboam as a cultic innovator, 1 Kgs 12:28–31 and 2 Chr 13:8–9 offer overlapping accounts of his apostasy that include the appointment of non-Levitical priests.

4 Construction reports: comparing three versions

When we read the accounts of Solomon's major building projects with three eyes open, we find that Kgdms or Chr is normally witness to the shorter and more original text: Chr to its extent, because Kgs/Kgdms has been more expansively

7 See the essays on Jeroboam pp. 109–115 and 117–129 above.

rewritten; Kgdms to its wording, especially where Chr has been co-ordinated with expansive Kgs (as just discussed). Two short portions of the generally briefer Chr have no parallel in Kgs (2 Chr 3:14; 4:7–9). In addition, the two versions sometimes use different terminology for what appear to be the same details.[8]

4.1

All three versions report the same start date, unique within synoptic narrative in its precision: *in the 2nd month* of the 4th year of Solomon's reign; and they are largely in agreement towards the end. Much of the second half of the report in Chr (all of 2 Chr 4:2–6a and 4:10–5:1) appears almost identically in 1 Kgs 7:23–26, 38–51 (3 Kgdms 7:10–13, 24–37). Where Chr is most similar to Kg[dm]s – as over the bronze sea, the ten bowls, the work of Hiram, and the conclusion (some 18 vv. in all) – there is also little difference between Kgs and Kgdms.

4.2

The most prominent differences between Kgs (MT) and Kgdms (LXX) are over material not represented in Chr. The construction of the royal apartments is a prime example: reported in a dozen verses at the start of 1 Kgs 7 but at the end of 3 Kgdms 7. Similarly, though at lesser extent, the preparation of stone and timber is reported before the start date in MT (5:31–32) but after 6:1 in LXX (and not at all in Chr). And there are several MT pluses and one significant LXX plus in 1[3] Kg[dm]s 6, where the material is not represented in Chr. 1 Kgs 6:11–14 is not represented in LXX. 6:11–13 (often called 'Deuteronomistic') in fact anticipate the wording of part of Solomon's second vision (1 Kgs 9:3–5//2 Chr 7:16–18) while 6:14 recapitulates ויבן את־הבית ויכלהו from 6:9a – a standard form of resumption after making an addition to the text.

Although 1 Kgs 6:11–14 is widely recognised as a later addition, it is less often remarked that the end of 6:3 in LXX includes the same formula: 'and he built the house and finished it'. Though not, or no longer, part of the standard Hebrew text, it is very likely that the presence of this formula at the end of 6:3 as well as the start of 6:9 helps identify 6:4–8 as an addition to the text still earlier than 6:11–14. The extension (יציע) it reports surrounding the temple building goes unmentioned in Chr; and in fact יציע is found in HB only in 1 Kgs 6:5, 6, 10. This is now a second portion of text that shares two characteristics with 6:11–14: (a) it

8 חפה piel is used only in Chr – 2 Chr 3:5, 5, 7, 8, 9 (cover, overlay – similar in sense to צפה synoptic in 3:6, 10//6:22, 28; 10:18//9:17; K+ in 1 Kgs 6:15, 15, 20, 20, 21, 21, 22, 30, 32, 35; and C+ in 3:4.

has no correspondent in Chr; and (b) recapitulation of a concluding formula offers evidence that it may have been secondary within Kg[dm]s.

4.3

היכל is always rendered in LXX by *naos* or 'nave' within the temple-construction reports. There are two certain synoptic instances (7:21//3:17 and 7:50//4:22); and the intervening occurrences in 2 Chr 4:7, 8 have no parallel in Kgs. All of 1 Kgs 6:3, 5, 17, 33, however, precede the synoptic pair. Of these, 1 Kgs 6:17 is MT+. In 6:5, both nouns להיכל ולדביר are rendered in LXX, but within a paragraph that may be secondary (see 4.2 above and 4.7 below). Similarly, 1 Kgs 6:33 (MT=LXX), though unproblematic in itself, is part of a long section (6:29–35) unrepresented in Chr (see 4.2 above). As for היכל הבית (6:3), 'nave of the house' is a curious expression and is represented in LXX^{B} by *naos* alone, though LXX^{L} attests היכל יהוה (Yahweh's nave). 2 Chr 3:4 has apparently lost (an expression including) היכל between the two occurrences of על־פני; it should therefore be reckoned a third synoptic instance.

	MT	Kgdms	Chr	
3	והאולם על־פני היכל הבית	והאולם על־פני ההיכל	והאולם אשר על־פני	4
	עשרים אמה ארכו	עשרים באמה ארכו	הארך	
	על־פני רחב הבית	על־פני רחב הבית	על־פני רחב הבית אמות עשרים	
	עשר באמה רחבו על־פני הבית	עשר באמה רחבו על־פני הבית		
			והגבה מאה ועשרים	

Kg[dm]s and Chr agree over the length of the hall (20 cubits); however, only Kg[dm]s specifies its width (10 cubits) and Chr its height (20 cubits – reading מאה as a slip for אמה).

4.4

Some features receive only brief mention in Chr but enjoy extended treatment in Kg[dm]s. The 'stands/supports' (מכונות) under the bowls (כירות) are mentioned in synoptic 1 Kgs 7:43//2 Chr 4:14; but only in 1 Kgs 7:27–37 are they extensively described. Then 2 Chr 3:7b notes briefly that 'he carved cherubim on the walls' (ופתח כרובים על־הקירות); and this topic is treated at length in 1 Kgs 6:29–35. There, while the cognate noun פתוח is used at the start (29), the recurring verb used for 'carve' (on the קירות הבית) is קלע (6:29, 32, 35) with cognate noun מקלעת in 6:29, 32. It appears that the original note has been expansively restated, using a different term for 'carve'. While פתח and פתוח are familiar elsewhere,[9]

9 פתח in Ex 28:9, 11, 36; 39:6; 1 Kgs 7:36; and Zech 3:9; and פתוח in Ex 28:11, 21, 36; 39:6, 14, 30; Zech 3:9; Ps 74:6; 2 Chr 2:6, 13.

the expansion uses a term found outside 1 Kgs 6:29–35 only in 6:18 and 7:31 (both MT plus).[10]

4.5

It is not always clear, in any of the three text-forms under scrutiny here, who is the implied subject of a verb. From one perspective, this may not matter: Solomon is king and ultimately responsible for the great project, while the half-Tyrian is his agent. There are six synoptic instances of ויעש ('and he made'). In none of the first four[11] is it immediately specified who made cherubim, pillars, sea, or bowls. Then Hiram is named in the fifth (7:40//4:11) and Solomon in the sixth (7:48//4:18). Yet there have been apparently secondary moves towards disambiguation in both Kgs (MT) and a strand within Kgdms. In the (main Greek) text of 3 Kgdms 6, the king is not named again after the opening verses. However, Solomon is specified as subject not only in the recapitulations in 1 Kgs 6:11,14 (the MT plus described above) but also in a further short plus in 6:21. Similarly, 3 Kgdms 2:5 reports 'and Solomon *made* the sea etc': a seemingly significant assertion that responsibility lay with the king and not Hiram.

4.6

As just noted, 'and he made' (ויעש) is regularly used to introduce individual elements of the grand project. And this is true not only in the six synoptic instances just noted, but also where Kgs[12] and Chr[13] diverge. In both books, 'build' (בנה) is used at the start of the report,[14] where the whole enterprise is in mind. From this perspective, the synoptic wording is similar to the start of Genesis, where 'created' (ברא) is used of the large project and 'made' of its constituent parts. Yet that is not the whole story in the case of temple-building. Kgs and Chr do diverge once explicitly over a shared topic: we find ויבן 2× in 1 Kgs 6:16 of *building* the *debir*/holy of holies while 2 Chr 3:8 uses ויעש 1× of *making* the holy of holies. Given that we also find 'and he built' (ויבן) in 1 Kgs 6:5, 10, 15, 36 – all material without parallel in Chr – this one explicit divergence over a shared topic is hardly surprising.

---

10 Joosten (Abdn IOSOT) stated that 6:18, though an addition, cannot be late, because it shares מקלעת and פטורי צצים with 6:29. However, the latter is MT+ in 6:29, though attested by LXX in 6:32, 35.)

11 1 Kgs 6:23; 7:18, 23, 38//2 Chr 3:10, 15; 4:2, 6.

12 1 Kgs 6:4, 5; 7:14, 27.

13 2 Chr 3:8, 14, 16, 16; 4:1, 7, 8, 8, 9, 18.

14 1 Kgs 6:1, 2 and 2 Chr 3:1, 2, 3.

4.7

The verb כלה piel (complete/finish) is found synoptically five times, four times in the narratives about David and Solomon where it always functions as a modal verb:[15]

- David blessed his people after *finishing* sacrificing (2 Sam 6:18//1 Chr 16:2).
- Hiram *finished* doing all his appointed task (1 Kgs 7:40//2 Chr 4:11).
- Solomon blessed his people after *finishing* praying at length (1 Kgs 8:54// 2 Chr 7:1).
- After *finishing* building the two houses Solomon received his second vision (1 Kgs 9:1//2 Chr 7:11).

In the fifth synoptic instance, כלה is not modal but independent: the king of Israel was to gore Aram till *finishing* them [off] (1 Kgs 22:11//2 Chr 18:10). The first, third, and fourth instances are of one sort: on the completion of the action described by the grammatically dependent infinitive, something else happens. Each of these two-verb reports about finishing sacrificing (or praying or building) is hence retrospective and transitional. However, the second case is different: Hiram 'finishing doing the task' does not immediately lead to a new topic; instead, it introduces a list of items that constituted the task.

1 Kgs 6:9, 14(MT+) and 3 Kgdms 6:3b(LXX+), 9 all combine the same two verbs: 'and he/Solomon *built* the house and *finished* it' (ויבן [שלמה] את־הבית ויכלהו). But what they say is something different. These non-synoptic summaries about Solomon building and finishing anticipate the *wording* of the fourth synoptic instance (9:1//7:11) but they more closely resemble the *function* of the second (7:40//4:11). In their present context, the function of each non-synoptic instance is not retrospective and transitional, but prospective. Each appears to introduce the next stage of the building work and all look forward to a completion before it has happened. However, read for itself, 'Solomon built the house and finished it' seems instead to draw a line under what has gone before so that the reader expects a move to a fresh topic. We have already observed (4.2 above), that each repetition of this note may have been recapitulatory, after first 6:4–8 and then 6:11–13 were added to the text: the repetition of the formula is a likely indication of a text that has undergone several expansions. We may speculate that an earlier version of the temple story (as in 6:2–3 LXX) simply detailed the measurements of nave and vestibule of Yahweh's house concluding 'and he built Yahweh's house and finished it'. Though some of the measurements differ, this would also enjoy the support of the introduction in 2 Chr 3:1–4. Indeed 'began to build' there (3:2)

15 כלה ל־ should be added to the list of unique pairs in the previous article.

may be a deliberate correction of any precipitate impression of completion suggested by the source-text, so confirming that 1 Kgs 6:3 once included and ended with ויכלהו (as attested in LXX). The pattern of pairings that we have identified (see 1 above) as constituting the DNA of the whole synoptic text may offer one supportive (even if negative) indicator. The 43 pairs unique to the accounts of David and Solomon (now 44 with the addition of כלה ל־ [fn. 15 above]), are spread remarkably evenly through the David story and also through most of the Solomon story but hardly appear in the report of the temple building. Had that originally been much shorter, the discrepancy would have been much less.

4.8

Importing cedar from Lebanon is envisaged in the early exchange of messages between Solomon and Hiram noted in the broadly parallel 1 Kgs 5:13, 22, 24 and 2 Chr 2:2, 7. That Solomon's building work in Jerusalem did utilise cedar can therefore be assumed; yet the actual report in 2 Chr 3–4 makes no mention of this wood. Jeremiah mocks a king who competes by building an extensive house 'covered with cedar' (Jer 22:14–15). Apart from Jer 22:14, only 1 Kgs 7:3, 7 uses the phrase ספון בארז and 1 Kgs 6:10 the related ויספן את־הבית בארזים (and he covered the house with cedar[s]). The wording of Jeremiah's mockery will have served the increasing critique of Solomon in the book of Kings. It will be no accident that three instances of ארז[ים] (1 Kgs 6:15, 16, 36)[16] follow ויבן (see 4.7 above).

4.9

Outside the Solomon story, דביר is used in HB only once (Ps 28:2b) and is intimately linked there with 'holiness', בנשאי ידי אל־דביר קדשך: 'as I raise my hands to your holy *debir* (or '... to the *debir* of your holiness/holy place'). Three instances in the temple narrative are synoptic: 1 Kgs 7:49; 8:6, 8//2 Chr 4:20; 5:7, 9; and two of these are followed (the second immediately) by the only two synoptic instances of קדש הקשדים (7:50; 8:6//4:22; 5:7). 'The most holy' (literally 'the holy of holies') normally refers to the quintessential elements of the sacrificial cult; but in Ezekiel's vision (41:4) קדש הקשדים 'identifies' the innermost part of the restored temple beyond the nave (היכל) – it characterises rather than names this very special space. It seems fair to suppose that the less common דביר would have been glossed by the more common קדש הקשדים (most holy [place]) where it was first used in the text. However, the two synoptic passages that make the equivalence

16 Cedar is also mentioned in 6:18, 36; 7:2, 2, 12.

explicit come towards the end of the temple-building report in both Kgs and Chr. דביר is not explained where we first meet it in 1 Kgs 6:5; and that may add credence to our earlier arguments (4.2 and 4.6 above) that 6:4–8 was a later addition to the building report. Of the other verses including *d*ᵉ*bîr* in 1 Kgs 6, two (6:16, 23) are (broadly) parallel with 2 Chr 3:8, 10. These two verses in Chr, however, use only קדש הקדשים.[17] If even a few of the remainder in Kgs (6:19, 21, 31 plus 20, 22 [MT only]) had been original to the narrative, the explanatory glosses in 7:50; 8:6//4:22; 5:7 would hardly have been necessary. In 6:16 the topic (inner sanctum) at least is synoptic; and there דביר is followed by the only non-synoptic instance in Kgs of קדש הקדשים (but it is widely supposed to be secondary).

4.10
Kgdms as prime witness for the Great Sea and Chr for the Bowls

17 The only non-synoptic instance of דביר in Chr (3:16) is almost certainly a corruption (בדביר there is often corrected to כרביד).

2	ויעש את־הים מוצק	ויעש את־הים	ויעש את־הים מוצק	23
	עשר באמה משפתו אל־שפתו	עשר באמה משפתו אל־שפתו	עשר באמה	
	עגול סביב וחמש באמה קומתו	עגול סביב חמש באמה קומתו	קומתו	
	וקו שלשים באמה	ו שלשים ושלש באמה	וקוה שלשים באמה	
	יסב אתו סביב	יסב אתו סביב	יסב אתו סביב	
3	ודמות בקרים תחת לו סביב	ופקעים מתחת לשפתו	ופקעים מתחת לשפתו	24
	סביב סבבים אתו	סביב סבבים אתו	סביב סבבים אתו	
	עשר באמה מקפים את־הים סביב	עשר באמה מקפים את־הים סביב	עשר באמה מקפים את־הים סביב	
	שנים טורים הבקר	<u>ושפתו כמעשה שפת־כוס</u>	שני טורים הפקעים	
	יצקים במצקתו	<u>פרח שושן ועביו טפח</u>	יצקים ביצקתו	
4	עמד על־שנים עשר בקר	ושני עשר בקר מתחת לים	עמד על־שני עשר בקר	25
	שלשה פנים צפונה	שלשה פנים צפונה	שלשה פנים צפונה	
	ושלשה פנים ימה	ושלשה פנים ימה	ושלשה פנים ימה	
	ושלשה פנים נגבה	ושלשה פנים נגבה	ושלשה פנים נגבה	
	ושלשה פנים מזרחה	ושלשה פנים מזרחה	ושלשה פנים מזרחה	
	והים עליהם מלמעלה	וכל־אחריהם ביתה	והים עליהם מלמעלה	
	וכל־אחריהם ביתה	והים עליהם מלמעלה	וכל־אחריהם ביתה	
5	<u>ועביו טפח</u>		<u>ועביו טפח</u>	26
	<u>ושפתו כמעשה שפת־כוס פרח שושנה</u>		<u>ושפתו כמעשה שפת־כוס פרח שושן</u>	
	מחזיק בתים שלשת אלפים יכיל		אלפים בת יכיל	
6	ויעש כיורים עשרה	ויעש עשרה כירות נחשת	ויעש עשרה כירות נחשת	38
		ארבעים בת יכיל הכיור האחד	ארבעים בת יכיל הכיור האחד	
			ארבע באמה הכיור האחד	
		כיור אחד על־המכונה האחת לעשר המכנות	כיור אחד על־המכונה האחת לעשר המכנות	
	ויתן	ויתן את־עשר המכנות	ויתן את־המכנות	39
	חמשה מימין	חמש על־כתף הבית מימין	חמש על־כתף הבית מימין	
	וחמשה משמאול	וחמש על־כתף הבית משמאל	וחמש על־כתף הבית משמאלו	
	לרחצה בהם			
	את־מעשה העולה ידיחו בם			
	והים לרחצה לכהנים בו			
10	ואת־הים נתן מכתף	ואת־הים מכתף הבית הימנית קדמה ממול נגב	ואת־הים נתן מכתף הבית הימנית קדמה ממול נגב	
	הימנית קדמה ממול נגב			

In their descriptions of the great sea, there are several differences between shorter Kgdms on the one hand and longer Kgs//Chr on the other. Three concern order: at the end of 25//4, the final two details about the position of the twelve oxen are in reverse order; 26a//5a appears earlier in Kgdms, at the end of 24//3, and with its two elements reversed. And there are three pluses in Kgs/Chr of which the first two are related: מוצק (cast) in the 1st line of 23//2 as set out above anticipates the related יצקים ביצקתו (cast at its casting) at the end of 24//3 describing the manufacture of two decorative rows. The third plus states the capacity of the sea (differently in Kgs and Chr). The technological implication of these pluses is huge: casting a regular shape of the size recorded would already have been a great feat; but including intricate decoration under the rim within such large-scale casting would have been metalworking of extraordinary expertise.

On most of these six points, shorter Kgdms is preferable. 'Pour/cast' (יצק) is found in Kgs, Kgdms, and Chr together only in 7:46//4:17 – there with reference to casting much smaller objects. And only in these concluding verses (7:45, 47//4:16, 18) do we find bronze (נחשת) specified in all three texts except where Hiram is introduced (7:14, 14//2:6, 13). As just discussed, the great sea and its decoration are said in Kgs and Chr to be cast but not in Kgdms. Similarly, the capitals on top of the great pillars are specified as bronze in Kgs and Kgdms, but not Chr. Both bronze (7:27, 30, 30) and cast (7:33) are stressed in relation to the long description in Kgs and Kgdms of the stands and their components; but this plays no part in Chr. And the same is true of the basins (7:38). In 7:30 (following the double mention of bronze) cast is part of a large plus in MT running from the last words of 30 to the first words of 32. This further detail of the stands also includes מקלעת in 7:31 (found only in Kgs pluses – see end of 4.4 above). Correspondingly, bronze is specified in two Chr pluses (4:1, 9).

The precise nature of the two decorative rows is difficult to evaluate. Kgs specifies rows of פקעים (gourd-shaped ornaments). This noun occurs only once more in HB (in Kgs MT). However, not only is 1 Kgs 6:18 absent from Kgdms but the whole account of making the most holy place (6:16–20) is very much more briefly reported in 2 Chr 3:8–9. Kgdms here specifies ὑποστηρίγματα, listed immediately after the sea in the summary list in 3 Kgdms 2:35e of objects made by Solomon and rendering מסעדים ('supports') in 10:12. In 2 Chr 4:3 (//1 Kgs 7:24) we read neither פקעים nor simply the (assonant?) בקרים (cf בקר in 7:25), but 'the likeness of oxen'; and these are under the sea, not under its lip – have they become assimilated to the twelve oxen that carry the sea? To complicate further the issue in Kgs (MT): in 6:18 (MT+) the gourds are 'carved' (מקלעת פקעים) in cedar while here they are 'cast' with the 'sea' itself, like the decoration on the 'stands' in 7:30 (again MT+). It appears that Kgs MT is the longest of the three construction reports because it is also the most expansionist.

We may deduce from the note in 39b//10 about the sea and its position that the ten bowls are presented in 38–39a//6a as an adjunct to this larger container. We may assume, therefore, that the position of the bowls (five to right or south and five to left or north) is defined in Chr's much briefer description in relation to the sea. In the second part of its short note Chr mentions the cultic function of both bowls and sea. Kgs and Kgdms say nothing about function but much more about the objects themselves: their capacity and that each was on a stand. This longer text also removes the potential for ambiguity in the brevity of Chr by adding that the stands were five on the shoulder of the house to the right and five on the shoulder of the house to the left. In Kg[dm]s the stands are described at great length (27–37 – Kgs at even greater length than Kgdms) before a first mention of the bowls (38–39). This involves a reversal of the order Kg[dm]s and Chr share when describing the great sea: object first and only then what supported it.

5 Prospect

"The most stable and oldest textual tradition is that attested by the three textual traditions ... The texts common to LXX and MT Kings, missing in 2 Chronicles, are not necessarily more recent because of this. They can also be ancient, although of a different provenance ..." (Trebolle 496). Adrian Schenker's magisterial demonstration of the high value of LXX in 1 Kgs 2–14 pays only limited attention to the houses of Yahweh and the king and the dowry of the queen (2000, 129–139) and makes even less mention of the Chronicler. Schenker rightly observes that Chr's parallel narrative does not take away the question of dependence between MT and LXX. But he does not explore whether on some topics Chr preserves a text earlier than either of the others. The analysis of sea and basins just adumbrated has taken "attest[ation] by the three textual traditions" quite strictly: as meaning shared wording whether best preserved in Kgdms or Chr.

Exploring the making of the report(s) is as complex as reconstructing the building of the temple and is the necessary first step. Before any further (historical) reconstruction is attempted of how Solomon's temple was built and furnished, a fresh account must be offered of how the several reports of its building and furnishing were constructed.

Follow the Words: What's in a King's Name?

1 Paired names

The majority of Jerusalem's kings bore names which made a statement about Yahweh, though the divine subject could be omitted. Some names, or at least some components, occur twice. Ahaziah (*'ḥz-yhw*) or 'Yahweh holds' and Ahaz illustrate both abbreviation and repetition. Importantly the pairing is not confined to the name: these are two of Jerusalem's kings who were not acceptable 'in Yahweh's eyes' – more specifically, who 'walked in the ways of the house of Ahab/kings of Israel' (2 Kgs 8:27; 16:3).

There are many more links between the boy-kings Joash and Josiah than between Ahaziah and Ahaz. The story of Athaliah and Joash (2 Kgs 11–12) has at least seven explicit links with the Josiah narrative (2 Kgs 22–23). Both reforms are masterminded by a named *priest* (כהן)[1] with a *scribe* (ספר)[2] also involved. Both kings *strengthen* (חזק piel) Yahweh's house; and both reports about their temple repairs speak repeatedly of *those doing the task* (עשי המלאכה).[3] *A covenant is made*[4] and the king *stands* (עומד) *by the pillar* (על־העמוד).[5] Then Athaliah like Josiah *tears her clothes* (ותקרע את־בגדיה).[6]

These equivalences are precise and many are unique. Others, though less precise, are no less important. Joash aged seven and Josiah aged eight are the youngest kings on accession; and, hardly surprisingly, they also follow the two kings with the shortest reigns (Amaziah and Amon). Their names too, J[eh]oash (*y̲h̲w̲-'š̲*) and Josiah (*y̲'š̲-y̲h̲w̲*), are much more similar in Hebrew than when translated into other languages. Whatever either may have meant originally, the complement describing Yahweh in each name-statement can be read as a form of אוש (give).[7] As with Ahaziah and Ahaz, the connections between Joash and Josiah operate on (at least) two levels: near identity of name and similarity of content and evaluation. The many overlaps between the latter pair also serve to highlight

---

1 2 Kgs 11:9, 10, 15; 12:3, 6, 11//2 Chr 23:8, 9, 14; 24:2, 5, 11; 2 Kgs 22:4//2 Chr 34:9 – כהן is + in 2 Kgs 12:7, 8, 9, 10(2×), 17; 22:8, 12, 14.

2 2 Kgs 12:11//2 Chr 24:11; 2 Kgs 22:9, 10, 12//2 Chr 34:16, 18, 20.

3 2 Kgs 12:12, 15, 16//2 Chr 24:12, 13; 2 Kgs 22:5, 9//2 Chr 34:10, 12, 13, 17 – compare 1 Kgs 7:40//2 Chr 4:11; however, the similar but non-synoptic expressions relating to Solomon's projects in 1 Kgs 9:23 and 2 Chr 8:9 appear secondary.

4 2 Kgs 11:17//2 Chr 23:16; 2 Kgs 23:3//2 Chr 34:31.

5 2 Kgs 11:14//2 Chr 23:13; 2 Kgs 23:3//2 Chr 34:31 (LXX).

6 2 Kgs 11:14//2 Chr 23:13; 2 Kgs 22:11, 19//2 Chr 34:19, 27.

7 אוש does not occur in classical Hebrew, but its sense can be inferred from cognate languages (KB I, 25).

https://doi.org/10.1515/9783111060279-015

the key differences: the surprise one priest produces from the temple is the boy-king; but the other, the torah-book (2 Kgs 11:12; 22:8–10).

The names Amaziah (*'mṣ-yhw*) and Hezekiah (*ḥzq-yhw*) have almost identical meanings: 'Yahweh is firm/strong'. Though Jotham also becomes king aged 25, only Amaziah and Hezekiah accede to the throne at 25 and go on to reign for 29 years (2 Kgs 14:2; 18:2) and only their reports mention Lachish: Amaziah flees there from Jerusalem and Assyrian forces are sent to Hezekiah's Jerusalem from there (2 Kgs 14:19; 18:17). Hezekiah's name (חזקיהו) is also deftly anticipated near the start of the report on Amaziah (14:5): כאשר חזקה הממלכה בידו (as the kingship strengthened in his hand).[8]

Like Tweedledum and Tweedledee in a 17th century satirical poem who 'resolved to have a battle', the pair of leaders who sundered Solomon's legacy also had similar names. Their names are not statements about Yahweh, although the second and shared element in the names Rehoboam (*rḥb'm*) and Jeroboam (*yrb'm*) may originally also have had divine significance (KB II, 414–415). Be that as it may, it seems most likely in the context of these rivals that *'m* became read in its most common sense of 'people'. What was described above as Solomon's legacy is known in these texts as [Yahweh's] 'people' (*'m*).[9] Protagonist Rehoboam (רחבעם) had been understood as 'the people has become wide'. Then the name of antagonist Jeroboam (ירבעם) may be usefully ambiguous: if the verb element *yrb* is read as related to *rbb*, 'the people becomes many' nicely rivals 'the people has become wide'; however, if related to *ryb*, a 'dispute' affecting the people makes equally good sense. That the culprits who divided this *'m* bore names suggesting either its increase or their conflict is grimly ironic.

There is a similarly rich cluster of links between David and Hezekiah as between Joash and Josiah; and these include חזק within two contexts in the David narratives. The divine envoy (מלאך יהוה) plays a key destructive role in 2 Sam 24:17 and 2 Kgs 19:35; and the census story, like the report on Amaziah, uses חזק to emphasise the authority of the king, in this case against the protests of Joab:

8 The play on their names may be anticipated in Isaiah's threat (28.2) against Ephraim of חזק ואמיץ לאדני.

9 While עם יהוה is never found in synoptic texts, the possessive suffix in 'my/your/his people' routinely refers to Yahweh. the combination *people of Yahweh* (עם יהוה) is never used in BoTH; however, the usage of עם with a sg sfx is instructive. In David and Solomon narratives, the possessive suffix with *people* (עמי\עמך\עמו) refers as often as 21× to Yahweh (עמי in 2 Sam 5:2; 7:7, 8, 10, 11//1 Chr 11:2; 17:6, 7, 9, 10; 1 Kgs 8:16//2 Chr 6:6; עמך in 2 Sam 7:23, 23, 24//1 Chr 17:21, 21, 22; 1 Kgs 3:9; 8:30, 33, 34, 36, 36, 38, 41, 43, 44//2 Chr 1:10; 6:21, 24, 25, 27, 27, 29, 32, 33, 34; and עמו in 2 Sam 5:12//1 Chr 14:2; 1 Kgs 8:66//2 Chr 7:10) – and only once to the king (2 Sam 8:15). *People* with a sg possessive is found only once more in BoTH, where Jehoshaphat responds to the invitation from the king of Israel that 'my people is as your people' (1 Kgs 22:4).

ויחזק דבר־המלך על־יואב (and the word of the king was strong upon[10] Joab). Then 2 Sam 10 uses the verb *be strong* (*ḥzq*) not once, but as many as four times in two verses (11–12), as David's generals prepare for successful battle against Ammon and Aram. One of these is in the *htp'l*: 'strengthen yourself' or 'show yourself strong'.

The narratives about Rehoboam and Amaziah (*'mṣ-yhw*) were also doubly linked. These were the only successors of David who sought to move militarily against northern Israel (1 Kgs 12:21; 2 Kgs 14:8); and only they suffered the plunder of the treasuries of Yahweh's house and the king's house, Rehoboam at the hands of Pharaoh and Amaziah at the hands of (northern) Jehoash (1 Kgs 14:26; 2 Kgs 14:14). *htḥzq* in 2 Sam 10:12 gives added significance to the sole instance of the verb *'mṣ* in the narrative of Sam-Kgs[11] -- it is also *htp'l*. As he mounts his chariot in Shechem to escape to Jerusalem, Rehoboam 'firms himself' or 'shows himself firm' (1 Kgs 12:18). In this text that is emerging as a hall of mirrors, the reader is presented with a puzzle. Was Rehoboam emulating the confidence of his grandfather's generals that Yahweh would do what was right in his eyes (2 Sam 10:12)? Or was Rehoboam's 'firmness' – precisely in flight! – but a poor reflection of the 'strength' called for and exhibited by Joab and Abishai? Amaziah returned to Jerusalem after being worsted by his northern neighbour. In colloquial English, we could portray Rehoboam fleeing from Shechem as 'doing an Amaziah' (*ht'mṣ*).

These links between similarly named Ahaziah and Ahaz, Joash and Josiah, Amaziah and Hezekiah, and Rehoboam and Jeroboam, are more readily grasped when their narratives are read in Hebrew. Each set of comparisons operates in both directions. Rehoboam in flight from northern Shechem may have been said to 'do an Amaziah'. Equally, Amaziah outdid his ancestor's folly in mustering against northern Israel: Rehoboam had accepted the warning from a man of God, but Amaziah ignored the advice in the parable of the trees. And each link is quite effective within the books of Samuel and Kings as we have inherited them. However, if we adjust our focus and zoom in on the 'synoptic' portions of Sam-Kgs (those shared with Chronicles), the pattern of paired relationships becomes even crisper. In the reports of Joash and Josiah we encounter the only named priests and the only torn clothes and the only scribe or secretary in synoptic narratives. On the other hand, *ḥzq* is used much more widely in Sam-Kgs than in the synoptic narratives of David and Amaziah; and these additional instances[12] need to be

---

10 Reading על for MT אל with LXX^{L} and other witnesses.

11 It is also found in 2 Sam 22:18 (Ps 18:18).

12 חזק qal 1 Sam 17:50; 2 Sam 2:7; 13:14, 28; 16:21; 1 Kgs 2:2; 16:22; 20:23, 23, 25; 2 Kgs 3:26; 25:3; piel 1 Sam 23:16; 2 Sam 11:25; hiph 1 Sam 15:27; 17:35; 2 Sam 1:11; 2:16; 3:29; 11:25; 13:11; 15:5; 1 Kgs 1:50; 2:28; 2 Kgs 2:12; 4:8, 27; 15:19; hitp 1 Sam 4:9; 30:6; 2 Sam 3:6; 1 Kgs 20:22.

cropped to achieve a clearer image. Reviewing the names of other sons of David within a synoptic perspective also pays dividends.

2 Names and narrative

Grounds for reading Amaziah with Hezekiah and Joash with Josiah as significant pairs were presented above (pp. 149–167), where many dozens of uniquely paired expressions were listed. Evidence (even if negative) was also offered there for seeing Josiah as the final king in the synoptic Book of Two Houses (BoTH): the pattern of pairings does not extend into the reports of the final four kings. The following discussion extends and complements that presentation. The use of the verb component in Amaziah in only one synoptic context proves far from accidental, for the same holds true for other royal names. The verb in Azar-iah ('Yahweh aids') occurs only in 2 Sam 8:5, where Aram of Damascus came to 'aid' (*'zr*) Hadad-ezer of Zobah, whose name ironically means (the god) 'Hadad aids'. However, these aiding Aramaeans were worsted by David 'whom Yahweh saved wherever he went' (8:6). The point of the story is clear: Yahweh not Hadad was the god who really 'brought aid'. Azariah's alternative name in Chronicles, Uzziah ('Yahweh's might'),[13] is even prefigured twice in a single David story: *Uzzah* (עזא) suffers death for touching the ark (2 Sam 6:3–8) while David goes on to dance *with all might* (בכל־עז) in front of it (6:14). Double or ambiguous prefiguring may be appropriate for a king who on the one side reigned for more than fifty years but on the other had to withdraw from public life after contracting a skin complaint. Similarly, if Asa does mean medical doctor (KB I, 70–71), it is somewhat ironic that he should have become diseased in his feet in old age (1 Kgs 15:23). In this emerging context, we may see a deliberate link between the meaning of *Jotham* (יותם), 'Yahweh is complete/whole/innocent' (*tm*), and the only synoptic instance of a cognate form (1 Kgs 22:34): an archer draws his bow and kills Ahab 'in his *innocence/perfection*' (לתמו). The archer demonstrated skill that was Yahweh-like or Yahweh-given. He may not have known he was to kill the king of Israel, but we may assume the narrator's view that Yahweh did know.

The narrative links with the names Amaziah and Jotham are in the accounts of Rehoboam and Jehoshaphat. As for the verb element in the name Jeho-shaphat ('Yahweh rules'), we find it in only two synoptic contexts: first, when reporting Solomon's vision at Gibeon (1 Kgs 3:9), and then in the account of Jotham's regency when his father Azariah had to self-isolate (2 Kgs 15:5). And the link between

13 2 Kgs 15:1–7 (on Azariah) is the source of the much expanded 2 Chr 26 (where the king is named Uzziah).

Solomon and Jehoshaphat is reinforced by a tale of maritime enterprise: like Solomon, though without his success, Jehoshaphat sought to despatch a fleet of Tarshish-ships from Ezion-Geber (1 Kgs 10:22; 22:47–48).

Saul is the only king in what Auld has called BoTH other than Ahab to be struck by an archer's arrow; and neither of these kings of Israel belonged to the house of David. Three further details of 1 Sam 31 reappear immediately, and only in the David stories: Philistines (פלשתים),[14] 'pierced' (חלל),[15] and 'armour-bearer' (נשא כלים).[16] The first two of these imply contrast: David succeeded where Saul failed. Because Saul's death is the opening scene of the synoptic narrative, we cannot hear echoes of his name until after his passing. Only David and Solomon within BoTH *ask* (שאל) or are *asked* by others. David, as soon as he became king in Saul's place, asked twice before confronting Philistines (2 Sam 5:19, 23). And that reminds us that the king called *Asked* (שאול) confronted the Philistines without first asking Yahweh (1 Sam 31). The story of Samuel at En-Dor (1 Sam 28) is a later narrative response to this situation.

The father of the line of Jerusalem's kings is not often mentioned explicitly outside his own narrative, apart from the recurring record of burials 'in the city of David'.[17] Exceptionally, Hezekiah and Josiah are explicitly compared with him (2 Kgs 18:3; 22:2) and Ahaz explicitly contrasted: he 'did not do what was right in the eyes of Yahweh like David his father' (2 Kgs 16:2). We began this royal roundup with Ahaziah and Ahaz; and one further exceptional reference to David occurs immediately before the short report on Ahaziah (2 Kgs 8:25–29). Despite the evil done by his father Jehoram, 'Yahweh was unwilling to destroy Judah, for the sake of his servant David' (2 Kgs 8:19). As with the names of so many of their relatives, BoTH uses the related verb only once. The name that Ahaziah and Ahaz share may properly have conveyed 'Yahweh [protectively] holds' (אחז). However, their link to the David narratives is uniquely unpropitious: Uzzah 'holds' the ark and suffers Yahweh's burning wrath (2 Sam 6:6–8). Given that hint, we should not be surprised to find much later in BoTH that both Ahaziah and Ahaz are among the smaller set of kings in Jerusalem introduced as doing evil (or not doing right) in Yahweh's eyes. The others are Rehoboam, Jehoram, Manasseh, and Amon. The names Ahaziah, Amaziah, Azariah, Uzziah, Ahaz, and Hezekiah, are all implicitly prefigured in synoptic David. However, Ahaziah (and Ahaz) are the only kings just listed, who have names compounded with Yahweh but did not do what was right in Yahweh's eyes. Saul too is implicitly contrasted with his successor.

---

14 2 Sam 5; 23.

15 2 Sam 23:8, 18.

16 2 Sam 23:37.

17 1 Kgs 15:8, 24; 22:51; 2 Kgs 8:24; 12:22; 14:20; 15:7, 38; 16:20.

Briefly reigning *Amon* (אמון) may have the most gloriously resonant name in BoTH: its echoes can be heard in the synoptic stories about David, Solomon, and possibly Hezekiah. In the culmination of Nathan's oracle, David's house and kingdom are to be *reliably established* (נאמן) before Yahweh (2 Sam 7:16). Solomon in his great prayer asks that [Yahweh's] word spoken to [his] servant David should be *reliable* (1 Kgs 8:26). Then Sennacherib's message to Jerusalem may have included 'Do not rely on him' (2 Chr 32:15).[18] Such triple introduction serves to emphasise just how different Amon is.

Only three successors of David and Solomon in Jerusalem have not featured in this review. Abijam/h is in any case very shadowy: 2 Chr 13:2 offers no evaluation while the introduction in 1 Kgs 15:3 appears secondary. However, in the light of the above, it seems surprising that Jeho-ram (Yahweh is high) in 2 Kgs 8:16–24 finds no echo. Hannah's Song has several echoes of royal ideology: Yahweh is subject of *rwm* pilpel in 1 Sam 2:7 and *rwm* hiphil is used in 2:8. The third, wicked Manasseh, is quite distinctive: *mnšh* is assonant with two verbs in BoTH; yet both are written with a different silent final letter: not *nšh* but *nš'*. One appears in a puzzling combination (ונשא־בו אלה להאלתו) in Solomon's petition about undertaking a self-exculpatory oath (1 Kgs 8:31//2 Chr 6:22). The other appears as the Assyrian envoy warns his Jerusalem audience against being deceived by Hezekiah: אל־ישיא לכם\אתכם (2 Kgs 18:29//2 Chr 32:15). The given spelling *mnšh* of the king's name seems to suggest 'making forgotten'; however, this has no cognate in BoTH, or indeed Sam-Kgs as a whole, and is attested in HB only once (Gen 41:51).

3 Other names

The first thing David asks of Yahweh is 'Do you give the Philistines into my hand' and receives the answer 'I give them into your hand' (2 Sam 5:19). After bringing the ark into Jerusalem, he requires further divine advice and speaks to the prophet Nathan (2 Sam 7), whose name means 'Grant/Give'. Micaiah (1 Kgs 22) means 'Who is like Yahweh?' Isaiah's name ('Yahweh is salvation', 2 Kgs 19–20) includes one of the keywords (save) found only in the narratives of David and Hezekiah. David's seer Gad means 'Lucky'. Rehoboam deals with Shemaiah ('Yahweh hears', 1 Kgs 12:22–24) and Jeroboam (and his wife) with Ahijah ('Yahweh is [my] brother', 1 Kgs 12:15; 14:1–18). The only puzzling name among these synoptic intermediaries

18 The ambassador uses בטח (trust) in his opening words according to both 2 Kgs 18:19 and 2 Chr 32:10. בטח will be repeated as many as 4× in 2 Kgs 18:21–24 and again in 19:10, but never in 2 Chr 32. Instead, ואל־תאמינו לו (32:15) may preserve an older form of the text, submerged in expanded 2 Kgs 18–19 under a flood of בטח additions.

comes last: what was the significance of Huldah (2 Kgs 22:13–20) being a 'Mole' (KB I, 303) or 'Weasel' (Clines 1996, 227)?

There are several similarities in names and clusters of names between the northern kings of Israel and kings of the house of David in the south. (Northern) Ahaziah and Jehoram rule in the same period as (southern) Jehoram and Ahaziah; and each Ahaziah reigns very briefly (only one or two years). Just as southern Ahaziah (*'ḥz-yhw*, 2 Kgs 8) reigns before Joash (2 Kgs 11–12), so too northern Jehoash is preceded by Jehoahaz (*yhw-'ḥz*, 2 Kgs 14:17). The first two of these northern pairs – with Jehu between them – are already part of BoTH, along with Omri, Ahab, and the first Jeroboam. The name of Hoshea, last king of northern Israel (2 Kgs 17:1–6), is based on the verb save (*yš'*) like that of Isaiah the prophet; and both overlap with king Hezekiah in whose story the verbs *save* and *deliver* are key elements.

We are clearly dealing in BoTH with an expertly crafted literary text. The allusions to David in the Amaziah report (2 Kgs 14:1–14, 17–20) provide a fine example. Apart from the standard heading, there are four components in the short narrative: how he dealt with his father's assassins (5–6); his campaign in Edom (7); most fully, his failed move against Jehoash of Israel (8–14); then his later years (17–20). And there are links with David in each of the first three: חזק (5) and חטא (6) with 2 Sam 24:4, 17; an almost identical report about Edom (7) in 2 Sam 8:13; the combination of נגף and נוס (12) as twice in 2 Sam 10; and finally, פרץ (13) as in 2 Sam 5:20 and 6:8. The last of these allusions is to Yahweh *bursting out* on Uzzah, whose name is echoed in Uzziah. And he was not just any other of Jerusalem's kings, but precisely Amaziah's son and successor. It is not just that each of these links is unique within BoTH. As with Joash and Josiah, these are a dense set of unique paired links within small compass. The inclusion (6) of a *torah* about the responsibility of each person for their own sin is an integral element in the texture of this report. The reference to a book of Moses may be secondary. However, the *torah* itself contributes to the debate within BoTH triggered by David's determined count of the people: was he alone guilty or did his successors also share his guilt?

4 Life in Kings and beyond

This review of the intimate relationship between the names of many of Jerusalem's kings and the texture of the narrative in which they appear adds further credence to the case advanced in Auld 2017 and extended above. Auld 2017, 91–94 provided a preliminary sketch of some 30 pairs, including the feature, noted also by Na'aman, of Amaziah and Hezekiah each starting their reigns aged 25 and reigning for 29 years! To this I added in confirmation that Lachish appears synoptically only in their stories. The listing tabulated on pp. 153–161 has multiplied fourfold and allowed the detection of many more interwoven patterns like those discussed by Na'aman. These start with the death of Saul, who is contrasted with David and compared with Ahab, and finish with the death of Josiah (the pattern of pairings includes no king after Josiah). David and Solomon are praised for practising משפט וצדקה; Solomon and Jehoshaphat are associated with trade from Ezion-geber in Tarshish-ships; and over a hundred more unique links in wording are preserved jointly by Sam-Kgs and Chr. The conclusion imposes itself: implicit comparisons and contrasts are the very DNA of the synoptic material.

Concentration on the synoptic text shared by Samuel-Kings and Chronicles allows two features of this material to come into clearer focus. Negatively, this 20% of Sam-Kgs is quite clearly distinctive within these books as a whole. Auld 2017 took its title from the observation that the 'life' word is very rare in BoTH but widely used in Sam-Kgs. That study also noted that יש ('there is') is completely absent from BoTH. BoTH includes only four instances of נפש – and in two pairs! (pp. 49–50 above) – while there are dozens in Sam-Kgs, many of them in close association with חי[ם]; and BoTH may have contained only two instances of נא (p. 32 above), which is even commoner in Sam-Kgs than יש. And this study listed above (fn 12) the many forms of חזק are used in Sam-Kgs over against the few in BoTH. Its review of royal names has added אוש*, אמץ, עז, עזר, תמם to the list on pp. 153–161 above of unique word-pairs while moving אחז, חזק, and שפט to the much shorter list of significant threes. Adding royal names to the tabulation just mentioned has allowed the detection of many more interwoven patterns similar to those discussed in Na'aman 2017. The conclusion imposes itself ever more securely: implicit comparisons and contrasts are the very DNA of the synoptic material.

5 History

The formulaic reports of the age of each king at his accession and the number of years he reigned give the impression of archival information; and this impression is strengthened when the reader is directed at the end of each section to further available information. The fact that the only precise dates provided in BoTH within the reign of a king of Jerusalem relate to visits by two kings of Egypt (in the 5th year of Rehoboam and the 31st of Josiah) tend in the same direction. However, other facts point us in a different direction. It is about David and Solomon, the most distant kings, that we are provided with most detail. And the density of pairing, the integration of names and narrative, and the implausible 25+29 years for already paired Amaziah and Hezekiah raise too many doubts.

BoTH with its richly patterned texture is hardly 'historical' in our sense, although of course it is *historia* in the older senses of that term: both 'narrative' and 'enquiry'. The narrative that features all these names tells of kings (and some queens), of power struggles and battles, and it provides some dates. It may be the oldest (written) record to which we have access; and yet it is hardly a historical record. To my great fortune, my first research supervisor was Père Roland de Vaux at the École Biblique et Archéologique Française in Jerusalem. At the end of 1966, the Director of the British School of Archaeology had invited me to join the excavation he was about to start at Teleilat Ghassul, the key Chalcolithic site just north of the Dead Sea (identified with Gomorrah by earlier excavators!). When I asked de Vaux if he would endorse my missing classes for some weeks, he was doubly enthusiastic: (a) Basil Hennessy was a very fine excavator; and (b) it was particularly important for a student of Bible to encounter archaeology 'uncontaminated' – in a prehistorical site. Half a century on, my concern is not with historical enthusiasms that can result in 'reading' the material 'record' too quickly. The problem here is a different one: how to read a text whose very 'texture' or 'textuality' appears more significant than its relatedness to history, even though it is clearly interested in history.

The texture is so dense that it even seems unwise to try to plot its development. Was Josiah modelled on Joash, or the other way round? Was trade from Ezion-geber in Tarshish-ships first reported of Jehoshaphat and then added to the traditions about Solomon, or the other way round? And who first killed 10,000 Edomites: Amaziah or Abishai or David? How many aspects of David are derived from the many successors he anticipates, and how far are the later kings modelled on him?

BoTH may be our earliest available 'edition' of the book of Kings and the seedbed of much that is later added to it. However, this in no way implies that it constitutes the oldest material in Sam-Kgs. Many individual tales about struggles with neighbours, inner-communal strife, the exploits of kings and prophets, had likely been available to those who retold the royal narrative. But we must also reckon with the role of story-tellers ready to explore generously gaps they found in the master-narrative. We know that literary prequels offer a new backstory to an established narrative – precisely by drawing on and exploiting some of its key features. The synoptic account of actions by David and his servants against Philistines including Goliath with his massive spear-shaft and a massive man with extra digits (2 Sam 21:18–22) is memorably and expansively retold in 1 Sam 17 as single combat between David and Goliath to settle the fate of their two peoples. Synoptic Jeroboam in flight from Solomon, his former master, may similarly have assisted the telling of David in flight from Saul (pp. 134–137 above). Equally, we should expect that narratives in 1 Samuel about Saul and David also drew on non-synoptic traditions.

BoTH may be far from 'historical' as we use that term; but it poses useful questions to our contemporary discussion of the 'United Monarchy'. That term itself is ambiguous: a union may result from the uniting of originally separate entities; and union is also the situation before division takes place. The second half of the 20th century was familiar with two German, Korean, and Vietnamese states where formerly there had been one. On the other hand, the single or united German state had been produced only in the 19th century by the uniting of smaller German states. In some 60% of the text of BoTH – under Saul, David, and Solomon – Israel was one and undivided. In all this text, Judah is mentioned only once; and the context is highly significant. The relevant tale includes the intervention of Gad, the king's seer, and the king himself seeing Yahweh's messenger with drawn sword. David has overreached himself and insisted on having Israel counted – and the total is brought to him in two subtotals. He has anticipated Rehoboam's folly and what was one is counted as if already divided.

The first and only mention of Benjamin in BoTH is part of the report of the division of Israel in the time of Rehoboam and Jeroboam. Benjamin is mustered with Judah against the north. Tribal affinities played no part in the older narrative about Saul or David or Solomon. Contemporary interest in Saul of Benjamin over against David of Judah derives from the book of Samuel and not its older source.

Comparing Amaziah and Jehoash

1 In Kings and Chronicles

The regnal account of Amaziah son of Joash, king in Jerusalem, is presented in similar terms in 2 Kgs 14:2–3a, 5–6, 8–14, 17–20 and 2 Chr 25:1–2, 3–4, 17–24, 25–28. The reports of his dealings with Jehoash, king of Israel (14:8–14//25:17–24) are particularly alike. The major differences between 2 Kgs 14 and 2 Chr 25 are easily described. On the one side, two pluses in Kgs relate to the combination of the Amaziah account with the regnal account of J[eh]oash of Israel (14:1 supplies the synchronistic detail; and 14:15–16, uniquely in Kgs, repeats the second half of the Jehoash account found already in 13:12–13). And two add detail to the almost standard initial positive assessment (14:2–3a//25:1–2): in all things Amaziah followed his father Joash (14:3b); only, 'the high places' (הבמות) were not removed (14:4).

The largest divergence concerns Amaziah's military exploit in Edom. This is reported briefly in 2 Kgs 14:7 but at length in 2 Chr 25:5–16, which includes two prophetic encounters (7–9, 13–16). 2 Kgs 14:7 can plausibly be seen as the text from which a "midrashic" expansion in 2 Chr 25:5–16 developed. The *grab* (תפש) of Sela or the Rock (הסלע) provides the location for the further slaughter of 10,000 prisoners reported only in Chr (25:12); and battle (מלחמה), also from 14:7, reappears in 25:13. Within the following, and otherwise very similar, story of Amaziah's provocation of Jehoash, Chr has added a note (25:20aβb) relating Judah's troubles to their worship of Edomite gods as reported within the large plus (25:14). There is also divergence in 14:10//25:19 to which we will turn below (2.2).

2 With the wider shared narrative

The synoptic verses on Amaziah within 2 Kgs 14//2 Chr 25 are particularly rich in multiple echoes of three other parts of the synoptic narrative shared by Sam-Kgs and Chr: on Hezekiah, David, and Rehoboam/Jeroboam.

2.1

Only Amaziah and Hezekiah of all the kings in Jerusalem both accede to the throne aged 25 and go on to reign for 29 years (14:2; 18:2).[1] Their names, אמציהו

1 All following references to Samuel and Kings are to synoptic portions unless made clear otherwise; each of them is also found in Chronicles. These details unique to Amaziah and Hezekiah are noted also in Na'aman 2017 and Auld 2017.

https://doi.org/10.1515/9783111060279-016

and חזקיהו, have similar meanings; and the early statement (14:5) that 'the kingdom was strongly (חזקה) in [Amaziah's] hand' reinforces this association.[2] Two further pairings unique within the synoptic royal story confirm these initial clues: only the reports on Amaziah and Hezekiah feature Lachish (14:19; 18:17) or the wall of Jerusalem (14:13; 18:26).[3]

The explicit verbal links between Amaziah and Hezekiah encourage readers to pay attention to other parallels there too: Jerusalem comes under external threat when each is king; and, just as Amaziah outlives Jehoash (though the latter has destroyed part of his city wall) so too Hezekiah outlives Sennacherib (though his envoy has menaced the inhabitants on that wall).

Accession to the throne at 25 and a following 29-year reign serve to underline the similar meanings of the names Amaziah and Hezekiah. But others among the uniquely shared elements in their stories suggest contrast. Lachish is where Amaziah's life ended in a coup (14:19) but where Sennacherib starts his ascent to Jerusalem (18:17). The wall of Amaziah's Jerusalem was partly destroyed by Jehoash (14:13), but Hezekiah's people stand defiantly on it to hear Assyrians haranguing them but not entering their city (18:26). Similarly, as we shall note below, Jehoash destroys a city wall near the Ephraim Gate, while Jeroboam had (re-)built a city in Ephraim.

2.2

Amaziah's substantial slaughter of 10,000 Edomites in 'the valley of salt' (14:7) repeats a victory there in the time of David. We find it variously attributed, and with different casualty numbers, to David himself (18,000, 2 Sam 8:13) or Abishai (18,000, 1 Chr 18:12) or Joab (12,000, Ps 60:2). Amaziah then challenges his northern neighbour (14:8); and Jehoash of Israel parries his threat in a fable or parable (14:9). On first hearing, we might suppose that the northern king was portraying himself as the noble cedar of his tale. But as we read further, we realise that what Amaziah was about to experience was more like being trampled by the *fieldlife* (חית השדה). In the most immediate context of the short fable, this lumbering animal[4] could as well have been called a "beast" (בהמה). But both elements of חית השדה are deliberately chosen. *Life*, the first, relates to the next-wider context. Jehoash did prevail against Amaziah; but the result was paradoxical. Despite experiencing defeat, including damage to the wall of his capitol,

2 As discussed above (pp. 183–192), this play on names is part of a much wider pattern in synoptic narrative.

3 Building the wall of Jerusalem is also part of the story of Solomon and Pharaoh's daughter in Kgs and Kgdms, but not Chr (pp. 170–171 above).

4 LXX in both Kgs and Chr renders 'wild animals', presumably reading חית as collective singular.

Amaziah the loser *lived* on (ויחי): in fact, he out*lived* the victor, field*life* Jehoash, by fifteen years (2 Kgs 14:17).[5] The second element of the phrase addresses a still wider context. The only other instances of *field* in synoptic texts are found within two portions of the David story. Each of these also concerns conflict; and both include further unique links with the Amaziah report. In the first, Aram in the *field* (2 Sam 10:8) twice *flees* (נוס) after *being smitten* (נגף);[6] and these two verbs reappear as a pair in synoptic narrative only in 2 Kgs 14:12 (close after *field* in 14:9), as Amaziah is defeated by Jehoash of Israel. Amaziah now suffers what had been Aram's fate then, while the king of Israel emulates David. In the second, Shamma defending the strip of *field* (2 Sam 23:11) belongs among David's heroes some of whose exploits will be noted below.

Jehoash draws his conclusion from the cautionary tale differently and more expansively in Chr than Kgs –

2 Kgs 14:10	ושב בביתך	הכבד	הכה הכית את־אדום ונשאך לבך	
2 Chr 25:19 LXX	עתה שבה בביתך	הכבד	הנה הכית את־אדום ונשאך לבך	אמרת
2 Chr 25:19 MT	עתה שבה בביתך	להכביד	הנה הכית את־אדום ונשאך לבך	אמרת

The key issues relate to syntax and meaning of the *k-b-d* word. In Kgs it opens the second half of the sentence and is read as *niphal* imperative, coordinate with the following imperative ושב. In Chr it closes the first half and is either adjective modifying לבך (LXX) or *hiphil* infinitive explaining ונשאך לבך (MT). In Kgs, he says: "You have doubtless smitten Edom and your heart has lifted you up; accept the honour and sit in your house." But in Chr LXX: "You have said, look you have smitten Edom and your heavy/insensitive heart has lifted you up. Now sit in your house." The adjustment in Chr MT is not dissimilar: "... your heart has lifted you up making [you] heavy/insensitive ...".[7] Following the prefaced "you have said" we would have expected "I have smitten" after "look". כבד *hiphil* in the sense "make insensitive" is always elsewhere construed with an object: "heart"[8] or "ears".[9] כבד *niphal* is much commoner and means "be honoured". The shorter Kgs version is crisper; and it is easy to see how a few small adjustments changed it into the longer Chr text. When the *k-b-d* word came to be read as concluding

5 Terms related to *live/life* are very rare in synoptic narratives (Auld 2017, 29–31); only in this one chapter do they appear twice.

6 2 Sam 10:14–15, 18–19.

7 Ex 7:14 (כבד לב פרעה) offers a further case of כבד as adj with לב. And four of the six cases of כבד hiphil meaning "make insensitive" immediately follow: Ex 8:11, 28; 9:34; 10:1.

8 Ex 8:11, 28; 9:34; 10:1.

9 Isa 6:10; Zech 7:11.

the first part of the sentence, "now" (a conjunction stronger than the simple connective) was appropriately added before "sit" at the start of the second.

Jehoash in Kgs advises Amaziah to *be satisfied with the glory* (הכבד) of taking Sela (14:10), echoing a term unique in synoptic texts (נכבד) that describes two of David's heroes, Abishai (2 Sam 23:19)[10] and Benaiah (23:23). Not only so – Benaiah's own additional exploits had just been introduced (23:20.21) by הוא הכה ('he it was that smote'), the very words that told of Amaziah's defeat of Edom in 14:7 – and are used in synoptic contexts only in these two passages.[11] Jehoash gives full and emphatic credit to Amaziah: "Smite Edom – that you certainly did" (הכה הכית את־אדום). By then repeating in הכבד ("enjoy the glory") the opening consonants of הכה הכית, he ensures that the double allusion to 2 Sam 23:18–23 is not missed. However, he is arguably doing far more. (a) By using the intensive infinitive absolute, he echoes only synoptic David and Micaiah. David used this verbal form once (2 Sam 24:24) and possibly twice (24:17) after his great error in having the people counted; and Micaiah used it (1 Kgs 22:28) in a narrative with many echoes of that census story. Then (b), by extending *hkh* into *hkbd*, he echoes a feature of an earlier short report (2 Sam 8:1) on David's final strike on Philistines. In *wyk* ... *wykny'm* ("he struck ... and subdued them"), the second verb extends the first in both form and meaning: "subdued" starts like "struck", but has even more serious consequences. Amaziah, after his campaign in Edom, may deserve to share the renown of some of David's heroes; but in battle with the present king of Israel he will suffer like Aram with David. David not only struck the Philistines but went further and subdued them. Amaziah struck Edom but should now bask in the credit and stay at home.

The Amaziah story also echoes two further portions of the David story where the king is particularly fragile. The remark so soon after the opening chronological note on Amaziah that he had a *strong* grip on his kingdom (חזקה הממלכה בידו) indicates comparison with Hezekiah. Yet, with a suggestion of menace, it also recalls David's forceful overreach when he *insisted* that Joab count Israel: ויחזק דבר־המלך אל־יואב (2 Sam 24:4). The second resonance is even more striking. Jehoash *bursting* (פרץ) through the wall of Jerusalem (2 Kgs 14:13) is a unique reprise within synoptic texts of two *outbursts* by Yahweh in the time of David. In

10 Abishai, to whom 1 Chr 18:12 ascribes the earlier victory in Edom – 2 Sam 8:13 will have claimed it for David.

11 This assumes that 2 Kgs 14:7 represents the older version of the text which has been expanded in 2 Chr 25:11. The analogous הוא בנה is used shortly afterwards in both 2 Kgs 14:22 and synoptic 2 Chr 26:2. הוא הכה is found only once more in HB, in non-synoptic 2 Kgs 18:8. This mirrors synoptic Amaziah more closely than synoptic David: Philistines like Edomites are a people and not just single heroic foes felled by David's Benaiah.

the first, he defeated Philistines (2 Sam 5:20); in the second, he destroyed Uzzah who had held the ark (6:7–8). Like David when he had the people counted, his descendant Amaziah has gone too far. More surprising: the role played by Jehoash of Israel is more like Yahweh's, and in two respects. First, he *bursts* through Jerusalem's wall like Yahweh at Baal-*Peraz*im. Next, having reached Jerusalem and threatened it Jehoash then withdraws, emulating the destroying divine emissary (מלאך יהוה, 2 Sam 24:16–17).

Since there are echoes of David in 14:5 (the king prevailing on Joab to count the people) and in 14:7 (similar defeats of Edom), we naturally detect another in 14:6. By executing only the regicides who had killed his father, but not their sons, Amaziah was attentive to the *torah*: only sinners should die for their sins, and not their parents or children with them. David had recognised his census as a sin and many of his people had died as a consequence of the count (2 Sam 24:10, 15). Solomon would later plead in his great prayer that, if sinners prayed towards the temple and turned from their sin, Yahweh should forgive them (1 Kgs 8:33–34). However, neither David nor Solomon received a direct answer to their confession or plea; and sin goes without further mention in synoptic narrative till this commendation of Amaziah.[12] The author may be hinting here at the answer that both founding kings were seeking.

2.3

After Hezekiah and David, the third significant set of echoes in the regnal report of Amaziah are heard in the report of Rehoboam (and Jeroboam). Jeroboam is responsible for building in *Ephraim*;[13] and the name *Ephraim* is synoptic only once more: in 2 Kgs 14:13, it identifies one of the gates between which Jehoash destroyed part of Jerusalem's wall. "To the tents" marks a further unique connection; spoken by Israel at Shechem (1 Kgs 12:16//3 Kgdms 12:24t, u), it is a call of defiance against southern Rehoboam; reported here by the narrator (2 Kgs 14:12), it confirms Judah's defeat. Jehoash follows victory at Beth-shemesh by *grabbing* Amaziah of Judah (14:13). The only other occurrence of the verb תפש in a synoptic context, has Ahijah *grabbing* and tearing a cloak (1 Kgs 11:30): a symbolic action indicating loss of most of Israel from Rehoboam to Jeroboam. However, the shorter synoptic parallel (3 Kgdms 12:24o) attests not תפש, but simply קח־לך;

12 *Sin* will receive only one more synoptic mention, in the summary of Manasseh's life (2 Kgs 21:17). The situation is wholly different in the book of Kings: every northern king from Nadab (1 Kgs 15:26) to Pekah (2 Kgs 15:28) 'did not turn from the sins of Jeroboam which he caused Israel to sin'.

13 At Shechem according to MT and the longer LXX (1 Kgs 12:25) and at Sarira in the shorter LXX (3 Kgdms 12:24b).

and its "cloak that has not entered water" is more reminiscent of Jeremiah's girdle (Jer 13:1).

Importantly, only Rehoboam and Amaziah suffer the plundering of the treasuries in Jerusalem of the "houses" of Yahweh and of the king, by Jehoash (2 Kgs 14:14) and Pharaoh Shishak (1 Kgs 14:26). These two paired situations are part of a wider synoptic pattern. When Judah is twice threatened by Israel, both Asa and Ahaz resort to these same treasuries to buy help, one from Aram (1 Kgs 15:17–21) and the other from Assyria (2 Kgs 16:5–9). And Judah twice partners Israel in military action against Aram at Ramoth-Gilead, under Jehoshaphat (1 Kgs 22:1–35) and Ahaziah (2 Kgs 8:28–29).

Unique pairings of individual words and phrases have the objectivity of marks on a page; they constitute links that cannot be denied. But they also help us detect others. Of all David's successors in Jerusalem, as just noted, only Amaziah (2 Kgs 14:8) and Rehoboam (1 Kgs 12:21) initiate action against Israel. The reports on Rehoboam and Amaziah are unusual within synoptic narratives, if not unique, by including a precise date *within* their reigns: Shishak arriving in the fifth year of Rehoboam (1 Kgs 14:25) and Amaziah outliving Jehoash by fifteen years (2 Kgs 14:17). Then, within the frame of a Rehoboam-Amaziah comparison, the king's fable discouraging Amaziah's ambitions (2 Kgs 14:9) corresponds to Shemaiah's warning oracle to Rehoboam (1 Kgs 12:22–24). We observed above that the names Amaziah and Hezekiah have similar meaning. The name Amaziah (אמציהו) has only one further synoptic echo: Rehoboam *firming himself* (התאמץ) as he mounts his chariot to flee from Shechem to Jerusalem (1 Kgs 12:18 MT and 12:24u [shorter] LXX) can only confirm that these other links are not accidental.

As just noted, the verb-element of אמציהו is replicated (only once) in the wider narrative: by the *hitpael* התאמץ in 1 Kgs 12:18. Similar form and meaning bring to mind Joab's encouragement of Abishai (חזק ונתחזק in 2 Sam 10:12) and serve to emphasize both a "like" and a "not like". At the end of the Shechem assembly, Rehoboam may *show himself firm* by mounting his chariot and fleeing to Jerusalem. Yet his return to his capitol from an Israel loyal to Jeroboam is as ignominious as Amaziah's return there after capture by Jehoash at Beth-Shemesh. In colloquial English, והמלך רחבעם התאמץ could be rendered "and king Rehoboam did an Amaziah". David's grandson did not behave as David's generals would have expected. The mix of comparison and contrast is reminiscent of the wisdom in Proverbs.

2.4

Given the abundant wordplay already described, it does not seem fanciful to propose another significant link. It has just been noted that each possible military relationship between Judah and Israel is described twice in synoptic narrative:

Judah moving against Israel, Israel attacking Judah, and Judah and Israel making common cause. Both joint ventures concern Ramoth-Gilead and end badly for the king of Israel; but at each end he wants to show he is still alive. Ahab dies at the end of the first, after being propped up in his chariot facing the enemy (1 Kgs 22:35). After the second, we read in 2 Kgs 8:29 וישב יורם המלך להתרפא ביזרעאל – "and king Joram returned to show himself being healed in Jezreel" – and then his erstwhile partner Ahaziah "went down to see Joram" (ירד לראות את־יורם). רפא *hitpael* is unique within HB to this story;[14] simple passive "be healed" is normally expressed (17×) by רפא *niphal*. In this next reported encounter between kings of Judah and Israel, Amaziah ambiguously proposes לכה נתראה פנים (14:8). "Come let us see each other face to face" is not an inaccurate rendering; however, it fails to do justice to a second phrase unique within HB that (a) involves a *hitpael* of the verb used in 8:29 of Ahaziah's action (לראות) and (b) is built from the very consonants – להתרפא – used in that verse of Joram's action. Wording and context perfectly conceal intention.

Some critics will remark that too much is being made here of expressions which were simply the way things were said in ancient Hebrew. However, two defences may be offered. (a) Much of the wording under review is unremarkable in itself. However, when found in unique clusters of pairs, it takes on fresh significance. (b) If we possessed many more texts in ancient Hebrew, we might find further examples of התרפא and of התראה פנים.[15] But we might not. All we know is that each is unique within the Hebrew Bible and it is dangerous to argue from silence. Both may have been coined to effect mutual resonance within this narrative.

Beyond the three clusters of links and this skilled allusion to Joram and Ahaziah, there are two further single unique links: *Lebanon* (לבנון) appears only in narratives about Solomon (1 Kgs 5:13, 20, 23)[16] and Amaziah (2 Kgs 14:9); and *found* (נמצא) occurs synoptically only in the reports of Amaziah and Josiah: treasures in 2 Kgs 14:14; 22:9; and the book in 2 Kgs 22:13; 23:2.[17]

---

14 Apart from the synoptic parallel (2 Chr 22:6) it is used only within the expansive reworking of the Jehu story (2 Kgs 9:15). The rendering here follows the Latin sense proposed in Lisowsky 1352: *se sanandum praebere*.

15 התראה without פנים is found once more in a passage that is textually uncertain (Gen 42:1).

16 We read לבנון also in 1 Kgs 9:19//2 Chr 8:6; but not in the synoptic parallel in 3 Kgdms 10:22a.

17 מצא qal is also rare in synoptic material: bowmen and then Philistines "find" Saul (1 Sam 31:3, 8); David "finds" heart to pray (2 Sam 7:27); and Hilkiah "finds" the *torah*-book (2 Kgs 22:8).

3 In synoptic narrative and the Book of Kings

The action of Jehoash in *grabbing* Amaziah aligns this king of Israel with one of the two prophetic interventions in the Rehoboam/Jeroboam narrative; advising Amaziah against menacing the north aligns him with the other (1 Kgs 12:22–24). The Jehoash whom we meet within the synoptic Amaziah report (2 Kgs 14:8–14) is a sympathetic counterpart to the Jeroboam of the shorter and older account in 3 Kgdms (LXX).[18] We find all the uniquely paired words noted above in both the longer and the shorter accounts of Jeroboam and Rehoboam; however, the implied comparisons with Jehoash are with the Jeroboam of the shorter account preserved only in the Greek Bible.

Jehoash also speaks and behaves like a wise reader of the David story. The several parallels between the stories of Amaziah and Jehoash and of Rehoboam and Jeroboam encourage reading Jeroboam much more favourably than the book of Kings has accustomed us. The Jehoash whom we meet briefly within the series of northern kings gives a very different impression. The report comprises simply the introduction (13:10–11) and the conclusion (13:12–13 = 14:15–16) that are standard for northern kings. Apart from the names of his father and his son and the length of his reign, we are only informed of "his might and that he warred with Amaziah king of Judah" (וגבורתו ואשר נלחם עם אמציהו מלך־יהודה). He is a faceless successor – one of many faceless successors – to the Jeroboam of the longer familiar account of Rehoboam and Jeroboam in 1 Kgs 11–14 (MT) who founded a false cult of Yahweh from which not one of his successors in the north detached himself. His father's name and his warring with Amaziah were already part of the synoptic record. In light of the reading just offered of that synoptic record, it is interesting that his son is called Jeroboam.

This king of Israel who embodies many elements of the David tradition bears the same name as southern Joash; and the name they share (יהו־אש) is also closely related to the name Josiah (יאש־יהו).[19] Joash had been anointed like David (2 Kgs 11:12; 2 Sam 5:3). The only two synoptic anointings mark fresh starts after Saul and Athaliah. And Josiah will be introduced as not deviating from David's way (2 Kgs 22:2b).

---

18 Schenker 1996 had argued for the priority of the shorter text preserved only in Greek after 3 Kgdms 12:24. Despite the critique in Sweeney 2007, it is argued above (pp. 114–115) that this shorter text fitted the synoptic text better than the developed book of Kings. Trebolle 2020, 44–95 makes available in English his pioneering but complex study of 'The Alternative Stories about Solomon and Jeroboam (MT 1 Kings 12, 14 and LXX 3 Kingdoms 12:24b–z)'; and 420–424 briefly return in a concluding essay to the priority of the shorter text.

19 See 'Follow the Words' above.

4 In story and history

It has been our custom to see – to look for – historical reference in the book of Kings. The chronological structure, the succession of (mostly) fathers and sons, and perhaps especially the synchronisms of northern and southern kings, encourage such reading. Combining the parallel northern story with the synoptic narrative gave the whole book of Kings the appearance of having been chronologically researched. However, once we peel off the linked reports of northern kings from Nadab to Hoshea and expose the older synoptic narrative with which they were merged, new perspectives emerge. When paired with an Israel story, the synoptic account had looked more like a Judah story. But, viewed on its own, it might better be characterised as a story about Israel and the house of David. And again, when viewed on its own, its repetitions and cycles are more to the fore.

Historical issues certainly abound. Many scholars have been exercised about Amaziah's chronology. Montgomery (1951, 438) is typical: "Ascription of *twenty-nine years* to the reign is impossible." Has a victory in Edom in David's time been reassigned to Amaziah, or *vice versa*. How would our understanding of their campaigns be affected by locating Sela/the Rock within Petra, or taking גיא־המלח to be *wadi al-milḥ* in southern Judah rather than the valley of the Dead (Salt) Sea? And how to read the account of the northern kings if, as it seems, it is significantly less well informed about Jehoash than the record focused on his southern counterpart. Taking the independent pronoun in הוא הכה as his clue, Montgomery deems 2 Kgs 14:7 (like 14:22) "a true archival item in its original form".[20] But what if the nexus of linkages, the series of comparisons and contrasts, is more important than the accuracy of any single statement. What if resolutely "following the words" leads in a different direction from historicity?[21] Emending the 29 years attributed to Amaziah's reign will certainly lose a link in the story-chain; but it is far from certain that historical clarity is thereby gained.

5 Outlook

This article marks a further stage in a larger project provisionally titled "Seeing Double in David's House". The more than twenty clustered links discussed above are just a sample of some 150 explicit pairings throughout synoptic narrative,

20 Montgomery 1951, 439 claims that the archival original had used the emphatic 1st person pronoun, like the Mesha stone. Gray 1977, 605 commended Montgomery as "very sensitive to the features of archival style".

21 The issue is explored further on pp. 190–192 above.

each a word or phrase found in the reports of only two kings.[22] Together they represent the perfectly formed skeleton of the synoptic narrative. Reading Amaziah and Jehoash between David, Rehoboam and Jeroboam, and Hezekiah illustrates how the whole composition must be read. Only two of David's successors initiate military action against the north. Only twice does a force return to its "tents". The one northern antagonist builds a city in Ephraim; the other destroys a city wall by Jerusalem's Ephraim Gate – and both men bear comparison with David. Rehoboam's resolute flight anticipates Amaziah's very name. A textual jewel has long lain hidden in plain sight within both Samuel-Kings and Chronicles.

Less immediately clear is what this finely crafted text of consummate artistry is about – or is principally about. The books of Samuel and Kings have both built on it. While Kings shares more of its content, Samuel exhibits more of its literary flair. However, both successors have developed its prophetic tradition in similar fashion.[23] David and Solomon occupy more narrative space than all their successors together and are very differently portrayed from the rest. They take care of the ark and its housing; only they offer sacrifice to Yahweh; yet the continuing role of Yahweh's house seems more as treasury than shrine. This rich tapestry of comparisons and contrasts does not so much offer instruction or provide historical data as it invites reflection.

---

22 Pp. 153–161 provide a list of some 130 of these.
23 See the discussion of 'Divination' on pp. 75–87 above.

Ruth: A Reading of Scripture?

Structure

The biblical book called Ruth is a very finely crafted short story. Although there are good reasons for the traditional title of the book, Ruth herself is named only 12 times over the course of the story while the two senior characters are mentioned more often: Naomi 21 times and Boaz 20 times. A case could be made for renaming it "Naomi". Naomi features even more widely throughout the narrative, from beginning (1:2) to end (4:14–17), while Ruth is mentioned first in 1:4 and last in 4:13. Ruth as title focuses on the means, while Naomi would direct our attention to the end – the restoration of a devastated Bethlehem family.

It is now very widely recognized that the medieval chapter divisions correspond to four natural stages in the story; and these are underscored by verbal links at the end of these "chapters" (Korpel, 2001, p. 222): "at the start of the *barley harvest*" (1:22), "until the end of the *barley harvest*" (2:23), and "unless he has ended the matter today" (3:18). In the traditional Hebrew text (MT), as represented in both the most ancient codices, only one major break is noted: by leaving a space at the end of 4:17. This comes at the end of the narrative, and marks off the closing genealogy (4:18–22) as separate material. Critics are divided over whether this genealogy of ten names (nine generations) from Perez to David (the details agree with 1 Chr 2:4–15) is original and integral to the book. Be that as it may, Perez is already mentioned in 4:12, and David is the last word of 4:17.

Chapter 1 reports a family forced out of Bethlehem by famine and taking up residence in Moab. Father Elimelech dies there; his sons both marry Moabite women, but within ten years of leaving home both also die, still childless. On hearing that the famine is over, their mother Naomi starts home to Judah. On the way, she asks her daughters-in-law to return to their mothers' homes: Orpah eventually leaves, but Ruth insists on continuing with Naomi. When they reach Bethlehem at the start of the barley harvest, the townswomen recognise Naomi; but they ignore her companion (Gitay, 1993, pp. 182–83).

Chapter 2 informs us before we meet him that Boaz is a man of substance related to Elimelech. Ruth proposes, supported by Naomi, to glean in the harvest fields; and she "just happens" (v. 3) on Boaz's field. When Boaz arrives and is told that the stranger in his field is the Moabite who has come back to Bethlehem with Naomi, he treats her generously; and Naomi understands the significance of Ruth's report to her.

Naomi prompts Ruth (ch. 3) to offer herself at night to a relaxed Boaz at his threshing floor. He accepts Ruth's challenge to act as redeemer. However, pointing out that he is not the closest relative, he insists that their tryst remain secret.

https://doi.org/10.1515/9783111060279-017

Naomi again understands Ruth's report of what Boaz has said and the meaning of the barley she brings from him.

At the city gate next morning (ch. 4), Boaz asks the unnamed potential redeemer to join him, recruits a quorum of elders, and announces that Naomi is selling her late husband's land. The redeemer is willing to buy till he learns that a future claim on this land may come from Ruth's offspring. Boaz is left free both to redeem the field and marry Ruth. Their son Obed is credited to Naomi by her neighbours, who are now loud in their praise of Ruth; and Obed turns out to be grandfather to the future king David.

The narrative has often been characterised as broadly symmetrical. Balanced structure is more obvious in the two central chapters: each features talk between Ruth and Naomi (2:2; 3:1–5) that leads to an encounter between Ruth and Boaz (2:3–16; 3:6–15), then Ruth's report back to Naomi (2:17–22; 3:16–18). Boaz expresses a wish for Yahweh's intervention in both 2:12 and 3:10. The earlier wish ends by noting that Ruth has come seeking refuge under Yahweh's "wings" (*knp*); and Ruth uses exactly this word (which literally means an "edge" or "extremity") when she asks Boaz to spread over her the "skirt/edge" of his garment (3:9). Boaz demonstrates complete understanding of Ruth's situation, and functions as representative of Yahweh; he also speaks like a king or prophet in Samuel-Kings when he emphasises what he says both directly to her (2:11) and to his staff about her (2:16) by using the cognate infinitive absolute.

There are several links between the outer chapters too. The story opens in the period of the judges and closes with mention of David. It starts with the death of all the men in an Ephrathite family (1:2) and finishes first with a wish for children in Ephrath (4:11) and then the report of a birth and a (short) genealogy (4:13–17). Yahweh intervenes explicitly only twice in the book: to return food to Bethlehem (1:6) and ensure conception for Ruth (4:13). And the women of Bethlehem, rather like a Greek chorus, greet both Naomi's return from Moab (1:19) and the birth of Ruth's (or Naomi's!) child (4:14–17). These similarities between first and last chapters throw into relief one principal difference: all the speaking in the first is done by women, while in the last it is almost all by men with the women's chorus as sole exception.

Korpel has offered the most sustained account of the structure of the Book of Ruth, which she describes as a narrative text in poetic form. In the main, the cola in Ruth are shorter than in classical Hebrew prose; and "parallelism accounts for many of the seemingly superfluous repetitions" (Korpel, 2001, p. 223). She notes, however, that still greater balance can be achieved in the structure she has detected if both 1:12b–13a and 1:16b are recognised as later supplements, and it is agreed that a report of Ruth naming her child was suppressed (after 4:13) when the fuller ten-name genealogy (4:18–22) was added. She bases her analysis on the full resources of the Masoretic text – not just its consonants and their vocalization, but also the traditional accentuation that defines phrasing. And she finds wide ancient support for the implied paragraphs (or Sub-cantos) in other ancient versions: not only the Aramaic Targum and Syriac Peshitta (both close to the Hebrew tradition), but also the Greek LXX. On the latter point, it is true that the start of each of her 13 "Sub-cantos" does correspond to the start of one of the 48 divisions in our earliest Greek manuscript (LXX^B) marked by the scribe with a negative indent; but the same is not always the case at her lesser levels of "canticle" or "strophe".

Ruth taking the initiative with Boaz at his threshing-floor (ch. 3) recalls two stories in the book of Genesis: Ruth's own forefather Moab had been produced by Lot's elder daughter getting him drunk and lying with him (Gen. 19); then Tamar, who tricked Judah into performing his family duty by her (Gen. 38), is explicitly mentioned (4:12); and Perez, her son, was an ancestor of Boaz. And Ruth's grandson David would send "[his] father and mother" to her land for safety (1 Sam 22:3–4). Such "genetic" links in the story-line encourage further probes of the book's lexical DNA.

Unique links

The first probe is of the several words or phrases that occur just once within this short story and once (or rarely) elsewhere in the Hebrew Bible. Some of these individual links appear significant as soon as they are mentioned. Considered together, their force is all the more compelling.

1 The opening words, "in the days when the judges judged", resonate in different directions, giving an early indication of what we may expect of other significant words and phrases. Firstly, the cognate subject and verb ("judges judged") appear together again only once: in the report of Josiah's reformed Passover (but only as reported in 2 Kings 23:22, and not in the parallel passage in 2 Chr 35:18). And Passover was celebrated at the time of barley harvest (1:22; 2:23). Then the final chapters of the book called Judges (17–21) deal with scandalous events related to Bethlehem.

2 As the story of Ruth begins to unfold, it may appear unremarkable that two refugees from Judah in Moab should marry "Moabite wives". However, only two other "biblical" contexts mention "Moabite wives": each within a larger list of "foreign wives", because of whom first Solomon (1 Kings 11:1) and later men from Judah (Neh 13:23) are blamed.

3 Only Job (27:2) and Naomi (1:20) make "the Almighty" (*šadday*) subject of "brought bitterness". This divine title is used almost twice as often in Job (31 times) as elsewhere in HB together (17 times); and it is only in Job (9 times) and Ruth (twice) that we find *šadday* as subject of a verb. Naomi names God "the Almighty" again in 1:21, blaming him for causing her evil.

4 Rizpah was another remarkably strong woman, courageous in support of her family. After David had seven members of Saul's family killed, Rizpah protected their exposed corpses, action that shamed David into granting them burial. The story in which she features also started in grievous famine (2 Sam 21:1) and it was at "the beginning of the barley harvest" (only 21:9 and Ruth 1:22) that her relatives were killed.

5 Apart from Ruth 2:2, the only biblical passage in which the words for "glean" and "ears of grain" are linked is Isa 17:5, within an oracle about the diminished glory of Jacob. There the harvest scene is set in the valley of Rephaim, which has Jerusalem at its head and Bethlehem nearby.

6 "Native land" (or "land of [your] birth") is a phrase used only in 2:11 and Gen 24:7, where Abraham recalls he had been taken by Yahweh from "his father's house and his native land", and instructs his servant to return there and find a wife for his son.

7 The only close parallel to Boaz's wish for Ruth (2:12), that "Yahweh may repay your deed", is spoken in Job 34:11 – "deed" (*pa'al*) is object of "pay" (*šlm*, piel) only in these two verses. In Job, the implied subject of "repay your deed" must be El or Shaddai, as both divine names are used in the two adjacent verses (34:10, 12). Naomi had cited Job himself in Ruth 1:20 (**2** above), and Boaz now responds to Ruth using words of Elihu.

8 The next key term in Boaz's wish for Ruth (2:12) takes us back to the book of Genesis. The Hebrew word for "wage" is found again only in the reports about the bargain struck by Jacob and Laban: in Gen 29:15, where their deal is made; and in 31:7, 41, where Jacob complains about Laban's trickery. The last of these Genesis parallels provides yet another link with Ruth. Had God not intervened against his father-in-law who was always changing his "wage" (31:41–42), Jacob would have been sent away "empty[-handed]". Naomi had used the same word when she complained against Yahweh (1:21), that he had "brought her back empty" to Bethlehem (Beyer 2014, 153). And Boaz will acknowledge the problem when he counts out six measures of barley, telling Ruth that she should not return to her mother-in-law "empty[-handed]" (3:17). *šlm*, an adjective meaning "full/complete" nowhere else in HB modifies a term for payment; but its use in 2:12 alongside "wage" effects a nice juxtaposition with the piel form of the verb *šlm* in the previous clause (7 above).

9 We have already noted the play on *kanap*, introduced by Boaz in 2:12, when he mentions that Ruth has "come to shelter under [Yahweh's] wings". "Shelter under his wings" is found only once more (Ps 91:4), early in a psalm whose opening verse ends "will lodge in the shade of the Almighty (*šadday*)". Only one other psalm uses that divine title (68:15), and we shall discuss below (**18**) the significance of "lodge" in Ruth 1:16; 3:13. But we can add here that the only two occurrences in Ezekiel (1:24; 10:5) of "the Almighty" (**3** and 7 above) are also associated with the "wings" [of the cherubim].

10 "… who has not abandoned his *ḥesed*" is said only of Yahweh" in Gen 24:27 and again in Ruth 2:20, though verb and noun are also linked in Jon 2:9. (At **6** above, another link with Gen 24 was noted.)

11 Outside Ruth 4:9–11, Josh 24:22 provides the only example of the challenge "you are witnesses" being met by the one-word response "[we are] witnesses".

Wider links

Other relevant links are with words or phrases which occur in Ruth and more often elsewhere, but just in one or two contexts.

12 When Ruth swears "So may [God] do" in 1:17, she uses an oath formula found elsewhere in HB only in Samuel-Kings (11 times). It is in fact uttered by her grandson David more than any other character. Normally "God" is the subject: only one more time (1 Sam 20:13) is "Yahweh" the subject, and there as here it introduces a pledge of commitment (Campbell 1975, 74–75).

13 The noun "chance" (*miqrēh*) is found outside Ruth 2:3 only in 1 Sam 6:9; 20:26 and in Qoh 2:14, 15; 3:19; 9:2, 3. In Qoh 2:14, 15, the cognate verb "happen" (*qrh*) is also used; and this verb is found on its own in Esther 4:7; 6:13. The Philistine diviners propose a test (1 Sam 6:9) for deciding whether the plagues that had afflicted them since they captured the ark were a matter of chance or were caused by Yahweh. However, a reader of Ruth within the biblical tradition will not readily accept that binary choice: what appeared to Ruth at the time to be pure chance was in fact divine guidance.

14 Only three women are described in HB as washing (*rḥṣ*); two of them are certainly foreign, the daughter of Pharaoh (Exod 2:5) and Ruth the Moabite (3:3), while Bathsheba (2 Sam 11–12) is wife to Hittite Uriah. Washing is only one of several similarities between the stories of Ruth, grandmother of David, and Bathsheba, mother of Solomon. Naomi instructs Ruth to wash and anoint herself and then, after Boaz has eaten and drunk and lain down, to uncover his "legs" and herself "lie down" (3:3–4). David instructs Uriah to go to his house and wash his "legs" (2 Sam 11:8); and Uriah's seemingly knowing refusal (11:11) includes the words "shall I go to my house, to eat and to drink, and to lie down with my wife?"

15 A daughter-in-law "better for you than seven sons" (4:15) may have double resonance in 1 Samuel: echoing both Elkanah claiming to Hannah (1:10) he is better for her than ten sons, and also David chosen by Samuel in preference to seven elder brothers (16:6–13).

Preliminary Assessment

If we assume that that these links represent conscious borrowing or allusion, then the following intertextual reading may be sketched of the book of Ruth in its biblical context. Ruth's risqué approach at night to a Boaz who had been celebrating harvest-home risked evoking national[ist] memories of the provocative sexuality of Moabite women (Num 25) and even the DNA of their foremother, who had encouraged her sister to join with her in sleeping with Lot, their father (Gen 19). However, by means of a dense series of deliberate allusions to portions of Genesis (**6**, **8**, **10**), Joshua (**11**), Samuel-Kings (**1**, **2**, **4**, **12**, **13**, **14**, **15**), Isaiah (**5**), Psalms (**9**), Job (**3**, **7**), Qohelet (**13**), and Nehemiah (**2**), Ruth's behaviour is warmly supported; and we are reminded that Boaz's own ancestor, Perez, had similar origins in Tamar's entrapment of a similarly celebrating Judah, and that David his descendant would make a similar attempt to entrap Uriah.

The story of Ruth may be set "in the days when the judges judged"; but it is with Samuel (and Kings) that the closest word-links exist: not only the two indicators of time (**1**, **4**) but also the oath-formula Ruth uses (**12**), the happenstance of her choice of Boaz's harvest field (**13**), and the claim of Bethlehem's women that Ruth was better for Naomi than seven sons (**15**). The opening time-reference deftly evokes both days of old and the precise season of Passover at barley-harvest (**1**). When this is reinforced by a specific mention of barley-harvest, the wording also recalls Rizpah and her courageous care of the corpses of her dead menfolk throughout a hot summer (**4**). Abraham following divine promise and guidance from a distant land (as well as the hope that Rebekah will follow suit) are recalled from Gen 24 (**6** and **10**). Naomi has protested against the Almighty like Job himself (**3**) and Boaz answers Ruth in Elihu's words from the same book (**7**).

Clustered links

Of the fifteen close links in wording noted above, almost all seemed immediately relevant to Ruth's story. We move next to identify cases where the same cluster of features occurs in Ruth and in one (exceptionally two) other biblical context(s).

16 There are several echoes through Ruth of the end of Gen 2 ("Therefore a man leaves his father and mother and clings to his wife, and they become one flesh. And the man and his wife were both naked ...")

- Naomi tries to send both women back to their mother's homes (1:8)
- Ruth instead "clings to her" (1:14)
- "and you left your father and mother" (2:11) – the verb "leave" governs this double object (father and mother) elsewhere only in Gen 2:24
- Ruth requests covering from Boaz (3:9)

17 "A woman of substance" (*'ēšet ḥayil*) is found in HB only in Ruth 3:11 and Prov 31:10; and this phrase is only one of several links between our short story and the acrostic poem that concludes the book of Proverbs (31:10–31). (a) Each uses *šll* (normally "spoil" or "plunder") in a striking way. The woman's husband (31:11) will not lack *šll* (NRSV softens the noun to "gain"). And a literal translation of Boaz's instruction to his servants (2:16) would be "and also really plunder for her from the sheaves". (b) "Her husband is known at the gates, taking his seat with the elders of the land" (31:23) is richly echoed in Ruth 4:1–2, where Boaz goes up "to the gate", "sits down" there, and gathers ten men of the "elders" of the city. (c) "The teaching of *ḥesed* is on her lips" (31:26); and, while Naomi attributes this quality to Yahweh (1:8; 2:20), Boaz attributes it to Ruth (3:10). (d) The closing words of Proverbs, "and let her works praise her in the gates" (31:31), resonate with Boaz's words to Ruth (3:11): "the whole gate of my people knows that you are a woman of substance".

18 The verb "spend the night" (*lîn*) is used twice at key points in Ruth: first within Ruth's solemn declaration to Naomi in 1:16 ("where you lodge, I will lodge"), and then within Boaz's response to Ruth on the threshing-floor in 3:13 ("stay here tonight"). The biblical story is which this verb is most densely used (as often as 11 times in 17 verses) concerns the Levite whose partner would be grossly abused in Gibeah (Judg 19); and it also features in contexts already discussed above: Gen 19 and 24 (**6** and **10**) and Ps 91 (**9**). The tale told in Judg 19 also starts in Bethlehem: the Levite returns there to "speak to the heart of" the woman (19:3), words used by Ruth in appreciation of Boaz (2:13). And eating, drinking, and making merry (like Boaz in 3:3, 7) was the entertainment offered to the Levite both by the woman's father in Bethlehem (Judg 19:4, 9) and by their host in Gibeah (19:21–22). The idiom "speak to the heart of" is used eight times more in HB, and the situation is generally a fraught one. In three of these, a man is making overtures to a woman: Hamor to Dinah, whom he has just raped (Gen 34:3), the Levite to his partner, who has run away from him (Judg 19:3), and Yahweh to Israel, his wife who has committed adultery (Hos 2:16). In three more, Joseph now viceroy in Egypt reassures the brothers who had earlier got rid of him (Gen 50:21), King David is urged to win over the troops he has insulted (2 Sam 19:8), and Yahweh comforts banished Jerusalem (Isa 40:1–2). In 1 Sam 1:13, distraught Hannah is speaking to her own heart; and it is unclear what is intended in Hezekiah speaking to the heart of the levites (2 Chr 30:22). In two of these passages (Gen 50:21 and Isa 40:1–2), as also in Ruth 2:13, the idiom "speak to the heart of" follows and intensifies the verb "console"; but only in Ruth (in 4:15) does it go on to share with Gen 50:21 the verb "provide for". And the linkage between Ruth and the Joseph story is even closer: in Ruth, the provision is precisely for Naomi's old age (literally "grey hair"), while Jacob's other sons had earlier (Gen 44:31) begged Joseph not to imperil their father's grey hair by insisting on seeing Benjamin. The four verbal links between Ruth and Judg 19 serve to underline how different the Moabite woman's treatment by Boaz just outside the town of Bethlehem was from the Bethlehemite woman's fate at the hands of Gibeathites inside the "protection" of their own town.

19 When Boaz declares that he is taking Ruth as wife (4:10) "to *raise* the name of the deceased over his property, so that the name of the deceased be not cut off from his brothers", his language seems to draw on two sources. The most obvious link is with the law in Deuteronomy (25:5–10) about levirate marriage: (a) The terms "wife of the deceased" and "name of the deceased" are found only in Ruth 4 and Deut 25. (b) The eldest son of a levirate union of widow with brother-in-law "should *rise* over the name of his deceased brother, so that his name is not blotted out from Israel" (25:6). Just as English "raise" and "rise" are linked in both sound and sense, so too Hebrew *hāqîm* ("raise") is a causative form of the verb *qûm* ("rise"). But there is one interesting change: Boaz replaces "not blotted out" with "not cut off", and the latter verb is a key component of the divine promise relating to the house of David: "a man of yours shall not be cut off from before me, seated on Israel's throne" (1 Kgs 8:25‖2 Chr 6:16; and similarly 1 Kgs 9:5). This royal man of promise is called (Yahweh's) "servant" (*'ebed*) in almost every verse of the whole paragraph in 1 Kgs (8:23–30); and the name Obed (*'ôbēd*) that will be given to Boaz's son (4:17) is cognate and means "Server". In the very same breath as Boaz declares he is doing his duty as (stand-in) brother-in-law, he is also anticipating the divine promise to David.

20 The legal problem relating to the property of Zelophehad, who died having fathered daughters only and no sons, is treated twice in Numbers: first in Num 27:1–11 near the end of an earlier version of that book, and then in Num 36 which closes the canonical version. *naḥ^{a}lâ*, meaning "[heritable] property", and often translated "inheritance", is used very widely in these chapters (6 times in Num 27:1–11, and 18 times in Num 36); and the same term features in Ruth 4:5, 6, 10. A second linguistic similarity is the use 7 times in Ruth (1:8^{2}, 9, 11, 13, 19; 4:11) and twice in Num 27:7–8 (though never in Num 36) of apparently masculine plural forms in contexts where feminine would be expected (Embry 2016, 38). I am not aware of a grammatical explanation that works well in both books; but it is interesting that the same oddity is part of both principal biblical contexts where, in the absence of sons, women play a central role relating to property.

Redemption?

The story of Ruth is also unique in drawing together levirate responsibility (*ybm*) and "redemption" (*g'l*). Apart from the legal paragraph in Deut 25:5–10, only Gen 38 uses the verb *ybm*, which means "perform the duty of the brother-in-law": Onan refuses to "brother-in-law" Tamar, widow of his elder brother (38:8). The story of Tamar is recalled in the way the story of Ruth is told, from beginning to end. When Naomi urges Ruth to follow Orpah back to her mother's house (1:15), she describes Orpah as *ybmtk* ("your sister-in-law") – outside Deut 25, that noun is used nowhere else. When she declares she is too old (even if she had a husband) to produce further sons for the widows to wait for (1:11–12), she implicitly recalls Judah asking Tamar to wait (in her father's house!) for Shelah, his youngest son (Gen 38:11). Then, at the end of the book (4:12), Judah and Tamar are finally named along with Perez their son. And yet, despite hinting at levirate (*ybm*) in 1:15, the solution that Naomi actually voices to Ruth is "a redeemer" (*g'l*). "Redeem" (*g'l*), with "redeemer" and "redemption", does not receive a mention until the middle of the story; but, once introduced (2:20), usage of this group of related words multiplies.

When Ruth finishes reporting to Naomi on her generous reception in the harvest-field, Naomi utters a brief blessing on the one who had paid attention to her (2:19). When Ruth goes on to name this benefactor, Naomi's blessing becomes much more profuse; and the older woman adds that Boaz is "near to us" and (hence) among those with the right and responsibility to "redeem" them (2:20). Accordingly, when the woman Boaz discovers with him at night on the threshing floor identifies herself as Ruth, she asks him to spread the skirt of his garment over her "because you are redeemer" (3:9). It may just be that her prosecution of this key theme (*g'l*) is already (3:7) hinted at in the words describing her approach: *wt<u>gl</u> mr<u>gl</u>tyw wtškb* ("and she uncovered [the place of] his legs and lay down") – each of the first two Hebrew words contains the first and last letters of *g'l* together. In any case, after praising her and accepting her challenge (3:10–11), he points out that there is another redeemer still closer (3:12). "If he will redeem you, good – let him redeem; and, if he is not willing to redeem you, I myself will redeem you, as Yahweh lives" (3:13). After this proliferation of the term (6 times in Ruth 3), the usage of *g'l* becomes still more intensive: 14 times in 4:1–8, as the two potential redeemers meet in front of ten elders. Finally, in rather clumsy wording, the women of Bethlehem address Naomi with a blessing of Yahweh "who has not stopped for you a redeemer today" (4:14). Both Boaz and Yahweh himself could be discerned as intended in these strange words (the implied double negative has a possible parallel in Lev 2:13); but the women go on to make clear (4:15) that Ruth's baby will be Naomi's redeemer. Boaz had "comforted" Ruth and "spoken to her heart"; but it will be Obed who "provides for" Naomi's old age, so completing the parallel with Joseph's declaration at the end of Genesis (end of **18** above).

The prevalence of words related to *g'l* in the second half of the story would appear to support the claim (Bronner 1993, 167) that Ruth is about redemption (*g'l*), not levirate (*ybm*). And yet it also presses the question whether "redeem" is after all the right way to translate this most common term in the book? Elsewhere, it is used in a relatively small number of quite different biblical contexts. Common to most (but not all) of the literal usages is action taken in family solidarity by a near relative:

- In Lev 25, *g'l* is one of several terms used for the support necessary within a wider family to recover the wellbeing of impoverished members who have had to sell their land or their children or themselves.
- Lev 27 uses *g'l* for the recovery of property "vowed" or "consecrated" to Yahweh – what we might now call "mortgaged": such property made over to the deity (for safe keeping) could be reclaimed for a percentage fee.
- Num 35, Deut 19, and Josh 20 are all concerned with temporary sanctuary for an alleged homicide in flight from the "blood-avenger" (*g'l hdm*).
- Many Psalms and the second half of Isaiah apply *g'l* metaphorically to Yahweh, who acts in support of Israel as if recovering his kinsfolk.

Pinpointing the meaning of the term *g'l* within Ruth is important for understanding the development of the plot of this short story. Naomi is the first to use it. When she says of Boaz: "He is related to us, he is one of our *gō'ēls*", presumably her second remark develops the first – but precisely how: (a) As a relative, he has certain family responsibilities towards us? Or (b) As a relative, he could make a move specifically towards recovering our land? Similarly, when Ruth takes up the issue with Boaz at night, and says "Spread your skirt over me for you are *gō'ēl*", has she offspring in mind, or is she talking about Naomi's land, or both? When Boaz takes the issue to the more closely related *gō'ēl*, he first raises the matter of Naomi selling her field; only later does he mention the claim on this property that a son of Ruth would have. By approaching the discussion this way, is he confirming for us that "[property] redeemer" is the basic sense of *gō'ēl*, or is he somewhat deviously persuading an even closer relative that it is not in his interest to undertake this particular "family duty"? And when the townswomen assure Naomi that Obed as *gō'ēl* will provide for her old age, do they mean simply that he will be a willing and responsible family member, or do they assume that he will have available to him the resources accruing from the land she once owned? This overview of the story suggests that, at each stage, offspring and land are integrally linked. It appears that Naomi sends Ruth to Boaz at night to offer sex with the aim of encouraging him to act over the family land. Her uncovering of his legs is integral to what Naomi has called "redemption". And yet the priority for Boaz is that she stays with him all night – the land question can wait till morning.

Naomi seems conscious of the story of Judah and Tamar in her dealings with her daughters-in-law. She ends the first chapter complaining like Job of bitterness brought by the Almighty (**3** above), but by the end of the second she is recalling Yahweh's loyalty in the words of Abraham's servant (**10**). Ruth's oath to Naomi will often be uttered by David (**12**); and she tells Boaz he has given her reassurance like Joseph to his brothers (**18**). But it is Boaz himself whose language is most "biblical". He compares Ruth's journey to Abraham's (**6**) and borrows Elihu's words to call for a reward fairer than Jacob received from Laban (**7**). She should enjoy the divine shelter promised in Ps 91 (**9**), for she is the epitome of the fine woman praised in Prov 31 (**17**). Though he both speaks to Ruth's heart and also eats, drinks, and is merry, Boaz behaves wholly differently from all the men in Gibeah that fateful night (**18**). When he declares the significance of his marriage to Ruth, he splices together the levirate law and the divine promise to David (**19**). And at the gate he calls for witness corroboration like Joshua at Shechem (**11**). In short, this Bethlehemite, this ancestor of David, is an exemplar of biblical tradition at its best (Wetter 2015, 93–94).

A women's book?

Despite this prominent role played by Boaz, the book has been called after Ruth since ancient times. The story starts with a couple and their two sons being forced by famine out of Bethlehem. It finishes with the birth of a boy who will both complete the restoration of his grandmother's wellbeing and be grandfather of king David. And it has at its core the steady, generous, presence of Boaz, affirming in practice the values that much of the biblical tradition holds dear. And yet – and surprising within that tradition – the female cast is even stronger. There are not only the two central characters of Naomi and Ruth; but, among the minor figures, Orpah and the women of Bethlehem play as large a role as Boaz's steward together with the unnamed *gō'ēl* and the elder-witnesses.

Some readers have discerned a homosexual component in the relationship between Ruth and Naomi: in the younger woman "clinging/cleaving" to the older (1:14), in Ruth's marriage-like declaration of loyalty till and through death (1:16–17), and in the realization among Naomi's neighbours that Ruth "loved" her mother-in-law (4:15). Leaving father and mother (2:11) and cleaving to a wife is part of heterosexual marriage as envisaged in Gen 2:24. However, if the opening chapter depicts the younger woman as something of a husband to the elder, by the end (at least as viewed by the neighbours) she has become surrogate mother, for the child she has produced is reckoned as Naomi's (4:17). Certainly the roles of Ruth and Boaz do not conform to patriarchal stereotypes. Yet, on the other side, their roles and Naomi's too are repeatedly compared to other biblical characters.

Canonical function and placing

We have noted a large number of links between Ruth and other "biblical" books. Several of these resonate with end-pieces in other books. (a) The empathetic concern and practical care in Ruth 2:13 and 4:15 are expressed in the same terms as Joseph's declaration near the end of Genesis (50:21) – and it is of course famine that has also driven Joseph's brothers to Egypt. (b) Women's rights to land where a father dies without sons are legislated for in Num 27 (possibly an earlier conclusion of Numbers) and again in Num 36 (which certainly now ends that book). (c) The exchange about witnesses (Ruth 4:9–11) has its only analogue in the final chapter of Joshua (24:22). (d) The narrative about the Levite and his concubine occupies the final chapters of Judges (19–21). (e) Rizpah's care for her brothers' corpses is recounted as the start of the coda to the book of Samuel (2 Sam 21–24). (f) And it is in the final chapter of Proverbs that we find the virtuous woman with whom Ruth is implicitly compared.

Final chapters by no means always contain the latest additions to a biblical book. Yet, at the very least, this set of associations suggests that the author of the book called Ruth knew Genesis, Numbers, Joshua, Judges, Samuel, and Proverbs, as separate entities. Given that all three elements of Joseph's reassurance to his brothers (Gen 50:21) are echoed in Ruth (two by Ruth talking about Boaz and the third by Naomi's neighbours talking about Obed) and that Joseph's next words to his brothers (50:24–25) concern taking his body home from Egypt, it will be no accident that Josh 24:32 reports his burial in Shechem just after Joshua has called Israel as witnesses (24:22).

Comparing and contrasting Ruth with Judg 19–21 may permit greater precision. Edenburg, in a careful and detailed study, has proposed that the end of Judges was drafted in two main stages: the first included all of Judg 19 and an earlier version of 20–21; the second comprised a substantial rewriting of Judg 20–21. She explores the first draft in relation to Abraham and Lot (Gen 18–19), the battle at Ai (Josh 7–8), the Saul narratives, the laws of Deuteronomy, the rape of Tamar (2 Sam 13:11–17), several isolated parallels, and the earlier outer structure of Judges (1 and 17–18) and finds at almost every point of connection that the authors of Judg 19–21 were the borrowers. She "view[s] the story as a reflection of conflicting interests between rival groups within Yehud – those who advanced the restoration of Jerusalem against those who backed the relatively new pre-eminence of Benjaminite towns" (Edenburg 2016, 330).

The author of Ruth has drawn on a similarly wide range of "biblical" materials, including several links with Judg 19. Ruth, accordingly, must have been written later than the first draft of the final appendix to the book of Judges. (Similarly, the linguistic link with Zelophehad's daughters was with the earlier Num 27:1–11 and not the later Num 36.) Another observation points in the same direction. The Ruth narrative might itself have been included within the book of Judges, had the tale of the outrage at Gibeah and its consequences not already been there. If the purpose of that narrative was to besmirch the reputation of Benjamin's towns, and especially Saul's birthplace at Gibeah, a key aim of Ruth had been to revive the reputation of Bethlehem. In Judg 17, Bethlehem had been home to a Levite who had shown himself prepared to become priest at an impromptu and irregular shrine in the north. In Judg 19, by contrast, Bethlehem (that would be home to David) featured as a town where hospitality was more generous than in Gibeah (that would be home to Saul). And this rehabilitation of David's town is further and vigorously promoted in the book of Ruth.

In the Christian Bible, and at least since the earliest bound Greek codices available to us from the 5th century CE, the story called "Ruth" is found between Judges and (what the Greek Bible calls) Kingdoms (Samuel-Kings in Hebrew or English). The situation in Jewish tradition is more complex, and for two reasons: the earliest book-like codices we possess of the "Hebrew Bible" are much more recent, from around 1,000 CE; and liturgical reading in synagogue was and is from scrolls. The relationships between individual scrolls are more flexible. Only when bound in a large volume does a biblical "book" receive a fixed location between prescribed neighbours.

Most often, Ruth is reckoned one of the five *M^egillôt* or "Scrolls", each read in its entirety once a year at a major festival; and these *M^egillôt* are a sub-group within the "Writings" (the collection of varied books that are neither "Torah" nor "Prophets"). In Sephardi tradition, Ruth comes first, as related to the earliest historical period of the five, and is followed by Song of Songs and Qohelet both related to Solomon. In Ashkenazi tradition, the order follows their use in the liturgical year: Ruth, read at the feast of Weeks, follows the Song of Songs at Passover. Jonah (within the Prophets) is also read once a year, during the Day of Atonement; and it is suggested that the five *M^egillôt* were selected from the six scrolls read at festivals to correspond to the five "fifths" of the Torah which are also read in their entirety in the course of each year. Within codices or large volumes, Ruth can also be neighbour to other books. Ruth is ancestress of David, and her book can be found before the Psalms. The several links between her and the fine woman at the end of Proverbs (**17** above) lead to her book being set immediately after Proverbs.

It has been argued (Stone 2015, 180–81), in support of its position in ancient Greek and continuing Christian Bibles, that Ruth was deliberately written to link at its start with the end of Judges ("lift" rather than normal "take" a wife in Judg 21:23 and Ruth 1:4), and at its end with the beginning of Samuel ("better than *n* sons" in Ruth 4:15 and 1 Sam 1:8). However, we have noted so many unique and apparently significant intertextual links with several other biblical books that it seems unwise to concentrate on these two.

The Words in Context: A Hall of Mirrors

This chapter reminds readers which sections of Sam-Kgs are found also in Chr, which topics they have in common and highlights where in this broadly shared text the paired terms are to be found. It does not attempt a reconstruction of the complete text of BoTH. That could be reasonably attempted in many portions while in others it seems quite impossible. Instead, within the narrative shared by Sam-Kgs and Chr, it identifies the (often) interwoven pairings that indicate the structure of BoTH.

The heading of each synoptic portion supplies a reference to both Sam-Kgs and Chr (and occasionally also to Kgdms). Thereafter, precise references are normally given only to chapter and verse within the Hebrew text of Sam-Kgs. The English rendering of every paired feature is italicised at each mention, with the Hebrew supplied at first mention. Almost all such paired features are textually attested triply: they are not only found in Sam-Kgs MT and Chr MT but are also witnessed in Kgdms (or Sam-Kgs LXX). Exceptions to this rule are specifically noted.

1 The death of Saul (1 Sam 31//1 Chr 10)

'*Philistines* (פלשתים) were warring in Israel' are the opening words of the whole narrative. We may know historically that Philistines remained a significant population for many centuries in the southern part of the east coast of the Mediterranean. However, these neighbours of Israel play no further part in BoTH after Saul and David: Saul fails against them while David succeeds. No mention is made of Yahweh in this short account of the death of Saul. But it is proclaimed to the temples of Philistine gods. These gods (or *idols* – עצבים) reappear after 1 Sam 31:9 only in 2 Sam 5:21, where David's men collect abandoned Philistine idols.

Differences between Saul and his successor are pointed up by three other terms unique to this narrative and 2 Sam 23//1 Chr 11. (a) We find *pierced* (חלל[ים]) at least twice[1] in the death narrative (1, 8). The implication is that the wounding is fatal; for the enemy come to strip those who have so fallen. Israel, including Saul, fall [fatally] *pierced* (1) and are then stripped by *Philistines* (8). Later, *Philistines* are *pierced* in their hundreds by David's heroes (23:8, 18). (b) One *bodyguard* (נשא כלי – literally equipment/weapons-carrier) is included in the

1 LXX and other ancient versions have read ויחל at the end of 3 as niphal of the related verb חלל, whereas MT has related it to חיל ('writhe').

https://doi.org/10.1515/9783111060279-018

listing of David's heroes in 2 Sam 23:37. The other is caught up in Saul's death (1 Sam 31:4–5); he refuses to administer the *coup de grâce* to his wounded master but follows him into death on his own sword. (c) *Man of valour* (איש חיל) describes the Jabeshites who rescued the bodies of Saul and his sons (12); and David's hero Benaiah is son of such a man (2 Sam 23:20). In a further link, Saul's order (4) to *draw [his] sword* (שלף חרבך) is echoed only where Joab and his group bring David the totals of their count (2 Sam 24:9). Hardly less explicit is the contrast between *the people* (העם) to whom (and of course their gods) the Philistines carry their good news and *his [Yahweh's] people* (עמו) that feature so often in the David stories.

Six explicit unique links contrast Saul with David, while a seventh compares Saul with another of the non-Davidic kings of Israel in the story. An arrow from a *bow* (קשת, 3) will also kill Ahab (1 Kgs 22:34–35).

2.1 David becomes king and takes Jerusalem (2 Sam 5:1–3, 6–10//1 Chr 11:1–9)

David is not mentioned in BoTH till Saul and his sons are dead. David and the many men loyal to him will have been the most significant absentees from Saul's last battle. Israel's elders now invoke Yahweh: they tell David that Yahweh has said that he should *shepherd* (רעה) Israel. Their words contrast with Micaiah's vision of Israel scattered like *sheep* with no *shepherd* – a vision delivered (1 Kgs 22:17) just before Ahab's death from a bow. Yahweh is represented as calling Israel '*my people*'. In BoTH, *people* (עם) carries a suffix referring to Yahweh only in the narratives about David and Solomon: first at the introduction to each king (2 Sam 5:2 and 1 Kgs 3:9), then most densely in 2 Sam 7 (7×) and 1 Kgs 8 (11×).[2] Those who come to Hebron to follow up Israel's first approach and do the formal business with David (5:3) are *the elders of Israel* (זקני ישראל) – and these too will re-appear only once, when Solomon calls them to participate in bringing the ark into the temple. David makes a *covenant* (ברית) with them (is he simply accepting their invitation, or imposing his own conditions on it?), and they *anoint* (משח) him king. BoTH will report only one other literal anointing – of young Joash. That occasion (2 Kgs 11:12, 17) is also associated with covenant-making and marks the only case among David's descendants of a succession not immediately from father to son or brother to brother.

2 Uniquely נגיד עמי in 2 Kgs 20:5 reflects נגיד [על־עמי] על־ישראל in 2 Sam 5:2; 7:8. Sfx forms relating to Yahweh are more common towards the end of Chr.

A short report follows on the new king's assault on Jerusalem. The details in Sam MT, Kgdms LXX, and Chr are remarkably different; but the main structure of the account is common to all versions:

> And David/the king and all Israel went to Jerusalem where the Jebusites were that inhabited the land. And they said to David, 'You shall not come here ...' And David captured the fortress of Zion (that is the city of David). And David said 'Whoever strikes down the Jebusite ...' And David lived in the fortress, and it is called the city of David. And he built the city around from the Fill and his house.

Jebusites (יבוסי) and *Zion* (ציון) will reappear only in the Solomon narrative. Being made king and then taking Jerusalem supply sufficient grounds for the twin judgments (5:10) that David was becoming greater and greater, and that Yahweh was with him. Solomon, and only Solomon, will also be called *great* (גדול). However, 'Yahweh was with him' is said only of David; the usage here anticipates 'for Yahweh is with you' said by Nathan (2 Sam 7:3) and 'and I was with you' put by Nathan in Yahweh's mouth (2 Sam 7:9) – and is seemingly unique within BoTH to these three verses.

2.2 David's strongmen (2 Sam 23:8–39//1 Chr 11:10–47)

The exploits of some of David's leading men against *Philistines* and a listing of still more of his men form the next section in 1 Chr 11. But in Samuel this block of material comes much later and immediately precedes the census at the end of the David story. The structure of 2 Sam 21–24, with its six elements in chiastic arrangement, is artistic and almost certainly secondary. Two of these elements (2 Sam 21:18–22 and 2 Sam 24) in the same relative order are also the last portions within 1 Chr of synoptic David material (20:4–8 and 21); and it appears that the list in 23:8–39 had been moved from the earlier position still maintained in 1 Chr 11:10–41 to join these and help create the chiastic conclusion.[3]

The exploits sketched in this block have a fourfold echo of the death of Saul: *Philistines* (23:9, 10, 11, 12), *pierced* (23:8, 18), *man of valour* (23:20), and *armour-bearer* (23:37). This second *armour-bearer* serves no less a figure than Joab and is himself listed among the 'Thirty'. Then there are three anticipations of Hezekiah. Only the Hezekiah story will also use either *save* (23:12)[4] or *deliver* (23:12), though in very different frequencies – הושע occurs several times in the David stories but only once in the Hezekiah of BoTH; by contrast הציל, frequent in synoptic

3 For further text-critical discussion, see Auld 2011, 9–11.

4 While 2 Sam 23:12 has ויעש תשועה, the parallel 1 Chr 11:14 has ויושע תשועה.

Hezekiah, appears only once in relation to David (23:12). However, this unique verse is significant: Shamma *delivered* ... and struck down Philistines ... and Yahweh achieved a great *salvation* (תשועה). *Saving* also occurs from other foes within the David narratives but *delivering* only from Philistines – so anticipating the question posed repeatedly in the Hezekiah narratives about the possibility of 'deliverance' from Assyria (here both verbs have a divine subject). And 'strongmen' (גברים) reappear in (Chr's version of) Hezekiah's response to the invasion of Sennacherib (2 Chr 32:3).[5]

There are also two implicit anticipations each of Solomon, Joash, Amaziah, and Hezekiah.

- The Solomon stories (1 Kgs 3:11; 8:48) include נפש (23:17) in the sense of *life* and also mention military *third men* (שלשים, 23:8). Associated with נפש here is the only instance of blood (דם) in all of BoTH.
- *Spear* (חנית) is a feature of David stories, not only in this section (8, 18, 21, 21, 21) but also in 21:19; and it reappears in BoTH only in 2 Kgs 11:10, where David's *spears* and shields are distributed from the temple. This further link with Joash (*anoint* and *covenant* were noted above) is reinforced by *slay* (הרג) in 2 Sam 23:21 (and also 10:18) and 2 Kgs 11:23.
- Shamma defending a *field*-strip (חלקת השדה, 23:11) anticipates the conflict implied in the trampling *field*-life of the parabolic warning delivered by northern Jehoash (2 Kgs 14:9). Then two of David's heroes are termed *honoured* (נכבד, 23:19, 23) and northern Jehoash will chide Amaziah (2 Kgs 14:10) that he should be satisfied with the *honour* he has acquired from one victory and not overreach himself.

The report that opens this section, of the chief wielding a spear and killing 800 at one 'time' (פעם) anticipates Joab attempting to dissuade David from counting his people and wishing that Yahweh might increase his people 100 'times'.

2.3 Tyre, David's family, and Philistines (2 Sam 5:11–25//1 Chr 14:1–17)

The larger part of this section concerns activity led by David against *Philistines* (17–25). However, the prior embassy from *Tyre* (צור, 11–12) anticipates a relationship that will also be important for Solomon; and David's double *asking* (שאל) of Yahweh (19, 23) whether he should 'go up against *Philistines*' finds its only echo in Yahweh commending Solomon for not *asking* for the *life* (נפש) of his enemies.

5 2 Kgs 18:20 has arguably reworked the older text (p. 254 below).

In Sam, we read of the embassy from Tyre immediately after the taking of Jerusalem and the narrator's comment about Yahweh's support as cause of David's rise. David reads the practical recognition by Hiram as evidence of two things: (1) his newly elevated position was due to Yahweh; (2) it was 'for the sake of' Yahweh's people Israel. We will meet בעבור again in the David narratives of BoTH (7:21; 10:3), but never outside them.[6] In Chr, this episode comes later, where it suggests that the elevation of David's kingship to which Hiram responds is not just his taking Jerusalem but also being supported by a long list of proven heroes.[7]

David freely acknowledges that it is Yahweh who *bursts* (פרץ) through his enemies like a flood (20, cf 6:8). BoTH will use this verb just once after David: of Jehoash of Israel *bursting* through the wall of Jerusalem in the reign of Amaziah. Immediately after recognising Yahweh's action, Sam MT has David and his men picking up the abandoned *idols* (עצבים, v 21) to whom, *Philistines* had brought the good news of victory over Saul; however, Kgdms and Chr call them 'gods'.

2.4 The ark starts its journey (2 Sam 6:1–11//1 Chr 13:1–14)

Bringing the *ark* (ארון) to Jerusalem is not only a narrative prelude to Solomon installing it in the temple but also provides several additional verbal anticipations of Solomon stories. The *ark* itself will never be mentioned again after Solomon brings it into the new temple (1 Kgs 8). The association with the *cherubim*-throne (כרובים) is signalled at the outset (2).[8] *Lyres and harps* (כנרות and נבלים) are among the instruments that accompany the dancing (5); and Solomon will make both with wood brought by the queen of Sheba. *Bless* (ברך, 11) occurs only in Solomon and David stories; but the subjects of the verb vary. At this first occurrence, Yahweh *blesses* the house of Obed-edom. David will later pray that Yahweh may *bless* his own house.

The action happens in two stages, separated by a frightening interruption and its aftermath. Yahweh who had *burst through* against Philistines now *bursts through* on *Uzzah* who had *grasped* (אחז) the *ark* (6–7). The verb *'ḥz* appears again in BoTH only in the royal names Ahaziah and Ahaz; and Yahweh disapproves of both these later kings. The name *Uzzah* also anticipates the later king *Uzziah*. David responds in anger to Yahweh's anger against Uzzah; but חרה

6 It is Sam+ in a fourth synoptic context at the end of 6:12. It occurs 8× in non-synoptic Sam, but never in Kgs.

7 See 3.2 below.

8 1 Kgs 6–8//2 Chr 3–5. The combination ישב הכרבים is found only here in BoTH – and elsewhere in 1 Sam 4:4; 2 Kgs 19:15//Isa 37:16; Ps 80:2; 99:1.

('blaze') will not reappear in BoTH, though it is attested at the start of the version in 2 Sam 24 of David's census. In Chr, this first section of the *ark*'s journey (1 Chr 13) is set before rather than after the embassy of *Hiram* and the defeats of *Philistines* (1 Chr 14).

The *ark* had been placed on a new *cart* (עגלה) for its journey to Jerusalem (3); and only the dead Josiah will be similarly transported at the end of BoTH – also to Jerusalem. A *threshing-floor* (גרן), again in Jerusalem, will feature in the culmination of the story of David's census – and the only other *threshing-floor* in BoTH is the meeting place of Jehoshaphat and the king of Israel at the gate of Samaria (7.2).

2.5 Ark arrives in Jerusalem (2 Sam 6:12–20a//1 Chr 15–16)

The *ark* is brought into Jerusalem with great celebration: David leaping and dancing before it *with all [his] power* (בכל־עז) is a further anticipation of *Uzziah* (עזיה). One observer is far from sharing the popular enthusiasm. Michal, daughter of Saul and perhaps his only surviving offspring, sees David through a window and despises him *in her heart* (בלבה). No more is said – indeed in BoTH neither Michal nor Saul will be mentioned again. Like *Philistines*, Saul is part only of his story and that of David. However, *in her heart* finds an immediate echo (2 Sam 7:3) and also anticipates *in his heart* (בלבו) of Solomon (1 Kgs 10:24). Michal daughter of Saul also resonates with Athaliah daughter of Ahab (8).

Only David and Solomon are reported in BoTH as offering *holocausts* (עלות) and *š^{e}lamîm*-sacrifices (שלמים, 17). When David had 'finished' (כלה) sacrificing, he *blessed* the people (18) *in Yahweh's name* (בשם יהוה). After distributing food to all the participants, he sent them home (19)[9] and returned to *bless* his own house(hold). Solomon will similarly *bless* the people after installing the *Ark* in the temple; but *in Yahweh's name* will occur only once more – and in the mouth of 'the king of Israel' to Micaiah. A progression may be intuited from (a) Yahweh blessing through (b) David blessing in Yahweh's name to (c) David blessing (with the name of Yahweh now unstated but assumed).

2.6 David seeks and receives counsel (2 Sam 7:1–17//1 Chr 17:1–15)

David is embarrassed that he is living in a cedar house, but the divine *ark* only in a tent. Michal had scorned David *in her heart*; Nathan tells him to do whatever

9 2 Sam 6:19a is stated more expansively than 1 Chr 16:3, notably with לכל־העם לכל־המון ישראל instead of לכל־איש ישראל – cf 2 Sam 12:31//1 Chr 20:3.

is *in his heart*: Yahweh is with him (cf 5:10; 7:9). 'Heart' (לב[ב]) recurs throughout BoTH, appearing in narratives about David, Solomon, Asa, Amaziah, and Josiah. Twice it will be paired with נפש but it is mostly used on its own.[10] Nathan is introduced as the *prophet* (נביא) and is one of four prophets loyal to Yahweh in BoTH. The accounts of Micaiah and Huldah are clearly twinned. In the context of BoTH and its multiple pairings, that invites exploring a link between the remaining two, Nathan and Isaiah. In Chr (and hence also BoTH), Isaiah simply accompanies Hezekiah and prays when his king prays. That may suggest that Nathan the prophet was (also) a royal companion/counsellor, and that David was seeking and received 'advice' from him, rather than a divine 'word'. Gad will be introduced later (2 Sam 24:11//1 Chr 21:9) as 'David's seer' (חזה).[11]

The prophet's advice is immediately overtaken by a divine word (4) delivered (17) in a 'vision' (חזון – cognate with חזה)[12]: Nathan had said 'Go (לך) do …' but is himself now told 'Go (לך) say …'. Nathan receives the divine 'vision' (17) *at night* (בלילה, 4) as Solomon will at Gibeon. There are many verbal links between David raising the question of a house for Yahweh and the report of Solomon the builder (1 Kgs 8). The three most pervasive anticipations in this section and the next are the actual phrase *build a house* (בנה בית, 5, 7, 13, and then 27), the description of David as *servant of Yahweh* (עבד יהוה, 5, 8, and then 19, 25, 26, 27, 28, 29), and the designation of Israel as Yahweh's *people* (עם, 7, 8, 10, 11, 23, 23, 23, 24, 24). Solomon also, but only twice, calls himself *your servant* to Yahweh; but no later king will be so designated in BoTH. The very first words of Yahweh's extended intervention (5–16) link the two key and oft-repeated themes:

> Go and say to *my servant David*, Thus has Yahweh spoken: Is it (or: It is not) you that will *build me a house* to live in?

In Chr, Yahweh's ruling opens with a direct negative, whereas in Sam the implied negative is stated in a rhetorical question. It is less of a surprise that building a house for Yahweh occurs only in the David and Solomon narratives: once it was built, it was built and there was no more need to talk about it. Much more surprising is that 'my/your servant' is only applied to David and Solomon.

Yahweh has never lived in a house (6–7). Instead, Yahweh will make a house for David – he will establish kingly rule by 'seed' raised 'after you' from David's body (11b-12):

---

10 2 Sam 6:16; 7:3, 21, 27; 1 Kgs 8:17, 18, 18, 23, 38, 39, 47, 66; 9:3; 10:2, 24; 15:14; 2 Kgs 14:10; 22:19.

11 הנביא before חזה דוד in 2 Sam 24:11 is Sam+.

12 We find the less usual form חזיון in 2 Sam 7:17 and the more regular חזון in synoptic 1 Chr 17:15.

> It is he that will *build* for me a *house*, and I shall establish his seat *for ever.* I shall be a father to him and he shall be a son to me. I shall not turn away my *loyalty* from him, as I turned it away from the one who was before you. (13–14a, 15)

He has given David success and status and his people Israel security (8–11a). He has cut off (ואכרתה, 9) David's *enemies* (איבים). Solomon's prayer will include the only certain mention[13] of *enemies* again in BoTH.

סור (qal) echoes throughout Kgs, mostly in contexts of disloyal human turning or lack of loyal turning. But it is rare in BoTH: only of the 'high places' not turning (1 Kgs 15:14; 22:44) and of Josiah not turning (2 Kgs 22:2). סור (hiph) is used a little more often in BoTH: 2 Sam 6:10; 7:15; 1 Kgs 15:13; 2 Kgs 18:22. *Loyalty* (חסד) is used very sparingly in BoTH, and only in narratives relating to David and Solomon. At this early point (15),[14] Yahweh insists on his own continuing *loyalty* to David's 'seed'.

There are several differences between the versions over what Nathan has just cited. A useful vantage point towards an assessment is provided by the substantial differences between Sam MT on the one side and Kgdms/Chr on the other over Yahweh's final declaration.

Sam (MT)	Kgdms (LXX)	Chr
ונאמן ביתך וממלכתך לפניך	ונאמן ביתו וממלכתו לפני	והעמדתיהו בביתי ובמלכותי
עד־עולם	עד־העולם	עד־העולם
כסאך יהיה נכון עד־עולם	וכסאו יהיה נכון עד־עולם	וכסאו יהיה נכון עד־עולם

In Sam (16), Yahweh pledges that 'your' (David's) house and kingdom will be set firm and 'your' throne will be established for ever. But in Kgdms (16), 'his' house and kingdom will be established before 'me'; and in Chr (14), 'he' (the successor) will be confirmed in 'my' (Yahweh's) house and kingdom and 'his' throne will be established for ever. There are two distinct issues: (1) Does the divine pledge to David relate to David himself ('your') or to the successor ('his'/'him')? (2) While the second clause clearly relates to the royal throne, does the first clause also relate to the royal house and kingdom (Sam/Kgdms) or to royal status within Yahweh's house and kingdom (Chr)? The closest echo of the pledge that is repeated in 2 Sam 7:13, 16(2×), 24, 25, 26, 29(2×) comes in the queen's words (1 Kgs 10:9):

13 See 3.1 below on Solomon's vision at Gibeon.

14 Not the first point: it had already been used in 2 Sam 6:10//1 Chr 13:13.

here, in a more nuanced way, the divine favour to Solomon is part of his love of Israel 'for ever'.

2.7 David responds in prayer (2 Sam 7:18–29//1 Chr 17:16–27)

Yahweh's word has been transmitted to David through Nathan, who has received it in a vision; but in what follows there is no further mention of the *prophet*. David instead now answers Yahweh directly and takes up several of the themes reported by Nathan, who had acted as Yahweh's intermediary. Just as only David and Solomon *ask* Yahweh, so too only they within BoTH *say* (אמר) something to him (18). Yahweh had spoken of David twice as *my servant* (5, 8); and he now speaks of himself to Yahweh repeatedly (19, 20, 21, 25, 26, 27, 28, 29) as *your servant*. Similarly, *for ever* (13, 16) is repeated 5× (24, 25, 26, 29, 29).

Yahweh's 'eyes' and how they evaluate behaviour will be one of the recurring narratorial themes of this early draft of a book of kings.[15] But this first instance of assessment (19) is reported by David, not the narrator; and the report is of Yahweh's own actions: it is a 'small' thing in his 'eyes' to do such *great* things (21, 23). Similar confidence will lead Joab to conclude his military orders to his brother Abishai with these words: 'And as for Yahweh, he will do what is good in his eyes.' (10:12)

In the ark story, Yahweh *blessed* David before David *blessed* others in Yahweh's name. David's answer to Yahweh's initiatives towards himself (*my servant* and *for ever*) is similar. Yahweh had sketched his relationship with Israel (6–11a); now David responds (22–26) with recognition of Yahweh's role in his people's remarkable story. Nathan had encouraged David to follow his heart (3) and Yahweh had recognised David's 'name', a reputation like the '*great*(est)' of the land/earth (9). So now David lauds Yahweh's role: he too was acting in accord with his own heart when working 'all this *greatness*' (21). We noted (5:10, 12) that *great* is another term found only in the David and Solomon narratives of BoTH. Michal, a survivor of Saul's house, despised David in her heart; Nathan was prepared to affirm what David had in his heart; and now Yahweh confirms what he has at heart in letting David know his intentions. David's response (27) is to find 'heart' to pray this prayer. 'Setting a name for ...' (לשום ל שם) in 23 looks back to 7:9 ('and I made for you a great name') and also forwards to 1 Kgs 9:3 etc ('to set my name there for ever').

A second link between David and Hezekiah stories requires elaboration; like Nathan and Isaiah both styled *prophet*, this is also a twosome within a foursome.

---

15 1 Kgs 15:11; 22:43; 2 Kgs 8:18, 27; 12:3; 14:3; 15:3, 34; 16:2; 18:3; 21:2, 20; 22:2.

The nations (הגוים) are only featured four times in BoTH. Twice this happens within a cluster of pairs: both Ahaz and Manasseh act 'like the abominations of the *nations*' (14, 16). 'The *nations*' also appear elsewhere only in the stories of David[16] and Hezekiah.[17]

2.8 Military actions and a list of officials (2 Sam 8//1 Chr 18)

Successes against Philistines, Moabites, Aramaeans, and Edomites are sketched (1–14) including mention of Ammon and Amalek (12); David's rule is assessed (15); and some officials are named (16–18). Such content gives the impression of a concluding appendix. This and the following two portions of BoTH are introduced identically by ויהי אחרי־כן. 'And it came to be after this', though apparently unremarkable wording, is found in HB only in these three linked portions of BoTH. If this is so, the repetition of the unique introductory formula in 2 Sam 10:1 and 21:18 may preserve evidence of the growth of BoTH.

'And David struck the Philistines and *humbled* them' (1). The initial ויך is a common term for attack, whether on an individual or army. The following ויכניעם skilfully extends the opening verb: (a) by lengthening it – its first three consonants (*wyk*) simply repeat those of the prior verb; (b) by spelling out its implication. We shall note a similar stylistic device in the Amaziah story (2 Kgs 14:10). The verb כנע reappears just once certainly in BoTH, though there, in the Josiah story, it is reflexive: the king has '*humbled* himself'.[18] The parallel in 1 Chr 18:2 reports the attack on Moab more briefly than Sam and its shorter version will represent BoTH here.[19] This makes no mention of putting some survivors to death and letting others live. In BoTH, only David and Solomon receive *tribute* (מנחה), while מנחה also names the sacrificial 'offerings' Solomon is reported as bringing to Yahweh (1 Kgs 8:64).

The third note is more extensive (3–8) and deals with more distant opponents, not only the king of Zobah but also the Aramaeans of Damascus who tried to *help* (עזר) him. This nice play on the name Hadad-ezer anticipates the name

16 All texts mingle עם and גוי in 23.

17 2 Kgs 18:33; 19:12 and 2 Chr 32:13, 14, 15, 17 elaborate in similar fashion the Assyrian claim that gods of (other) nations have been unable to withstand Assyria. 2 Chr 32:23 reports Hezekiah's reputation among the nations.

18 כנע niph is used 3× in SK +s and 16× in C +s (2 of these in synoptic contexts); and כנע hiph is C+ 2×. BoTH includes just one instance each of hiph (2 Sam 8:1//1 Chr 18:1) and niph (2 Kgs 22:19//2 Chr 34:27): 1 Sam 7:13; 1 Kgs 21:29, 29; 1 Chr 20:4 (//2 Sam 21:18); 2 Chr 7:14 (in Solomon's second vision); 12:6, 7, 7, 12; 13:18; 30:11; 32:26; 33:12, 19, 23, 23; 34:27; 36:12.

19 Auld 2017, 24–26.

of king Azar-iah. The *river* (נהר) Euphrates reappears once in connection with David and Hadad-ezer (10:16); and it features again as a boundary in the Solomon story (1 Kgs 5:1//2 Chr 9:26). *Horsemen* (4, פרשים), and again in 10:18, only reappear in Solomon portions of BoTH. This second campaign also results in receipt of *tribute* (6). *Saved* (6) is a recurrent link between David and Hezekiah. Gold *shields* (שלטים) are specified (7) and will reappear in the story of Joash, adding to the several links already noted there with David.[20] Gold and silver are the metals that appear more frequently in BoTH;[21] bronze is rarer, though repeated here in 10.

Toi/u of Hamath (9–10) responded to what had happened to his Aramaean neighbours by approaching David with congratulations and gifts. *Ask* and *bless* mark further links with Solomon. An interim conclusion (11–12) tells that David added the gifts from Toi/u to the dedications of gold and silver he had made to Yahweh from the *nations* (גוים): Edom, Moab, Ammon, Philistines, and Amalek. 'Nations' is read by Sam MT, Chr MT and Chr LXX, and would make another link with Hezekiah; however, Kgdms LXX attests 'cities'. *Dedicate* (הקדיש) is used only in David and Solomon narratives, but differently: here David dedicates, but it is Yahweh in 1 Kgs 9:3, 7.

Two uniquely paired longer combinations follow. The report that David (Sam) or Abishai (Chr) *smote eighteen thousand Edomites in Salt Valley* (13)[22] will be repeated about Amaziah (11); and the summary that David was *practising justice and righteousness* (עשה משפט וצדקה, 15) anticipates the Queen of Sheba's words about Solomon.[23]

2.9 Ammonite insult avenged (2 Sam 10:1–11:1; 12:26, 30–31//1 Chr 19:1–20:3)

The Ammonites were listed (8:12) among the nations from whose tribute or spoil or gifts David had dedicated to Yahweh. But report of a campaign against them

20 At the end of this verse Sam LXX and 4Q51 and Josephus all include the note that these were removed by Pharaoh in the days of Rehoboam.

21 Gold and silver in 1 Kgs 10:22; 2 Kgs 14:14; and silver and gold in 2 Sam 8:10–11; 1 Kgs 10:25(MT – no silver in LXX); 15:15, 19.

22 Some commentators advocate identifying *gy'-mlḥ* not with the valley of the Salt (Dead) Sea but the nearby *wadi 'al-milḥ*.

23 This phrase is never repeated in the narrative books. The instances elsewhere in HB are Jer 9:23; 22:3, 15; 23:5; 33:15[MT]; Ezek 18:5, 19, 21, 27; 33:16; 45:9; Ps 99:4. Only first and last are statements about God. Are Jeremiah and Ezekiel comparing the person who does right with David and Solomon, or God? See further in 3.15.

comes only now, and at much greater length than with Moab, Aram, or Edom. Philistines reappear throughout the David narratives.

Divine *loyalty* to David has been stated in 7:15 and will be repeated in Solomon's vision at Gibeon and his prayer; but here (2) the חסד is between kings mutually. *Explore* (חקר, 3) anticipates Solomon; but here its sense is sharpened by the added 'spy' (רגל), found only here in BoTH. Hadadezer brought out Aram (16) who were *across the river* (מעבר הנהר); and that geographical term reappears in BoTH only within the Solomon narrative (1 Kgs 5:1). הפך (3) reappears in 1 Kgs 22:34, but possibly in a different sense: *turn* here has the sense of over*turn*. נחם (10:2,3 – here piel) is repeated in BoTH only at the end of the David-story (24:16 – there niphal). *Destroy* (השחית) is also repeated in 24:16[24] from 11:1, and reappears only in the Jehoram portion, where Yahweh is unwilling to *destroy* precisely because of the promise made to David.[25]

David's decisive response (7) in sending out the *heroes/strongmen* (הגברים) may be contrasted with Hezekiah taking counsel with his *strongmen* (2 Chr 32:3). *Slay* (הרג) is twice part of the David story (18 and 23:21) and reappears only at the *slaying* of Mattan in the Joash story.[26] Then only in the Amaziah story will we find נגף (*be smitten* 15, 19) and נוס (*flee* 13, 14, 18) together again, probably to contrast David's victories with Amaziah's defeat by Jehoash of Israel.[27] A comparison with his success in Edom was noted in the previous section. Aram in the *field* (בשדה) in 2 Sam 10:8 anticipates the hostile *field*-life in the parable of Jehoash (2 Kgs 14:9). *Approach* (נגש, 13) is synoptic once more (1 Kgs 22:24) where is it also hostile.

Save (11, 19) occurs repeatedly in David narratives (also 23:10; 8:6) and anticipates the same verb in the Hezekiah narrative. Both clauses in 11 relate being *strong* (חזק) to saving, further hinting towards Hezekiah. The verb is also used in the census story (24:4), and similarly again when we are told of Amaziah's *strong* grip on the kingdom (2 Kgs 14:5). Then *our god* (12) is synoptic again only in 2 Kgs 18:22//2 Chr 32:11.

To meet (לקראת) is used four times in this narrative: meeting the shamed envoys in Jericho (5), meeting Aram (9, 10), and Aram meeting David (17). It will reappear only when Josiah goes to meet the Egyptian king (2 Kgs 23:29). NB בעד immediately below.

---

24 אדון is used of Hanun here (Sam but not Chr), as of David in the same census story.

25 2 Sam 11:1; 24:16//1 Chr 20:1; 21:15; 2 Kgs 8:19//2 Chr 21:7.

26 2 Sam 10:18; 23:21//1 Chr 19:18; 11:23; 2 Kgs 11:18//2 Chr 23:17.

27 2 Sam 10//1 Chr 19; 2 Kgs 14//2 Chr 25. נגף occurs independently of נוס in 1 Kgs 8:33, and נוס of נגף in 1 Sam 31:1, 7, 7.

Each of two interesting parallel expressions includes עם (people): מכל־בחור בישראל\\ואת יתר העם (10–11) and בעד־עמנו ובעד ערי אלהינו (12). There is only one further instance in HB of עם with a pl sfx – in Jer 46:16 (אל־עמנו ואל־ארץ מולדתנו). For עם הארץ see below on Joash. בעד (12) recurs only in the Josiah story (2 Kgs 22:13) and, in both contexts, Yahweh's favour is hoped for.

The Ammonite crown captured by David (12:30) includes *gold* (זהב) to the *weight* (משקל) of a *talent* (ככר). These three terms reappear in the same unique linkage in the report that *gold weighing* 666 *talents* came yearly to Solomon. *Precious stone* (אבן יקרה) in the crown is also an element in the gifts to Solomon by the Queen of Sheba that reappears nowhere in BoTH. *Iron* (ברזל) tools feature in the puzzling conclusion to the Ammon story (31),[28] and this metal too will reappear in BoTH only once – in *iron* horns brandished by the prophet Hananiah (1 Kgs 22:11).

2.10 Philistine giants killed (2 Sam 21:18–22//1 Chr 20:4–8)

In Chr, because originally in BoTH, this short portion (again introduced by ויהי אחרי־כן) immediately follows the end of the previous section (19:1 – 20:3).[29] There is 'war' with *Philistines*, and Goliath is mentioned. In *spear* (חנית) these notes include a further link with Joash; and in *scorn* (חרף), a further unique link with Hezekiah – the Assyrians in Hezekiah's time will behave like the Philistines in David's.

2.11 David has Israel counted (2 Sam 24//1 Chr 21)

This striking narrative is well connected both with the preceding David narratives and with later portions of BoTH: it has both a concluding and a transitional role. A *threshing floor* links this story with Jehoshaphat and the king of Israel, but also with David bringing the *ark* to Jerusalem. Then, just as David offers up *holocausts* plus *šelamîm*-sacrifices at the end of this narrative just as when the *ark* reaches Jerusalem, so too they are paired elsewhere only at the climax of Solomon's dedi-

28 Again, as in 2 Sam 6:19a//1 Chr 16:3, Sam is stated more fully: במגרה ובחריצי הברזל ובמגזרת הברזל instead of במגרה ובחריצי הברזל ובמגרות – cf also 1 Kgs 9:20//2 Chr 8:6.

29 There are at least two formal indicators that 21:15–17 is secondary: אחרי־כן at the end of v. 14 is a relic of the formula that opens v. 18 – it is clause-final in Gen 41:31 and Josh 10:26, but never verse-final let alone pericope-final as here; then אז in v. 17 anticipates the original אז in v. 18.

cation of the temple. Cattle (בקר) are specified in both contexts. In a further transitional linkage, *destroy* (השחית) has been used of the success of Joab in the campaign against Ammon (2 Sam 11:1) – precisely Joab, who in this story loyally discourages his king from the count. It is used here of the *divine emissary* about to *destroy* Jerusalem; and its only reappearance in BoTH will note Yahweh's unwillingness to *destroy* Judah in the time of Jehoram for the sake of David (2 Kgs 8:19). Each of these expressions that bind the census and its aftermath to the rest of the David tradition in BoTH also tie it to narratives that will follow.[30]

Several features within this narrative come in threes; and the first such are the technical terms relating to 'census': מנה (*count*), ספר (*tell/tally*), and פקד (*reckon*). David's insistence that Joab *tally* and *count* Israel is echoed in the quantity of Solomon's sacrifices: as he brought the ark into the temple, these could not be *tallied* or *counted.* פקד qal reappears only in the Joash story (but differently). A choice is offered between three punishments for ordering the census, and *plague* (דבר) for three days is chosen. *Plague* will reappear once in BoTH as one of the disasters foreseen in Solomon's prayer (1 Kgs 8:37). The same verse in Solomon's prayer uses the same verb *distress* (צרר) in hiphil as David employs in qal (2 Sam 24:13 immediately before *plague* in 24:14).

David twice admits his guilt. The first admission (10) follows receipt of the two totals, when he asks Yahweh: 'Remove my *offence* (עוני)'. The related verb (העוה) is part of a confession proposed by Solomon in his prayer (1 Kgs 8:47). On the second occasion (17), David in Sam MT includes this same verb; however, in 4QSam^{a} and LXX^{L}, as also in Chr, he says not העויתי but הרעתי, 'I have been wicked'. In a further unique link, the verb נעצר, used for the plague being *held back* (21), will only reappear in BoTH, where Solomon's prayer speaks of the heavens being *held back* from giving rain (8:35).

Both Joab (3) and Araunah/Ornan/Orna the Jebusite (21) address David as אדני המלך (*my lord king*). No one else in BoTH uses this wording; but its closest echo sounds after Micaiah sees Israel as *sheep* without a *shepherd* (22:17) and Yahweh notes in response that they have no *lords* (אדנים). David calling his people *sheep* (17) again uniquely anticipates Micaiah (1 Kgs 22:17). In a third anticipation of Micaiah, David 'sees' the divine messenger (בראתו את־המלאך) just as Micaiah saw Yahweh himself (ראיתי את־יהוה ישב).[31] David insistently over-ruling Joab (ויחזק דבר־המלך אך־יואב) anticipates Amaziah taking firm rule of his kingdom (חזקה הממלכה בידו).

30 Whether an original feature or not, it is not surprising that the story opens in Sam with Yahweh's wrath: a further link back to the ark-story and Perez-uzzah.

31 By contrast, the two visions of Solomon are introduced, not by ראה qal but by ראה niphal.

We have noted several significant links between narratives about David and about Hezekiah. The destroying *envoy of Yahweh* (מלאך יהוה) reappears in the Hezekiah story; and foreign Arauna *prostrating* (השתחוה) before David anticipates the (foreign) Assyrian envoy claiming that Hezekiah had instructed prostration before this/one altar.

This story of a census with malign consequences incorporates visionary components and includes the first synoptic mention of Judah separate from Israel. The task set by David has been simply to number Israel; but the totals he receives are for both Israel and Judah.[32] This will hardly be an accident in a story with several unique links with the story of Micaiah, where a king of Israel and a descendant of David in Judah pledge common military action – and fail. Equally significant: Yahweh's (destroying) envoy will only reappear when Jerusalem is again in danger, this time from the king of Assyria. A site for sacrifice is *acquired* (קנה) by David (24:21, 24); and this verb reappears only once in BoTH, where stone and wood are *acquired* for Josiah's restoration of the temple (2 Kgs 22:6). The verb itself reappears only once; however, the idiomatic emphasis in 2 Sam 24:24//1 Chr 21:24, with the finite אקנה reinforced by the infinitive absolute קנו\ה, nicely echoes the same idiom a few verses earlier (in 1 Chr 21:17 and perhaps also 2 Sam 24:17 in 4QSam^{a}): 'bad, I have been bad ... buy, I must buy'. The command (24:18) to *raise an altar to Yahweh* (הקם ליהוה מזבח) will be echoed only once (2 Kgs 21:3) where Manasseh *raised altars to Baal* (ויקם מזבחות לבעל). In each case, raising an altar or altars is immediately followed by altar-building (2 Sam 24:21, 25; 2 Kgs 21:4, 5).

3.1 Solomon's vision at Gibeon (1 Kgs 3:4–15//2 Chr 1:3–13)

Continuities with David narratives are immediately to the fore in the report of Solomon's inaugural vision. There are significant differences in wording between Kg[dm]s and Chr and these make reconstructing an earlier form of the text difficult (Auld 1992, 1993). However, and more significant for our purposes, there are at least ten unique shared links between the narratives of father and son: Solomon offers up *holocausts* (עלות) at Gibeon; his encounter with Yahweh is *at night* (בלילה), as when Nathan had received his answer for David; he *speaks* (אמר) of Yahweh's *loyalty* (חסד) – in fact *great* (גדול) *loyalty* – to his *servant* (עבד) David; he *asks* (שאל) Yahweh and is commended for not *asking* him for the *life* (נפש) of his *enemies* (Kgs)/'those who hate him' (Chr). Israel is not named but is referred

32 BHS suggests Gk MS evidence for 1 Chr 21:5b being secondary.

to as *your people* (עמך). One of these pairings marks an important contrast with his father. The only time David is reported *asking* of Yahweh, it is whether to engage with Philistine forces; however, Solomon makes no such request and is specifically commended for this. Relevant also is the way ואחריך (3:12) resumes the promise to David: והקימתי את־זרעך אחריך (7:12), and even more explicitly in 1 Kgs 3:12 (ואחריך לא־יקום כמוך) than 2 Chr 1:12 (ואחריך לא יהיה־כן).[33]

Half of these ten or eleven links with David will recur in the Solomon story. However, there will be no further *explicit* mention in BoTH of Gibeon and its *high place* (במה); and Solomon will go on to build a temple for Yahweh in Jerusalem instead. And yet the combination of the 'high places' on the 'hills' at which Ahaz will later 'sacrifice' present an *implicit* contrast with Solomon – 'hill' (גבעה) echoes 'Gibeon' (גבעון) and 'enthusiastic sacrificing' (זבח piel) is reported only of Solomon at the completion of the temple and of Ahaz at the 'high places'. This trio of links helps explain why Ahaz will be uniquely introduced as NOT acting like David.

Solomon asks, 'Who will (be able to[34]) judge/rule this your people?' (Kgs 9b// Chr 10b). The issue of judging or ruling is resumed within Yahweh's response in the vision report, but differently: in Chr 11b he grants wisdom and knowledge with which 'you will judge/rule my people' but in Kgs 11b he grants discernment 'to hear a case/judgment'. Especially when the vision report is read as in Chr, and hence without the Kgs sequel of the case of the two harlots, the repeated verb שפט more naturally bears the wider sense of 'rule' rather than the narrower 'judge'. The verb שפט (and again with עם as its object) will be used of only one other king in BoTH – of Jotham who rules 'the people of the land' – though it is also resumed in the name Jeho-shaphat. 'This people', though found on a few occasions in 1 Kgs (4 below) appears to be unique here in BoTH.

3.2 Solomon and Hiram of Tyre (1 Kgs 5:15–25//2 Chr 2:2–15)

The strictly synoptic elements of these two versions of the narrative are quite brief. There are only two pieces of more extended shared wording: (a) Solomon's statement of his aim to *build a house* for his God (5:19//2:3); and (b) the start of Hiram's response (5:21b//2:11). The significant links are of two sorts. There are two with David: Hiram of *Tyre* makes contact with the son of his old friend; and their correspondence relates, as with David (2 Sam 5:11), to *building a house*. Other

33 Each Solomon variant is resumed in a subsequent Kgs+: ואחריו לא־היה כמהו (2 Kgs 18:5) and ואחריו לא קם כמהו (2 Kgs 23:25).

34 יוכל added to the question in 1 Kgs 3:9 is construed with ל + inf only in synoptic Hezekiah.

features anticipate subsequent parts of the Solomon story. As with the vision report that precedes and the building operations that follow, it is very hard to reconstruct an earlier version. Solomon follows his statement of aim by a request, introduced by ועתה (5:20//2:6), asking for both cedars and a promise of co-operation, stated as עבדי עם עבדיך (5:20//2:7). ועתה has been differently developed in each version. 2 Chr 2 has no parallel to 1 Kgs 5:18; but there is broad correspondence between 5:20 and 2:6–8 – 'So now send me cedar from Lebanon ... my servants will be with your servants.' Then עצים + הכין in 2 Chr 2:8 is reflected in 1 Kgs 5:32.[35]

Hiram's reply opens with shared content: ברוך יהוה אשר נתן לדוד בן חכם,[36] though 2:11 is much expanded.[37] The final words of 5:21b (על־העם הרב הזה) combine and restate elements of 3:9 and 12. Hiram also anticipates the Queen of Sheba blessing Yahweh for Solomon's fortune. 1 Kgs 5:23 and 2 Chr 2:15 are similar in sense but share only מן־הלבנון and ים. Even their terms for 'rafts' are different, each being *hapax*: דברות (5:23) and רפסדות (2:16) – LXX renders both σχεδία[ι]ς.

Some developments in each version may have been suggested by the unusual wording in Solomon's declaration of intent. יהוה אלהי (Yahweh my God) is strictly synoptic only here and in 1 Kgs 8:28.[38] Perhaps even more surprising, 1 Kgs 10:9 provides the unique synoptic occurrence of the corresponding יהוה אלהיך (Yahweh your God). We should note that the few non-synoptic instances of 'Yahweh my/your God' are restricted to Solomon narratives in 1 Kgs (3:7; 5:18) and the story of David's census in both books (2 Sam 24:3, 23, 24; 1 Chr 21:17). *My/your god* was the counterpart of *your/my servant*, and similarly restricted to the narratives about David and Solomon. The corresponding plural suffixes occur only towards the end of BoTH. 'Yahweh our God' is attested synoptically only in the narratives about Hezekiah (2 Kgs 18:22; 19:19; 2 Chr 32:11) and 'Yahweh your (pl.) God' in the Josiah Passover narrative (2 Kgs 23:21; 2 Chr 35:3).

חפץ (in 1 Kgs 5:22, 23, 24) is synoptic again only in 10:13//9:12 (the queen's 'pleasure') – that immediately follows the cognate verb in 10:9//9:8 which has Yahweh as sbj (while the noun here expresses the 'pleasure/wish' of each king – cf חסד in 2 Sam 10).

---

35 Noth, 88 describes 15–26 as Dtr and observes how its elements are culled from elsewhere; 27–32 were a further supplement.

36 היום is attested in Kgs MT after ברוך יהוה but not in LXX^{L} or Chr (Auld 2017, 40–41).

37 This is the only synoptic instance of adj חכם; but cf also 1 Kgs 2:9; 3:12 and 2 Chr 2:6, 6, 12, 13.

38 'Strictly' in MT only: LXX reads 'Lord God of Israel' in 8:28 and 'Lord God' in 6:19. יהוה אלהי ישראל has been standard in 8:15, 17, 20, 23, 25, 26//6:4, 7, 10, 14, 16, 17. God is not invoked by name in the remainder of this long prayer.

This is the introduction to an important recurring theme of the Solomon story: an appointee of the king of *Tyre* works on the temple: 1 Kgs 7:13–14, 40, 45// 2 Chr 2:13–14; 4:11, 16; cities are passed between the two kings (9:10–14//8:1–2); and Hiram and Solomon jointly send a fleet to Ophir (9:26–28//8:17–18; 10:11–12// 9:10–11; 10:21–22//9:20–21.

3.3 Local labour (1 Kgs 5:29–30a//2 Chr 2:17)

Kg[dm]s and Chr are very different here, with Kgs much longer. Both use *porter* (סבל), so anticipating the Jeroboam story, and agree that there were seventy thousand (1 Kgs 5:29//2 Chr 2:17).

3.4 Making the temple (1 Kgs 6:1–7:39//2 Chr 3:1–4:10)

Paired links with the rest of BoTH are very few, possibly because of the uniqueness of the topic and the extent (in Kg[dm]s at least) of the treatment. However, it is also true that our three main witnesses differ more widely and less consistently on this subject than on any other. This is discussed more fully on pp. 172–181 above. One pairing returns us to the language of the David/Nathan exchange: 'build' + 'house'. Then *the (southern) shoulder of the house* (כתף הבית הימנית), where the great sea was placed, reappears only where the disposition of the guards for the presentation of the boy king Joash is reported.

3.5 Temple implements (1 Kgs 7:40–51//2 Chr 4:11–5:1)

Most of the content is again unique to this report. However, there are links at the start to David and at the end to Asa. The object of חקר (*explore*), used in 7:50 of the weight of the bronze, was the Ammonite city in 2 Sam 10:3.[39] The verb כלה piel (*complete/finish*) is found synoptically five times, four times in the narratives about David and Solomon where it always functions as a modal verb:

- David blessed his people after *finishing* sacrificing (2 Sam 6:18//1 Chr 16:2).
- Hiram *finished* doing all his appointed task (1 Kgs 7:40//2 Chr 4:11).
- After *finishing* praying ... (1 Kgs 8:54//2 Chr 7:1).
- After *finishing* building the two houses Solomon received his second vision (1 Kgs 9:1//2 Chr 7:11).

39 Exploring is paired with spying in 2 Sam 10:3. Exploring so much bronze in the treasury might be reckoned a form of trespass.

The first, third, and fourth instances are of one sort: when the action described by the grammatically dependent infinitive is completed, something else happens. Each of these two-verb reports about finishing sacrificing (or praying or building) is hence retrospective and transitional. (In the third instance, Kgs and Chr diverge over what Solomon did immediately after finishing praying.) However, the second case is different: Hiram 'finishing doing the task' does not immediately lead to a new topic; instead it introduces the list of items that constituted the task.[40] Then the closing note about the *completion of the whole task* (ותשלם כל־המלאכה) hints at the name of the king while the rich *dedications of his father* (קדשי אביו) confirm the hint, because this phrase is repeated only in the report on Asa (1 Kgs 15:14–15) – and alongside a further hint (שלם) at Solomon's name.

3.6 Ark installed (1 Kgs 8:1–11//2 Chr 5:2–14)

The installation of the *ark* in the new temple is unsurprisingly dominated by multiple occurrences of the key term. The texts of Kgs MT and Chr are almost identical; but Kgdms is much briefer in 1–5 and should be accepted as the prior form of the text.[41] The *elders of Israel* make their only reappearance here, after their key role in making David king (2.1). There they acted independently – here by contrast they have been *assembled* (הקהיל) by the king to represent the people. The verbs *count* and *number* reappear here from David's census instructions, unless 'unnumbered' (Kgdms) attests a more original and briefer אין מספר. Possibly because the *ark* will not reappear in BoTH (at least not after 8:21), this narrative contains only one unique and possibly ironic echo of a future synoptic narrative. Solomon *assembles* (הקהיל) *the elders of Israel* to represent the people, while his son *assembles* (only) Judah and Benjamin to fight with Israel (12:21). The final verse includes the only synoptic instance of שרת ('minister'); it will reappear in the non-synoptic account of the Babylonian despoliation of the temple implements (2 Kgs 25:14//Jer 52:18).

3.7 Promise fulfilled (1 Kgs 8:14–26//2 Chr 6:3–12, 14–17)

Solomon is the only king after David who *blesses* (ברך) the people (14). His opening words to Yahweh (15) are prefaced simply by 'and he *said*' (אמר); and such

---

40 In the fifth synoptic instance, כלה is not modal but independent: the king of Israel was to gore Aram till *finishing* them [off] (1 Kgs 22:11//2 Chr 18:10).

41 In the shorter text, the king is joined by the elders of Israel and the priests; the longer text adds all the heads of the tribes, the leaders of the fathers' houses, and the Levites.

direct address to Yahweh is reported only of David and Solomon. As he blesses 'all Israel', he invokes Yahweh as *god of Israel* (6× in 8:15–26).[42] BoTH will not use 'God of Israel' again till it reports on Hezekiah and Josiah (in whose reigns no king of Israel is mentioned). The first instance of *assembly* (קהל) is M+, but this noun is well anchored in Solomon's prayer (14, 22, 65) and resumes the related verb at the start of the report (8:1). We find *your servant David* in 24 and 25. 26 is shorter in Kgdms which attests only 'David my father' (without 'your servant') at the end. Kgdms also reads 'to your servant' (sg) in 23 – not pl as in Kgs and Chr. *Build a house* recurs 6× in 16–20. Three times in 17–18 it follows 'it was with David's heart', a phrase that resumes Nathan's words to David (2 Sam 7:3). *Heart* (לב[ב]) is a key term in Solomon's prayer and occurs there as often (8×)[43] as all the other instances in BoTH (8×);[44] and it is used four times in this early portion of the prayer.[45] However, Solomon's idiom (עם־לבב) is different from David's (בלבב). Only three instances of *heart* relate to later kings: Asa (1×) and Josiah (2×). As in 1 Kgs 3:6, Yahweh's *loyalty* (23) is resumed from 2 Sam 7:15, where the divine promise to David had concerned his 'seed'. Appropriately 'your servant walking before you' is sg in Kgdms 23[46] – cf also 9:4. Only David and Solomon are ever termed Yahweh's *servant* in BoTH.

3.8 Where does God live? (1 Kgs 8:27–30//2 Chr 6:18–21)

As this transitional question is explored, continuities with David are again to the fore, such as *house building* (27). But Solomon now calls himself *your servant* as he speaks to *my God* in 28, 30. Part of his request is unique: that 'Yahweh's eyes' should always be 'open towards this house' (29) – a positive divine response comes in 9:3.

3.9 First four petitions (1 Kgs 8:31–40//2 Chr 6:22–31)

Of five further links with David, four need no comment: *enemy* (33, 37), *be restrained* (35), and *distress* and *plague* (37). Solomon's first three requests include

42 The expression is also found in David's prayer, but not at a stable position within 2 Sam 7:26–27 (MT or LXX)//1 Chr 17:24–25.

43 1 Kgs 8:17, 18, 18, 23, 38, 39, 47, 48.

44 2 Sam 6:16; 7:3, 27[Sam+]; 1 Kgs 8:66; 9:3; 15:14; 2 Kgs 22:19; 23:3.

45 Kozlova, 263.

46 LXX^{L} includes 'David my father' here too.

sin within their opening words (31, 33, 35), resuming the terms of David's repeated confession (24:10, 17); and *be restrained* and *plague* are also elements of the same census-story. *Stroke* (נגע, 37) anticipates Azariah's fate. The *ruling/judging* (שפט) of which Solomon speaks here (32) is Yahweh's, not his own as in his vision.[47] Twice again Kgdms offers a different text to 'servants' (pl) in Kgs/Chr: in 32 those to be judged/ruled are 'your people Israel'; and in 36 the sins are those 'of your servant and of your people Israel' and not 'of your servants, your people Israel'. In Kgdms (as probably originally in BoTH), Yahweh's people Israel may have special status, but they are never termed his 'servants'. Equally, '(my/your/his) servant' is reserved for David and Solomon, and not extended to their successors.

3.10 Last three petitions (1 Kgs 8:41–50a//2 Chr 6:32–39)

Most of the unique links are again with David: *far* (41, 46), *build a house* (43, 44, 48), *enemy* (44, 46), and *do wrong* (47). But two of them look forwards: *all the peoples* (43) anticipates the last reported words of Micaiah; and *with all heart and with all life-force* (48) anticipates Josiah's covenanted declaration. As already noted, the *heart* is by far the most frequently mentioned divine organ in Solomon's prayer. However, Solomon does mention Yahweh's 'eyes' once (28). And now in בכל־לבבם ובכל־נפשם the long series of eight mentions of *heart* concludes with נפש reinforcing לבב. The series opens with what David had *with his heart* (17, 18, 18) and continues with another servant walking before Yahweh *in all his heart* (23). In his fourth petition, Solomon asks that anyone may bring before Yahweh a *blow to his heart* (38), for he alone knows every human *heart* (39). Then the final petition asks that those who *return to their hearts* (47) and turn to Yahweh 'in all their *heart* and *nephesh'* (48) will be heard and forgiven. Intent and purpose are important components of *heart* in this series; and the addition of *nephesh* reminds readers of the extreme seriousness of purpose that had led David's heroes to hazard their 'lives' to bring him water.

3.11 Yahweh's chosen dwelling

Schenker (2000, 130–135) argues well for the greater originality of the 4-line poem in Kgdms and its position before 8:54a (//7:1a) and following Solomon's prayer: only without its 1st line do the three lines fit better after 8:11 (as in Kgs//Chr). But

47 Neither element of להצדיק צדיק (32) is resumed anywhere in BoTH.

he says nothing about the prior literary history and is mistaken about the absence of these two verses from Chr. Also 'build a house' (13) fits well with 16–20 [48]

3.12 Inauguration climax (1 Kgs 8:54a, 62–66//2 Chr 7:1a, 4–5, 7–8, 10)

Kgs and Chr go separate ways immediately after the opening link and each is expansive.[49] In this concluding section on the inauguration of the temple, almost all the unique links are again with David: the verbs *completed* [doing] (כלה ל־, 54) and *sacrificed* (זבח, 62, 63), the two specific sorts of sacrifice (64), David as *servant* (66), and *blessing* (66) – though this time Solomon is blessed by the people. In the Solomon narratives, a *court* (חצר) of the temple is only precisely synoptic here,[50] and will reappear only to be desecrated by Manasseh. 'All the people' will be *joyful* (שמחים, 66) again only at the restoration of Joash, though the cognate *in joy* (בשמחה) is part of David's ark-story. Both Kgs and Chr are expansive: זבח השלמים (63) is found elsewhere only in Lev-Num.[51]

3.13 Second vision (1 Kgs 9:1–9//2 Chr 7:11–22) and Pharaoh's daughter (3 Kgdms 9:9*//1 Kgs 9:24//2 Chr 8:11)

The finishing of the *house building* (1), though not the last mention of it, leads to a second vision (2–9). In the opening verses, most of the links are with David. Solomon has completed the physical construction; now Yahweh *declares* (3) that he has consecrated the building to himself, placing his name there for ever. *Walk*

48 Ska's approach (OT Abstracts 42, 2019, 396) is convergent with Schenker's: '[His] comparison of the MT text of 1 Kgs 8:12 and that of LXX 8:53 leads him to two interesting conclusions. First, the Greek text is, in all likelihood, the older one. Second, the theology of this Greek text is different from that of the MT parallel: in the former, the God who comes to dwell in the temple is the traditional storm God, who is well known, e.g. from Ugarit. In the MT, by contrast, a close connection is made between the tent of meeting constructed by Moses in the desert and the temple in Jerusalem. Here, the God who dwells in the temple is the God of the Exodus and a continuity is created between Moses and the dynasty of David and Solomon.' The move of this text from the one position to the other may have been eased by the fact that Moses is mentioned in both 8:9 and 8:53. Yet, from a BoTH perspective, only 8:9 (Moses at Horeb after the Exodus) is synoptic. כור הברזל (in non-synoptic 8:51) is found elsewhere only in Deut 4:20; Jer 11:4.

49 LXX attests the more grammatical ויקם after ויהי ככלות; however, all of 54b may be secondary – only Kgs refers after the prayer to Solomon kneeling, while 2 Chr 6:13 has added this at the start.

50 חצר occurs also in non-synoptic 1 Kgs 6:36; 7:8, 9, 12, 12; and in 2 Chr 4:9.

51 Lev 3:3, 9; 4:10, 26; 7:11. 20, 21, 37; 9:18; Num 6:18; 7 (13×).

before me (4) recalls 8:23 (and is singular like Kgdms there) with its link back to the promise to David (2 Sam 7:15). *Walking before* [Yahweh] had been reinforced in 8:23 by 'with all his heart'. Now Yahweh reciprocates: his undertaking that *my eyes and my heart will be there for all time* (3) resumes 'eyes' from Solomon's request in 8:29 in support of the pervasive 'heart'. Yahweh's eyes are first mentioned in BoTH by David (2.7 above on 2 Sam 7:19). Most of the kings to follow will be measured by what is right or bad in these divine eyes. Appropriately, the topics of the next verses are following the example of David and acting according to divine standards.

Keeping (or 'not forsaking') *commandments* and *statutes* (4, 6) are part of both 1–5 and 6–9 and anticipate Huldah and Josiah. All the remaining unique links similarly look forwards: *all nations* (עמים, 7) to Micaiah and Jehoshaphat; *prostrate oneself* (השתחוה, 9) to Manasseh; and *forsake* (עזב, 9) to Huldah and Josiah. However, there will still be many links back to David in both sections of 1 Kgs 10.

The juxtaposition in Kgdms (and presumably in BoTH – see below) of forsaking Yahweh who had 'brought out' (הוציא) the fathers from Egypt (9:9) and Solomon who now 'brought up' (העלה) the daughter of Pharaoh to the house he had built for himself (9:9a) is quite striking. Each verb is used as often as the other in HB in references to the Exodus.

3.14 Solomon and Hiram: Cities and trade (1 Kgs 9:10–14, 26–28//2 Chr 8:1–2, 17–18)

In the first portion, only 9:10 and synoptic 8:1 are identical. What follows is a brief return to issues between Solomon and Hiram of *Tyre* over *housebuilding*. However, the (different) syntax that follows in 9:11 and 8:2 is difficult. The fact that the building of Yahweh's house and of the king's own house is noted both before and after the second vision may suggest that the second vision was a later supplement to the Solomon story.

None of *shipping* (אני), *Tarshish* (תרשיש), or the port of *Ezion-geber* (עציון־גבר) reappears even separately in BoTH except in the report of Jehoshaphat where all feature again together. Azariah will restore *Eilat* to Judah. It may be in order to link these two connections that *Ezion-geber* is said here to be near *Eilat*. Cf 10:11, 22.

In Kgdms, 9:14 immediately anticipates the greater detail in 27–28 – in both, Hiram sends Solomon a large quantity of gold. 9:14, 28 include both וישלח חירם and 120 talents of gold (so B – MT and L have 420 in 27). Chr 18 has Huram sending (וישלח) and the talents have increased to 450, but in 2 he gives cities (והערים אשר נתן חורם).

3.15 Queen of Sheba (1 Kgs 10:1–13//2 Chr 9:1–12)

The first part of this story (10:1–10) is bracketed by reports of the benefits to Solomon of Hiram's trade with Ophir (9:28; 10:11). The visit of the queen of Sheba may therefore be seen as a further example of the international role of Solomon exemplified in his relations with Hiram.

She brought Solomon without compulsion *precious stone* (אבן יקרה) such as David conquered in Rabbah, and *weight of the gold* makes a further link. However, the association of gold with balsam (10:2, 10) links Solomon instead with Hezekiah (2 Kgs 20:13//2 Chr 32:27) as does האמין (10:7) with 2 Chr 32:15 (//בטח in 2 Kgs).

'Wise' (חכם) and 'wisdom' (חכמה) are associated only with Solomon in BoTH. The references throughout 1 Kgs 10 (4, 6, 8, 23, 24) are most obviously synoptic; NB also 3:12//1:12 and 5:21//2:11.

Towards the end of the episode about her visit, there are three significant links, all with David material. Echoing the narrator on David (2 Sam 8:15), the queen links 'Israel' and 'reign' with *practise justice and righteousness* (לעשות משפט וצדקה, 9). From wood she supplied, Solomon made *lyres and harps* (12, cf 2 Sam 6:5). And she *asked for* (שאל) things from Solomon (13), as Toi had done (somewhat differently) of David (2 Sam 8:10).

3.16 Gold (1 Kgs 10:14–22//2 Chr 9:13–21)

Three topics are handled here briefly: the riches Solomon acquired were used to embellish the Lebanon Forest House (14–17); a magnificent throne was constructed (18–20); and trade in the Red Sea by 'ships of Tarshish' helped furnish the Lebanon Forest House (21–22).

Solomon's yearly income in gold (14–15) is turned into armour (mostly rendered 'shields') of two sorts: צנה (16) and מגן (17).[52] These – either the latter or both – were put in the House of the Forest of Lebanon. The gold that Solomon beat into מגן (17) would be quickly lost by his son Rehoboam to Pharaoh. Kgs, Kgdms, and Chr differ over several details (Schenker 2000, 126–128). Ancient readers were apparently grappling with actual or perceived tension between five synoptic reports: (a) David brought captured gold armour to Jerusalem (2 Sam 8:7); (b) Solomon brought into the completed those of Yahweh items dedicated by David (1 Kgs 7:51); (c) Solomon deposited in his Lebanon Forest House armour (of

52 Alter (2019, 477) renders מגן by 'buckler, but notes that the distinction from צנה 'cannot be determined'.

two sorts!) created from his huge receipts in gold; (d) Rehoboam lost gold armour made by Solomon among the treasures Pharaoh seized from the houses of both Yahweh and the king (1 Kgs 14:26–27); (e) young Joash was guarded by armour that had been David's preserved in Yahweh's house.

'Ships/Tarshish' (22) anticipate Jehoshaphat where Ophir (11) is also mentioned. Beyond the emphasis on gold for the great house, this trade by Tarshish-ships included 'silver, hewn [wood][53] and [wood] worked in relief' – so LXX, neatly introducing the theme of building works (3.17). When the following paragraph was moved to its new position in 1 Kgs 9:15–22 (MT), 1 Kgs 10:22 MT reported these cargoes differently: 'gold, silver, ivory, apes, and peacocks'. Two sorts of high-quality construction material have metamorphosed into three luxury imports. Each of the three is unique within HB to this verse and its parallel in 2 Chr 9:21. At the end of 18, Syr renders not מופז but מאופיר.

3.17 Solomon's labour force (3 Kgdms 10:22a–c[54] [cf 1 Kgs 9:15–22 and 2 Chr 8:3–16])

These verses record diverse or miscellaneous materials; and there is considerable textual diversity between Kgs, Kgdms, and Chr. The surrounding material in Kgs/Chr (but not Kgdms) concerns relations between Solomon and the king of Tyre.

Third men (22) and *holocausts* (25) are terms found elsewhere in BoTH only in narratives about David; however, *holocausts* are already part of the Solomon story in 3:4 and 8:64, and ושריו ושלשיו is textually uncertain (it is absent from 3 Kgdms 10:22c and from Pesh in 2 Chr 8:9). 9:25b and 8:16b are closely related; but 8:16 reads better in LXX which retroverts to עד־כלות שלמה בית יהוה (cf 2 Chr 7:11, but not quite 1 Kgs 9:1).

Plural forms of איש such as אנשי מלחמה (9:22//8:9) are uncommon in BoTH; but we find two further cases in the Solomon narratives in 10:8, 15//9:7, 14. Cf also האנשים in 2 Sam 10:5; 23:17//1 Chr 19:5; 11:19.

Like the neighbouring issue of the indigenous peoples, this topic may have come late to BoTH.

3.18 Three notes (1 Kgs 10:23–25//2 Chr 9:22–24)

Solomon as *great[er]* (23) recalls the early judgment on David (2 Sam 5:10). However, all the [kings of the] earth *seeking* (מבקשים) Solomon to hear his wisdom (24) is

53 'Hewn' is the literal rendering of the Greek; but we should note that it corresponds in 10:11, 12 to אלמגים.

54 a corresponds to 15, 17b-19; b to 20–21; and c to 22 (9:9a corresponds to 16–17a).

in striking contrast with Philistines *seeking* David (2 Sam 5:17). In our discussion of Solomon's first vision, we noted a similar contrast between David *asking* Yahweh about engaging Philistines in battle and Solomon praised for not *asking* for the life of his enemies. Yet there is continuity with David (2 Sam 8:2, 6) in foreigners bringing him *tribute* (מנחה, 25). שלמה (*mantle*) will reappear in the Jeroboam story (11:29, 30//o); and בשמים (*balsam*) both recalls 10:2 and looks forward to Hezekiah (2 Kgs 20:13, cf 2 Chr 32:17). Neither wealth (עשר) nor wisdom (חכמה) is attributed to any other character in BoTH (23); these topics bring us back to the opening vision – just as Hiram is omnipresent.[55] Synoptic Solomon corresponds well to 2 Sam 5–8 – what follows in the David story repeats several links, but hardly adds any; and 8 makes a good conclusion.

3.19 Maritime trade with Ophir (1 Kgs 10:26–29//2 Chr 9:25–28)

2 Chr 9:25–28 is the shortest and probably oldest version. The additional 1 Kgs 10:26a and 29 also bracket the longer variant in 2 Chr 1:14–17. The note about Solomon's 'dominion' includes the only instance in BoTH in which the verb משל is text-critically unambiguous.[56] In the report of Solomon's second vision, איש מושל בישראל of 2 Chr 7:18 is also attested in synoptic 3 Kgdms 9:5; but in 1 Kgs 9:5 we find איש מעל כסא ישראל. The cognate ממשלתו occurs in 1 Kgs 9:19// 2 Chr 8:6, while the parallel following 3 Kgdms 10:22 may attest משל (Schenker 2000, 54). ממשלתו may have been part of the Hezekiah report in BoTH. However, the canonical versions place it differently: early in 2 Chr 32:9 but late in 2 Kgs 20:13. מושל may play on the name שלמה, just like ותשלם in 7:51.

4 Rehoboam and Jeroboam (1 Kgs 11–14 and parallels)

Three elements of the Jeroboam part of the Rehoboam story form unique links back to Solomon: *porter* (סבל), *assembled* (הקהיל), and *cloak/mantle* (שלמה). In the three cases of הקהיל, Solomon assembles all the elders of Israel; Jeroboam assembles the tribes/sceptres of Israel; and Rehoboam assembles the 'man' of Judah and Benjamin.[57] The *elders of Israel* had approached David after Saul's

55 Chr attributes this quality to Jehoshaphat – because of trade story?

56 מושל is rendered by ἡγούμενος in 3 Kgdms 10:26* and 2 Chr 9:26 (LXX), but by ἄρχων in 3 Kgdms 2:46k, as elsewhere only in Gen 24:2.

57 In 1 Kgs 12:3 (MT) and 2 Chr 10:3 (LXX) Jeroboam is accompanied by כל־קהל ישראל, but in 2 Chr 10:3 (MT) by כל־ישראל. However, LXX attests 'the people' (העם) in both 3 Kgdms 12:3 and 12:24p.

death; they had been assembled by Solomon as the ark was borne into the temple; now *elders* are *consulted* (נועץ) by Rehoboam, but their advice rejected. *Consulting* is echoed only in (Chr's version of) the Hezekiah story. The principal detail of Pharaoh Shishak's spoil was מגני הזהב, the *gold 'bucklers'* (Alter 2019, 495) made for Solomon. *Consult* and *advice* (עצה) do not feature in the narratives about David and Solomon; but they reappear in the Hezekiah story.[58]

Shishak's spoiling of the Jerusalem temple and palace in Rehoboam's fifth year (1 Kgs 14:25–26//2 Chr 12:2, 9) is one of the very few precise dates provided in the Book of Two Houses, apart from the ages of kings at accession and the length of their reigns. Three others are the move against (the irregular rule of) Athaliah in her seventh year, Amaziah living on for 15 years after the death of Jehoash, and Josiah's temple-work and Passover in his eighteenth. However, only the last of these is stated in the same way: 'in the nth year of king X' (2 Kgs 22:3; 23:23).

Oracular הנני anticipates Huldah's words in 2 Kgs 22:16, 20. However, *cut off* (הכרית, 14:10) looks in two directions: both back to 2 Sam 7:9 and forwards to (2 Kgs 9:8//)2 Chr 22:7 – in all three passages Yahweh is subject while the objects are (a) David's enemies, (b) Jeroboam's son, and (c) [not] Judah. Rehoboam *firming himself* (התאמץ) as he mounted his chariot to escape to Jerusalem is an ironic anticipation of the name of king *Amaziah* (אמציהו) who had to return to Jerusalem after defeat by his northern neighbour. The Rehoboam and Amaziah reports share three further unique links: (a) Jeroboam was closely associated with *Ephraim* (אפרים, 1 Kgs 12:25) and Amaziah's destruction of Jerusalem's wall started at the *Ephraim* gate (2 Kgs 14:13). (b) Israel said to Rehoboam 'To your tents, Israel' (לאהליך ישראל, 1 Kgs 12:16), while Judah fled 'to their tents' on defeat by Jehoash (איש לאהלו, 2 Kgs 14:12). (c) Ahijah *took hold of* (תפש) a new robe (1 Kgs 11:30) while Amaziah *took hold of* Sela', and Jehoash of Amaziah in Beth-Shemesh (2 Kgs 14:7, 13). See further pp. 197–198 above.

5 Abijam/h (1 Kgs 15:1–8//2 Chr 13:1–23)

The synoptic material is meagre and hardly any element of it is textually assured. There are no unique links with other kings.

58 For several unique (though non-verbal) links between David and Jeroboam see pp. 132–133 above.

6 Asa (1 Kgs 15:9–24//2 Chr 14:1–2; 15:16–19; 16:1–6, 11–12a, 13a, 14)

The report on Asa in Kg[dm]s also starts with a synchronism: stated as Jeroboam's 20th year in MT but his 24th year in LXX; however, Chr does not include a synchronism and also does not report the length of Asa's reign at the outset. Kgs MT also attributes to him the same mother as Abijam, Maacha daughter of Absalom; but in LXX (15:10, 13) she is Ana daughter of Absalom. No name is given in Chr at the start, but she is Maacha in 2 Chr 15:16 (both MT and LXX).

Asa removed some sort of representation of *Ashera* (אשרה, 13) and Manasseh had one manufactured.[59] Asa *burned* the Ashera at the Kidron (13);[60] and the only other plausibly synoptic burning [שרף] is by Josiah of human/priestly bones on altars.[61] Only in the synoptic reports of Asa and Jehoshaphat is it noted that *the high places did not disappear* (14);[62] and only in these same reports do we find *desist* (21), and each time the subject of חדל is a king of Israel (Baasha, then Ahab) while Aram is integral to each context.[63] In the case of Asa (15:14//15:17), despite the continuance of the *bamoth*, his heart was שלם – Kgs adds 'with Yahweh'. This is the only synoptic instance of לבב שלם. It is arguable that it suggests an implicit pairing with Solomon: *heart* is a key term in Solomon's great prayer and *complete heart* here has similar force to 'heart and life-force' at the conclusion of the prayer. In Chr pluses[64] the phrase is never followed by 'with Yahweh', unlike 1 Kgs 8:61; 11:4; 15:3 (but not 2 Kgs 20:3=Isa 38:3). A nearby and undeniable link with Solomon is provided by the unique pairing of the following whole clause: *brought into the house of Yahweh his father's dedications – gold, silver, and vessels* (15).[65] In Kgs, Asa (12) and Jehoshaphat (22:47) are also linked over קדש[ים] differently vocalised; and these may have been removed by Chr from the text he inherited (in Asa's case by substituting the pejorative שקוצים). Only Asa and Ahaz use the resources of the two 'houses' to buy help when threatened by Israel. Asa is implicitly paired with Solomon; and in Kgs but not Chr he is explicitly compared with David (11). Mention of his sickness (15:23) links him with two further successors: Ahaziah and Hezekiah.

---

59 1 Kgs 15:13//2 Chr 15:16; 2 Kgs 21:3, 7//2 Chr 33:3, 7.

60 1 Kgs 15:13//2 Chr 15:16.

61 2 Kgs 23:20 and 2 Chr 34:5.

62 1 Kgs 15:14//2 Chr 15:17; 1 Kgs 22:44//2 Chr 20:33.

63 1 Kgs 15:21//2 Chr 16:5; 1 Kgs 22:6, 15//2 Chr 18:5, 14.

64 1 Chr 12:39; 28:9, 9; 29:19; 2 Chr 16:9; 19:9; 25:2.

65 Montgomery 275 finds the reference obscure while other commentators such as Gray and Sweeney ignore it. Kgdms has κίονας ('pillars') for קדשי, having possibly read קרשי.

7.1 Jehoshaphat summary (3 Kgdms 16:28a–c, f–h//1 Kgs 22:41–44, 46, 49–51//2 Chr 20:31–37)

In both Kgs MT and Chr, the summary information on Jehoshaphat follows the Micaiah story, while in Kgdms, it precedes it. There are several differences in detail between the three versions. In neither case is the longer report included within the report of this king's reign. Since this may have been secondarily added, it is treated separately below (7.2). Jehoshaphat and Solomon shared a concern for *shipping* (אני[ו]ת) and in each case the ships are of *Tarshish* (תרשיש). Since both reports include unique mention of *Ezion-geber* (עציון־גבר),[66] the trade was on the Red Sea. Hence 'of Tarshish' will designate the type of the ships. Links with Asa are *bamoth not disappeared* (44) and possibly קדש (47).

7.2 Jehoshaphat, the king of Israel, and the prophets (1 Kgs 22:1–35// 2 Chr 18:1–34)

Only David and Jehoshaphat are involved with action at a *threshing floor* (גרן).[67] In explanation of his vision, Micaiah adds that [Israel and Judah] have no *lords* (אדנים), while in synoptic texts only David is addressed as 'my lord [king]' (אדני [המלך]).[68] Shepherding brackets the entire David story in BoTH: 'all Israel' at the start cites David's divine appointment to *shepherd* (רעה)[69] Israel, while David at the end calls his people *sheep* (צאן)[70] as he witnesses the divine messenger destroying them; and now Micaiah tells the two kings that he had seen 'all Israel scattered … like sheep without a shepherd'. Links with David are concentrated in one verse (1 Kgs 22:17) and relate to details of the census story. Additionally, only the synoptic accounts of Micaiah and (at least in MT and LXX^{B}) of David's census use the particle נא.[71] Yet נגש is synoptic only in 22:24 and 2 Sam 10:13; and in both contexts the *approach* is hostile; and iron only appears in BoTH at the cruel end to the capture of Rabbat Ammon and in the horns worn by the prophet Zedekiah as he encourages the two kings to victory over Aram.[72] Hostility, even if not cruelty, is common to both contexts.

66 1 Kgs 9:27; 10:22//2 Chr 8:18; 9:21; 1 Kgs 22:49–50//2 Chr 20:36–37.

67 2 Sam 6:6; 24:16, 18, 21, 24//1 Chr 13:9; 21:15, 18, 21, 22; 1 Kgs 22:10//2 Chr 18:9.

68 2 Sam 24:3//1 Chr 21:3; 1 Kgs 22:17//2 Chr 18:16.

69 2 Sam 5:2; 7:7//1 Chr 11:2; 17:6; 1 Kgs 22:17//2 Chr 18:16.

70 2 Sam 24:17//1 Chr 21:17; 1 Kgs 22:17//2 Chr 18:16.

71 2 Sam 24:10, 14, 17//1 Chr 21:8, 13, 17; 1 Kgs 22:5, 13//2 Chr 18:4, 12. Both versions of Solomon's prayer attest it, but at different points (1 Kgs 8:26 and 2 Chr 6:40.) By contrast, it is found in almost half of all the chapters in Sam-Kgs (49/102).

72 2 Sam 12:31//1 Chr 20:3; 1 Kgs 22:11//2 Chr 18:10.

The name Jeho-shaphat includes the verb *rule* (שפט) that features throughout the Solomon story: in both visions, at start and end of his prayer, and in the assessment of the visiting queen. There is a possible further link: in each of 1 Kgs 8:43 and 9:7 and at the end of 22:28, we find *nations* (עמים). עמים pl occurs nowhere else in BoTH and in each case it is strengthened by all (כל); however, the clause is lacking in 22:28 LXX. After the David and Solomon narratives, where עם with sg possessive sfx referring to Yahweh is densely used, כעמי כעמך within the initial bargain between Jehoshaphat and the king of Israel sounds almost impious.

A link with Asa is *desist* (חדל, 6, 15). Chariot-commanders (שרי הרכב, 32–33) reappear only when J[eh]oram attacks Edom. *Ramoth in Gilead* features only as goal of two joint expeditions against Aram: one mounted by Jehoshaphat and Ahab and the other by Ahaziah (grandson of Jehoshaphat) and Joram (son of Ahab).[73] Both *hide* (חבא\ה)[74] and *chamber* (חדר)[75] provide unique links between the reports of Jehoshaphat and Joash. In Micaiah's vision *the host of heaven* (צבא השמים) attend on Yahweh while for Manasseh they themselves are objects of worship.[76] Ahab like Saul is killed by an arrow from a *bow* (קשת, 34).

There are several links between Jehoshaphat/Micaiah and Josiah/Huldah. Jehoshaphat and Ahab *seek* (דרש)[77] Yahweh through Micaiah the *prophet* (הנביא), as only synoptic Josiah will do again – in his case through Huldah the prophetess (הנביאה).[78] *Small* (קט[ו]ן) and *great* (גדול) are also paired only in the Jehoshaphat and Josiah reports.[79] Then *in peace* (בשלום) is uttered three times in the exchanges between Micaiah and the king of Israel,[80] and reappears only in the response of Huldah to Josiah.[81] (The only other synoptic mention of 'peace' occurs in a greeting received by David.[82]) Given these several links between the reports of Jehoshaphat and Josiah and their respective prophets, perhaps we should treat Micaiah's חי יהוה as a virtual pair with Huldah's נאם יהוה – each confirmatory phrase is unique in BoTH.[83] The extended story of the two kings with Micaiah and the other prophets is very well connected, within Kgs as already within BoTH.

---

73 1 Kgs 22:3, 4, 15, 20//2 Chr 18:2, 3, 14, 19; 2 Kgs 8:28//2 Chr 22:5.

74 1 Kgs 22:25//2 Chr 18:24; 2 Kgs 11:3//2 Chr 22:12.

75 1 Kgs 22:25//2 Chr 18:24; 2 Kgs 11:2//2 Chr 22:11.

76 1 Kgs 22:19//2 Chr 18:18; 2 Kgs 21:3//2 Chr 33:3.

77 1 Kgs 22:5, 7, 8//2 Chr 18:4, 6, 7; 2 Kgs 22:13, 18//2 Chr 34:21, 26.

78 1 Kgs 22:7//2 Chr 18:6; 2 Kgs 22:14//2 Chr 34:22.

79 1 Kgs 22:31//2 Chr 18:30; 2 Kgs 23:2//2 Chr 34:30.

80 1 Kgs 22:17, 27, 28//2 Chr 18:16, 26, 27.

81 2 Kgs 22:20//2 Chr 34:28.

82 2 Sam 8:10//1 Chr 18:10.

83 2 Kgs 22:19//2 Chr 34:27; 1 Kgs 22:14//2 Chr 18:13.

Its close links with major elements of the cycle dominated by Elijah and Elisha (1 Kgs 17–2 Kgs 10) have long been noted; but some twenty links throughout BoTH, from Saul at the start to Josiah and Huldah at the end are no less important.

Ahab is named only once in the synoptic Micaiah portion; and historians often suppose that not Ahab but Jehoram was the original 'king of Israel' in the story. Jehoram of course is explicitly partner of Ahaziah in a similar venture. However, the historians may be missing a double rhetorical point. The name of the 'king of Israel' is withheld until the very mid-point of the story (20), exactly when the true prophecy is given (Alter 2019, 524). Then, given the several links with stories of David, himself king of Israel, it seems likely that the author found it significant that one of David's descendants was operating in close association with the current 'king of Israel': 'all Israel' occurs beside 'shepherd' in both 2 Sam 5:1–2 and 1 Kgs 22:17. (When Kgs [MT] was created, including a synchronistic account of Israel's kings, was the Micaiah narrative reassigned from Jehoshaphat to Ahab?)

8 Jehoram (2 Kgs 8:17–22, 24a//2 Chr 21: 5–10a)

Jehoram is spared *destruction* (השחית) by Yahweh, reminding us of Yahweh relenting from his decision to *destroy*, as his plague-dealing envoy approached Jerusalem after David's count (2 Sam 24:16). Because of Yahweh's commitment to David, Jehoram did not suffer like so many of David's own people had (19). His response to Edom's rebellion involved an attack on their *chariot-commanders* (21), mentioned elsewhere only in Aram's conflict with Ahab and Jehoshaphat (1 Kgs 22:31–33). Athaliah, Jehoram's wife, is not named till the following report on their son (8:26). At her first mention (8:18), she is simply 'the daughter of Ahab'. Just as Saul and Ahab are the only kings in BoTH to meet death from a bow, so too only their daughters, Michal and Athaliah, are named and play a role in the text – Athaliah more fully than Michal. (Michal becomes David's wife only in non-synoptic Samuel.)

9 Ahaziah (2 Kgs 8:26–29; 9:21, 27b//2 Chr 22:2–6, 7–9)

In addition to the connection with the house of Ahab, Ahaziah has further links with the wider narrative. Like Jehoshaphat, he has an unsuccessful campaign against Aram at *Ramoth-Gilead*, in his case along with Jehoram of Israel. Though told in only a few clauses, these reports share the terms הלך למלחמה (2 Kgs 8:28 and 1 Kgs 22:4, 6, 15), ויכ־ (2 Kgs 8:28 and 1 Kgs 22:24, 34), and חלה (2 Kgs 8:29 and 1 Kgs 22:34) with the previous and much longer narrative as well as mention of

Ahab. If 2 Chr 22:7 does preserve the text of BoTH, Ahaziah visits the wounded Jehoram at the time of the revolt by Jehu who was divinely ordained to *cut off* (הכרית) the house of Ahab, so implicitly making them enemies of David (2 Sam 7:9) and comparing them to Jeroboam's unfortunate son (who was also 'sick'). הכרית is also linked with the house of Ahab in the fuller narrative of 2 Kgs 9:7–8. One king descended from both the house of David and the house of Ahab was spared destruction because of the divine commitment to David; but his son became collateral damage when the house of Ahab was cut off. Then in name and also by deeds he anticipates Ahaz.

10 Joash (2 Kgs 11–12//2 Chr 22:10–24:26)

Only synoptic David and Joash are reported as being *anointed* (משח),[84] and each anointing is associated with *making a covenant* (כרת ברית) – intimately so in the briefer account of David's anointing. In the case of Joash, two covenants are narrated, one before and the other after the anointing.[85] The people being or becoming called *a people for Yahweh* (לעם ליהוה) is unique to David and Joash.[86] This explicit wording is unparalleled; however, the relationship between God and people is already implicit in the widespread talk of 'my/your/his people' in the David and Solomon narratives. *Shields* (שלטים)[87] or *quivers* (Clines 2011, 391b) provide a further link with David. Then David's Benaiah *slays* (הרג) an Egyptian with his own *spear* (חנית); and *spears* are handed out before Mattan is *slain*;[88] and the use of פקד qal (2 Kgs 11:15//2 Chr 23:14) is anticipated in David's census (2 Sam 24//1 Chr 21).

But there is also a difference between the two situations. David had had responsibility for Israel's forces: 'it was you who brought us out and in' (צאת ובא). By contrast, Jehoiada must alert his temple guards to a converse responsibility: they must support their new young king *as he goes out and comes in* (11:8). This expression is not unique to David and Joash. Baasha builds Ramah to blockade Asa: 'not to allow going out and coming in' (לבלתי תת יצא ובא).[89] While Solomon, at least according to 1 Kgs 3:7, had professed to be a junior, Joash really is a youngster.

---

84 2 Sam 5:3, 17//1 Chr 11:3; 14:8; 2 Kgs 11:12//2 Chr 23:11.
85 2 Sam 5:3//1 Chr 11:3; 2 Kgs 11:4, 17//2 Chr 23:3, 16.
86 2 Sam 7:24//1 Chr 17:22; 2 Kgs 11:17//2 Chr 23:16.
87 2 Sam 8:7//1 Chr 18:7; 2 Kgs 11:10//2 Chr 23:9.
88 2 Sam 23:21//1 Chr 11:23; 2 Kgs 11:10, 18//2 Chr 23:9, 17.
89 1 Kgs 15:17 refers to a blockade.

Both at the end of Solomon's dedication of the temple and at the restoration of Joash, the people were *happy* (שמח[ים]).[90] *Runners* (רצים) to whom Rehoboam entrusts *shields* (מגנים) reappear only in the Joash narrative.[91] *Hide/chamber* make a unique double link with Jehoshaphat. Athaliah in the Joash story like Sennacherib in the time of Hezekiah dies *by the sword* (בחרב).[92] שבר piel (*smash*) is synoptic only in 2 Kgs 11:18; 18:4//2 Chr 23:17//31:1 but the objects differ.[93] Athaliah also anticipates Manasseh as a follower of *Baal*. Despite being very prominent in non-synoptic Kings, this god appears only in these two synoptic reports.[94]

In addition to its several links with David, the report of Athaliah and Joash has at least eight explicit unique links with the Josiah narrative: Athaliah like Josiah *tears her clothes* (ותקרע את־בגדיה),[95] Joash's reforms are masterminded by a named *priest* (כהן)[96] with a *scribe* (ספר)[97] also involved, *a covenant is made*,[98] the king stands *by the pillar* (על־העמוד),[99] and each report speaks repeatedly of *those doing the task* (עשי המלאכה).[100] In both reports Yahweh's house is *firmed* (חזק piel)[101] and artisans (חרשים) are mentioned. Then, the king's names are closely related (p. 183 above). Finally, two destructive verbs: tear down (נתץ) and shatter (שבר) are clearly synoptic in 2 Kgs 11:18//2 Chr 23:17; and both Kgs and Chr use the verbs in their reports on Josiah.[102] Also unique to this story are 'the (chiefs of the) hundreds' (שרי המאות).[103]

---

90 1 Kgs 8:64//2 Chr 7:10; 2 Kgs 11:14, 20//2 Chr 23:13, 19. Cognate שמחה is used in the synoptic ark narrative (2 Sam 6:12//1 Chr 15:25).

91 1 Kgs 14:27–28//2 Chr 12:10–11; 2 Kgs 11:13//2 Chr 23:12.

92 2 Kgs 11:20//2 Chr 23:21; 2 Kgs 19:37//2 Chr 32:21.

93 צלמיו or מזבחתיו in the case of Joash, but המצבת in the case of Hezekiah. שבר piel is also used in 2 Kgs 23:14 and 2 Chr 34:4.

94 2 Kgs 11:18–20//2 Chr 23:17–21; 2 Kgs 21:3//2 Chr 33:3.

95 2 Kgs 11:14//2 Chr 23:13; 2 Kgs 22:11, 19//2 Chr 34:19, 27.

96 2 Kgs 11:9, 10, 15; 12:3, 6, 11//2 Chr 23:8, 9, 14; 24:2, 5, 11; 2 Kgs 22:4//2 Chr 34:9 – כהן is + in 2 Kgs 12:7, 8, 9, 10(2×), 17; 22:8, 12, 14.

97 2 Kgs 12:11//2 Chr 24:11; 2 Kgs 22:9, 10, 12//2 Chr 34:16, 18, 20.

98 2 Kgs 11:17//2 Chr 23:16; 2 Kgs 23:3//2 Chr 34:31.

99 2 Kgs 11:14//2 Chr 23:13; 2 Kgs 23:3//2 Chr 34:31 (LXX).

100 2 Kgs 12:12, 15, 16//2 Chr 24:12, 13; 2 Kgs 22:5, 9//2 Chr 34:10, 12, 13, 17 – compare 1 Kgs 7:40// 2 Chr 4:11; however, the similar but non-synoptic expressions relating to Solomon's projects in 1 Kgs 9:23 and 2 Chr 8:9 appear secondary.

101 2 Kgs 12:6, 7//2 Chr 24:5.

102 נתץ in 2 Kgs 23:7, 8, 12, 15; 2 Chr 34:4, 7; and שבר in 2 Kgs 23:14; 2 Chr 34:4. In 2 Kgs 23:12, 15 and 2 Chr 34:4, 7 the object of נתץ is altars (מזבחות) as in 2 Kgs 11:18. But the objects of שבר vary: צלמיו (2 Kgs 11:18//2 Chr 23:17); המצבות (2 Kgs 23:14); and האשרים (2 Chr 34:4).

103 2 Kgs 11:4, 10, 15, 19//2 Chr 23:1, 9, 14, 20 – and also in 11:9, while in 23:8 they have become 'the Levites and all Judah' (הלוים וכל־יהודה).

Alongside the role of named priest and scribe, 'the people of the land'[104] also play a role in the narratives of both boy-kings (BoTH mentions them again only in the Azariah/Jotham story). 'Die' is not a unique link, but two of the relatively rare occurrences of this common verb in BoTH close the reports of Joash (2 Kgs 12:25) and Josiah (23:29). It is also true that מות is used in connection with each of the three instances of קשר: Joash, Amaziah, and Amon.

One further probable link should be noted: נתץ qal is synoptic in 2 Kgs 11:18// 2 Chr 23:17 and qal is also found in the report of Josiah's reform in 2 Kgs 23:7, 8, 12, 15 while 2 Chr 34:4, 7 has piel.[105]

11 Amaziah (2 Kgs 14:1–3a, 5–14, 17–20//2 Chr 25:1–4, 11, 17–28)

There are several unique links between the synoptic portions of the Amaziah report and David narratives in 2 Sam 8, 10, 23, and 24. Both David (or Abishai his nephew[106]) and Amaziah *strike down* (הכה) 10,000 or 18,000 [Edomites] *in Salt Valley* (בגיא־מלח);[107] and both experience *irruption* (פרץ).[108] Then *flee* (נוס) follows *be smitten* (נגף) in reports of two of David's campaigns (2 Sam 10:14–15, 18–19); and these verbs reappear as a pair in BoTH only as Amaziah is defeated by Jehoash of Israel (14:12). The note about his *strong* grip on the kingdom (2 Kgs 14:5) employs חזק qal. This certainly makes a further link with David (2 Sam 10:11–12; 24:4); but it may also play on the very similar meanings of חזק and אמץ that the Amaziah/Hezekiah links will exploit. Then, assuming that הוא הכה in 2 Kgs 14:7 reflects the earlier text in BoTH before that was expanded to produce 2 Chr 25:11, it will form a further David/Amaziah pairing (2 Sam 23:20, 21). An additional link with the same portion of the David story is provided by *honoured* (נכבד) in both 2 Sam 23:19, 23 and 2 Kgs 14:10. Then trampling *field*-life (חית השדה) in 14:9 recalls two of these David portions: both hero Shamma defending the strip of *field* (2 Sam 23:11) and Aram in the *field* (2 Sam 10:8) – each a conflict situation. We shall note below an additional significant David-link (in 14:6), though not a further unique pair.

A second significant link is with the report on Rehoboam and Jeroboam. Only Amaziah and Rehoboam initiate action against Israel; only they suffer the

104 Trebolle 2020, 191–210 discusses עם הארץ and המליך in the Joash story.
105 Auld 2017, 248–251 includes several items of implicit critique of Na'aman 1998, 337–340.
106 Or Joab in Ps 60:2.
107 2 Sam 8:13//1 Chr 18:12; 2 Kgs 14:7//2 Chr 25:11.
108 2 Sam 5:20; 6:8//1 Chr 14:11; 13:11; 2 Kgs 14:13//2 Chr 25:23.

plundering of the two 'houses' in Jerusalem (by Shishak and Jehoash); and Rehoboam *firming himself* (התאמץ) as he mounts his chariot confirms that these other links are not accidental. Jeroboam builds in Ephraim while Jehoash destroys part of the Jerusalem wall from[109] the Ephraim Gate. Only in these two narratives do people take 'to [their] tents'. Then, though not unique, the reports on Rehoboam and Amaziah also include a precise date *within* their reigns.

Amaziah is paired four times with Hezekiah: (1) each is *aged 25* on succeeding to his father; then (2), while a start at 25 is reported of two further kings (Jotham and Jehoiakim), only Amaziah and Hezekiah go on to reign *for 29 years*.[110] (3) *Lachish* (לכיש) also plays a role in the Hezekiah account: Amaziah fled there when conspired against in Jerusalem (19), and it was from there that Sennacherib sent forces to Jerusalem[111] – this apparently important city of Judah is not even mentioned in any other synoptic account. Similarly (4), the *wall* (חומה) of Jerusalem appears synoptically only in these two reports.

Finally, there are two single links: *Lebanon* (לבנון) appears only in narratives about Solomon (1 Kgs 5:13, 20, 23)[112] and Amaziah (2 Kgs 14:9); and *be found* (נמצא) relates synoptically only to Amaziah and Josiah: treasures in 2 Kgs 14:14; 22:9; and the book in 2 Kgs 22:13; 23:2.[113]

12 Azariah/Uzziah (2 Kgs 14:21–22; 15:2–3, 5–7//2 Chr 26:1–4, 21–23)

Both names by which we know Azariah/Uzziah are anticipated in narratives about David.[114] The other paired links in the report are with Solomon. Azariah restored to Judah the port of *Eilat*[115] (אילת) last mentioned in connection with Solomon; and his *stroke* (נגע) from Yahweh is one of the disasters anticipated in Solomon's prayer.[116]

---

109 LXX^L and V in 2 Kgs 14:13 agree with 2 Chr 25:23 reading משער for MT בשער, and also ויביאהו for ויבאו (Trebolle 2020, 348).

110 2 Kgs 14:2//2 Chr 25:1; 2 Kgs 18:2//2 Chr 29:2.

111 2 Kgs 14:19//2 Chr 25:27; 2 Kgs 18:17//2 Chr 32:9.

112 We read לבנון also in 1 Kgs 9:19//2 Chr 8:6; but the synoptic parallel in 3 Kgdms 10 attests לבנה.

113 מצא qal is also rare in BoTH: bowmen and then Philistines 'find' Saul (1 Sam 31:3, 8); David 'finds' heart to pray (2 Sam 7:27); and Hilkiah 'finds' the *torah*-book.

114 Help (עזר) in the ironical mention of Hadad-ezer in 2 Sam 8:3–8; and both Uzza and 'strength' (עז) in 2 Sam 6:6–7, 14.

115 1 Kgs 9:26//2 Chr 8:17; 2 Kgs 14:22//2 Chr 26:2.

116 1 Kgs 8:37//2 Chr 6:28; 2 Kgs 15:5//2 Chr 26:20. נגע piel only occurs once elsewhere in HB: of Yahweh striking Pharaoh (Gen 12:17).

13 Jotham (2 Kgs 15:33–34, 35b-36, 38//2 Chr 27:1–2a, 3a, 7, 9)

When Azariah became affected by a serious skin complaint, possibly 'skin blanch' (Alter 2019, 576), his son Jotham *judged/ruled* (שפט) in his place – a verb associated elsewhere in BoTH only with Solomon.[117] The 'free house' to which he moved (15:5) may be a quarantine house.[118]

14 Ahaz (2 Kgs 16:2–4, 5, 17–18//2 Chr 28:1–2a, 3b-4, 5–15, 16–25, 26–27)

Solomon-links continue from Azariah and Jotham to Ahaz who worshipped at high places on every high *hill* (גבעה)[119] – and his enthusiastic *sacrificing* (piel of זבח) at these locations mirrors only Solomon's large-scale sacrificing at Jerusalem as the ark was brought into his new temple.[120] Ahaz is unique in being introduced as *unlike* David. But the intended contrast may not have been with distant David himself, but rather with one or other of the nearer kings. Hezekiah and Josiah are each described as *like* David. Then Ahaz is the only king other than Asa to use the resources of the two 'houses' in Jerusalem to buy help when menaced by Israel. Like his namesake Ahaziah and Jehoram the latter's father, he 'walked in the way of the kings of Israel/house of Ahab'. Then Ahaz anticipates Manasseh (3) in *passing his son through the fire in accord with the abominations of the nations which Yahweh dispossessed in face of the sons of Israel* (כתעבות הגוים אשר הריש יהוה מפני בני ישראל)[121] and practises enthusiastic ritual *burning* (piel of קטר) which will be condemned by Huldah in the days of Josiah.[122] Only in the synoptic reports of Ahaz and Hezekiah do we find (the king of) *Assyria* (7, 8, 9).[123]

---

117 1 Kgs 3:9; 8:32//2 Chr 1:10; 6:23; 2 Kgs 15:5//2 Chr 26:21.

118 Alter (2019, 576) asks whether the freedom is brought by death or is freedom from civic obligations.

119 1 Kgs 3:4//2 Chr 1:3; 2 Kgs 16:4//2 Chr 28:4.

120 1 Kgs 8:5//2 Chr 5:6; 2 Kgs 16:4//2 Chr 28:4. The verses reporting his sacrificing at Gibeon (1 Kgs 3:2,3) are both non-synoptic.

121 2 Kgs 16:3//2 Chr 28:3; 2 Kgs 21:2//2 Chr 33:2.

122 2 Kgs 16:4//2 Chr 28:4; 2 Kgs 22:17//2 Chr 34:25.

123 2 Kgs 16:7, 8, 9//2 Chr 28:16, 20, 21; 2 Kgs 18–20(22×)//2 Chr 32(8×).

15 Hezekiah (2 Kgs 18–20//2 Chr 29–32)

Synoptic material is concentrated in the report of the Assyrian embassy to Jerusalem.

Hezekiah shares up to seven unique linkings with David. Four of them need no comment. Of the several enemies encountered throughout the synoptic narrative, only Philistines and Assyrians are said to *scorn* (חרף) Israel or Israel's god.[124] *Save* (הושׁע)[125] and *deliver* (הציל),[126] though common in much of the Hebrew Bible including elsewhere in Samuel-Kings,[127] are used in the synoptic material only in narratives about David and Hezekiah. *Yahweh's messenger* (מלאך יהוה) provides a fourth unique link[128] – in each case the fate of Jerusalem is in his hands. In the next three significant links, the term in question occurs four times in synoptic contexts: but each quartet consists of two pairs of pairs. The (foreign) Hittite *prostrating himself* (השׁתחוה) before David is paired with the (foreign) Assyrian envoy claiming that Hezekiah had commanded his people to *prostrate* before an altar.[129] Again, as noted above, *the nations* (הגוים) are part of a larger formula linking Ahaz and Manasseh. However, given the cluster of unique links, it will be significant that the only other instances of הגוים occur in narratives about David and Hezekiah.[130] *Prophet* (נביא) too appears four times synoptically, again in two pairs: Nathan and Isaiah with David and Hezekiah,[131] and Micaiah and Huldah with Jehoshaphat and Josiah (see below).

Solomon has several paired links with Hezekiah; but the Hezekiah material has been so substantially rewritten that it is hard to know what was original. (1) בשׂמים are brought to Solomon (10:2, 25) and are among Hezekiah's riches (2 Kgs 20:13//2 Chr 32:27), there following gold and silver (Chr is expansive and adds to links with Solomon). (2) יכל + inf is certainly synoptic in both 1 Kgs 8:11// 2 Chr 5:14 and 2 Kgs 18:23//2 Chr 32:13–15; but it is also attested in 1 Kgs 14:4//i. (3) האמין is found in 2 Kgs 17:14 and 2 Chr 32:15 and may have been altered to בטח

124 2 Sam 21:21//1 Chr 20:7; 2 Kgs 19:4, 16, 22, 23//2 Chr 32:17.

125 2 Sam 8:6, 14; 10:11, 19//1 Chr 18:6, 13; 19:12, 19; and 23:10//11:14 (תשׁועה); 2 Kgs 19:19, 34//2 Chr 32:22.

126 2 Sam 23:12//1 Chr 11:14; 2 Kgs 18–20 (9×)//2 Chr 32 (8×).

127 הושׁע in 1 Sam 4:3; 7:8; 9:16; 10:27; 11:3; 14:6, 23, 39; 17:47;23:2, 5; 25:26, 31, 33; 2 Sam 3:18; 14:4; 22:3, 28; 2 Kgs 6:26, 27, 27; 14:27; 16:7; and הציל in 1 Sam 4:8; 7:3, 14; 10:18; 12:10, 11, 21; 14:48; 17:35, 37, 37; 26:24; 30:8, 18, 18, 22; 2 Sam 12:7; 14:6, 16; 19:10; 20:6; 22:1, 18, 49.

128 2 Sam 24:16//1 Chr 21:15–16; 2 Kgs 19:35//2 Chr 32:21.

129 2 Sam 24:20//1 Chr 21:21; 2 Kgs 18:22//2 Chr 32:12.

130 2 Sam 7:23; 8:11//1 Chr 17:21; 18:11; 2 Kgs 18:33; 19:12//2 Chr 32:14.

131 2 Sam 7:2//1 Chr 17:1; 2 Kgs 19:2//2 Chr 32:20.

when synoptic 2 Kgs 18:30 was remodelled. (4) Hezekiah's riches belong בביתו ובכל־ממשלתו (2 Kgs 20:13) and Solomon was building ובכל־ארץ ממשלתו – but 2 Chr 32 uses ממשלה much earlier in the story, at v. 9. (5) A further likely candidate is יהוה אלהי ישראל: densely used in the opening section of Solomon's long prayer[132] and reappearing in the Assyrian letters scorning 'Yahweh God of Israel' (2 Chr 32:17) – in the much expanded 2 Kgs 19, the letter (ספר) is mentioned in v. 14, Hezekiah prays to 'Yahweh God of Israel' in v. 15, and in v. 16 the scorning is now of 'the living god'. The only synoptic instance of יהוה אלהינו is 2 Kgs 18:22[133]// 2 Chr 32:11 – and in proximity to 'this/one altar'.

Hezekiah has at least five pairings with Amaziah: each is *aged 25* on succeeding to his father; then, while a start at 25 is reported of two further kings (Jotham and Jehoiakim), only Amaziah and Hezekiah go on to reign *for 29 years*;[134] *Lachish* (לכיש) and the wall (חומה) of Jerusalem play a role in both accounts; and we are told that the kingdom became *strong* (חזקה) in Amaziah's hand.

We find two further clear echoes in synoptic Hezekiah: of Ahaz (*Assyria*), and of Huldah (the critique of other gods as *the work of human hands* [מעשה ידי אדם][135]). Two more need a little discussion. 2 Chr 32:3 reports Hezekiah's response to the early threat from Sennacherib: 'he *took counsel* with his chiefs and strongmen' (ויועץ עם־שריו וגבריו).[136] On arrival in Jerusalem, the Assyrian envoy appears to allude to this when he asks (2 Kgs 18:20): 'are spoken words counsel and strength for war?' (אך־דבר שפתים עצה וגבורה למלחמה). Both his verb (took counsel) and noun (counsel/advice) echo Rehoboam's discussions with older and younger advisers. However, if we suppose that 2 Chr 32:3 represents the older text (BoTH), 'his strongmen' (גבריו) makes a further unique link with David (2 Sam 23:8, 9, 22). In Kgs' rewriting of the story, the envoy denies strongmen/heroes to Hezekiah and allows him mere fighting talk. Real strongmen have become abstract strength.[137]

16 Manasseh (2 Kgs 21:1–10, 17–18//2 Chr 33:1–10, 18–20)

Early in the Manasseh report we find a three-fold echo of the end of the David story: the verb-series ויקם\ובנה\ויבן in vv. 3, 4, 5 resonates with the conclusion

132 And not securely located in 2 Sam 7:26–27 and parallels (see 2.7 above).

133 But Kgs LXX attests simply 'god' without 'our'.

134 2 Kgs 14:2//2 Chr 25:1; 2 Kgs 18:2//2 Chr 29:2.

135 2 Kgs 19:18//2 Chr 32:19; 2 Kgs 22:17//2 Chr 34:25.

136 גבור חיל in 1 Kgs 12:28 MT offers another link; but it is not attested in the older shorter version in LXX.

137 גבורה is never synoptic, never found in Sam, and much more common in Kgs (11×) than Chr (4×).

to the census story in 2 Sam 24:18, 21, 25 – 'raised … and built … and built'. When David confesses his sin, he is commanded by Gad to raise/erect an altar, buys a threshing floor in order to build it, then does build for Yahweh and offers sacrifice. But when Manasseh raises and builds altars in the house of Yahweh, they are for Baal[138] and they are instances of his sin and not a remedy for it.[139] There are three echoes of the Solomon story: *prostration* (3), *building* in Yahweh's *house* (5), and *court* (of the temple); and two of the Ahaz report: *abominations of the nations* (2); and *son passed through fire* (6). Then we find single echoes of Asa (*Asherah*: 3, 7), of Jehoshaphat and Micaiah (*host of heaven*: 3, 5), of Joash and Athaliah (*Baal*:[140] 3); and an anticipation of Josiah and Huldah (*provoke*: הכעיס, 6).

17 Amon (2 Kgs 21:19–21, 23–24//2 Chr 33:21–22, 24–25)

Amon continues the false worship of his father, summarised as service of הגלולים (Kgs) or הפסילים (Chr). הגלולים could imply an undoing of the work of Asa, but 1 Kgs 15:12b is Kgs+. פסילים appear in Chr's reports of Manasseh, Amon, and Josiah (2 Chr 33:19, 22; 34:3, 4, 7); but within Kgs only in the late 2 Kgs 17:41.

18 Josiah (2 Kgs 22–23//2 Chr 34–35)

The largest number of echoes (8) are with Joash who bore a variant of the same name: the role of a named priest and of a scribe (22:4), חזק piel (*strengthen* [the house], 22:5, 6) עשי המלאכה (*those performing the task*, 22:5), *artisans* (חרשים, 22:6), *rent clothes* (22:19), king standing by *pillar* (עמוד, 22:3), and *covenant-making* (22:3). The שמרי הסף responsible for temple collections (22:4) are additionally specified as Levites in synoptic 2 Chr 34:9, while the same officials according to 2 Kgs 12:10 are simply renamed the Levites in 2 Chr 24:11.

As with Micaiah in the Jehoshaphat report (1 Kgs 22:17), Huldah's first response (17) has multiple resonances with unique echoes of no less than four predecessors: Solomon (אלהים אחרים), Ahaz (קטר), Hezekiah (מעשי ידי), and Manasseh (הכעיס).[141] There is a probable single link in 2 Kgs 23:20 with Asa who

---

138 Baal in sg in Kgs MT but pl in LXX and Chr. Sg in MT fits better the comparison with Ahab and may have been adjusted towards it.

139 Schenker 2004, 47 suggests that the location changes in 4 with the explicit mention of the Jerusalem temple. It can also be argued that 4–7 simply unpack the opening summary.

140 Baal (3) is sg in Kgs (MT and LXX) but pl in Chr. Ashera (7) is sg in Kgs (MT) but pl in LXX and Chr.

141 2 Kgs 21:6//2 Chr 33:6; 2 Kgs 22:17//2 Chr 34:25.

also *burned* a detestable object. There are two (and possibly three) further linked echoes of Jehoshaphat (22:13, 14): only these two kings *enquire* (דרש) of Yahweh – and in both cases through a *prophet* (נביא[ה]); then *right and left* (ימין ושמאל) are paired only in 1 Kgs 22:19 and 2 Kgs 22:2. There are three linked echoes of David (בעד: 13, לקראת: 23:29, הרכיב: 30); two more with Solomon (*heart and soul*, 3; מצותי[ו] וחקתי[ו] 3); and three with Rehoboam (oracular הנני, in 22:16, 20; *in the* n^{th} *year of king X*, in 22:3 and 23:23; the arrival of a Pharaoh, in 23:29).

An Interim Balance

1 What's been done?

This collection of essays has extended and adjusted and strengthened the argument of *Life in Kings* (Auld 2017). The distinctiveness of the synoptic elements within Sam-Kgs has been further demonstrated. Text-critical issues have been more sensitively explored in relation to Jeroboam, Solomon, and Jehoshaphat. Major non-synoptic narratives in Sam-Kgs – about David and Jeroboam, about Samuel, Elijah, and Elisha – have been shown, like the Hezekiah story in Isaiah and Kings, to have their roots in synoptic tradition. And the key role of clustered comparisons and contrasts in that older, productive narrative has been more fully explored. The issues identified deserve more extended monographic treatment. If an earlier 'Book of Kings' has been at least plausibly identified, how should it be read?

A prior version of 'Comparing Amaziah and Jehoash' (pp. 193–202) was submitted to a Journal to see whether its argument could stand on its own. On advice from the readers invited by the editor, the article was rejected for publication. Reviewer #1 found the submission

> completely unconvincing. ... About the only aspect of this paper that makes sense is the assertion that the lengthy account of Amaziah's victory over Edom in 2 Chr 25 may be a midrashic expansion of the account in 2 Kings 14.

Reviewer #2 had

> a mixed reaction to this article. On the one hand, it observes the literary artistry or "textual jewel," as the author describes it, in the material treated in Kings. ... At the same time, there are major problems with the article's presentation in that the author's references to structure and the article's conclusion imply intention on the part of the biblical author both in the cross references and in the overall point of the work. This implication of authorial intent is not pursued to any real extent.

Both readers had encountered the article 'cold'. By contrast, the Journal ready to accept it was already familiar with the previous three essays (pp. 149–192 above). The reviewers might have come to different judgments had they met it towards the end of the present collection, and especially after the discussion of names (pp. 183–192). Perhaps, but perhaps not.

The 'sorites' paradox from ancient Greece pondered how many individual grains need to be removed from a heap (σωρός) of grain until it is no longer a heap. The question can also be posed from the other end: how many grains need to be assembled on top of each other before they become recognised as – before

https://doi.org/10.1515/9783111060279-019

they impose themselves as being – a heap of grain? Happily, reviewer #2 did not dispute that literary artistry had imposed itself, had been recognised. But why did reviewer #1 prefer the *unargued suggestion* that 2 Chr 25:5–16 may be a midrash on 2 Kgs 14:7 to the *argued demonstration* of intertextual relationships (which were never claimed, at least in so many words, to be 'authorially based')? Did this represent a greater preparedness to reckon with serious word-games in Chronicles than at the heart of Samuel-Kings?

The study of Ruth (pp. 203–216) has been included in this collection not just because it was written in the same period as the others nor even thanks to a review (Briggs 2019) more sympathetic than those just cited. I became confident in preparing it that its author must have been familiar with many other (now) biblical books – that Boaz, Naomi, and Ruth are set in a *collage* of quite diverse materials. Similar method may be at play in writing the Book of Two Houses. David (or Abishai or even Joab) defeating Edom in Salt Valley may be retrojected from Amaziah doing the same; or Solomon with a partner in Red Sea trade, from Jehoshaphat; and Rehoboam in flight from the north may recall the same Amaziah. Saul-David-Philistines share several features of Ahaz-Hezekiah-Assyrians. Uzzah 'grasping' (*'ḥz*) the Ark on its way to Jerusalem may help explain why Ahaziah (and Ahaz) were the only Jerusalem kings who bore Yahweh-names in BoTH but were also introduced as doing evil in his eyes.

Adequate reason has been provided for recovering from within Sam-Kgs and Chr the main lineaments of a well-structured BoTH, out of which they grew. Future study will pay closer attention to indications within this older narrative of how it too had developed. We have noted that a prior form of the David story may have ended at the close of 2 Sam 8. Moveable elements in the Solomon story such as Pharaoh's daughter and the personnel at work on his major constructions may have been more recently added topics without sure location. Then the major episode of Micaiah and the prophets with the two kings is distinctive is several ways. (a) It is placed alongside not within the brief report of Jehoshaphat's reign (pp. 245–247). (b) It includes the only secure attestation in BoTH of the particle נא that becomes more widely used in later biblical texts (pp. 21–34). And (c) it is one of the best-connected narratives in BoTH. Both composing and recomposing exhibited a tendency to pair. Whichever of לא כלום (now in 2 Chr 8:8) or לא יכלו להחרימם (now in 1 Kgs 9:21) was drafted before the other, neatly rewording one into the other accompanied a change in unique pairing – from the Micaiah to the Hezekiah story, or the other way round (pp. 161–162).

If I know a heap of grain when I see one, if I recognise a midrash as soon as identification is proposed, just how much artistry must be detected in a text before it becomes unlikely that this quality is coincidental or unintentional? How and by whom – or by how many – the text was authored would be interesting to know. But much more important, once the nature of its artistry has been glimpsed, is how this older text that underlies both Samuel-Kings and Chronicles must (not) be read.

2 History and (syn)chronology

Non-synoptic prophetic narratives in Sam-Kgs breathe a different air from the prophets of BoTH. 'Of Proust and Prophets' (pp. 131–142) sketched how Samuel-Kings portrays a different prophetic world from synoptic narrative. Samuel, Elijah, and Elisha share some characteristics of synoptic prophets and men of God, yet there is no one like them in synoptic story. The large presence in Samuel-Kings of these giants will have helped these books impose themselves as 'Prophets'.

These books are also traditionally recognised as (among the) 'Histories' within the Bible. Arguably this characterisation too is worn more comfortably by Samuel-Kings than by the older synoptic story. That earlier account is both 'narrative' and 'enquiry'; and both are aspects of ancient Greek ἱστορία. But the book of Kings with its synchronisms of northern and southern kingdoms is at least superficially more congenial to the modern historian than its main source. Several dates in non-synoptic Chr add precision to an older vaguer indication of earlier and later. The 23rd year of Joash (2 Kgs 12:7) is an occasional example in Kgs of the same phenomenon. Its introduction there uses a non-synoptic formula found only in the synchronisms of northern and southern reigns in Kings; and it serves to align a shift in policy in Jerusalem with the accession in Samaria of Jehoahaz (Auld 2017, 250). That in turn invites attention to the difference in chronological 'feel' between the Book of Kings with its synchronisms of north and south and the Book of Two Houses without.

With synchronisms removed, that older story exhibits a different world. The age of each king at his accession is reported and the length of his reign supplies a time frame. Yet the kaleidoscope of patterns that repeat themselves seems to trump the time-line in which it is set. If the arguments from textual and literary history developed in these essays are persuasive, the historical implications are serious.

The English language has borrowed Spanish *mañana* (literally 'tomorrow') to refer to some indefinite time in the future. Lowland Scots story tells that a highland Gaelic speaker, asked if that language had any similar terms, replied that there were perhaps five or six, but none so precise as *mañana*. BoTH lacks synchronisms yet is not innocent of chronology. We are told at the outset of every royal report the age of the new king and how many years he will reign. And yet … in some cases these data (seem designed to) suggest and reinforce comparisons and contrasts among Jerusalem's kings rather than measure the passing of time. When they become computed with others, they acquire a newly literal precision.

3 David's house and Israel

Synchronising separate accounts of kings in Jerusalem and Samaria involved reconceiving more than what chronology had contributed to BoTH. The accompanying changed conception of 'Israel' was no less significant. There is critique of some northern kings in BoTH. Southern Jehoram and Ahaziah and Ahaz are blamed for following in the ways of kings of Israel. But this older narrative breathes no whisper of Jeroboam founding a cult to rival Jerusalem and ensnare all his successors. Instead, Rehoboam appears the more culpable of the two rivals at the division of Solomon's inheritance; and, when Amaziah is later poised to repeat Rehoboam's mistakes, it is northern Jehoash that embodies a sanely critical mix of David and that older Jeroboam.

The narratives about Saul, David, and Solomon – kings of Israel – occupy some 60% of the text of BoTH and include one (prophetic?) mention of Judah. Some later kings of Israel are blamed, as are some kings of Judah. The god of Israel is still invoked in narratives about Hezekiah and Josiah. There is not a word about a sanctuary to rival Jerusalem. Israel has not yet been 'othered' as it will be in the book of Kings. Recognising that the world of BoTH is different from that of Sam-Kgs is one thing. Interpreting its worldview is quite another – and intuiting its silences is the hardest.

- Anointing is reported only of David and Joash. Was no other king anointed? Was it only necessary in these two cases because they followed an interregnum?
- Sacrifice in Jerusalem is reported only of David and Solomon, and then only as part of dedication ceremonies. Ahaz sacrifices enthusiastically, but at 'high places'. In post-Solomon narrative, Yahweh's house features in BoTH only as a treasury.
- Blood is related neither to bloodguilt as in Sam-Kgs nor to sacrifice as in Chr – at its sole mention, it is not even 'real', but is the water David had longed for from Bethlehem's well.
- Successors could bear names such as Jehoshaphat (Yahweh is Judge/Ruler). Jotham (Yahweh is Whole/Innocent) was reported as 'ruling' (שפט). Yet only David and Solomon were said to 'practise justice and righteousness' (עשה משפט וצדקה). Had all their successors in Jerusalem been irreparably diminished by the loss of Israel?

The story ends in an enigma. We are told at the outset of its final chapter that Josiah (uniquely) 'did what was right in the eyes of Yahweh and walked in all the way of his father David – he did not turn to right or left'. Only David and he are addressed by a prophet about lying down with/being gathered to their fathers.

Nathan speaks to David about Yahweh bringing Israel out of Egypt and Solomon in the house he has built for Yahweh uniquely returns to the theme. In the same 18th year as Josiah gave instructions about temple repairs, he held a Passover such as had never been held since before David. As to what features of the nation's 'past' may have been 'remembered' at that festival, the narrative gives no clue. Did it include facing down Pharaoh and spoiling the Egyptians? However that may be, Josiah went some years later to 'meet' the Egyptian Pharaoh and was killed by him.

Bibliography

Adam, Klaus-Peter. 2010. 'Warfare and Treaty Formulas in the Background of Kings,' in Mark Leuchter and Klaus-Peter Adam (eds), *Soundings in Kings. Perspectives and Methods in Contemporary Scholarship*. (Minneapolis MN: Fortress Press) 35–68.

Alter, Robert. 2018. *The Hebrew Bible. A Translation with Commentary.* II *Prophets*. New York: W. W. Norton.

Amar, Itzhak. 2020. 'Expansion and exile in the Chronicler's narrative of the two and a half tribes (1 Chr. 5.1–26)', *JSOT* 44, 357–376.

Auld, A. Graeme. 1983. 'Prophets through the Looking Glass: between Writings and Moses', *JSOT* 27, 3–23, reprinted in Auld 2004, 45–61.

Auld, A. Graeme. 1984. 'Prophets and Prophecy in Jeremiah and Kings', *ZAW* 96, 66–82, reprinted in Auld 2004, 29–43.

Auld, A. Graeme. 1990. 'The Cities in Joshua 21: The Contribution of Textual Criticism', *Textus* XV, 141–152 (reprinted in *Joshua Retold. Synoptic Perspectives* [Edinburgh: T&T Clark, 1998], 49–62).

Auld, A. Graeme. 1992. 'Vision of a New Future?', *ThZ* 48, 343–355.

Auld, A. Graeme. 1993. 'Solomon at Gibeon. History Glimpsed', Avraham Malamat Volume (EI 24; Jerusalem: IES), 1–7.

Auld, A. Graeme. 1994. *Kings Without Privilege* (Edinburgh: T&T Clark).

Auld, A. Graeme. 2002. 'Counting Sheep, Sins, and Sour Grapes: The Primacy of the Primary History?', in Alastair G. Hunter and Philip R. Davies (eds), *Sense and Sensitivity: Essays on Reading the Bible in Memory of Robert Carroll*, JSOTS 348, 63–72.

Auld, A. Graeme. 2004. *Samuel at the Threshold* (SOTSM), Aldershot: Ashgate.

Auld, A. Graeme. 2005. '*imago dei* in Genesis', *ExT* 116, 259–262.

Auld, A. Graeme. 2011. *I & II Samuel: A Commentary.* Old Testament Library. Louisville, KY: Westminster John Knox.

Auld, A. Graeme. 2012. 'Re-telling the Disputed "Altar" in Joshua 22', in Ed Noort (ed.), *The Book of Joshua*. (BETL CCX. Leuven: Peeters), 281–293.

Auld, A. Graeme. 2014. 'The Shaping of Israelite History in Samuel and Kings,' *RB* 121, 204–212.

Auld, A. Graeme. 2015. 'Isaiah and the Oldest "Biblical" Prophetic Narrative', in Bob Becking and Hans M. Barstad (eds), *Prophecy and Prophets in Stories: Papers Read at the Fifth Meeting of the Edinburgh Prophecy Network, Utrecht, October 2013* (OTS 65. Leiden: Brill), 45–63.

Auld, A. Graeme. 2017. *Life in Kings. Reshaping the Royal Story in the Hebrew Bible* (AIL 30; Atlanta GA: SBL).

Auld, A. Graeme. 2020a. 'Ahaz and Jeroboam', in Keith Bodner and Benjamin J. M. Johnson (eds), *Characters and Characterization in the Book of Kings* (LHBOTS 670. London: T&T Clark), 17–31.

Auld, A. Graeme. 2020b. 'Chronicles – Isaiah – Kings', in Reinhard G. Kratz and Joachim Schaper (eds), *Imperial Visions. The Prophet and the Book of Isaiah in an Age of Empires* (FRLANT 277. Göttingen: Vandenhoeck und Ruprecht), 115–128.

Auld, A. Graeme. 2020c. 'Some Thoughts on the First Jeroboam'. *BN* 185, 45–53.

Auld, A. Graeme. 2021a. 'David and his *Alter Ego* in the Desert', in Hannes Bezzel and Reinhard G. Kratz (eds), *David in the Desert. Tradition and Redaction in the "History of David's Rise"* (BZAW 514. Berlin: de Gruyter), 145–157.

Auld, A. Graeme. 2021b. 'Divination in Hebrew and Greek Bibles: A Text-historical Overview', in Hannes Bezzel and Stefan Pfeiffer (eds), *Prophecy and Hellenism* (FAT2 129. Tübingen: Mohr Siebeck), 55–67.

https://doi.org/10.1515/9783111060279-020

Auld, A. Graeme. 2021c. 'נפש אדם and the Associations of 1 Chronicles 5 in the Hebrew Bible', in Jaeyoung Jeon and Louis C. Jonker (eds), *Chronicles and the Priestly Literature of the Hebrew Bible* (BZAW 528. Berlin: de Gruyter), 2021.

Auld, A. Graeme. 2021d. 'Of Proust and Prophets: Samuel, Elijah, and Charles Swann', *ExT* 133, 143–148.

Auld, A. Graeme. 2021e. '"Tell נא How It Is". Describing הגד־נא within Biblical Hebrew', in Samuel Hildebrandt, Kurtis Peters, and Eric N. Ortlund (eds), *From Words to Meaning. Studies on Old Testament Language and Theology for David J. Reimer* (HBM 100. Sheffield: Phoenix Press), 63–76.

Auld, A. Graeme. 2021f. 'Tracing the Writing of Kings with Nadav Na'aman and Klaus-Peter Adam', *SJOT* 35, 2021.

Auld, A. Graeme. 2021g. 'Deuteronomy and the Older Royal Narrative', in Diana Edelman, Benedetta Rossi, Kåre Berge, and Philippe Guillaume (eds), *Deuteronomy in the Making. Studies in the Production of* Debarim (BZAW 533. Berlin: de Gruyter), 219–239.

Auld, A. Graeme. 2022a. 'Reading Solomon with Three Eyes Open', *SJOT* 36, 22–35.

Auld, A. Graeme. 2022b. 'Follow the Words: What's in a King's Name?', *SJOT* 36, 138–148.

Benzinger, Immanuel. 1901. *Die Bücher der Chronik* (KHAT XX. Tübingen: Mohr-Siebeck).

Beyer, Andrea. 2014. *Hoffnung in Bethlehem. Innerbiblische Querbezüge als Deutungshorizonte im Ruthbuch* (BZAW 463. Berlin: de Gruyter).

Blenkinsopp, Joseph. 2006. *Opening the Sealed Book. Interpretations of the Book of Isaiah in Late Antiquity* (Grand Rapids MI: Eerdmans).

Bodner, Keith. 2012. *Jeroboam's Royal Drama* (Biblical Refigurations. Oxford: OUP).

Braun, Roddy. 1986. *1 Chronicles* (WBC 14. Waco: Word Books).

Brenner, Athalya. 2011. 'Ruth: The Art of Memorizing Territory and Religion' in David J. A. Clines and Ellen van Wolde (eds), *A Critical Engagement. Essays on the Hebrew Bible in Honour of J. Cheryl Exum* (HBM 38. Sheffield: Sheffield Phoenix Press), 82–89.

Bronner, Leila L. 1993. 'A Thematic Approach to Ruth in Rabbinic Literature', in Athalya Brenner (ed.), *A Feminist Companion to Ruth* (Sheffield: Sheffield Academic Press), 146–69.

Campbell, Edward F. 1975. *Ruth* (AB 7. New York: Doubleday).

Chavel, Simeon. 2011. 'The Literary Development of Deuteronomy 12: Between Religious Ideal and Social Reality', in Thomas B. Dozeman, Konrad Schmid, and Baruch J. Schwartz (eds), *The Pentateuch: International Perspectives on Current Research* (FAT 78. Tübingen: Mohr Siebeck), 303–326.

Clines, David J. A. 1996. (ed.), *The Dictionary of Classical Hebrew*, Vol. III (Sheffield: Sheffield Academic Press).

Clines, David J. A. 2001. (ed.), *The Dictionary of Classical Hebrew*, Vol. V (Sheffield: Sheffield Academic Press).

Clines, David J. A. 2007. (ed.), *The Dictionary of Classical Hebrew*, Vol. VI (Sheffield: Sheffield Academic Press).

Clines, David J. A. 2011. (ed.), *The Dictionary of Classical Hebrew*, Vol. VIII (Sheffield: Sheffield Academic Press).

Cross, Frank M. 1973. *Canaanite Myth and Hebrew Epic: Essays in the History of the Religion of Israel* (Cambridge MA: HUP).

Cryer, Frederick H. 1994. *Divination in Ancient Israel and its Near Eastern Environment. A Socio-Historical Investigation* (JSOTS 142. Sheffield: Sheffield Academic Press).

Cudworth, Troy D. 2016. *War in Chronicles. Temple Faithfulness and Israel's Place in the Land* (LHBOTS 627. London: T&T Clark).

Dahood, Mitchell. 1968. *Psalms* II 51–100 (AB 17. New York: Doubleday).

Dorival, Giles. 1994. *Les Nombres* (BA 4. Paris: Cerf).
Edenburg, Cynthia. 2016. *Dismembering the Whole. Composition and Purpose of Judges 19–21* (AIL 24. Atlanta: SBL).
Embry, Brad. 2016. 'Legalities in the Book of Ruth: A Renewed Look'. *JSOT* 41: 31–44.
Fernández Marcos, Natalio and José Ramón Busto Saiz. 1992. *El Texto Antioqueno de la Biblia Griega* II *1–2 Reyes* (Madrid: Instituto de Filología del CSIC).
Fernández Marcos, Natalio and José Ramón Busto Saiz. 1996. *El Texto Antioqueno de la Biblia Griega* III *1–2 Crónicas* (Madrid: Instituto de Filología del CSIC).
Flower, Michael A. 2008. *The Seer in Ancient Greece* (Berkeley CA).
Gitay, Z. 1993. 'Ruth and the Women of Bethlehem', in A. Brenner (ed.), *A Feminist Companion to Ruth* (Sheffield: Sheffield Academic Press), 178–90.
Gray, John. 1977. *I & II Kings*, 3rd ed (OTL; London: SCM).
Grillet, Bernard et Michel Lestienne 1997. *Premier Livre des Règnes* (BA 9.1. Paris: Cerf).
Guillaume, Philippe. 'Binding "Sucks": A Response to Stephan Schorch.' *VT* 61 (2011), 1–3.
Harl, Marguerite, *La Génèse*, BA 1, Paris 1987.
Himbaza, Innocent. 2016. '"Le lieu que YHWH aura choisi". Une perspective narrative, historique et philologique.' *Semitica* 58, 115–34.
Japhet, Sara. 1993. *I & II Chronicles* (OTL. London: SCM).
Jepsen, Alfred. 1956. *Die Quellen des Königsbuches* (Halle: Max Niemeyer).
Johnstone, William. 1993. 'The Deuteronomistic Cycles of "Signs" and "Wonders" in Exodus 1–13', in A. Graeme Auld (ed.), *Understanding Poets and Prophets. Essays in Honour of George Wishart Anderson* (JSOTS 152; Sheffield: Sheffield Academic Press), 166–185.
Klein, Anja. 2014. *Geschichte und Gebet. Die Rezeption der biblischen Geschichte in den Psalmen des Alten Testaments* (FAT 94. Tübingen: Mohr Siebeck).
Klein, Ralph W. 2006. *1 Chronicles*. Hermeneia (Minneapolis: Fortress)
Klein, Ralph W. 2010. 'The Chronicler's Theological Rewriting of the Deuteronomistic History: Amaziah, a Test Case', in K. L. Noll and Brooks Schramm (eds), *Raising Up a Faithful Exegete. Essays in Honor of Richard D. Nelson* (Winona Lake: Eisenbrauns), 237–245.
Klein, Ralph W. 2012. *2 Chronicles*. Hermeneia (Minneapolis: Fortress).
Knoppers, Gary N. 1999. 'Treasures Won and Lost: Royal [Mis]Appropriations in Kings and Chronicles' in M. Patrick Graham and Steven L. McKenzie (eds), *The Chronicler as Author* (JSOTS 263. Sheffield: Sheffield Academic Press), 181–208.
Knoppers, Gary N. 2012. *1 Chronicles* (AB. New York: Doubleday)
Korpel, M. 2001. *The Structure of the Book of Ruth* (Pericope 2. Assen: Van Gorcum).
Kozlova, Ekaterina E. 2021. 'King Solomon and the "Anatomy" of Wisdom', JSOT 46, 249–268.
Kratz, Reinhard G. 2015. 'Isaiah and the Siege of Jerusalem', in Rannfrid I. Thelle, Terje Stordalen, and Mervyn E. J. Richardson (eds), *New Perspectives on Prophecy and History in Honour of Hans M. Barstad* (VTS 168. Leiden: Brill), 143–160.
Kucová, Lydie. 2007. 'Obeisance in the Biblical Stories of David', in Robert Rezetko and others (eds), *Reflection and Refraction. Studies in Biblical Historiography in Honour of A. Graeme Auld* (SVT 113. Leiden: Brill), 241–260.
Lisowsky, Gerhard. 1957. *Konkordanz zum Hebräischen Alten Testament* (Stuttgart: Württembergische Bibelanstalt).
Milgrom, Jacob. 2000. *Leviticus 17–22* (AB 3A. New York: Doubleday).
Monroe, Lauren A. S. 2011. *Josiah's Reform and the Dynamics of Defilement: Israelite Rites of Violence and the Making of a Biblical Text* (Oxford: Oxford University Press).
Montgomery, James A. 1951. *The Books of Kings* (Edited by Henry S. Gehman. ICC. Edinburgh: T&T Clark).

Myers, Jacob M. 1965. *1 Chronicles* (AB. New York: Doubleday).
Na'aman, Nadav. 2003. 'Updating the Messages: Hezekiah's Second Prophetic Story (2 Kings 19.9b–35) and the Community of Babylonian Deportees', in Lester L. Grabbe (ed.), *"Like a Bird in a Cage". The Invasion of Sennacherib in 701 BCE* (JSOTS 363. London: Sheffield Academic Press), 201–220.
Na'aman, Nadav. 2017. 'Was an Early Edition of the Book of Kings Composed During Hezekiah's Reign', *SJOT* 31, 80–91.
Nelson, Richard D. 2002. *Deuteronomy* (OTL. Louisville: WJK).
Nelson, Richard D. 2017. *Judges. A Critical and Rhetorical Commentary* (London: T&T Clark).
Noth, Martin. 1965. Könige (BK IX 2; Neukirchen-Vluyn: Neukirchener).
Park, Song-Mi Suzie. 2015. *Hezekiah and the Dialogue of Memory* (Emerging Scholars. Minneapolis MN).
Person, Raymond. 1997. *The Kings-Isaiah and Kings-Jeremiah Recensions* (BZAW 252. Berlin: de Gruyter).
Proust, Marcel. 2021. *Les Soixante-Quinze Feuillets et autres manuscrits inédits* (Paris: Gallimard).
Rad, Gerhard von. 1962. *Old Testament Theology* I, Edinburgh: Oliver & Boyd.
Reimer, David J. 1993. *The Oracles against Babylon in Jeremiah 50–51. A Horror among the Nations* (San Francisco: Mellem Research University Press).
Schenker, Adrian. 1996. 'Jéroboam et la division du royaume dans la Septante Ancienne', in Albert de Pury and others (eds), *Israël construit son histoire* (Le Monde de la Bible 34. Geneva: Labor et Fides) = *Israel constructs its History. Deuteronomistic historiography in recent research.* (JSOTS 306. Sheffield: Sheffield Academic Press, 2000).
Schenker, Adrian. 2000. *Septante et texte massorétique dans l'histoire la plus ancienne du texte de 1 Rois 2–14* (Cahiers de la Revue Biblique 48. Paris: Gabalda).
Schenker, Adrian. 2008. 'Jeroboam's Rise and Fall in the Hebrew and Greek Bible. Methodological Reflections on a Recent Article ...', *JSJ* 38, 367–373.
Schenker, Adrian. 2010. 'Textgeschichtliches zum Samaritanischen Pentateuch und Samareitikon. Zur Textgeschichte des Pentateuchs im 2. Jh. v. Chr.', in Menachem Mor and Friedrich V. Reiterer (eds), *Samaritans: Past and Present: Current Studies* (Studia Judaica 53; Studia Samaritana 5. Berlin: de Gruyter), 105–21.
Schorch, Stefan. 2010. 'A Young Goat in its Mother's Milk? Understanding an Ancient Prohibition.' *VT* 60, 116–30.
Shulman, A. 1999. 'The Particle נא in Biblical Hebrew Prose', *HS* 40, 57–82.
Stade, Bernhard. 1886. 'Anmerkungen zu 2 Kö. 15–21', ZAW 6, 156–192.
Stone, Timothy J. 2015. 'The Search for Order: The Compilational History of Ruth', in J. Steinberg and T. J. Stone (eds), *The Shape of the Writings* (Siphrut 16. Winona Lake IN: Eisenbrauns), 175–85.
Sweeney, Marvin A. 2007a. *I & II Kings* (Old Testament Library. Louisville KY: WJK).
Sweeney, Marvin A. 2007b. 'A Reassessment of the Masoretic and Septuagint Versions of the Jeroboam Narratives in 1 Kings/3 Kingdoms 11–14', *JSJ* 38, 165–195.
Talshir, Zipora. 1993. *The Alternative Story. 3 Kingdoms 12:24 A–Z* (Jerusalem Biblical Studies 6. Jerusalem: Simor).
Thelle, Rannfrid. 2009. 'Babylon in the Book of Jeremiah (MT): Negotiating a Power Shift', in Hans M. Barstad and Reinhard G. Kratz (eds), *Prophecy in the Book of Jeremiah* (BZAW 388. Berlin: de Gruyter), 187–232.
Trebolle Barrera, Julio. 2007. 'Kings (MT/LXX) and Chronicles: The Double and Triple Textual Tradition', in Robert Rezetko and others (eds), *Reflection and Refraction. Studies in Biblical Historiography in Honour of A. Graeme Auld* (SVT 113. Leiden: Brill), 483–501.

Trebolle Barrera, Julio. 2020. *Textual and Literary Criticism of the Books of Kings. Collected Essays* (Edited by Andrés Piquer Otero and Pablo A. Torijano. VTS 185. Brill: Leiden).
Turton, Megan B. 2021. 'Deuteronomic Law, Deuteronomic Narrative, or Exodus Narrative?', in Diana Edelman, Benedetta Rossi, Kåre Berge, and Philippe Guillaume (eds), *Deuteronomy in the Making. Studies in the Production of* Debarim (BZAW 533. Berlin: de Gruyter), 243–270.
Wetter, Anne-Mareike. 2015. *"On Her Account". Reconfiguring Israel in Ruth, Esther, and Judith* (LHBOTS 623. London: T&T Clark).
Wildberger, Hans. 1982. *Jesaja* (3 vol.; BK X. Neukirchen-Vluyn: Neukirchener).
Willi, Thomas. 1991. *Chronik* (BK xxiv.1. Neukirchen: Neukirchener).
Williamson, Hugh G. M. 2006. *Isaiah 1–5* (ICC. London: T&T Clark).
Wilt, Timothy. 1996. 'A Sociolinguistic Analysis of nā'', *VT* 46, 237–55.
Würthwein, Ernst. 1984. Die Bücher der Könige (2 vol.; ATD 11,2. Göttingen: Vandenhoeck & Ruprecht).
Zakovitch, Yair. 2000. *Joshua* (Tel Aviv: Revivim).

Index of Names

https://doi.org/10.1515/9783111060279-021

Index of Biblical passages

Genesis

Exodus

Leviticus

Numbers

https://doi.org/10.1515/9783111060279-022

Deuteronomy

Joshua

Judges

1 Samuel

2 Samuel

1 Kings

2 Kings

1 Kingdoms

2 Kingdoms

3 Kingdoms

4 Kingdoms

Isaiah

Jeremiah

Ezekiel

Hosea

Amos

Micah

Jonah

Zechariah

Psalms

Job

Proverbs

Ruth

Qohelet

Esther

Daniel

Ezra

Nehemiah

1 Chronicles

2 Chronicles

Index of Hebrew words

https://doi.org/10.1515/9783111060279-023

Index of Authors

https://doi.org/10.1515/9783111060279-024